D1592537

Amos

———

VOLUME 24G

THE ANCHOR YALE BIBLE is a project of international and interfaith scope in which Protestant, Catholic, and Jewish scholars from many countries contribute individual volumes. The project is not sponsored by any ecclesiastical organization and is not intended to reflect any particular theological doctrine.

THE ANCHOR YALE BIBLE is committed to producing commentaries in the tradition established half a century ago by the founders of the series, William Foxwell Albright and David Noel Freedman. It aims to present the best contemporary scholarship in a way that is accessible not only to scholars but also to the educated nonspecialist. Its approach is grounded in exact translation of the ancient languages and an appreciation of the historical and cultural contexts in which the biblical books were written, supplemented by insights from modern methods, such as sociological and literary criticism.

John J. Collins
General Editor

THE ANCHOR YALE BIBLE

Amos

A New Translation with
Introduction and Commentary

GÖRAN EIDEVALL

THE ANCHOR YALE BIBLE

Yale UNIVERSITY PRESS

New Haven and London

Yale University Press books may be purchased in quantity for educational, business, or promotional use. For information, please e-mail sales.press@yale.edu (U.S. office) or sales@yaleup.co.uk (U.K. office).

Set in Adobe Garmond type by Newgen North America.

Printed in the United States of America.

Library of Congress Control Number: 2017934302
ISBN: 978-0-300-17878-4 (hardcover : alk. paper)

A catalogue record for this book is available from the British Library.

This paper meets the requirements of ANSI/NISO Z39.48–1992 (Permanence of Paper).

10 9 8 7 6 5 4 3 2 1

Contents

Acknowledgments

———————

While writing this commentary, I have been in constant conversation with other scholars, both in Sweden and abroad. Thanks are due to all of them. In particular, I thank John J. Collins and Saul Olyan for helpful feedback on preliminary versions of this manuscript.

As expected from a commentary in the Anchor Yale Bible series, this volume contains a new translation of the book of Amos. In this case, however, the translation is the result of a collective and collaborative process. Chapter by chapter, drafts I prepared were discussed in a series of workshops in Uppsala, where both Hebrew Bible scholars and specialists in Semitic languages participated. I have profited immensely from a wide range of constructive suggestions the participants made concerning semantic, syntactic, and text-critical issues pertaining to the translation of individual passages.

Many people were involved in one or several of these workshops; hence, it is not possible to mention everyone. However, I extend a special thanks to (in alphabetical order) Ulf Bergström, LarsOlov Eriksson, Mats Eskhult, Tord Fornberg, Pedro Gonçalves, Bo Isaksson, Natalie Lantz, Mikael Larsson, Emil Lundin, Stig Norin, Sverrir Ólafsson, Dag Oredsson, Lina Petersson, Richard Pleijel, Cian Power, Helena Riihiaho, and Karin Tillberg. This being said, it is important to point out that I am solely responsible for the published end result of the collective process: this new translation of the book of Amos, with its merits and its deficiencies.

Abbreviations

ABD	*Anchor Bible Dictionary.* Edited by D. N. Freedman. New York: Doubleday, 1992.
ADPV	Abhandlungen des Deutschen Palästina-Vereins
AGJU	Arbeiten zur Geschichte des antiken Judentums und des Urchristentums
AOAT	Alter Orient und Altes Testament
ATD	Das Alte Testament Deutsch
AYB	Anchor Yale Bible
BASOR	*Bulletin of the American Schools of Oriental Research*
BBB	Bonner biblische Beiträge
BEATAJ	Beiträge zur Erforschung des Alten Testaments und des antiken Judentum
BEvT	Beiträge zur evangelischen Theologie
BHQ	*Biblia Hebraica Quinta*
BHS	*Biblia Hebraica Stuttgartensia*
BHSapp	Text-critical apparatus in *Biblia Hebraica Stuttgartensia*
BN	*Biblische Notizen*
BSac	*Bibliotheca Sacra*
BWANT	Beiträge zur Wissenschaft vom Alten und Neuen Testament
BZ	*Biblische Zeitschrift*
BZAW	Beihefte zur Zeitschrift für die alttestamentliche Wissenschaft

CAD	*The Assyrian Dictionary of the Oriental Institute of the University of Chicago.* Chicago: Oriental Institute of the University of Chicago, 1956–2006.
CBC	Cambridge Bible Commentary
CBQ	*Catholic Biblical Quarterly*
CBQMS	Catholic Biblical Quarterly Monograph Series
ConBOT	Coniectanea Biblica: Old Testament Series
CTU	*The Cuneiform Alphabetic Texts from Ugarit, Ras Ibn Hani, and Other Places.* Edited by M. Dietrich, O. Loretz, and J. Sanmartín. Münster: Ugarit-Verlag, 1995.
DCH	*Dictionary of Classical Hebrew.* Edited by D. J. A. Clines. 9 vols. Sheffield: Sheffield Phoenix Press, 1993–2014.
DSD	*Dead Sea Discoveries*
EA	El Amarna tablets. According to J. A. Knudtzon, *Die el-Amarna-Tafeln,* Leipzig: Hinrichs, 1908–15.
EBR	*Encyclopedia of the Bible and Its Reception.* Edited by Hans-Josef Klauck et al. Berlin: De Gruyter, 2009–.
Eng.	English translation
ETL	*Ephemerides Theologicae Lovanienses*
ETR	*Études théologiques et religieuses*
EvT	*Evangelische Theologie*
ExAud	*Ex Auditu*
ExpTim	*Expository Times*
FAT	Forschungen zum Alten Testament
FRLANT	Forschungen zur Literatur und Religion des Alten und Neues Testaments
FS	Festschrift
Ges18	Gesenius, *Hebräisches und aramäisches Handwörterbuch über das Alte Testament,* 18th ed. Edited by D. R. Meyer and H. Donner. Berlin: Springer, 1987–2010.
GKC	*Gesenius' Hebrew Grammar.* Edited by Emil Kautzsch. Translated by Arthur E. Cowley. 2nd ed. Oxford: Clarendon, 1910.
HALOT	*The Hebrew and Aramaic Lexicon of the Old Testament.* Ludwig Kehler, Walter Baumgartner, and Johann J. Stamm. Translated and edited under the supervision of M. E. J. Richardson. 4 vols. Leiden: Brill, 1994–99.
HAR	*Hebrew Annual Review*
HAT	Handbuch zum Alten Testament

HKAT	Handkommentar zum Alten Testament
HTR	*Harvard Theological Review*
HUCA	*Hebrew Union College Annual*
ICC	International Critical Commentary
JANER	*Journal of Ancient Near Eastern Religions*
JAOS	*Journal of the American Oriental Society*
JBL	*Journal of Biblical Literature*
JCS	*Journal of Cuneiform Studies*
JETS	*Journal of the Evangelical Theological Society*
JHebS	*Journal of Hebrew Scriptures*
JNES	*Journal of Near Eastern Studies*
JPOS	*Journal of the Palestine Oriental Society*
JPS	Jewish Publication Society
JRT	*Journal of Religious Thought*
JSOT	*Journal for the Study of the Old Testament*
JSOTSup	Journal for the Study of the Old Testament Supplement Series
JSS	*Journal of Semitic Studies*
JTS	*Journal of Theological Studies*
KAI	*Kanaanäische und aramäische Inschriften.* Herbert Donner and Wolfgang Röllig. 2nd ed. Wiesbaden: Harrassowitz, 1966–69.
KAT	Kommentar zum Alten Testament
KHC	Kurzer Hand-Commentar zum Alten Testament
KJV	King James Version
KTU	*Die keilalphabetischen Texte aus Ugarit.* Edited by M. Dietrich, O. Loretz, and J. Sanmartín. Münster: Ugarit-Verlag, 2013. See also *CTU*.
LHBOTS	Library of Hebrew Bible/Old Testament Studies (continues JSOTSup)
LXX	Septuagint
MT	Masoretic text
NEB	New English Bible
NedTT	*Nederlands Theologisch Tijdschrift*
NET	New English Translation
NIBCOT	New International Biblical Commentary on the Old Testament

NIV	New International Version
NovT	*Novum Testamentum*
NRSV	New Revised Standard Version
NTT	*Norsk Teologisk Tidsskrift*
OBO	Orbis Biblicus et Orientalis
OrAnt	*Oriens Antiquus*
OTE	*Old Testament Essays*
OTL	Old Testament Library
OTS	Old Testament Studies
OtSt	*Oudtestamentische Studiën*
RA	*Revue d'assyriologie et d'archéologie orientale*
RB	*Revue biblique*
ResQ	*Restoration Quarterly*
RIBLA	*Revista de interpretación bíblica latino-americana*
RSV	Revised Standard Version
SAA	State Archives of Assyria
SBL	Society of Biblical Literature
SBS	Stuttgarter Bibelstudien
SOTSMS	Society for Old Testament Study Monograph Series
SEÅ	*Svensk exegetisk årsbok*
SWBA	Social World of Biblical Antiquity
TDOT	*Theological Dictionary of the Old Testament.* Edited by G. J. Botterweck and H. Ringgren. Translated by J. T. Willis et al. 8 vols. Grand Rapids, MI: Eerdmans, 1974–2006.
TQ	*Theologische Quartalschrift*
TTZ	*Trierer theologische Zeitschrift*
TWNT	*Theologisches Wörterbuch zum Neuen Testament.* Edited by G. Kittel and G. Friedrich. Stuttgart: Kohlhammer, 1932–79.
TynBul	*Tyndale Bulletin*
TZ	*Theologische Zeitschrift*
UF	*Ugarit-Forschungen*
VT	*Vetus Testamentum*
VTSup	Supplements to Vetus Testamentum
WAW	Writings from the Ancient World
WMANT	Wissenschaftliche Monographien zum Alten und Neuen Testament

WUNT	Wissenschaftliche Untersuchungen zum Neuen Testament
ZAH	*Zeitschrift für Althebraistik*
ZAW	*Zeitschrift für die alttestamentliche Wissenschaft*
ZDPV	*Zeitschrift des deutschen Palästina-Vereins*
ZTK	*Zeitschrift für Theologie und Kirche*

A Note on the Translation
and Transliteration

The guiding principles behind the new translation of Amos presented in this commentary can be stated briefly. It is, first and foremost, based on thorough text-critical, philological, and contextual analysis. Rather than striving after perfectly idiomatic English formulations (so-called dynamic equivalence), the aim has been to produce an English text that, as far as possible, does justice to the semantic and syntactic properties (including some oddities) of the Hebrew text.

Transliteration of Hebrew words and letters has been made in accordance with the guidelines for "academic purpose" transliteration in *The SBL Handbook of Style* (2nd ed.; Atlanta: SBL, 2014, 56–58). However, I have made a couple of minor modifications, in order to avoid confusion with accents or quotation marks. Thus, ʾ stands for the Hebrew letter א (*aleph*) and ʿ for ע (*ayin*). This is in line with praxis within philological studies of Semitic languages.

INTRODUCTION

I.

Aim and Profile of This Commentary

"Amos" may refer either to a prophet or to a book. Owing to the lack of sources, we know almost nothing about Amos as a historical person—except for an early tradition according to which he earned his living as a livestock breeder, and perhaps also as a tender of sycamore trees (Amos 1:1; 7:14). His hometown seems to have been Tekoa. That is all we know about the person Amos; however, he left a long-lasting legacy. As part of the Old Testament/Hebrew Bible, the book carrying his name has been continually studied and interpreted for more than two thousand years.

One interesting aspect of the process of reading ancient literature with an unknown author is that it will almost inevitably generate an image of the implied speaker, or author—in this case: of the eponymous prophet who appears to be the one who pronounces all the oracles that have been collected in the book. Some of these images become powerful, since they are shared by large reading communities. Within biblical scholarship during the past two centuries, Amos has mainly been regarded as a harbinger of ethical monotheism and/or as a prototypical prophet of doom. Outside the exegetical guild this prophet is nowadays above all known as an advocate of justice, as someone who had the courage to speak out against the maltreatment of the poor. In that capacity Amos from Tekoa has served (and still serves) as a source of inspiration for protest and reform movements in various parts of the world.

It is easy to understand the attraction of the traditional Amos story, which has been told over and over again: about a simple man from a small village who became a prophet of doom, a rhetorically skilled dissident, and/or a champion of justice. But to a large extent these popular images of Amos, as a religious teacher or as a political reformer, are based more on fiction than on facts. Such conceptions are, I suggest, best understood as personifications of central aspects of the message(s) conveyed by the book of Amos.

One important point of departure for my exegetical approach to Amos can be formulated in the following way: We have no access to the eponymous prophet as a

3

historical person, but we do have access to the book that carries his name (see further "From the Prophet Amos to the Book of Amos" in this introduction). Leaving speculations about the life and work of the *person* Amos aside, the present commentary aims to provide a comprehensive literary and historical analysis of the *book* of Amos. In order to achieve this goal I have chosen to combine synchronic and diachronic exegetical approaches. This means, to begin with, that the book of Amos is studied as an artistically structured literary *composition*. At the same time, however, this complex composition is regarded as the result of *redaction* (most likely in several stages). More detailed discussions of the book's compositional structure and its editorial history are found in the ensuing sections of this introduction.

The textual analysis provided by this commentary has been guided by a twofold purpose: (1) to elucidate the rhetorical function of each passage, and each prophetic message, included in the book of Amos (in relation to the literary context as well as to a specific historical and rhetorical setting), and (2) to explore the theological and ideological aspects of (different parts of) this prophetic book, viewed as a multilayered literary composition. Working in dialogue with other scholars, and in constant interaction with recent studies within the field of prophetic literature in general and the book of Amos in particular, I have tried to produce an up-to-date commentary that reflects the current state of research. However, a new biblical commentary should preferably also be informed by the long and rich tradition of exegetical studies. I therefore have sought to integrate valuable insights from previous generations of Amos commentators at every point of the analysis.

The synthesis of various perspectives, old and new, that is presented in this commentary is my own. Since no consensus is in sight concerning the dating of individual passages or the reconstruction of the gradual growth of the book of Amos, some readers will probably find my conclusions regarding such matters controversial. Nonetheless, I hope that all readers of this commentary will find it useful as a resource for study or research, whether or not they agree with me on the usefulness of redaction criticism.

It has been my primary aim to elucidate the biblical text, not to persuade readers that my historical reconstructions are superior to those of other scholars. I therefore would like to emphasize that it is by no means necessary to subscribe to my redaction-critical hypotheses, for instance that Amos 7–9 as a whole should be dated to the post-monarchic period, in order to avail oneself of the Notes (containing philological and text-critical information) or the Comments (containing contextual and intertextual analysis of words and phrases) in this volume. This can be illustrated by the example of Amos 7:10–17. The detailed rhetorical analysis of the debate between Amos and Amaziah that is offered in the Comments on that passage has intentionally been written in such a way that readers from both camps (those who think that this narrative goes back to the eponymous prophet himself and those who doubt that) may benefit from the analysis in equal measure.

II.

From the Prophet Amos
to the Book of Amos

The Quest for the Historical Amos

From Julius Wellhausen on, many biblical scholars have taken a great interest in the protagonist of the book, the eponymous prophet/seer Amos, who supposedly left his home in Judah in order to prophesy against the Northern Kingdom, Israel. Until recently, commentaries on Amos often included a section dedicated to discussion of Amos from Tekoa as a historical person. Thus, one important strand within previous Amos studies may be called the "quest of the historical Amos" (Auld 1986: 39). This line of research has produced a vast literature, for instance regarding Amos's intellectual milieu (Wolff 1964) and his diverse agricultural occupations (see Steiner 2003). On closer examination, however, the available sources for reconstructing the life of Amos turn out to be sparse.

In my opinion, there is no reason to regard Amos from Tekoa as an entirely fictitious character. But from a scholarly point of view it is important to keep in mind that all reconstructions of his life and career have to be based on one source only, namely, the book of Amos. A prophet or seer named Amos is not mentioned elsewhere—neither in any other text in the Hebrew Bible nor in any roughly contemporaneous extrabiblical source. The earliest references to Amos are found in writings that are later than, and hence clearly dependent on, this prophetic book, such as the book of Tobit and *Vitae Prophetarum*.[1] All we have, then, are a few hints within the book of Amos itself. More precisely, biographical information is purportedly provided by two passages: (1) the *editorial* superscription (1:1), which by definition is not part of the book itself, and (2) the *legendary* account in 7:10–17 (see especially 7:14–15). There are strong reasons to assume that the synchronistic reference to the reigns of two kings (Jeroboam II in Israel and Uzziah in Judah) was added to the book's superscription during the postmonarchic era (see the Comments on 1:1). As regards the narrative in 7:10–17, the fact that it interrupts the cycle of visions clearly indicates that it is a later addition (with Kratz 2003: 58). Nevertheless, these two passages (1:1 and 7:10–17) have been mined for information about the book's eponymous hero. Taking for granted that the superscription and the narrative really provide accurate pieces of information, which can be combined in an unproblematic way, many commentators have arrived at the following picture: The historical Amos came from Tekoa in Judah, where he earned his living as a breeder of livestock—sheep (1:1) and/or cattle (7:14)—and, in addition, as a tender of sycamore trees (7:14). He received visions and delivered prophetic messages concerning Israel during the reigns of Jeroboam II and Uzziah, that is, somewhere in the 760s or 750s B.C.E., two years before the occurrence of a particularly memorable earthquake (1:1).

With these "data" as their point of departure, a number of exegetes have tried to reconstruct the biography of Amos in more detail. He has been described as "a simple countryman" (S. Driver 1897: 94) whose character was shaped by "the atmosphere of the moorland and the desert."[2] By contrast, he has also been portrayed as a learned and sophisticated speaker (Kapelrud 1958) and as a representative of the traditional clan wisdom that was taught in Tekoa (Wolff 1964 and 1977: 91). On a somewhat different note, Anthony Ceresko writes that the prophet's "moral outrage was provoked by the suffering and hardship he saw around him" (1992: 180).

Attempts to Date the Activities of Amos with Precision

It has sometimes been claimed that the book's superscription, which mentions the reign of Jeroboam II as well as an earthquake, provides information that enables us to pinpoint the time of Amos's public appearance with great precision. With reference to alleged (but disputable) archaeological evidence for a major quake around 760 B.C.E., several scholars have maintained that Amos started prophesying circa 762 B.C.E., that is, "two years before the earthquake" (Amos 1:1).[3] However, it turns out that Yigael Yadin, the author of the excavation report from Hazor, based his interpretation of the destruction layer in question on a traditional interpretation of Amos 1:1 (1960: 36). In other words, this is a case of circular argumentation.[4] It is indeed likely that at least one major earthquake occurred in this region during the eighth century B.C.E., but it is hardly possible to date it with such precision (see Zwickel 2015).

According to John Hayes, who opts for a slightly later date, "Amos's preaching at Bethel probably lasted only a single day at the least and a few days at the most. It took place just prior to the fall festival beginning the year 750–749, which witnessed the coronation of Pekah as a rival king to Jeroboam II" (1988: 38).[5] Other commentators have sought to reconstruct several successive stages within a prophetic career that spanned several years.[6] Subsequent to the conflict with Amaziah (7:10–17), several scholars aver, Amos returned to Tekoa, where he wrote down his messages.[7] According to Andersen and Freedman, however, the provocative prophet was executed on account of his oppositional speech, or at least put in jail for the rest of his life (1989: 86–87). Aside from being slightly in accord with a late legendary account of Amos's martyrdom, recorded in *Vitae Prophetarum* (The Lives of the Prophets), this is sheer speculation.[8]

Amos as a Cultic Professional or as an Anti-Cultic Prophet

The historical Amos's attitude toward the sacrificial cult has been construed in strongly divergent ways. On one hand, it has been suggested that Amos was employed as a cultic functionary.[9] Some scholars have asserted that the term *nōqēd*, which occurs in 1:1, designated a shepherd or sheep breeder belonging to the temple staff.[10] According to Bič (1951), the term *nōqēd* denoted a cultic specialist who inspected the livers of animals in order to obtain omens. However, this theory turned out to be based on unfounded etymological speculations (Murtonen 1952). Scholars such as Vuilleumier (1960) and Reventlow (1962) envisaged Amos acting within a purely hypothetical type of (largely nonsacrificial) cult centering on covenant renewal ceremonies; however, recent scholarship has abandoned all such hypotheses.[11]

On the other hand, several scholars have described the historical Amos as radically anti-cultic, that is, as someone who was opposed to all kinds of worship involving sacrifices (thus, e.g., Krüger 2006 and Barton 2012: 84–92). Arguably, though, this approach is flawed by a somewhat anachronistic view of the role of sacrificial cults in societies such as ancient Israel and Judah (Eidevall 2012a: 9–30). On the basis of a thorough investigation of all passages in the book of Amos that refer or allude to cultic matters, I have reached the conclusion that this prophetic book displays a basically positive attitude toward sacrificial cults in general and toward worship performed in Jerusalem during the Second Temple era in particular (see Eidevall 2016). I suggest that the so-called cult-critical passages in Amos (above all, 4:4–5 and 5:21–24) are best understood as instances of situationally conditioned rejection of sacrifices.[12] This means that the people and the leaders of the Northern Kingdom were not condemned because of their active participation in a sacrificial cult (as if such worship could have been seen as sinful in itself). Rather, their sacrifices were rejected because of the numerous sins and crimes that they had (allegedly) committed outside the cult.[13]

Calling Off the Quest: Outline of an Alternative Approach

In retrospect, the scholarly quest for the historical Amos has not yielded any reasonably secure results at all. The difficulties inherent in this project are well illustrated by Graeme Auld's volume on Amos in the series Old Testament Guides (1986). Having argued (quite reasonably) that both the book's superscription (1:1) and the story about the confrontation in Bethel (7:10–17) must be discarded as secondary, Auld proposes that "it is from Amos's words that his biography must be produced" (1986: 38–40). On the basis of an examination of those oracles in the book that he claims can be ascribed to Amos, he concludes that Amos was a rhetorically skilled poet, rather than a prophet, and that he appears to have held the views expressed by the studied passages (1986: 73–80). As far as I can see, however, what Auld actually describes in this way is not "the historical Amos" (1986: 12), but rather some kind of personification of the message of certain parts of the book of Amos.

In my opinion, it is time to call off the quest for the historical Amos, for pragmatic and methodological reasons (with Gowan 1996: 341). Rather than denying the existence of such a historical person, I am suggesting that any reconstruction of Amos's biography would by necessity be too speculative to serve as the basis for scholarly interpretation (with Davies 2006: 123–24 and Joyce 2011: 107–8). We have no direct access to the eponymous seer/prophet (who may indeed have uttered oracles against Israel during the eighth century B.C.E.), but we do have access to the book that carries his name, and in that book "Amos" can be studied as a literary character. Hence, the focus of scholarly attention should be the contents of the *book* of Amos, not Amos the *prophet*. Important steps toward a shift in focus, from the prophet as a person who would seem to have been active in *Israel*, to the book of Amos as a literary composition that was edited in *Judah*, were taken in the commentary by Jörg Jeremias (1998). Today one may speak of a growing trend in Amos studies characterized by abstention from biographical speculations, on one hand, and by the application of new methods and perspectives on the literary and theological dimensions of this prophetic book, on the other.[14]

III.

The Book of Amos as a Literary Composition

Genres within the Book

Like most other prophetic books in the Hebrew Bible, the book of Amos contains a rich variety of literary genres drawn from different domains of life. Each of the three main sections in this book has its own characteristic mixture of formal and stylistic ingredients. Whereas chapters 1–2 are dominated by prophetic oracles of doom and destruction directed against other nations, chapters 3–6 exhibit an abundance of forms, ranging from rhetorical questions to hymns and laments. Some of these forms recur in chapters 7–9. In addition, however, the last section of the book features a number of genres that do not appear in the preceding sections: the vision report, the prophetic legend, and the oracle of salvation (or restoration). In my opinion, the unique combination of genres that we find in Amos is best explained as a result of this book's long and complicated history of redaction and composition (see further "History of Composition and Redaction," below).

Here I list all forms and genres found in the book of Amos (with the exception of the superscription and some introductory phrases) in the order of their first appearance:

Oracle against another nation: 1:3–2:8
Historical retrospective: 2:9–12; 3:2a; 4:6–11
Oracle of disaster: 2:13–16; 3:2b, 14–15; 5:3, 16–17, 27; 6:11; 7:9; 8:3, 9–10, 11–12, 13–14; 9:2–4, 8–10
Rhetorical question: 3:3–8; 5:25–26; 6:12a; 8:8; 9:7
Summons, appeal: 3:9, 13
Pronouncement of judgment and punishment: 3:10–11; 4:1–3; 5:11–12; 6:13–14
Extended simile: 3:12
Cultic formula (modified): 4:4–5; 5:21–23
Doxology/hymn: 4:13; 5:8(9); 9:5–6
Lament: 5:1–2
Exhortation: 5:4–6, 14–15
Accusation: 5:7, 10; 6:12b; 8:4–6
Woe exclamation: 5:18–20; 6:1–7
Miniature narrative: 5:19; 6:9–10
Oath: 6:8; 8:7
Vision report: 7:1–3, 4–6, 7–8; 8:1–2; 9:1
Prophetic legend: 7:10–17
Oracle of salvation/restoration: 9:11–15

Only a few passages in the book of Amos can be classified as prose (e.g., 6:10 and some parts of 7:1–8:2). Hence, the large bulk of the book ought to be described as poetry or, in some cases, perhaps as a blend of poetry and prose (see Andersen and Freedman 1989: 145–47).[15] It is worth noting, though, that when compared with other prophetic texts in the Hebrew Bible, such as Hosea or Jeremiah, the book of Amos contains surprisingly few instances of metaphor or simile.[16] According to a possible (but far from necessary) interpretation of the opening oracle, Amos 1:2, YHWH is implicitly pictured as a lion (see also 3:8). In many other passages, the reader is led to assume that YHWH acts/speaks as a judge or as a heavenly king. However, one looks in vain for explicit metaphors that depict the deity himself or some aspect of divine agency. The inhabitants of Samaria are occasionally portrayed as sheep (3:12) or cattle (4:1), but extended metaphorical depictions of the relationship between YHWH and his people are, as far as I can see, missing in this book.

With its mixture of genres, Amos resembles the other parts of the book of the Twelve (except for Jonah). At the same time, this prophetic book has an unmistakably distinct character, emanating from its quite unique combination of eloquently variegated messages of doom, passionately formulated indictments of injustice, and intriguingly dark doxologies. Searching for a factor that would explain this book's special character, scholars have opted either for the cult or for the wisdom tradition. As shown below, none of these hypotheses has been successful in the long run.

As already mentioned, several scholars who were active around the middle of the twentieth century subscribed to (some version of) the theory that Amos himself was a cultic functionary (see "Amos as a Cultic Professional or as an Anti-Cultic Prophet"). As a rule, these exegetes claimed that many forms and genres in the book of Amos had a cultic origin. According to Bentzen, for instance, the entire series of oracles against neighboring nations in chapters 1–2 can be linked to a ritual, known from Egypt, that involved words of execration accompanied by the crushing of ceramic bowls symbolizing various enemies (1950: 85–91). As far as I can see, however, this hypothesis cannot be corroborated by any single formulation in Amos 1:3–2:16. Similar flaws are attached to the subsequent attempt by Kapelrud to demonstrate that the entire book is "strongly influenced by the cult" (1956: 69). Especially given that Kapelrud used a wide definition of "cult," including "more than festivals, sacrifices and offerings" (1956: 68), he could demonstrate (possible) cultic influence (regarding forms and/or formulations) in a surprisingly few number of passages.

Yet other scholars have postulated the existence of an alternative temple cult, allegedly focusing on covenant renewal rather than regular sacrifices and featuring exactly the type of curses, warnings, and indictments that appear frequently in the book of Amos (thus Vuilleumier 1960 and Reventlow 1962). This is, of course, another case of perfectly circular argumentation. At the end of the day, not much remains of cultic or cult-connected genres and forms in the book of Amos. In two instances, the "cult-critical" passages 4:4–5 and 5:21–23, one may speak of prophetic (and slightly satirical) adaptations of priestly formulas and declarations deriving from the domain of sacrificial worship. Finally, the so-called doxologies (4:13; 5:8; 9:5–6) might attest to liturgical *use* of the book of Amos during the postexilic era (Koch 1974: 536 and Jeremias 1998: 78). To sum up, the cult does not seem to constitute a unifying factor behind the plurality of genres that the book of Amos displays.

According to an alternative hypothesis, many forms and formulations used in the book betray influence from the wisdom tradition (Terrien 1962; and Wolff 1964; 1977: 91–100). According to Wolff, the use of genres originating in wisdom circles goes back to the eponymous prophet himself, who was well acquainted with "clan wisdom," because this tradition "had been taught to him by the clan elders in the gate" (1977: 91). Presumably alluding to the wise woman from Tekoa mentioned in 2 Sam 14:2, Wolff adds that the hometown of Amos seems to have been a rural center for sapiential teaching: "perhaps this tradition had been preserved more zealously in Tekoa than elsewhere" (1977: 91). Leaving such speculations aside, Wolff's theory has another serious problem, namely, the fact that very little of this book's style and vocabulary can be safely linked to the wisdom literature (see McLaughlin 2014). On closer examination, the amount of sapiential forms in Amos boils down to no more than two: the repeated (though somewhat irregular) use of a formula associated with so-called graduated numerical sayings (in 1:3–2:8) and the occurrence of a number of rhetorical (but perhaps not particularly didactic) questions (in 3:3–8 and 6:12). As pointed out by Rainer Kessler, the observation that the emphasis on just treatment of the poor constitutes a shared motif between the book of Amos and Proverbs does not permit any definite conclusion concerning sources of origin or direction(s) of influence (2015: 54–57).

Structural Symmetry

The book of Amos can be described as a carefully structured literary composition. A symmetric overall structure is visible in the almost universally accepted tripartite division of the book: chapters 1–2 // 3–6 // 7–9. The middle part, consisting of a collection of oracles (chapters 3–6), is framed by a prologue and an epilogue, often referred to as the cycle of oracles against the nations (chapters 1–2) and the cycle of visions (chapters 7–9). Thus, the book can be viewed as a triptych: chapters 1–2 (oracles against the nations) // 3–6 (the words of Amos) // 7–9 (visions).

Within chapters 3–6 it is possible to make a further subdivision into two parts of roughly equal length, comprising chapters 3–4 and 5–6, each introduced by a summons to hear: 3:1 and 5:1 (Jeremias 1998: 6). However, this does not exhaust the possibilities of describing the book's structure. There is nowadays a wide scholarly consensus that the section 5:1–17, which constitutes the centerpiece of the composition, displays an artistically crafted concentric structure: A, lamentation (vv. 1–3)—B, exhortation (vv. 4–6)—C, injustice (v. 7)—D, doxology (vv. 8–9)—C′, injustice (vv. 10–13)—B′, exhortation (vv. 14–15)—A′, lamentation (vv. 16–17). This was convincingly demonstrated by Jan de Waard in a groundbreaking study (1977; see also Tromp 1984). (This is discussed further in "Introduction to 5:1–17.")

Developing this approach further, other scholars have extended the scope of the concentric structure. Although opinions differ concerning the exact boundaries, many scholars agree that the bulk of the book's middle section (chapters 3–6) has been arranged according to such a principle. Lust (1981: 154) sees the concentric composition as comprising 4:1–6:7. Others have suggested that 3:9–6:14 or chapters 3–6 in their entirety exhibit such a pattern (see Möller 2003a: 69–72). Arguably, though, the strongest case can be made for 5:1–17. In my opinion, the concentric structure of 4:1–6:7, as reconstructed by several scholars, is likewise sufficiently neat to be convincing (with

Table 1. Amos 3–6 as a Concentric Composition

A. 3:1–2 Words of judgment against the secure
    B. 3:3–8 Rhetorical questions
        C. 3:9–15 Buildings become ruins
            D. 4:1–3 Against the elite in Samaria (feasts, deportation)
                E. 4:4–5 Sacrificial cult
                    F. 4:6–12 (13) Disasters (past)
                        G. 5:1–3 Lamentation
                            H. 5:4–6 Exhortation: Seek!
                              I. 5:7 Injustice
                                J. 5:8 (9) Doxology
                            I. 5:10–13 Injustice
                          H. 5:14–15 Exhortation: Seek!
                      G. 5:16–17 Lamentation
                  F. 5:18–20 Disaster (day of YHWH)
                E. 5:21–17 Sacrificial cult
             D. 6:1–7 Against the elite in Samaria (feasts, deportation)
        C. 6:8–11 Buildings become ruins
    B. 6:12a Rhetorical questions
A. 6:12b–14 Words of judgment against the secure

Hadjiev 2009: 179–84). It is somewhat more difficult to make the various subsections of chapter 3 correspond to the series of oracles in 6:8–14. Table 1, which covers Amos 3:1–6:14, is based on the analysis presented by Rottzoll (1996: 3).

Since this intricate concentric pattern (to the extent that it can be seen as intentional) operates in a sophisticated way and on a macrostructural level, average readers (or listeners) will probably not discover it. It is more likely that they will notice the repeated use of certain stylistic devices, such as rhetorical questions or various numerical patterns (Limburg 1987; O'Connell 1996).[17] Another structuring feature that many readers must have noted, but which has not yet been systematically studied, is the presence of a number of literary themes (or "thematic threads") that pervade the book and thereby help to tie its different parts together.

Thematic Threads

In addition to structural symmetry, the book of Amos is characterized by a high degree of thematic coherence. To begin with, most passages in the book are connected to one dominant topic, namely, judgment over Israel (the Northern Kingdom). Over and over again, accusations are followed by proclamations of punishment. While the accusations mainly concern corruption in the courts, rejected cultic practices, and social and economic oppression, the divine judgment may take the form of either military invasion (with ensuing deportations) or some kind of natural disaster. In the book's final section, 9:11–15, all these threats are reversed and transformed into a utopian vision.

However, it is also possible to speak of thematic coherence of a different kind. As shown by Terry Collins (2001), a number of "thematic threads" run through the book of Amos. Here, the notion of a "theme" is used analogously to the way one speaks of themes in musical compositions. Thus, it denotes a series of variations on a specific literary motif (see Eidevall 1996: 40). Some of the thematic threads identified by Collins, such as "the lion" (see below) and "destruction of buildings" (which includes instances of the earthquake motif), begin in the book's introduction, in 1:1–2, and continue into chapter 9 (Collins 2001: 95–98). Others permeate only parts of the composition. Some are mainly metaphorical; others are predominantly based on literal usage of the key term(s). Each thread is first introduced, often rather vaguely; then it unfolds, gradually, taking on sharper contours and acquiring further nuances and aspects as it resurfaces at a number of junctures in the text.

The theme of "the lion," which is perhaps preferably labeled "the roaring lion and other dangerous animals," may serve as an illustrative example (cf. Collins 2001: 95–96). It is introduced in 1:2, albeit indirectly, by means of the phrase "YHWH roars (*yišʾag*) from Zion." In the passage 3:3–8, this theme is developed further, step by step. At first, in 3:4, a roaring lion is mentioned in a rhetorical question, which illustrates the relation between cause (capture of prey) and effect (roar). As the series of questions reaches its climax, the motif of the roaring lion becomes firmly linked to YHWH's awe-inspiring (or terrifying) self-revelation, as well as to the prophetic vocation: "The lion has roared. Who is not frightened? / The Lord YHWH has spoken. Who can but prophesy?" (3:8). Somewhat later, this thread surfaces again, as the devastation that will befall Samaria is likened to a situation where all that remains of a sheep torn by a lion is "a couple of bones or a piece of an ear" (3:12). A further variation on this theme is found in 5:18–20, the famous passage dealing with expectations related to the day of YHWH. In the miniature narrative told in 5:19, a wretched person manages to escape first a lion and then a bear, but ends up being bitten by a snake as he returns home. Finally, the motif of the biting snake recurs in 9:3 in a passage that emphasizes the inescapability of the divine judgment.

Collins (2001) discusses the following thematic threads: "the lion," "the destruction of buildings," "encounter with the Lord," and "the reversal motif." In addition, he identifies several other themes of potential interest for future studies: "feasting and mourning, cultic worship, vegetation, the land, election, exile, rich and poor, the role of the prophet, cities and numbers" (2001: 101–2, n. 6). However, these themes appear to have been defined and labeled in a somewhat impressionistic way. In my opinion, it is imperative to formulate clear criteria for analytical categories of this kind and to apply them consistently. The themes listed below fit the two criteria that I find most important: shared motif(s) and shared vocabulary. On the basis of these criteria alone, however, it is possible to detect a large number of thematic threads of varying length. Arguably, threads running through (more or less) the entire book are of particular interest for a study focusing on thematic coherence. Here I list nine such themes, all of which start in one of the opening utterances of the book (1:1–5), in the order of their first appearance:

> Earthquake/no escape: 1:1 (earthquake); 2:13–16 (quake, no escape); 3:14–15
> (destroyed buildings); 4:11 (overthrown like Sodom and Gomorrah,

hpk); 6:11 (destroyed buildings); 8:8 (quake); 9:1–4 (earthquake, no escape); 9:5 (quake)

Shepherding: 1:1, 2; 3:12; 7:14–15

Mountains: 1:2 (Zion; "the top of Carmel"); 3:9; 4:1 (Samaria); 4:3 (Hermon [?]); 4:13 (high places); 6:1 (Zion; Samaria); (7:9, high places); 9:3 ("the top of Carmel"); 9:13

The roaring lion and other dangerous animals: 1:2; 3:4, 8; 12; 5:19; 9:3

Drought/thirst: 1:2; 4:7–8; 8:11–13

Mourning/lament: 1:2; 5:1–3, 16–17; 6:9–10; 8:3, 8, 10; 9:5

Fortresses/palaces: 1:4, 7, 10, 12, 14; 2:2, 5; 3:9–11; 5:9; 6:8

Destruction by fire: 1:4, 7, 10, 12, 14; 2:1, 2, 5; 4:11; 5:6; 7:4

Deportation/exile: 1:5, 6, 15; 4:2–3; 5:5, 27; 6:7; 7:11, 17; 9:4 (cf. also 9:9, 15)

The presence of multiple thematic threads, some of them frequently interwoven with other threads, enables the reader to follow different paths through the book. Thus, a sense of coherence may be construed, albeit in a number of different ways. It is important to point out that thematic coherence of this kind need not imply authorial unity.[18] As I argue in more detail below, the book of Amos most likely went through multiple redactions. Apparently, though, the editors took an interest in creating and/or developing thematic threads as well as maintaining structural symmetry.[19]

Reading the Book of Amos as a Drama

Despite the fact that only the final chapters contain texts representing narrative genres (see especially 7:1–8:2 and 9:1), I suggest that it is possible (from a "synchronic" point of view) to read the book of Amos in its entirety as a drama of sorts. Notably, a narrative dimension is introduced in 1:2 (with Möller 2003a: 159). I want to stress that I use the term "drama" in a very loose sense in the following. There is no recognizable plot in the book of Amos, and there is only one powerful agent: YHWH. This peculiar drama unfolds in three acts, corresponding to the traditional tripartite subdivision presented above.

In Act I, comprising chapters 1–2, the divine protagonist, YHWH, acts as a judge over all the nations in the Syro-Canaanite region. Catalogues of war-related crimes and atrocities are interspersed with announcements of punishment, invariably in the form of fire and consistently directed against major cities and fortifications (see 1:3–2:3). From 2:4 onward one might speak of a "zooming in" effect, as the accusations suddenly begin to concern internal affairs, such as cultic transgressions or instances of social and economic oppression: first in Judah (2:4–5) and finally in Israel, the Northern Kingdom (2:6–12).

Act II (chapters 3–6) is about acts and their consequences. This is efficiently underlined by the series of rhetorical questions in 3:3–8. However, throughout this part of the drama the focus lies on the Northern Kingdom (Israel)—or, to be more precise, on YHWH's rejection of the Northern Kingdom and on the dire consequences of this rejection of a nation that cherished the exodus tradition and regarded itself as YHWH's elect people (see 3:1–2). The divine monologues in chapters 3–6 consist mainly of condemnations of the ruling elite in Samaria. While indulging in a luxurious lifestyle (4:1; 6:1–6), which involves lavish cultic celebrations (4:4–5; 5:21–24), they allegedly fail to uphold justice, as they manipulate the courts and prey on the poor (3:9–10; 4:1; 5:7, 10–12; 6:12b). As a consequence, the entire nation is threatened by destruction. However, apparently blinded by their chauvinist pride (6:8, 13), the people and their leaders fail to heed the prophetic warnings and exhortations (3:13; 4:6–12; 5:4–6, 14–15). They do not realize the imminent danger: Because of all these (alleged) crimes and transgressions, it is declared that the nation's patron deity, YHWH, is about to withdraw his protection. As a consequence, bright expectations will be turned into dark despair (5:18–20). The judgment seems to be irrevocable. It is announced that a hostile army will invade and occupy the country (3:11; 6:14). According to the oracles pronounced by the prophet, many buildings will be demolished (3:15; 6:11), large parts of the population will be killed (5:1–2, 16–17; 6:9–10), and the few survivors will be deported (4:3; 6:7). The cities of the Northern Kingdom are going to be destroyed and depopulated.

The setting of Act III, the final act of this drama (chapters 7–9), appears to be an agrarian landscape (see 7:1–2, 4, 14–15; 8:1; 9:13–15). With the notable exception of Bethel (7:10–12), cities are hardly mentioned; however, temples and sanctuaries are foregrounded in some passages (7:12; 8:14; 9:1). Instead of focusing almost exclusively on the fate of the Northern Kingdom, the monologues and dialogues in chapters 7–9 are primarily concerned with the fate of YHWH's people. From now on, "Israel" may sometimes include (or refer exclusively to) the people of Judah (see especially 9:14). In the first part of Act III a human character, Amos, suddenly appears at center stage (7:1–8:2). By means of introductory phrases and messenger formulas the reader has been constantly reminded that the divine messages proclaimed in Acts I and II should be construed as speeches delivered by a prophet interacting with various audiences (see Möller 2003a: 125–32). Until now, however, this prophet, acting as the deity's mouth-piece, has remained almost invisible. This changes in chapter 7. In reaction to terrifying visions, Amos enters into dialogue with YHWH and intercedes for the people, called "Jacob" (7:1–6). Although his initial attempts to avert impending catastrophes are successful (7:3, 6), it turns out that Amos cannot in the long run persuade YHWH to spare the people (7:7–8). At this crucial juncture another human character appears on the stage: Amaziah, "priest in Bethel" (7:10). The debate between Amos and Amaziah (7:12–17) demonstrates that the political and religious authorities had a hostile attitude to the prophetic message. In response to yet another vision, Amos is compelled to declare, "The end has come for my people Israel" (8:2).

At this point the prophet Amos leaves the stage, but the drama (recounted by a prophetic voice) continues. Renewed accusations and announcements of disasters (8:4–14) lead to a climax: a vision of total destruction (9:1). It is stated, repeatedly, that no one will be able to escape (9:2–4). Yet this is not the end. A hymnic piece that praises the deity's power to destroy but also to (re)build implies that there might be some hope, after all (9:5–6). In the next utterance, 9:7, the reader is reminded that YHWH is "an exodus kind of God" (Strawn 2013: 122–23). Declarations to the effect that parts of YHWH's people will be spared (9:8–10) are followed by a promise of future restoration (9:11–12). This promise develops into a utopian vision of peace and prosperity (9:13–15). But despite this rather unexpected happy ending, it is debatable whether the book of Amos, viewed as a drama, should be characterized as a comedy, rather than a tragedy. Admittedly, this observation attests to the limitations of a predominantly synchronic perspective on this prophetic book.[20]

IV.
History of Composition and Redaction

Theological Diversity and Questions Regarding Authorship

As we have seen, the book of Amos is characterized by structural as well as thematic coherence. Far from being a haphazard collection or a quick transcript of oral oracles, this prophetic book deserves to be studied as an artistic literary composition. But who wrote it? When were the symmetrical structures created? It is important to realize that the above observations concerning concentric patterns and thematic threads do not necessarily mean that the book of Amos is the product of one single author. On the contrary, such compositional features are perfectly compatible with the assumption that the final version of this prophetic book is the result of extensive editorial work involving several stages (with Rottzoll 1996: 1–7).

Moving from the level of macrostructure to the actual contents of the book, it is possible to detect dissonance and diversity. I am not primarily referring to the obvious fact that the book of Amos contains a rich variety of topics and genres. There is also a rather high degree of ideological diversity. It is customary to speak about the "theology" of Amos (the book and/or the prophet) in the singular. In my opinion, it would be more to the point to speak of a number of theologies, or (perhaps preferably) ideologies, within this book (see Barton 2012: 70–160). In the following, I briefly indicate some areas where strong tensions exist between divergent ideological perspectives. I supply further details in the Comments on the relevant passages.

One such area is the role of *prophets and prophecy*. According to a rather straightforward interpretation of the utterance in Amos 3:8, anyone who hears the word of YHWH would, or should, start prophesying. This appears to stand in tension with other utterances in the book that seem to refer to the prophets as members of a well-defined guild. Such intermediaries, we learn, are "raised" by YHWH himself (2:11). The prophets, YHWH's "servants," are even granted access to the divine council, where they receive information in advance concerning the deity's plans (3:7). One may infer that the most important task of this special group of prophets is to issue instructions and warnings, in order to give others the opportunity to repent and thereby avoid divine punishment. From these passages one may further infer that "Amos," the prophet speaking throughout the book, belongs to such a category of prophets. However, the oracles in the book of Amos contain very few words of instruction or warning. In many cases, the message seems to be that it is already too late; nothing can be done to prevent the coming disaster (see 2:13–16; 3:9–15; 4:1–3; 5:1–3, 16–17; 6:7–14; 7:7–9; 8:1–3). Somewhat surprisingly, moreover, the literary character Amos seems to deny that he is a member of a prophetic guild (7:14).

Another central topic where tensions are tangible is divine *judgment and mercy*. In most passages within chapters 1–6, the punishment decreed by YHWH is described as irrevocable and inescapable (see 1:3–2:16; 3:1–12; 3:13–15; 4:1–5; 5:1–3, 11, 16–27; 6:1–14). A few passages stand out as more hopeful, since they contain exhortations to repent (5:4–6, 14–15; see also 3:13; 4:6–12). In the latter group of utterances the idea seems to be that a radical change of human behavior might appease YHWH and make the deity somewhat more merciful. However, there is no hint in chapters 1–6 that YHWH might be prepared to forgive all the crimes and sins committed by the people and their leaders. Therefore, it comes as a surprise when the notion of radical forgiveness is introduced in chapter 7. Now, all of a sudden, YHWH repents and relents, in response to prophetic intercessory prayer (nothing is said about repentance among the people). As a result, planned disasters are canceled (7:1–6). But then YHWH changes his mind once more and declares, through Amos the seer, that "the end has come for my people Israel" (8:2).

Thus far, two alternative (and utterly incompatible) visions, of either all-encompassing destruction or collective forgiveness, have been juxtaposed. In 9:7–10, a string of theological reflections that form a preamble to the book's hopeful epilogue (9:11–15), attempts are made to resolve the tension between these two perspectives. Step by step, the scope of YHWH's punitive actions is limited. It is stated that these will be directed against only "the sinners among my people" (9:10). Interestingly, though, such a distinction between sinners and righteous within YHWH's people has not been made anywhere in the preceding parts of the book. For the reader, therefore, the tension between contrasting theological perspectives remains.

In my opinion, these and other tensions are best explained as the result of diachronic developments spanning several centuries. The book of Amos seems to attest to a continuous process of reflection on such matters as divine wrath and mercy in the light of the two great national disasters—when the Assyrians conquered the Northern Kingdom in 722 B.C.E. and when the Babylonians destroyed Jerusalem and the temple in 587 B.C.E.—and subsequent experiences of deportation and exile. In other words, the actual contents of the book suggest that it is the product of gradual growth (with Jeremias 1998: 7–9). As a consequence, it is necessary for the interpreter to take more than one historical context into consideration.

Historical Contexts for the Book's Messages

When it comes to outlining the historical context(s) for the prophetic message(s) contained in the book of Amos, most modern commentaries are rather uniform. With few exceptions they concentrate on one particular period in the history of the kingdom of Israel (or the Northern Kingdom), namely, the last decades of the reign of Jeroboam II (ca. 787–747 B.C.E.). Although the commentators' depictions of this era vary considerably in length and depth, they have several traits in common.

As a rule, the long reign of Jeroboam II is characterized as a period of unprecedented peace and prosperity for the Northern Kingdom.[21] Two other recurring key concepts are corruption and oppression. More precisely, it is maintained that decisive military conquests (2 Kgs 13:25; 14:25), followed by decades without large-scale warfare, led to a flowering of trade that generated considerable economic wealth. However, the accumulated wealth was unevenly distributed. In this situation, the traditional judicial system seems to have collapsed, more or less. As a consequence, it is claimed, the rich and few became much richer, while the masses of poor people became even poorer (so, e.g., Fendler 1973: 35–42 and Wolff 1977: 89–90). In order to maintain their position, and if possible increase their incomes even further, those who belonged to the elite manipulated the market, bribed the judges, and forced those who were less fortunate into debt slavery: "Slavery for debt took on vicious forms" (Wolff 1977: 90). Some scholars have described the societal and economic conditions prevailing in Israel during the eighth century B.C.E. in terms of "rent capitalism" (so Lang 1981: 483–84 and 1983: 114–27).

As regards the opulent upper classes in Samaria and their "luxurious" lifestyle (Paul 1991: 2), the depictions provided by the commentaries are often infused with indignation. The reader is told that "the rich enjoyed an indolent, indulgent existence" (Mays 1969: 3). According to Paul, these rich people were, in addition, involved in "an intensive and zealous religious life"; however, this "panoply of pomp and ceremony" was ultimately of no avail, since the rich oppressors were "blinded by their boundless optimism" (1991: 2).

This picture of the situation in Samaria and Israel around the middle of the eighth century B.C.E. has been repeated so often that it has almost acquired the status of an unquestionable truth. But on closer examination, this colorful historical reconstruction turns out to be nothing more than a relatively plausible scenario, based on a weak foundation. Whereas it appears to be a fact that this era was unusually peaceful (the Aramean wars had ceased and the Assyrian campaigns had not yet begun), some of the remaining features in the standard description of the Israelite society lack support from reliable historical sources.[22]

How do we know that large parts of the population were impoverished and enslaved in the midst of an economic boom? Or how do we know that legal corruption escalated during the reign of Jeroboam II? The truth is that we have no information at all concerning these issues, apart from what we possibly might extract from some polemical utterances in the book of Amos! The only sources adduced by Wolff and Mays in order to support their far-reaching reconstructions are in fact a number of passages in Amos, such as 2:6–7; 3:9–10, 15; 4:1–3; 5:10–12; 6:1–7; 8:4–6 (see Wolff 1977: 89–90 and Mays 1969: 2–3). As pointed out by Carroll R., Lang's reconstruction of a rather advanced (and extremely oppressive) system of rent capitalism during the days of Jeroboam II rests to a large extent on a specific (and far from self-evident) interpretation of a few verses in Amos, in particular 2:6 and 8:6 (1992: 32–44).[23] What we have here, as well as in the commentary introductions referred to above, is yet another case of blatant circular argumentation. In order to throw light on various texts in the book of Amos, these exegetes draw on a reconstructed historical context that is, in its turn, based on interpretations of these and other passages in the book that they seek to interpret.

What I have chosen to call the standard description of the primary historical context for Amos is not only based on a weak textual foundation. It is furthermore based on several questionable presuppositions: (1) that it is possible to identify *one* central message in the book of Amos, (2) that this message is linked to oral performances by a certain prophet named Amos, (3) that this prophet was active during the reign of Jeroboam II, and (4) that many oracles in the book appear to have been uttered during an era of peace and prosperity.

The present commentary represents an alternative approach, based on the observation that the book of Amos contains a number of different messages that seem to presuppose multiple voices connected to a number of different historical settings. Moreover, because the chronological data found in the superscription most likely originated at a later stage in the book's editorial history (see the Comments on 1:1), there is no compelling reason to assume that the years around the middle of the eighth century B.C.E. constitute the most important historical context for the reader of this prophetic book. Finally, it is far from self-evident that prophecies filled with references to war and violence (such as Amos 1:3–2:16; 3:9–15; 4:2–3, 10–11; 5:1–3; 6:8–10, 13–14) originated in the midst of a peaceful era. Personally, I find this idea counterintuitive.

I suggest that the professional interpreter, instead of concentrating on one particular period within the history of Israel and Judah, should assume that a range of periods and historical events may have had an impact on (parts of) the book of Amos. In the following I briefly indicate some major aspects of the history of the region (from the eighth until the fourth century B.C.E.) that need to be considered in such a broad search for the historical contexts of the diverse messages found in the book of Amos.

The period preceding the fall of Samaria. One cannot, admittedly, exclude the possibility that a few oracles in the book go back to a prophet who was active in the days of Jeroboam II (see Fritz 1989: 34–40 and Blum 2008: 96–107). However, one should keep in mind that the traditional dating of the earliest oracles in the book to Jeroboam's reign is based on meager and late evidence, consisting of the superscription and the legendary account in 7:10–17. In my opinion, several features in those prophecies that are commonly regarded as belonging to the oldest layer in Amos make better sense if one posits a somewhat later date of origin, in the 730s and/or 720s B.C.E.[24] During that period the people and the leaders in Israel and Judah would (or should) have been aware of the Assyrian threat (Wöhrle 2006: 128).

Therefore, the turbulent years between 738 (the first military campaign of Tiglath-Pileser III affecting this region) and 722 B.C.E. (the Assyrian capture of Samaria) would seem to constitute a likely setting for exactly those kinds of oracles that constitute the core of Amos 3–6: woe-cries (4:1; 5:18; 6:1), laments (5:1–2, 16–17), critique against the ruling elite for not taking the situation seriously (6:4–6), and predictions of disasters, including military defeat (5:3) and deportations (4:2–3; 6:7). Such a dating of the book's earliest layer would make the eponymous prophet contemporary with Isaiah and Hosea (Kratz 2003: 85–86). It is worth noting that the combination of woe-sayings and critique against the rich elite, which is often seen as characteristic of Amos, is also found in the book of Isaiah (Isa 5:8–23; 28:1–4). To this may be added that the textual basis of the widespread idea that Amos delivered his prophecies in Bethel and Samaria is restricted to the legend in 7:10–17. According to 1:1, the words of Amos concerned Israel, Judah's neighbor. However, the superscription fails to mention that Amos ever left Judah (Tekoa) in order to preach in the Northern Kingdom. It is thus conceivable that the oracles that constitute the earliest layer of the book of Amos were formulated by a prophet, or by a group of prophets, in Judah.

The period subsequent to the fall of Samaria. The present commentary is based on the hypothesis that the book of Amos is a product of the period after the great national disaster in 722 B.C.E. when Israel became a province in the Assyrian empire and parts of the population were deported. Although some individual oracles may have originated before 722, and possibly in the Northern Kingdom, the perspective of the book is markedly different. It is, to begin with, decidedly pro-Judean (see Koch et al. 1976b: 121–22 and Sweeney 2000: 192–95). Notably, Amos begins with a reference to Jerusalem as the abode of YHWH (1:2) and ends with a promise to restore the "hut" of David (9:11). Hence, it is reasonable to posit that this prophetic book was composed and edited in Jerusalem.

Moreover, one may speak of a "past-fulfillment perspective" (Möller 2003a: 119). Throughout the book of Amos the downfall of Samaria and the Northern Kingdom seems to be treated either as a fact that has to be explained or as a past event that may serve as a historical lesson. Several scholars have recently argued that even the earliest version of this prophetic book has the character of *vaticinium ex eventu* (a prophecy formulated after the event), with regard to the disaster that occurred in 722 B.C.E.[25] The downfall of the Northern Kingdom is explained in terms of (well-deserved) divine punishment for serious crimes committed by the leaders of this nation, with a particular emphasis on oppression of the poor and corruption of the judicial system (Amos 2:6–8, 13–16; 3:9–12; 5:10–12, etc.). In addition, this historical event is used as a warning for the book's first (Judean) addressees (3:13–14; 5:6, 14–15).

The period preceding the destruction of Jerusalem. It is possible that some of the book's anti-Bethel prophecies, such as 3:13–14 and 5:6 (cf. also 4:4–5 and 5:4–5), should be dated to the Josianic era (so Wolff 1977: 111–12). However, the historicity of the cultic reform ascribed to Josiah, as described in 2 Kings 22–23, is a matter of intense scholarly dispute (see Pakkala 2010 and Pietsch 2013). In the light of Bethel's enduring significance as a cultic center, both earlier and later dates of origin are conceivable (see Blenkinsopp 2003).

The period subsequent to the destruction of Jerusalem. The disaster in 587 B.C.E., which put an end to the kingdom of Judah, is never explicitly mentioned in the book of Amos. No unambiguous reference is made to the destruction of the Jerusalem temple (but see the Comments on 9:1); nevertheless, there are good reasons to assume that this catastrophe, and its aftermath, had a major impact on the book as we now have it. Not only the epilogue (9:11–15) betrays a post-587 perspective. In chapters 7–8 several central features—such as the motif of intercession, the prophet's dialogues with YHWH, and his conflict with a priest—have close counterparts in the book of Jeremiah.[26] In my opinion, this indicates that the series of vision reports in Amos 7:1–8:2, as well as the interspersed narrative (7:10–17), should be dated to the postmonarchic era. To this one may add that some utterances in chapters 1–6 contain typically Deuteronomistic phraseology and theology (e.g., 2:4–5, 9–11; 3:1b, 7; 5:25).[27] On the basis of these and other observations I suggest that the second (revised and expanded) version of the book of Amos was produced during the exilic or the early postexilic era.

The Persian era. In a recent commentary James Linville (2008) made a daring and innovative attempt to study the book of Amos in its entirety as a literary product of the Persian era (539–333 B.C.E.). In my opinion, this experiment can be described as both a failure and a success. On one hand, large parts of Amos, for instance those passages that refer to the luxurious lifestyle among the upper classes in Samaria before the demise of the Northern Kingdom (4:1–3; 6:1–7), including references to their predilection for ivory ornamentation (3:15; 6:4), become awkwardly pointless when they are detached from an eighth-century setting. I agree with John Barton that this prophetic book's depictions of "Israel" are so far removed from the situation prevailing in the Persian era that it is utterly unlikely that someone living during that time could author such texts: "The Israel of the book of Amos has an army, a king, no foreign overlord; and it has recently recaptured two Transjordanian towns from the Arameans" (2012: 30). Hence, Linville fails to persuade me that the whole book actually originated in the post-monarchic era. On the other hand, Linville's reading of certain passages with cosmic or eschatological overtones, such as the so-called doxologies (4:13; 5:8–9; 9:5–6), can be seen as both congenial and convincing (see Linville 2008: 92–97, 105–6, 165–68). This speaks in favor of the hypothesis that these hymnic fragments were inserted during the Persian era. According to my reconstruction, substantial parts of chapter 8 (the chain of reinterpretations of earlier prophecies in 8:4–14) and some expansions in chapter 9 should likewise be dated to that period (cf. similarly Jeremias 1998: 144–45, 162).

The Hellenistic era. One cannot exclude the possibility that additions were made as late as the third century B.C.E., for instance as a result of editorial processes extending over the (evolving) book of the Twelve as a whole. As far as I can see, however, none of the utterances in the book of Amos points specifically to such a late historical context.

On the Advantages and Limitations of Redaction Criticism

I have argued above that the book of Amos contains more than one theology and that this implies that the oracles collected in the book originated (and were edited) in a number of different historical situations. If this is correct, redaction criticism cannot be avoided in a commentary such as this, which aims to study both historical and literary aspects of the text. In other words, the observations made in the preceding sections of this introduction seem to require a theory of the book's history of composition that assumes more than one version.

In conversation with previous and contemporary research, I have made an attempt to connect every utterance in the book of Amos to its present literary context, as well as to its original historical (or rhetorical) situation. I am well aware of the method-ological problems associated with redaction criticism.[28] Conclusions concerning such matters as the dating of individual oracles are inevitably hypothetical. Perfectly reliable criteria for distinguishing between different strata within a given text are lacking. As a consequence, all reconstructions of editorial stages have a tentative character and should be seen as exploratory models rather than as faithful representations of factual development—or, to put it differently, they should primarily be regarded as suggestions intended to aid the interpretation of certain passages.

Redaction criticism is a tool that can be used to distinguish different voices in a debate between different ideologies/theologies—a debate that seems to have been preserved at least (to some extent) in the book of Amos. A tentative reconstruction of the book's stages of redaction can thus help the reader to discover the multilayered and dialogic character of the prophetic discourse. Within the boundaries of one passage, more than one standpoint may be formulated, and more than one group of addressees may be addressed. It has been my aim to formulate redaction-critical hypotheses with a high explanatory potential. Ideally, such hypotheses should be based on observations pertaining to several different levels: context, form, style, topic, terminology, phraseology, intertextuality, and ideological tendency.

The redaction-critical methodology used in this commentary can be illustrated by the example of Amos 3:7.[29] Within the rhetorical unit 3:3–8, v. 7 is often treated as a secondary insertion (see Auld 1986: 30–31 and Jeremias 1998: 54).[30] There are several reasons for this. First, as regards form and style, v. 7 is written in prose, whereas the remainder of 3:3–8 consists of poetic utterances. Second, as concerns the relation of this utterance to its immediate context, 3:7 evidently interrupts the chain of rhetorical questions. Third, this verse discontinues the topic of cause and effect (or observation and implication). Finally, and perhaps most important, the message conveyed by 3:7 is hardly compatible with the remainder of the passage 3:3–8. Although this utterance apparently comments on the surrounding sayings, it has a theological tendency that sets it apart from its context.[31] According to a likely interpretation of 3:6, calamities sent by YHWH may indeed occur in a city without previous notice. In v. 7, however, we learn that YHWH invariably informs "his servants the prophets" about such events in advance. According to v. 8, anyone is allowed to (or, perhaps better, is compelled to) prophesy when YHWH speaks to him or her. This stands in sharp contrast to 3:7, which speaks of "the prophets" as a confined group with an extraordinary status.

The rather awkward position of v. 7 within 3:3–8 has been described as follows: "Far from offering a rhetorical enhancement, it actually appears to do violence to the argument of the whole section" (Auld 1986: 31). Still, it is part of the text as we now have it. I find it likely that v. 7 was placed in its present context in order to modify or correct the views expressed in vv. 6 and 8. Notably, this utterance adds an aspect that makes the passage's portrayal of YHWH less harsh, as it asserts that the deity always issues warnings, which would give people a chance to repent. Since the notion that the prophets are YHWH's "servants" is unique within the book of Amos but frequently attested in the book of Jeremiah (7:25; 25:4; 26:5; 29:19; 35:15; 44:4) and in 2 Kings (17:13, 23; 21:10; 24:2), it is reasonable to assume that Amos 3:7 was inserted by a Deuteronomistic editor (W. H. Schmidt 1965: 183–85). Alternatively, this editorial strand should be termed "post-Deuteronomistic" (Auld 1986: 30). At any rate, 3:7 was most probably added in the sixth century B.C.E. or later.

I hope to have demonstrated that at least in some cases it may indeed be possible to identify later insertions and expansions with a relatively high degree of certainty. Using the type of methodology illustrated above, scholars may in fact draw some well-founded conclusions concerning the book's gradual growth. However, during the process of writing this commentary I have not regarded redaction criticism as an end in itself. Sometimes the reconstruction of different layers is presented as the main result of an exegetical study. In this case, my tentative reconstruction should rather be seen as a starting point. Let us return to the example of Amos 3:3–8. Instead of being the end result of the analysis, the hypothesis that 3:7 is a later insertion can serve as a point of departure for a rhetorical analysis that seeks to illuminate the rhetorical strategy and function of two different versions of this prophecy, comprising 3:3–6 + 8 and 3:3–8 (with v. 7), respectively, in relation to two different rhetorical situations.

The reconstruction of editorial stages that I present in the ensuing section has been developed in close interaction with recent research.[32] It has, above all, much in common with the reconstruction made by Jörg Jeremias (1998). The most important difference between Jeremias's model and mine concerns the dating of the collection of vision reports in 7:1–8:2. Like most other commentators, Jeremias regards the so-called vision cycle (often thought to include 9:1–4 as well) as stemming originally from the eponymous prophet himself (1996: 157–71; 1998: 6, 124–34). However, it is widely accepted among scholars that larger additions tend to be placed at the end of prophetic books. The concluding chapters of Isaiah and Zechariah are well-known cases. I suggest that, in terms of the history of composition, Amos 7–9 provides a parallel of sorts to Isaiah 40–66 and Zechariah 9–14. According to my analysis, the three last chapters of Amos (7–9) differ from chapters 1–6 in one fundamental respect: Chapters 7–9 do not contain a core of prophecies from the monarchic era (with Becker 2001: 160 and 2011: 214–16). This is a minority position within Amos studies. Hence, a rather elaborate argument is called for, especially regarding the proposed postmonarchic date of origin for the vision cycle.

It is commonly acknowledged among exegetes with an interest in diachronic issues that chapter 9 contains exilic and/or postexilic material (thus already Wellhausen 1893). As regards chapter 8, some scholars have adduced weighty (and, in my opinion, convincing) arguments for the view that the section 8:3–14 consists of a string of late scribal prophecies, which reuse and reinterpret oracles found within chapters 1–6 (see Jeremias 1998: 144–53 and Hadjiev 2009: 96–108). Whereas the passage 8:4–6 reuses and updates parts of Amos 2:6–8, the prophecy in 8:11–12 would seem to be based on a metaphorical and "spiritualizing" exegesis of 4:6–8, with a special emphasis on the motifs of famine and thirst. More examples are provided in the commentary (see "Introduction to 8:4–14").

But what about the vision cycle and the narrative in 7:1–8:2? Can an exilic or postexilic date of origin be defended for this section in its entirety? As already mentioned, a vast majority among scholars subscribes to the hypothesis that these vision reports, written in the first person, originated in the eighth century B.C.E. However, I suspect that this near consensus regarding the dating is a consequence of a collective exegetical desire to find something in the book that could give us direct access to the prophet. If the visions somehow reflect authentic experiences of Amos himself, then it might be possible to reconstruct some aspects of his personal development and of his self-understanding as a prophet. Moreover, with an eighth-century dating of the vision reports, one might argue that the conflict narrative (7:10–17) provides accurate biographical information, too, despite the fact that it looks like a later insertion. However, as noted by Jeremias (1998: 126), it is indeed very strange that the vision reports, which are often said to function as a kind of call narrative, are placed toward the end of the book.

Once the assumption that the first-person and third-person accounts in 7:1–8:2 contain authentic biographical data about the "real" Amos from Tekoa is dropped, another picture emerges. There are in fact several strong arguments for a later dating (see Becker 2001 and 2011, and Steins 2010: 29–75). From the reader's perspective, the transition from 6:14 to 7:1 is abrupt. Despite the lack of a new superscription, the divide is easily recognizable (cf. Isa 40:1). As already mentioned, Amos 7 introduces new genres that were missing in chapters 1–6 (vision report and narrative). In addition, the section 7:1–8:2 contains a radically new theological perspective that emphasizes God's mercy and willingness to forgive, as well as an entirely new focus on the prophet/seer Amos. Nothing in the previous chapters has prepared the reader for this. It is therefore unlikely, in my opinion, that (the original core of) chapters 3–6 and the vision cycle originated at the same time or within the same circles. Indeed, as demonstrated by Georg Steins, a thorough examination of both terminology and theology in 7:1–8:2 indicates that the vision cycle should be dated to the exilic or the postexilic period (2010: 57–67). Arguably, the closest parallel texts are found in the book of Jeremiah (Jer 1:11–14; 24:1–5).

As will be shown in more detail in the commentary below, the texts within Amos 7:1–8:2 can be read as theological reflections on the dramatically changed situation that the Judeans experienced in the wake of the disaster that occurred in 587 B.C.E. Here Amos, the protagonist, is not pictured as an uncompromising prophet of doom (as he is, at least implicitly, throughout chapters 1–6). He is instead portrayed as a prophet like Moses, or even more to the point, as a prophet like Jeremiah. For such a prophet it is not enough to proclaim words of judgment. He is supposed to act as an intermediary, in both directions. In this capacity he suffers with his people and entreats YHWH to show mercy. Just like Jeremiah, Amos of the vision cycle intercedes for the victims of the disasters orchestrated by the deity (7:1–6; cf. Jer 7:16; 11:14; 14:11). Moreover, several features in Amos 7:7–8 and 8:1–2, such as the element of wordplay and the shape and content of the human-divine dialogue, recall the vision reports in Jer 1:11–14. In the prophetic legend in Amos 7, finally, the prophetic protagonist is involved in a confrontation with a priest, just like Jeremiah (7:10–17; cf. Jer 20:1–6). Arguably, this "Amos" looks like a literary character created in the sixth century B.C.E. or later.

Before the Book: The Very First Stage

I find it likely that the book of Amos is based on a collection of oracles from the turbulent decades that preceded the national disaster in 722 B.C.E. These oracles (e.g., Amos 6:1–7*), directed against the Northern Kingdom and its ruling elite, may have been delivered by one or more prophets in Israel or—perhaps more likely—in Judah.[33] In some respects, I suggest, the oldest layer in Amos can be compared to the oldest layer in the book of Isaiah, which most likely originated in the 730s and 720s B.C.E. and which consists of oracles with a decidedly anti-Israel (and pro-Judah) perspective (e.g., Isa 7:4–9; 8:1–4; 17:1–3; 28:1–4*).[34]

Another illuminating parallel to the earliest layer in the book of Amos is provided by an enigmatic inscription from the eighth century B.C.E. (or earlier), consisting of a number of plaster fragments, that was discovered at Deir 'Alla in the Jordan valley (see Hoftijzer and van der Kooij 1976). There are some conspicuous similarities between this text and parts of the prophetic literature in the Hebrew Bible, as regards "phraseology, structure, and form" (Dijkstra 1995: 60). In the first part of the reconstructed text (Combination I), a "seer" (ḥzh) named Balaam, son of Beor (cf. Numbers 22–24!), recounts a disturbing vision of an impending catastrophe, apparently decreed by one of the deities in the pantheon. The depiction of this disaster includes a formulation (in lines 6–7) that closely parallels parts of Amos 5:18–20: "there is darkness, not brightness" (see further the Comments on 5:18). Arguably, the dark vision ascribed to Balaam shows that the genre of oracles of doom and destruction was known among Israel's neighbors, and most likely in Israel (and Judah) as well.[35]

In addition, and most important, the plaster text from Deir 'Alla can be cited as evidence that the literary and scribal competence required in order to write down rather lengthy compositions containing oracles and visions existed in this region as early as the eighth century B.C.E. (with Jeremias 2013: 98–100). However, because of the speculative character of such a venture, I will not make any attempt to reconstruct the shape and contents of a hypothetical collection of "Amos" oracles predating 722 B.C.E. Such tentative reconstructions are found in many previous redaction-oriented commentaries.[36] In accordance with a current trend in Amos studies, I prefer to focus on the compositional and editorial history of the book, leaving various prestages aside. As recent studies argue and demonstrate, the prophetic *book* bearing Amos's name is, even in its first version, a product from *Judah* in the period *after* the downfall of the kingdom of Israel in 722 B.C.E. (see Möller 2003a: 104–52 and Radine 2010: 46–79).

Three Versions of the Book: A Tentative Reconstruction

What follows is a tentative reconstruction of the book's gradual growth through approximately four centuries. Instead of making a division into a large number of successive redactions (like Rottzoll 1996), I have chosen to describe what I take to be the three major stages in the book's editorial history (cf. similarly Coote 1981). Each editorial stage has a distinct ideological (or theological) profile, linked to the interests of a certain historical period. Possibly, though, this picture represents an oversimplification.

Thus, it is conceivable that what is here referred to as the "first" version of the book of Amos actually consists of two separate layers: one from the reign of Hezekiah (715–687 B.C.E.) or Manasseh (687–642 B.C.E.), which preserved some even older oracles, and another from the time of Josiah (640–609 B.C.E.). As regards the "second" version, it is evident that the story in 7:10–17, which interrupts the series of vision reports, should be seen as a later insertion into its present literary context. Thus, the second major version appears to be the result of a process that involved at least two separate stages. Finally, I find it unlikely that all the additions I have tentatively ascribed to the "third" and final version were made at the same time; nevertheless, I have refrained from attempts to reconstruct these processes in more detail. The doxologies, for instance, may have been inserted at a late stage, when the bulk of chapters 8–9 was already in place. However, the opposite is equally possible.

One of several intriguing questions left unanswered by my reconstruction of compositional stages is the following: When and why was the concentric structure in chapters 3–6 created? Was it constructed in one or more steps? Did this process involve extensive rearranging of an existing collection of oracles?[37] My own guess would be that already the first version of the book contained some kind of concentric arrangement, which was developed further by later editors (so also Jeremias 1998: 85).

It is difficult to give a precise date for the *first version* of the book of Amos. All that can be said with any certainty is that it was composed after 722 and before 587 B.C.E. Its main purpose was to explain the catastrophe that put an end to the kingdom of Israel and to spell out some important implications for Judah. The disaster that occurred in 722 was seen as YHWH's punishment for Israel's crimes, with an emphasis on corruption and oppression of the poor. In keeping with ancient Near Eastern royal ideology, the underlying idea would seem to be that the kingdom of Israel was doomed because its rulers had failed to fulfill their obligations as guarantors of justice. At the same time, the downfall of the Northern Kingdom was used as a warning example for the intended readership in Judah. According to my hypothesis, the first version comprised substantial parts of what is now the book's central section, namely, chapters 3–6. Parts of chapters 1–2 may have served as a prologue. Alternatively, parts of the cycle of oracles against the nations (chapters 1–2*) formed a separate collection, which was later augmented and incorporated into the second version. This is a tentative reconstruction of the contents of the first version: 1:1*, 3–5, 6–8, 13–15; 2:1–3, 6–8, 9, 13–16; 3:1a, 3–6, 8, 9–12, 15; 4:1–3, 4–5; 5:1–5, 7, 10–12, 14–17, 18–24, 27; 6:1–7, 8, 11–14 (Table 2).

The next major stage, resulting in the *second version* of the book, happened after 587 B.C.E. Its main purpose was to reframe and update the words of Amos concerning Israel in the light of the catastrophe that had struck Judah. In the wake of the destruction of Jerusalem and its temple, a more hopeful message was called for (cf. Isaiah 40–55). At the same time, a distinctly ideological type of explanation of the divine judgment, focusing on idolatry and disregard of YHWH's Torah, was introduced (see, e.g., 2:4 and 5:26). Juxtaposed with prophecies of doom and words of warning, new elements of intercession and forgiveness were presented (7:1–6). Several of the additions, such as the references to the exodus and the conquest (2:10–12; 3:1b–2) and the statement that YHWH always informs the prophets (his "servants") in advance (3:7), seem to betray an influence from Deuteronomistic ideology. In some cases (e.g., 7:7–8 and 8:1–2) the literary motifs and the ideological conceptions featured in the text have close counterparts in the book of Jeremiah. I suggest that the following passages may, with due caution, be ascribed to the second stage: 1:2, 9–12; 2:4–5, 10–12; 3:1b–2, 7,

Table 2. Three Versions of the Book of Amos

	Verses
Version 1 (after 722 and before 587 B.C.E.)	1:1*, 3–5, 6–8, 13–15; 2:1–3, 6–8, 9, 13–16; 3:1a, 3–6, 8, 9–12, 15; 4:1–3, 4–5; 5:1–5, 7, 10–12, 14–17, 18–24, 27; 6:1–7, 8, 11–14
Version 2 (after 587 B.C.E.)	1:2, 9–12; 2:4–5, 10–12; 3:1b–2, 7, 13–14; 4:6–12; 5:6, 25–26; 7:1–8 (9); 8:1–2; 9:1, 4b, 7–11, 14–15 (?)
Version 3 (Persian period, 539–333 B.C.E.)	4:13; 5:8–9; 6:9–10 (?); 8:3, 4–6, 7, 8, 9–10, 11–12, 13–14; 9:2–4a, 5–6, 12–13

13–14; 4:6–12; 5:6, 25–26; 7:1–8 (9); 8:1–2; 9:1, 4b, 7–11, 14–15 (?) (see Table 2). In a separate move, 7:10–17 was inserted into the vision cycle.

The *third version,* corresponding to the book of Amos as we now have it, is probably a product from the Persian period.[38] In this final edition, the perspective has shifted from the past to the future, from *explanation* (of the great national disasters in the past) to *expectation.* To a certain extent, the emphasis on historical events (and on their causes and consequences) has been replaced by an eschatological perspective. The passages that I have ascribed to the third and final edition of Amos tend to emphasize the cosmological and soteriological aspects of divine agency. It is likely that accretions and *Fortschreibungen* were made in successive stages. During this process, which may have involved the work of numerous scribes over a couple of centuries, several earlier prophecies, recorded in chapters 1–6, were reinterpreted (see 8:4–14).[39] Furthermore, doxologies with cosmic perspectives were inserted at strategic junctures (4:13; 5:8–9; 9:5–6; cf. also 8:8), and a truly utopian ending was composed (9:11–15), probably on the basis of an already existing hopeful epilogue (consisting of 9:11 and, possibly, 9:14–15*). According to my reconstruction, the following passages were added during the final phase of redaction: 4:13; 5:8–9; 6:9–10 (?); 8:3, 4–6, 7, 8, 9–10, 11–12, 13–14; 9:2–4a, 5–6, 12–13 (see Table 2).

Amos and the Book of the Twelve

In recent years, the book of the Twelve (also known as the Minor Prophets) has emerged as an object of study (that is, as a composition, or "book") in its own right. Several studies of the gradual growth of this collection of prophetic writings have appeared.[40] According to one of the most interesting and influential theories that have been propounded by these scholars, there once existed an exilic collection, a "book of the Four," comprising Hosea, Amos, Micah, and Zephaniah.[41] I find this hypothesis quite plausible, although it is important to keep in mind that it rests on a rather limited amount of data. The most intriguing detail indicating that these four books may have formed a collection is the fact that they have similar superscriptions containing references to the reign of one or several kings in Judah and/or Israel (Hos 1:1; Amos 1:1; Mic 1:1; Zeph 1:1).

Some of the results of this line of research have bearing on the interpretation of individual passages in the book of Amos. Thus, Nogalski (1993a: 24–30, 113) has called attention to catchword links and verbatim quotations that connect the beginning and the end of Amos to the immediately surrounding books, namely, Joel and Obadiah: Amos 1:2a—Joel 4:16a (Eng. 3:16a); Amos 9:12—Obadiah 17–19; Amos 9:13—Joel 4:18 (Eng. 3:18). Thus it is evident that there was some kind of overlap between the last stage in the editorial history of the book of Amos and the process of collecting and editing the evolving book of the Twelve. But it is difficult to decide whether, for instance, the programmatic proclamation in Amos 1:2a was borrowed from Joel 4:16a or vice versa.

As far as I can see, the intertextual links between passages in Amos and texts in other parts of the book of the Twelve are in fact rather few. In many cases the most significant intertextual points of comparison for a certain utterance in the book of Amos are found elsewhere in the Hebrew Bible: in Isaiah or Jeremiah, in the Deuteronomistic History, or in the Pentateuch. On the whole, therefore, I tend to agree with John Barton's rather negative assessment of the new scholarly trend that treats the book of the Twelve as a carefully edited composition: "In general, then, theories of the growth of the Twelve as a single book are not necessarily as strong as the effort expended on them might lead one to expect" (2012: 36).[42] Arguably, the Twelve should be regarded as a collection of twelve rather different prophetic books (with a total size that would fit one single scroll), and not as a unified literary composition made up of twelve closely interrelated parts.

V.

Ancient and Modern Interpretations of the Book of Amos

It lies beyond the scope of this commentary to provide a detailed survey of how the book of Amos has been used and interpreted through the centuries. Other scholars have supplied helpful overviews.[43] What follows is merely an outline, focusing on a few important aspects of this prophetic book's long and rich history of reception.

Early Amos Reception

The earliest reference to Amos outside the prophetic book itself is found in a passage in the book of Tobit, which quotes Amos 8:10. This quotation is introduced by the clause "Then I remembered the prophecy of Amos, how he said against Bethel" (Tob 2:6, NRSV). In other words, Amos is here associated with depictions of disasters and hardships similar to those experienced by Tobit and his family. The words from Amos 8:10, announcing that joyous feasts will be turned into occasions of lamentation, are cited as a fitting comment on the situation described in the opening scenes of the narrative.[44] However, the author of Tobit does not provide an interpretation of Amos 8:10. In that respect, the quotations from Amos in the Dead Sea Scrolls and the New Testament are of greater interest.

Amos at Qumran

We know for certain that the book of Amos was studied in the Qumran community. The Dead Sea Scrolls (that is, the scrolls that have been preserved) do not include a *pesher* on Amos. However, an unmarked quotation from Amos 8:11 (a prediction of a severe thirst for YHWH's words) occurs in an exegetical text, the Apocryphon of Jeremiah C (see Weissenberg 2012: 372–73). Even more important, passages from this prophetic book are cited as authoritative scripture in two writings, namely, the *Damascus*

Document and 4QFlorilegium (Weissenberg 2012: 368–74; cf. Park 2001: 178–91).

In a section of the *Damascus Document,* the so-called Amos-Numbers Midrash (CD A 7:13b–8:1a), two passages from the book of Amos, 5:26–27 and 9:11, have been conflated. Notably, both quotations are introduced by a formula indicating that authoritative scripture is being cited: "as it/he says (*kaʾăšer ʾāmar*)." Using a creative exegetical technique involving selective and sometimes liberal quotation, the author of the Amos-Numbers Midrash managed to transform Amos 5:26–27 (an allegation followed by a prediction of deportation) into a messianic prophecy (Brooke 1980; Weissenberg 2012: 368–71). According to this midrash-like interpretation, two enigmatic words in the Hebrew text, which most likely represent the names of Babylonian deities (Sakkut and Kaiwan), are to be read as references to the books of the law and the books of the prophets, respectively (see further Osten-Sacken 1979). At the same time, an association is made to the promise in 9:11 that YHWH will restore "David's fallen hut (*sukkat dāwîd*)."

The latter passage, Amos 9:11, is also cited in 4QFlorilegium (4Q174 1:12), where it is introduced by a similar formula ("as it is written," *kaʾăšer kātûb*). The immediate context is different, since the quotation from Amos 9:11 occurs within an exposition of Nathan's oracle to David in 2 Sam 7:11–14 (see Brooke 1985: 130–44). In this case, too, references are made to the Torah, as well as to a messianic figure (see Weissenberg 2012: 371–72).[45]

As far as I can see, these observations indicate that the Qumran exegetes were mainly interested in those prophecies in the book of Amos that, owing to their eschatological and/or obscure character, could be directly applied to their own experiences and expectations. It is worth noting that passages containing social or cultic critique are not cited in the extant sectarian material (cf. Weissenberg 2012: 373–74). From the point of view of modern scholarship, which tends to view the indictments of injustice as more central to the book's message than passages like 5:25–27 and 9:11–15, such a perspective on Amos stands out as narrow and distorted. However, the contextually and eschatologically oriented interpretation practiced at Qumran appears to have been representative for the latter part of the Second Temple era. According to the reconstruction presented above, those passages in Amos that tend to shift the emphasis from history to eschatology were added at a late stage, during the Persian or the Hellenistic period. Furthermore, a strong interest in eschatology and messianism is observable in the Septuagint version of Amos (see Glenny 2009: 201–40), as well as in the use of this prophetic book in the New Testament.

Amos in the New Testament

Only one of the New Testament authors, Luke in the Acts of the Apostles, quotes the book of Amos. Luke has inserted passages from this prophetic book in two speeches: one by Stephen and the other by James. In Acts 7:42–43, the passage Amos 5:25–27 is cited, in a version that closely resembles the Septuagint, in order to make the point that the Babylonian exile was a well-deserved punishment for the people's idolatry (see Martin-Achard 1984a: 180–82). In Acts 15:16–17, the Septuagint version of Amos 9:11–12 is quoted by James in a selective and creative way.[46] The Amos passage has here been conflated with some other scriptural quotations in order to serve as justification for the mission to the gentiles.

Remarkably enough, these two prophecies, Amos 5:25–27 and 9:11–12 (or, to be more precise, 5:25–26 and 9:11), are also the ones that (together with 8:11) are quoted and interpreted in the Qumran texts. This is probably not a pure coincidence. Especially Amos 9:11–12 appears to have been a focal point for eschatological and messianic interpretations of the prophetic writings during this period (with Glenny 2009: 223).[47]

Amos in Premodern Jewish and Christian Exegesis

In comparison to some other books in the Hebrew Bible, Amos is rarely mentioned in early Jewish and Christian writings. As suggested by Donald Gowan, this is probably due to the fact that large parts of the book of Amos are dominated by passages conveying uncompromisingly harsh messages: "Both Jewish and Christian interpreters typically sought messages of comfort and hope in the Old Testament, and there is little of that to be found in Amos" (1996: 340). Nevertheless, the amount of rabbinic and patristic interpretations of the book of Amos is far too extensive to be completely covered by a survey such as this.

In rabbinic literature, passages from Amos are cited in discussions on a wide range of topics.[48] The following list of subjects and texts from Amos that are treated in the Talmud or Midrash is by no means exhaustive but may nevertheless indicate some areas of interest: the prophet's social status (Amos 7:14, in m. Nedarim 4:3), divine creation (Amos 4:13; in m. Berakot 8:5 and Genesis Rabbah 1:9), sin (Amos 5:10, in Genesis Rabbah 31:3), punishment (Amos 3:2, in m. Abodah Zarah 1:1), forgiveness (Amos 2:6, in m. Yoma 8:8–9), mourning (Amos 8:10, in m. Berakot 2:8), the destruction of the first temple (Amos 9:1, in Leviticus Rabbah 33:3 and Lamentations Rabbah 25:1), the Messiah (Amos 9:11, in m. Sanhedrin 11:1–2), and the world to come (Amos 9:13, in Ruth Rabbah 9:1). According to one tradition, attributed to Rabbi Simla, Amos summarized all the commandments of the Torah in one sentence, in 5:4 (see Martin-Achard 1984a: 192). One may note that the social critique in the book of Amos does not constitute a prominent topic in the rabbinic interpretations.[49]

A similar neglect of those passages in Amos that denounce oppression and corruption is observable in the patristic literature (Martin-Achard 1984a: 201–6 and Barton 2012: 171–72).[50] This prophetic book was quoted in discussions on a variety of theological subjects. Significantly, though, the passage most frequently cited by the church fathers is 4:13, a hymnic piece that extols the works of the creator (Kelly 1977). By contrast, such passages as 2:6–8, 5:10–12, and 8:4–6, which denounce oppression and corruption in society, are very sparsely attested. In his work The City of God (De Civitate Dei, book XVIII), Augustine praises Amos as a rhetorically skilled prophet who heralded the coming of Christ. Augustine cites Amos 4:12–13 and 9:11–12, but he does not highlight those passages in the book that contain social and cultic critique (see further Martin-Achard 1984a: 206–10).

Throughout the history of premodern and early modern Christian interpretation of Amos the social and political aspects of the book's message continued to be downplayed. The most notable exception occurred in Florence during the Renaissance. In a series of sermons delivered in 1496, Girolamo Savonarola, a controversial Dominican friar and political reformer, made extensive use of the book of Amos (see Mein 2011). Savonarola contemporized passages such as Amos 2:6–8 and 2:9–12, as he condemned corruption among the political and religious leaders in the Italy of his time, in an attempt to gain support for his own political reforms.[51]

Although the particular emphases have varied considerably, all premodern and early modern interpreters of Amos seem to have adapted the messages in this prophetic book (or a selection thereof) to their own theological agendas (or to the interests of their interpretive communities). Thus, according to Martin Luther, who admittedly provided a thorough and complex exegesis of this book (Martin-Achard 1984a: 220–25), Amos admonished his addressees to seek a righteousness based on faith, not on works (Markert 1978: 485).[52] In his commentary on Amos, Jean Calvin treated each passage in the book in a scholarly manner, which has much in common with modern exegesis (see Martin-Achard 1984a: 225–42). Far from surprising, however, Calvin claimed that the teachings of Amos involved a sharp division between elected and rejected individuals, in accordance with his own doctrine of predestination.[53]

Amos in the Modern Era: A Spokesman for the Poor

In its modern history of reception and interpretation, the book of Amos has often been regarded as "an important source for the claim that Israel's classical prophets had a fundamental concern with social justice" (Auld 1986: 9). This (relatively) new emphasis on the ethical, social, and political aspects of the book's message(s) coincided with the emergence in the nineteenth century of academic research on the prophetic literature.[54] According to Julius Wellhausen and other scholars, so-called classical prophets such as Amos were forth-tellers rather than foretellers and more concerned with ethics (or ethical monotheism) than with eschatology (see Clifford 2011). Thus, the emerging historical-critical perspective on the prophetic literature is one important factor behind the "rediscovery" of the ethical and social dimensions of the book of Amos. Another major factor is, of course, the societal changes in the nineteenth century that gave rise to movements and organizations striving for democracy, human rights, and economic equality. Andrew Mein has explained the development of the modern concept of the prophet Amos as an advocate of social and economic justice in a succinct formulation: "If the burden of prophecy was not messianic prediction but social analysis and moral critique, then Amos was well placed to emerge from the shadows and take centre stage" (2011: 117).

Because the topic of social and economic (in)justice is prominent in some of its passages, the book of Amos has become a source of inspiration for various protest movements, especially during the second half of the twentieth century. In his commencement address at Lincoln University in Pennsylvania (June 1961), Martin Luther King, Jr., quoted Amos 5:24: "So let us be maladjusted, as maladjusted as the prophet Amos, who in the midst of the injustices of his day could cry out in words that echo across the centuries, 'Let justice run down like waters and righteousness like a mighty stream'" (see Carroll R. 2002: 57–59). In the subsequent decades, the image of Amos as a spokesman for the poor and the oppressed became common in liberation theology, above all in Latin America.[55] This line of interpretation has left its imprint in historical-critical scholarship, as well.[56]

According to Haroldo Reimer, a biblical scholar from Brazil, the main theme of the book of Amos is justice (1992: 22–23). Like most modern interpreters, he emphasizes those passages that criticize mistreatment of the poor and corruption in the courts (e.g., Amos 2:6–8; 5:7, 10–12). Unlike many other biblical scholars, however, Reimer maintains that the prophecies of doom and destruction (e.g., 2:13–16; 3:12; 5:1–3; 8:1–3) do not concern the entire population of the Northern Kingdom.[57] Only the oppressors—that is, the royal house, the priests, the administrators, and the military officers—were going to be hit by the coming disaster(s) decreed by YHWH. For the victims of the oppression, Reimer claims, Amos spoke a message of liberation.

Reimer's interpretation of Amos 5:16–17 illustrates the somewhat anachronistic character of his approach.[58] There is a near consensus among modern commentators regarding the general interpretation of the passage.[59] Most likely, the aftermath of a national disaster—a catastrophe affecting cities and countryside, rich and poor families alike—is depicted. Because so many had died, one may infer, unskilled peasants would have to assist the professional lamenters (see further the Comments on 5:16–17). According to Reimer, however, the disaster described was in fact confined to the cities, and the mourning rites were organized by the agricultural workers, in a situation where their former oppressors had miraculously disappeared as a result of divine intervention (1992: 119–22). As far as I can see, this interpretation of Amos 5:16–17 cannot be supported by the actual wording in the text or by any formulations in the immediate literary context.

Although such readings of the book of Amos, which present its message as a call for action against oppression and corruption, may seem sympathetic, they are problematic. Most important, interpretations of this kind fail to account for the observation that there is a troubling discrepancy in this book between, on one hand, passages criticizing the rich elite (e.g., 2:6–8; 4:1–3; 6:1–7) and, on the other hand, proclamations of judgment and punishment that seem to include also the poor majority of the population (e.g., 3:12; 5:1–3, 16–17; 8:1–3).[60] Moreover, a reader of the book of Amos who takes an interest in social action for the poor looks in vain for the contours of a reform program, or the like. James Linville has made the following remark, which captures vital aspects of the hermeneutical problem attached to uncritical liberationist interpretations of this book: "Despite a call to repent and let righteousness well up like rivers (Amos 5:24) and to seek God and the good (5:14–15), there is precious little in Amos that actually calls for the relief of the misery of the poor. Rather, the preferred response to corruption is divine violence" (2008: 116). Indeed, as demonstrated by Mary Mills (2010), divine violence constitutes a significant and challenging theological theme in this prophetic book.

Interpretive Guidelines for This Commentary

In the present commentary, I attempt to account for the existence of a plurality of topics and perspectives in the book of Amos without assigning a privileged position to any one of them (such as, for instance, injustice and corruption in society or eschatological expectations). I suggest that different aspects of the book's complex message can often be ascribed to different stages in its history of redaction and composition. However, as far as possible, I intend to abstain from value judgments or from implying that certain aspects are more central than others. I discuss the biblical text from a strictly scholarly point of view. It is, of course, impossible to be perfectly objective, but I try to avoid interpretations and comments that are based on (open or hidden) religious or political bias.

As shown by David Clines (1993), there is a risk that commentators of texts such as the book of Amos, which some religious communities consider to be authoritative, tend to sympathize openly with (what they take to be) the perspective of the prophet/author. However, as Clines points out, "it would be uncritical of us to accept Amos's analysis of his society, to simply buy the ideology of the text" (1993: 147). He continues: "Somehow, we need to distance ourselves from the prophetic voice, and recognize that the prophet's is only one voice in his community. The prophet, and the text, have a corner to fight, a position to uphold, and we for our part need to identify that position, and to relativize it, not so as to discard it but only so as to give it its proper due" (Clines 1993: 147). My ambition in writing this commentary has been to combine such a critical distance to the text's ideological (or theological) perspective with a sustained effort to uncover and understand the function and message of each passage, in the light of its original historical setting and its present literary context.

VI.

Text and Translation

The Masoretic Text

The primary textual basis for the new translation offered in this commentary is the Masoretic text (MT), according to the editions *Biblia Hebraica Stuttgartensia* (*BHS*) and *Biblia Hebraica Quinta* (*BHQ*), which reprint the text of a medieval manuscript (from 1008 C.E.), Codex Leningradensis. The reason for this choice is quite simple: There is no realistic alternative. Since a critical eclectic edition, based on all extant Hebrew manuscripts, does not yet exist, every scholar has to use the standard editions of the MT as his or her point of departure and make necessary corrections on the basis of a critical examination of the textual evidence available for each individual passage.[61]

All instances where my translation is based on a variant reading, attested in a Qumran manuscript or in one (or more) of the ancient versions, are registered in the Notes. I have refrained from conjectural emendations, no matter how ingenious some scholarly suggestions may seem, if these emendations involve substantial changes of the consonantal text. In some cases, however, I have adopted a different vocalization, or a different division of the consonants, from the one found in the MT (that is, in *BHS* and *BHQ*).

Fragmentary Manuscripts from the Judean Desert

The textual discoveries made in the Dead Sea region include the earliest known Hebrew manuscripts of the book of Amos (see Fuller 1996 and Weissenberg 2012). Unfortunately, no complete scroll has been preserved. Nevertheless, the manuscripts from the

Judean desert throw new light on the textual history of this prophetic book. Most important, they testify to the existence of a certain textual diversity during the last century B.C.E. and the first century C.E. (Fuller 2000 and Weissenberg 2012). Taken together, these four fragmentary scrolls cover large parts of Amos.[62] Frequently, however, only one or two words of a certain oracle are legible.

In cave 4 at Qumran, two out of seven scrolls containing (parts of) the book of the Twelve include fragmentary portions of the text of Amos: 4QXII[c] (2:11–4:2; 6:13–7:16) and 4QXII[g] (1:3–7; 1:9–2:1; 2:7–9; 2:15–3:2; 4:4–9; 5:1–2; 5:9; 5:11–18; 6:1–4; 6:6; 6:8–7:1; 7:7–12; 7:14–8:5; 8:11–9:1; 9:5–6; 9:14–15). These two manuscripts are commonly dated to the first century B.C.E. (Fuller 2000: 555–56). Another manuscript, found in cave 5, may have contained the text of one single book among the Twelve, namely, Amos. However, in this scroll, 5QAmos, only parts of 1:2–5 have been preserved.

Deviations from the MT are found in all three manuscripts, ranging from details in the orthography to variants that convey a divergent sense. Some of the latter examples will be discussed in the commentary. In a few cases, such as 1:3 (5QAmos) and 5:15 (4QXII[g]), a Qumran manuscript supports the Septuagint's reading over against the MT. This proves beyond reasonable doubt that the earliest Greek version was based on a Hebrew text that was not identical to the MT.

The remains of a fourth scroll, MurXII (or Mur88), containing parts of the book of Amos (1:5–2:1; 7:3–17; 8:3–7; 8:11–9:15), were discovered in Wadi Murabba'at, to the south of Qumran. This manuscript, dating to the first century C.E., has been characterized as proto-Masoretic (see Fuller 1996: 88–89). Interestingly, MurXII confirms the consonantal text of the MT even in some cases where many scholars have advocated conjectural emendations (see the Notes to 8:14 and 9:1).

The Septuagint and the Other Ancient Versions

Among the ancient versions (or translations) of the book of Amos, the first Greek translation, commonly referred to as the Septuagint of Amos (or LXX-Amos), constitutes the most important textual witness.[63] It is usually dated to the middle of the second century B.C.E. In some instances, the Septuagint of Amos may help us to correct the MT and to reconstruct a more original text.

The consonantal text of the Hebrew *Vorlage* (= original, or source text) used by the Greek translator was certainly not identical with the MT. This is evidenced by the fact that the Qumran manuscripts sometimes deviate from the MT in exactly the same way as the Septuagint. However, this *Vorlage* was probably quite close to the textual tradition represented by the MT. In many cases (indeed, in most cases), the differences between the LXX and the MT are better explained as the result of other factors, such as the use of a certain translation technique or elements of what might be called creative theological exegesis (Dines 1991; Glenny 2009). Occasionally, the Greek translator seems to have misunderstood the Hebrew text (Gelston 2002; but cf. Arieti 1974 and Glenny 2007); however, it is hardly possible to make a sharp distinction between misinterpretation and creative exegesis. Sometimes, when confronted with a difficult passage, the translator apparently seized the opportunity to express his own theological perspective.

Drawing on such observations, W. Edward Glenny (2009: 240) has concluded that the translator responsible for the Septuagint version of Amos had an interest in eschatology, the coming of the Messiah (LXX-Amos 4:13), the defeat of Gog (7:1 LXX), and the conversion of gentiles (9:12 LXX). Owing to the combined effect of its Hebrew *Vorlage*, its translation technique, and its theological tendencies, the LXX-Amos can be regarded as a distinct version of this prophetic book. Hence, it can be studied in its own right, without comparisons to the MT (Glenny 2013).

In some instances, I have used the Vulgate (the Latin translation made by Jerome) and Peshitta (the Syriac version) in order to correct the MT, when the latter seems to be in disorder. In addition, I have consulted Targum Jonathan, an Aramaic version of the Prophets that evolved during the first centuries C.E. (see further Cathcart and Gordon 1989: 1–19). However, because of the paraphrastic character of the Targum, which features numerous explicative and exegetical additions and expansions, it is often very difficult to draw conclusions concerning its Hebrew *Vorlage*.

BIBLIOGRAPHY

Achtemeier, Elizabeth
1996: *Minor Prophets I.* NIBCOT 17; Peabody, MA: Hendrickson.

Ackerman, Susan
1989: "A *marzēaḥ* in Ezekiel 8:7–13?" *HTR* 82: 267–81.

Ackroyd, Peter R.
1956: "Amos vii 14." *ExpTim* 68: 94.
1977: "A Judgment Narrative between Kings and Chronicles? An Approach to Amos 7:9–17." Pp. 71–87 in: G. W. Coats and B. O. Long (eds.), *Canon and Authority: Essays in Old Testament Religion and Theology,* Philadelphia: Fortress.

Adamo, D. T.
1992: "Amos 9.7–8 in an African Perspective." *Orita* 24: 76–84.

Aḥituv, Shmuel
2008: *Echoes from the Past: Hebrew and Cognate Inscriptions from the Biblical Period.* Jerusalem: Carta.

Ahlström, Gösta W.
1981: "King Josiah and the *dwd* of Amos vi 10." *JSS* 26: 7–9.

Albertz, Rainer
2003: "Exile as Purification: Reconstructing the 'Book of the Four.'" Pp. 234–52 in: P. L. Redditt and A. Schart (eds.), *Thematic Threads in the Book of the Twelve,* BZAW 325; Berlin: De Gruyter.

Allen, Spencer L.
2008: "Understanding Amos vi 12 in Light of His Other Rhetorical Questions." *VT* 58: 437–48.

Alter, Robert
1985: *The Art of Biblical Poetry.* Edinburgh: T&T Clark.

Altmann, Peter
2011: *Festive Meals in Ancient Israel: Deuteronomy's Identity Politics in Their Ancient Near Eastern Context.* BZAW 424; Berlin: De Gruyter.

Amsler, Samuel
    1965: "Amos." Pp. 157–247 in: *Osée—Joël—Abdias—Jonas—Amos.* Commentaire de l'Ancien Testament XIa; Neuchâtel: Delachaux & Niestlé.

Andersen, Francis I., and David Noel Freedman
    1989: *Amos: A New Translation with Introduction and Commentary.* AYB 24A; New York: Doubleday.

Arango, J. R.
    1992: "Opresión y profanación del santo nombre de Dios: Estudio del vocabulario de Amos 2,7b." *RIBLA* 11: 49–63.

Arieti, James A.
    1974: "The Vocabulary of Septuagint Amos." *JBL* 93: 338–47.

Asen, Bernhard A.
    1993: "No, Yes, and Perhaps in Amos and the Yahwist." *VT* 43: 433–41.

Auld, A. Graeme
    1983: "Prophets through the Looking Glass: Between Writings and Moses." *JSOT* 27: 3–23.
    1986: *Amos.* Old Testament Guides; Sheffield: JSOT Press.
    1991: "Amos and Apocalyptic: Vision, Prophecy, Revelation." Pp. 1–13 in: D. Garrone and F. Israel (eds.), *Storia e tradizioni di Israele* (FS Soggin), Brescia: Paideia Editrice.

Aurelius, Erik
    1988: *Der Fürbitter Israels. Eine Studie zum Mosebild im Alten Testament.* ConBOT 27; Stockholm: Almqvist & Wiksell.
    2006: "'Ich bin der Herr, dein Gott.' Israel und sein Gott zwischen Katastrophe und Neuanfang." Pp. 325–45 in: R. G. Kratz and H. Spieckermann (eds.), *Götterbilder, Gottesbilder, Weltbilder: Polytheismus und Monotheismus in der Welt der Antike. Band 1: Ägypten, Mesopotamien, Persien, Kleinasien, Syrien, Palästina,* FAT II 17; Tübingen: Mohr Siebeck.

Austin, S. A., G. W. Franz, and E. G. Frost
    2000: "Amos's Earthquake: An Extraordinary Middle East Seismic Event of 750 B.C." *International Geology Review* 42: 657–71.

Axskjöld, Carl-Johan
    1998: *Aram as the Enemy Friend: The Ideological Role of Aram in the Composition of Genesis—2 Kings.* ConBOT 45; Stockholm: Almqvist & Wiksell International.

Baltzer, Klaus
    1991: "Bild und Wort: Erwägungen zu der Vision Amos in Am 7: 7–9." Pp. 11–16 in: W. Gross et al. (eds.), *Text, Methode und Grammatik* (FS Richter), St. Ottilien: EOS.

Barré, Michael L.
    1985: "Amos 1:11 Reconsidered." *CBQ* 47: 420–27.
    1986: "The Meaning of *l' šybnw* in Amos 1:3–2:6." *JBL* 105: 611–31.
    1990: "Amos." Pp. 209–16 in: Raymond Brown et al. (eds.), *The New Jerome Biblical Commentary,* Englewood Cliffs, NJ: Prentice-Hall.

Barstad, Hans M.

1975: "Die Basankühe in Amos iv 1." *VT* 25: 286–97.

1984: *The Religious Polemics of Amos: Studies in the Preaching of Am 2,7B-8; 4,1–13; 5,1–27; 6,4–7; 8,14.* VTSup 34; Leiden: Brill.

Bartczek, Günter

1977: *Die Visionsberichte des Amos: Literarische Analyse und theologische Interpretation.* Münster: Münster Universität.

Barthélemy, D.

1992: *Critique textuelle de l'Ancien Testament: Tome 3 Ézéchiel, Daniel et les 12 Prophètes.* OBO 50/3; Fribourg: Universitätsverlag; Göttingen: Vandenhoeck & Ruprecht.

Bartlett, J. R.

1977: "The Brotherhood of Edom." *JSOT* 4: 2–27.

1989: *Edom and the Edomites.* JSOTSup 77; Sheffield: JSOT Press.

1992: "Edom in History." *ABD,* vol. 2, 287–95.

Barton, John

1980: *Amos's Oracles against the Nations: A Study of Amos 1:3–2:5.* SOTSMS 6; Cambridge: Cambridge University Press.

2004: "The Day of Yahweh in the Minor Prophets." Pp. 68–79 in: C. McCarthy and J. F. Healey (eds.), *Biblical and Near Eastern Essays,* JSOTSup 375; London: T&T Clark.

2005: "The Prophets and the Cult." Pp. 111–22 in: J. Day (ed.), *Temple and Worship in Biblical Israel,* London: T&T Clark.

2009: "The Theology of Amos." Pp. 188–210 in: J. Day (ed.), *Prophecy and the Prophets in Ancient Israel: Proceedings of the Oxford Old Testament Seminar,* London: T&T Clark.

2012: *The Theology of the Book of Amos.* Old Testament Theology; New York: Cambridge University Press.

Bauckham, Richard

1996: "James and the Gentiles (Acts 15:13–21)." Pp. 154–81 in: B. Witherington III (ed.), *History, Literature, and Society in the Book of Acts,* Cambridge: Cambridge University Press.

Baumann, E.

1903: *Der Aufbau der Amosreden.* BZAW 7; Giessen: Rickert.

Becker, Uwe

1997: *Jesaja: von der Botschaft zum Buch.* FRLANT 178; Göttingen: Vandenhoeck & Ruprecht.

2001: "Der Prophet als Fürbitter: Zum literar-historichen Ort der Amos-Visionen." *VT* 51: 141–65.

2011: "Historisch-kritisch oder kanonisch? Methodische Zugänge in der Prophetenauslegung am Beispiel des Amos-Buches." *Theologie der Gegenwart* 54: 206–20.

Behrens, A.

2002: *Prophetische Visionsschilderungen im Alten Testament. Sprachliche Eigenarten, Funktion und Geschichte einer Gattung.* AOAT 292; Münster: Ugarit-Verlag.

Bentzen, Aage

1950: "The Ritual Background of Amos i 2–ii 16." *OtSt* 8: 85–99.

Ben Zvi, Ehud, and James D. Nogalski

2009: *Two Sides of a Coin: Juxtaposing Views on Interpreting the Book of the Twelve/ The Twelve Prophetic Books.* Analecta Gorgiana 201; Piscataway, NJ: Gorgias.

Berg, W.

1974: *Die sogenannten Hymnenfragmente im Amosbuch.* Bern: Herbert Lang.

Bergler, Siegfried

2000: "'Auf der Mauer—auf dem Altar.' Noch einmal die Visionen des Amos." *VT* 50: 445–71.

Berlin, Adele

1985: *The Dynamics of Biblical Parallelism.* Bloomington: Indiana University Press.

Berquist, Jon L.

1993: "Dangerous Waters of Justice and Righteousness: Amos 5:18–27." *Biblical Theology Bulletin* 23/2: 54–63.

Beyerlin, Walter

1988: *Bleilot, Brecheisen oder was sonst? Revision einer Amos-Vision.* OBO 81; Freiburg: Universitätsverlag.

1989: *Reflexe der Amosvisionen im Jeremiabuch.* OBO 93; Freiburg: Universitätsverlag; Göttingen: Vandenhoeck & Ruprecht.

Bič, Milos

1951: "Amos: Ein Hepatoskopos." *VT* 1: 293–96.

1954: "Maštîn beqîr." *VT* 4: 411–16.

Biran, Avraham

1981: "To the God Who Is in Dan." Pp. 142–51 in: Biran, Avraham (ed.), *Temples and High Places in Biblical Times,* Jerusalem: Nelson Glueck School of Biblical Archaeology of Hebrew Union College.

Bjørndalen, Anders J.

1980: "Erwägungen zur Zukunft des Amazja und Israels nach der Überlieferung Amos 7,10–17." Pp. 236–51 in: R. Albertz et al. (eds.), *Werden und Wirken des Alten Testaments* (FS Westermann), Göttingen: Vandenhoeck & Ruprecht.

Blenkinsopp, Joseph

2003: "Bethel in the Neo-Babylonian Period." Pp. 93–107 in: O. Lipschits and J. Blenkinsopp (eds.), *Judah and the Judeans in the Neo-Babylonian Period,* Winona Lake, IN: Eisenbrauns.

2014: "The Theological Politics of Deutero-Isaiah." Pp. 129–43 in: A. Lenzi and J. Stökl (eds.), *Divination, Politics, and Ancient Near Eastern Empires,* Ancient Near East Monographs 7; Atlanta: SBL.

Blum, Erhard

1994: "'Amos' in Jerusalem. Beobachtungen zu Am 6,1–7." *Henoch* 16: 23–47.

2008: "Israels Prophetie im altorientalischen Kontext: Anmerkungen zu neueren religionsgeschichtlichen Thesen." Pp. 81–115 in: I. Cornelius and L. Jonker (eds.), *"From Ebla to Stellenbosch": Syro-Palestinian Religions and the Hebrew Bible,* ADPV 37; Wiesbaden: Harrassowitz.

Bohlen, Reinhold
1986: "Zur Sozialkritik des Propheten Amos." *TTZ* 95: 282–301.

Bokovoy, David E.
2008: "שמעו והעידו בבית יעקב: Invoking the Council as Witnesses in Amos 3:13." *JBL* 127: 37–51.

Bons, Eberhard
1996: "Das Denotat von כזביהם 'ihre Lügen' im Judaspruch Am 2,4–5." *ZAW* 108: 201–13.
2012: "Amos et la contestation des pouvoirs." Pp. 95–110 in: D. Luciani and A. Wenin (eds.), *Le pouvoir. Enquêtes dans l'un et l'autre testament,* Paris: Cerf.
2013: "Hosea und Amos auf Griechisch. Kulturelle Hintergründe und theologische Akzente in der Septuaginta." *Bibel und Kirche* 68: 32–36.

Borger, R.
1988: "Amos 5, 26, Apostelgeschichte 7, 43 und Šurpu II, 180." *ZAW* 100: 70–81.

Botterweck, G. Johannes
1958: "Zur Authentizität des Buches Amos." *BZ* 2: 176–89.

Bovati, P., and R. Meynet
1994: *Le livre du prophète Amos.* Paris: Cerf.

Boyle, Marjorie O'Rourke
1971: "The Covenant Lawsuit of the Prophet Amos: iii 1–iv 13." *VT* 21: 338–62.

Bramer, S. J.
1999: "The Literary Genre of the Book of Amos." *BSac* 156: 42–60.

Brettler, Marc Zvi
2006: "Redaction, History, and Redaction-History of Amos in Recent Scholarship." Pp. 103–12 in: B. E. Kelle and M. B. Moore (eds.), *Israel's Prophets and Israel's Past* (FS J. H. Hayes), LHBOTS 446; London: T&T Clark.

Bronznick, Norman M.
1985: "More on *hlk 'l.*" *VT* 35: 98–99.

Brooke, George
1980: "The Amos-Numbers Midrash (CD 7:13b–8:1a) and Messianic Expectations." *ZAW* 92: 397–404.
1985: *Exegesis at Qumran: 4QFlorilegium in Its Jewish Context.* JSOTSup 29; Sheffield: JSOT Press.
2006: "The Twelve Minor Prophets and the Dead Sea Scrolls." Pp. 19–44 in: A. Lemaire (ed.), *Congress Volume Leiden 2004,* VTSup 109; Leiden: Brill.

Brown, Walter E.
1995: "Amos 5:26: A Challenge to Reading and Interpretation." *Theological Educator* 52: 69–78.

Brueggemann, Walter
    1965: "Amos iv 4–13 and Israel's Covenant Worship." *VT* 15: 1–15.
    1969: "Amos' Intercessory Formula." *VT* 19: 385–99.

Brunet, Gilbert
    1966: "La vision de l'étain: Réinterpretation d'Amos vii 7–9." *VT* 16: 387–95.

Budde, Karl
    1897: "Die Ueberschrift des Buches Amos und des Propheten Heimat." Pp. 106–10
        in: G. A. Kohut (ed.), *Semitic Studies in Memory of Rev. Dr. Alexander Kohut,*
        Berlin: S. Calvary.
    1910: "Amos i 2." *ZAW* 30: 37–41.

Bulkeley, Tim
    2009: "Amos 7,1–8,3: Cohesion and Generic Dissonance." *ZAW* 121: 515–28.

Burger, J. A.
    1992: "Amos: A Historical-Geographical View." *Journal for Semitics* 4: 130–50.

Campbell, Edward F.
    1994: "Archaeological Reflections on Amos's Targets." Pp. 32–52 in: M. D. Coogan
        et al. (eds.), *Scripture and Other Artifacts: Essays on the Bible and Archaeology in*
        Honor of Philip J. King, Louisville, KY: Westminster John Knox.

Campos, Martha E.
    2011: "Structure and Meaning in the Third Vision of Amos (7:7–17)." *JHebS* 11,
        article 3, 2–28; doi:10.5508/jhs.2011.v11.a3, http://www.jhsonline.org.

Carlson, Agge
    1966: "Profeten Amos och Davidsriket." *Religion och Bibel* 25: 57–78.

Carroll R., M. Daniel
    1992: *Contexts for Amos: Prophetic Poetics in Latin American Perspective.* JSOTSup
        132; Sheffield: Sheffield Academic Press.
    1996: "God and His People in the Nations' History: A Contextualised Reading of
        Amos 1–2." *TynBul* 47: 39–70.
    2000: "'For So You Love to Do': Probing Popular Religion in the Book of Amos."
        Pp. 168–89 in: M. Daniel Carroll R. (ed.), *Rethinking Contexts, Rereading Texts:*
        Contributions from the Social Sciences to Biblical Interpretation, JSOTSup 299;
        Sheffield: Sheffield Academic Press.
    2002: *Amos: The Prophet and His Oracles.* Louisville, KY: Westminster John Knox.
    2008: "Imagining the Unthinkable: Exposing the Idolatry of National Security in
        Amos." *ExAud* 24: 37–54.

Cathcart, Kevin J.
    1994: "*rōʾš*, 'Poison,' in Amos ix 1." *VT* 44: 393–96.

Cathcart, Kevin J., and Robert P. Gordon
    1989: *The Targum of the Minor Prophets.* The Aramaic Bible, vol. 14. Wilmington,
        DE: Michael Glazier.

Ceresko, Anthony R.
    1992: *Introduction to the Old Testament: A Liberationist Perspective.* Maryknoll, NY:
        Orbis.

1994: "Janus Parallelism in Amos's 'Oracles against the Nations' (Amos 1.3–2.16)." *JBL* 113: 485–93.

Charlesworth, James H. (ed.)
1985: *The Old Testament Pseudepigrapha. Vol. 2.* London: Darton, Longman & Todd.

Chisholm, Robert B.
1990: "'For Three Sins . . . Even for Four': The Numerical Sayings in Amos." *BSac* 147: 188–97.

Christensen, Duane L.
1974: "The Prosodic Structure of Amos 1–2." *HTR* 67: 427–36.

Clements, Ronald E.
1996: "Amos and the Politics of Israel." Pp. 23–34 in: Clements, Ronald E., *Old Testament Prophecy: From Oracle to Canon,* Louisville, KY: Westminster John Knox.

Clifford, Hywel
2011: "Amos in Wellhausen's *Prolegomena.*" Pp. 141–56 in: A. C. Hagedorn and A. Mein (eds.), *Aspects of Amos: Exegesis and Interpretation,* LHBOTS 536; New York: T&T Clark.

Clines, David J. A.
1992: "Was There an 'bl II 'Be Dry' in Classical Hebrew?" *VT* 42:1–10.
1993: "Metacommentating Amos." Pp. 142–60 in: H. McKay and D. J. A. Clines (eds.), *Of Prophets' Visions and the Wisdom of Sages* (FS Whybray), JSOTSup 162; Sheffield: JSOT Press.

Cogan, Mordechai
1983: "'Ripping Open Pregnant Women' in Light of an Assyrian Analogue." *JAOS* 103: 755–57.

Coggins, R. J.
2000: *Joel and Amos.* New Century Bible; Sheffield: Sheffield Academic Press.

Cohen, C.
1979: "Neo-Assyrian Elements in the First Speech of the Biblical Rab-Šāqê." *Israel Oriental Studies* 9: 32–48.

Collins, John J.
1998: "From Prophecy to Apocalypticism: The Expectation of the End." Pp. 130–34 in: Collins, John J. (ed.), *The Encyclopedia of Apocalypticism,* vol. 1, New York: Continuum.

Collins, Terry
2001: "Threading as a Stylistic Feature of Amos." Pp. 94–104 in: J. C. de Moor (ed.), *The Elusive Prophet: The Prophet as a Historical Person, Literary Character and Anonymous Artist,* OTS XLV; Leiden: Brill.

Cooper, Alan
1988: "The Absurdity of Amos 6:12." *JBL* 107: 725–27.
1997: "The Meaning of Amos's Third Vision (Amos 7:7–9)." Pp. 13–22 in: M. Cogan et al. (eds.), *Tehillah le-Moshe* (FS M. Greenberg), Winona Lake, IN: Eisenbrauns.

Coote, R. B.
    1971: "Amos 1:11: *rḥmyw.*" *JBL* 90: 206–8.
    1981: *Amos among the Prophets: Composition and Theology.* Philadelphia: Fortress.

Couey, J. Blake
    2008: "Amos vii 10–17 and Royal Attitudes toward Prophecy in the Ancient Near East." *VT* 58: 300–314.

Craigie, P. C.
    1982: "Amos the *nōqēd* in the Light of Ugaritic." *Studies in Religion* 11: 29–33.

Cramer, K.
    1930: *Amos. Versuch einer theologischen Interpretation.* BWANT 51; Stuttgart: Kohlhammer.

Crenshaw, James L.
    1968: "Amos and the Theophanic Tradition." *ZAW* 80: 203–15.
    1970: "A Liturgy of Wasted Opportunity (Am. 4:6–12; Isa. 9:7–10:4; 5:25–29)." *Semitics* 1: 27–37.
    1972: "Wᵉdōrēk ʿal-bāmŏtê ʾāreṣ." *CBQ* 34: 39–53.

Cresson, B. C.
    1972: "The Condemnation of Edom in Postexilic Judaism." Pp. 125–48 in: J. M. Efird (ed.), *The Use of the Old Testament in the New and Other Essays,* Durham, NC: Duke University Press.

Cripps, R. S.
    1929: *A Critical and Exegetical Commentary on the Book of Amos.* London: SPCK.

Dahmen, Ulrich
    1986: "Zur Text- und Literarkritik von Am 6,6a." *BN* 31: 7–10.

Dahood, Mitchell
    1961: "To Pawn One's Cloak." *Biblica* 42: 359–66.

Danell, G.
    1951: "Var Amos verkligen en nabi?" *SEÅ* 16: 7–20.

Davies, Philip R.
    2006: "Amos, Man and Book." Pp. 113–31 in: B. E. Kelle and M. B. Moore (eds.), *Israel's Prophets and Israel's Past* (FS J. H. Hayes), LHBOTS 446; London: T&T Clark.

Davis, Andrew
    2013: *Tel Dan in Its Northern Cultic Context.* Archaeology and Biblical Studies 20; Atlanta: SBL.

Delcor, M.
    1978: "Les Kéréthim et les Crètois." *VT* 28: 409–22.

Dell, Katherine J.
    1995: "The Misuse of Forms in Amos." *VT* 45: 45–61.
    2011: "Amos and the Earthquake: Judgment as Natural Disaster." Pp. 1–14 in: A. C. Hagedorn and A. Mein (eds.), *Aspects of Amos: Exegesis and Interpretation,* LHBOTS 536; New York: T&T Clark.

Dempsey, Carol J.
2000: *The Prophets: A Liberation-Critical Reading*. Minneapolis: Fortress.

Dempster, S.
1991: "The Lord Is His Name: A Study of the Distribution of the Names and Titles of God in the Book of Amos." *RB* 98: 170–89.

Dever, W. G.
1992: "A Case-Study in Biblical Archaeology: The Earthquake of *ca.* 760 BCE." *Eretz-Israel* 23: 27–35.

Dietrich, Jan
2010: *Kollektive Schuld und Haftung: Religions- und rechtsgeschichtliche Studien zum Sündenkuhritus des Deuteronomiums und zu verwandten Texten.* Oriental Religions in Antiquity 4; Tübingen: Mohr Siebeck.

Dietrich, Manfried, and Oswald Loretz
1977: "Die ug. Berufsgruppe der *nqdm* und das Amt des *rb nqdm.*" *UF* 9: 336–37.

Dietrich, Walter
1992: "JHWH, Israel und die Völker beim Propheten Amos." *TZ* 48: 315–28.

Dijkstra, Meindert
1994: "Gelijkenessen in Amos." *NedTT* 48: 178–90.
1995: "Is Balaam Also among the Prophets?" *JBL* 114: 43–64.
1998: "Textual Remarks on the Hymn-Fragment in Amos 4:13." Pp. 245–53 in: K.-D. Schunck and M. Augustin (eds.), *Lasset uns Brücken bauen: Collected Communications to the XVth Congress of the International Organization for the Study of the Old Testament, Cambridge 1995,* BEATAJ 42; Frankfurt am Main: Peter Lang.
2001: "'I Am Neither a Prophet Nor a Prophet's Pupil.' Amos 7:9–17 as the Presentation of a Prophet like Moses." Pp. 105–28 in: J. C. de Moor (ed.), *The Elusive Prophet: The Prophet as a Historical Person, Literary Character and Anonymous Artist,* OTS XLV; Leiden: Brill.

Dines, Jennifer M.
1991: "The Septuagint of Amos: A Study in Interpretation." Ph.D. diss., University of London.
2001: "Amos." Pp. 581–90 in: J. Barton and J. Muddiman (eds.), *The Oxford Bible Commentary,* Oxford: Oxford University Press.

Dorsey, David
1992: "Literary Architecture and Aural Structuring Techniques in Amos." *Biblica* 73: 305–30.

Dossin, G.
1948: "Une révélation du dieu Dagan à Terqa." *RA* 42: 316–20.

Driver, G. R.
1953: "Two Astronomical Passages in the Old Testament." *JTS* 4: 208–12.
1954: "A Hebrew Burial Custom." *ZAW* 66: 314–15.
1955: "Amos vii 14." *ExpTim* 67: 91–92.

Driver, Samuel R.

1897: *The Books of Joel and Amos*. Cambridge Bible for Schools and Colleges; Cambridge: Cambridge University Press.

Ego, Beate, Armin Lange, Hermann Lichtenberger, and Kristin de Troye (eds.)

2005: *Biblia Qumranica, Vol. 3B: Minor Prophets*. Leiden: Brill.

Eidevall, Göran

1996: *Grapes in the Desert: Metaphors, Models, and Themes in Hosea 4–14*. ConBOT 43; Stockholm: Almqvist & Wiksell.

2009: *Prophecy and Propaganda: Images of Enemies in the Book of Isaiah*. ConBOT 56; Winona Lake, IN: Eisenbrauns.

2012a: *Sacrificial Rhetoric in the Prophetic Literature*. Lewiston, NY: Edwin Mellen.

2012b: "Sounds of Silence in Biblical Hebrew: A Lexical Study." *VT* 62: 159–74.

2012c: "Amos och kulten: Ett bidrag till forskningshistorien." Pp. 11–31 in: T. Davidovich (ed.), *Plogbillar & svärd: En festskrift till Stig Norin*, Stockholm: Molin & Sorgenfrei.

2013: "Rejected Sacrifice in the Prophetic Literature: A Rhetorical Perspective." *SEÅ* 78: 31–45.

2014: "Propagandistic Constructions of Empires in the Book of Isaiah." Pp. 109–28 in: A. Lenzi and J. Stökl (eds.), *Divination, Politics and Ancient Near Eastern Empires*, Atlanta: SBL.

2016: "A Farewell to the Anticultic Prophet: Attitudes towards the Cult in the Book of Amos." Pp. 99–114 in: L.-S. Tiemeyer (ed.), *Priests and Cults in the Book of the Twelve*, Ancient Near Eastern Monographs 14; Atlanta: SBL.

Eissfeldt, Otto

1966: "Etymologische und archäologische Erklärung alttestamentlicher Wörter." *OrAnt* 5: 165–76.

1971: "Der Zugang nach Hamath." *OrAnt* 10: 269–76.

Engnell, Ivan

1967: *Studies in Divine Kingship in the Ancient Near East*. Oxford: Blackwell.

Erlandsson, Seth

1968: "Amos 5:25–27, ett crux interpretum." *SEÅ* 33: 76–82.

Ernst, Alexander B.

1994: *Weisheitliche Kultkritik: Zu Theologie und Ethik des Sprüchebuchs und der Prophetie des 8. Jahrhunderts*. Biblisch-theologische Studien 23; Neukirchen-Vluyn: Neukirchener.

Eslinger, Lyle

1987: "The Education of Amos." *HAR* 11: 35–57.

Fabry, Heinz-Josef

1998: "מַרְזֵחַ *marzēaḥ*." *TDOT*, vol. X, 10–15.

Fendler, Marlene

1973: "Zur Sozialkritik des Amos: Versuch einer wirtschafts- und sozialgeschichtlichen Interpretation alttestamentlicher Texte." *EvT* 33: 32–53.

Fenton, T. L.
1969: "Ugaritica—Biblica." *UF* 1: 65–70.

Fey, Reinhard
1963: *Amos und Jesaja: Abhängigkeit und Eigenständigkeit des Jesaja.* WMANT 12; Neukirchen-Vluyn: Neukirchener.

Firth, David G.
1996: "Promise as Polemic: Levels of Meaning in Amos 9:11–15." *OTE* 9/3: 372–82.

Fischer, Charis
2002: *Die Fremdvölkersprüche bei Amos und Jesaja: Studien zur Eigenart und Intention in Am 1,3–2,3.4f und Jes 13,1–16,14.* BBB 136; Berlin: Philo.

Fishbane, Michael
1970: "The Treaty Background of Amos 1:11 and Related Matters." *JBL* 89: 313–18.
1972: "Additional Remarks on *rḥmyw* (Amos 1:11)." *JBL* 91: 391–93.

Fleischer, Gunther
1989: *Von Menschenverkäufern, Baschankühen und Rechtsverkehrern: Die Sozialkritik des Amosbuches in historisch-kritischer, sozialgeschichtlicher und archäologischer Perspektive.* BBB 74; Frankfurt am Main: Athenäum.
2001: "Das Buch Amos." Pp. 115–292 in: U. Dahmen and G. Fleischer, *Die Bücher Joel und Amos,* Neuer Stuttgarter Kommentar Altes Testament; Stuttgart: Katholisches Bibelwerk.

Fleming, Daniel E.
2010: "The Day of Yahweh in the Book of Amos: A Rhetorical Response to Ritual Expectation." *RB* 117: 20–38.

Fohrer, Georg
1964: "Zion-Jerusalem im Alten Testament." *TWNT,* vol. 7, 292–318.

Foresti, Fabrizio
1981: "Funzione semantica dei brani participiali di Amos: 4,13; 5,8s; 9,5s." *Biblica* 62: 169–84.

Förg, Florian
2007: "Beobachtungen zur Struktur von Amos 2,6–12." *BN* 132: 13–21.

Fred, Stig
2003: *Varför säger Herren så? Profeterna, kontexten, retoriken: En jämförelse mellan Amos och Malaki.* Lund: Lunds universitet.

Freedman, David Noel
1985: "But Did King David Invent Musical Instruments?" *Bible Review* 1: 49–51.

Freedman, David Noel, and Francis I. Andersen
1970: "Harmon in Amos 4:3." *BASOR* 198: 41.

Freedman, David Noel, and Andrew Welch
1994: "Amos's Earthquake and Israelite Prophecy." Pp. 188–98 in: M. D. Coogan, J. C. Exum, and L. E. Stager (eds.), *Scripture and Other Artifacts: Essays in Honor of Philip J. King,* Louisville, KY: Westminster John Knox.

Fritz, Volkmar

    1987: "Die Fremdvölkersprüche des Amos." *VT* 37: 26–38.

    1989: "Amosbuch, Amos-Schule und historischer Amos." Pp. 29–43 in: V. Fritz, K.-F. Pohlmann, and H.-C. Schmitt (eds.), *Prophet und Prophetenbuch* (FS Otto Kaiser), BZAW 185; Berlin: De Gruyter.

Fuhs, Hans F.

    1977: "Amos 1,1. Erwägungen zur Tradition und Redaktion des Amosbuches." Pp. 271–289 in: H.-J. Fabry (ed.), *Bausteine Biblischer Theologie* (FS J. Botterweck), BBB 50; Cologne: Peter Hanstein.

    1999: "עָבַר *ʿābar.*" *TDOT,* vol. X, 408–25.

Fuller, Russell

    1996: "The Form and Formation of the Book of the Twelve: The Evidence from the Judean Desert." Pp. 86–101 in: J. W. Watts and P. R. House (eds.), *Forming Prophetic Literature: Essays on Isaiah and the Twelve in Honor of John D. W. Watts,* JSOTSup 235; Sheffield: Sheffield Academic.

    2000: "Minor Prophets." Pp. 554–57 in: L. Schiffman and J. Vanderkam (eds.), *Encyclopedia of the Dead Sea Scrolls,* vol. 1, New York: Oxford University Press.

García-Treto, Francisco O.

    1993: "A Reader-Response Approach to Prophetic Conflict: The Case of Amos 7.10–17." Pp. 114–24 in: J. C. Exum and D. J. A. Clines (eds.), *The New Literary Criticism and the Hebrew Bible,* JSOTSup 143; Sheffield: Sheffield Academic Press.

Garrett, Duane A.

    2008: *Amos: A Handbook on the Hebrew Text.* Waco, TX: Baylor University Press.

Gass, Erasmus

    2009: *Die Moabiter: Geschichte und Kultur eines ostjordanisches Volkes im 1. Jahrtausend v. Chr.* ADPV 38; Wiesbaden: Harrassowitz.

    2012: "'Kein Prophet bin ich und kein Prophetenschüler bin ich': Zum Selbstverständnis des Propheten Amos in Am 7:14." *TZ* 68: 1–24.

Gelston, Anthony

    2002: "Some Hebrew Misreadings in the Septuagint of Amos." *VT* 52: 493–500.

    2010: "Introduction and Commentaries on the Twelve Minor Prophets." Pp. 5–162 in: *Biblia Hebraica Quinta, Vol. 13: The Twelve Minor Prophets,* Stuttgart: Deutsche Bibelgesellschaft.

Gertz, Jan Christian

    2003: "Die unbedingte Gerichtsankündigung des Amos." Pp. 153–70 in: F. Sedlmeier (ed.), *Gottes Wege suchend,* Würzburg: Echter.

Gese, Hartmut

    1962: "Kleine Beiträge zum Verständnis des Amosbuches." *VT* 12: 417–38.

    1981: "Komposition bei Amos." Pp. 74–95 in: J. A. Emerton (ed.), *Congress Volume: Vienna 1980,* VTSup 32; Leiden: Brill.

    1989: "Amos 8:4–8: Der kosmische Frevel händlerischer Habgier." Pp. 59–72 in: V. Fritz, K.-F. Pohlmann, and H.-C. Schmitt (eds.), *Prophet und Prophetenbuch* (FS Otto Kaiser), BZAW 185; Berlin: De Gruyter.

Gevirtz, Stanley
1968: "A New Look at an Old Crux: Amos 5:26." *JBL* 87: 267–76.

Giles, Terry
1992: "A Note on the Vocation of Amos in 7:14." *JBL* 111: 690–92.

Gillingham, Susan
1993: "'Der die Morgenröte zur Finsternis macht.' Gott und Schöpfung im Amos-buch." *EvT* 55: 109–23.

Gitay, Yehoshua
1980: "A Study of Amos's Art of Speech: A Rhetorical Analysis of Amos 3:1–15." *CBQ* 42: 293–309.

Glenny, W. Edward
2007: "Hebrew Misreadings or Free Translation in the Septuagint of Amos?" *VT* 57: 524–47.
2009: *Finding Meaning in the Text: Translation Technique and Theology in the Septuagint of Amos.* VTSup 126; Leiden: Brill.
2012: "The Septuagint and Apostolic Hermeneutics: Amos 9 in Acts 15." *Bulletin of Biblical Research* 22: 1–26.
2013: *Amos: A Commentary Based on Amos in Codex Vaticanus.* Septuagint Commentary Series; Brill: Leiden.

Goff, Matthew
2008: "Awe, Wordlessness and Calamity: A Short Note on Amos v 13." *VT* 58: 638–43.

Gordis, R.
1940: "The Composition and Structure of Amos." *HTR* 33: 239–51.

Gosse, Bernard
1988: "Le recueil d'oracles contre les nations du livre d'Amos et 'l'histoire deutero-nomique.'" *VT* 38: 22–40.

Goswell, Greg
2011: "David in the Prophecy of Amos." *VT* 61: 243–57.

Gowan, D. E.
1996: "The Book of Amos: Introduction, Commentary, and Reflections." Pp. 337–431 in: L. E. Keck et al. (eds.), *New Interpreter's Bible,* vol. VII, Nashville: Abingdon.

Grätz, Sebastian
1998: *Der strafende Wettergott.* Bodenheim: Philo.

Greenfield, J. C.
1974: "The Marzeaḥ as a Social Institution." *Acta Antiqua Scientarium Hungaricae* 22: 451–55.

Greer, Jonathan
2007: "A *Marzeaḥ* and a *Mizraq:* A Prophet's Mêlée with Religious Diversity in Amos 6.4–7." *JSOT* 32: 243–62.

Grosch, Heinz
1969: *Der Prophet Amos.* Gütersloh: Gerd Mohn.

Guillaume, Philippe

2007: "A Reconsideration of Manuscripts Classified as Scrolls of the Twelve Minor Prophets (XII)." *JHebS* 7, article 16, 2–12; doi:10.5508/jhs.2007.v7.a16, http://www.jhsonline.org.

2011: "Binding 'Sucks': A Response to Stefan Schorch." *VT* 61: 335–37.

Gunneweg, Antonius

1960: "Erwägungen zu Amos 7, 14." *ZTK* 57: 1–16.

Haak, Robert D.

2008: "Response to Carroll." *ExAud* 24: 55–59.

Hadjiev, Tchavdar S.

2007: "'Kill All Who Are in Front': Another Suggestion about Amos ix 1." *VT* 57: 386–89.

2008: "The Context as Means of Redactional Reinterpretation in the Book of Amos." *JTS* 59: 655–68.

2009: *The Composition and Redaction of the Book of Amos.* BZAW 393; Berlin: De Gruyter.

Hagedorn, Anselm C.

2011: "Edom in the Book of Amos and Beyond." Pp. 41–57 in: A. C. Hagedorn and A. Mein (eds.), *Aspects of Amos: Exegesis and Interpretation,* LHBOTS 536; New York: T&T Clark.

Haldar, Alfred

1945: *Associations of Cult Prophets among the Ancient Semites.* Uppsala: Almqvist & Wiksell.

Hammershaimb, Erling

1970: *The Book of Amos.* Oxford: Basil Blackwell [1946].

Hardmeier, Christof

1985: "Alttestamentliche Exegese und linguistische Erzählforschung. Grundfragen der Erzähltextinterpretation am Beispiel von Amos 7,10–17." *Wort und Dienst* 18: 49–71.

Harper, William R.

1905: *A Critical and Exegetical Commentary on Amos and Hosea.* ICC; Edinburgh: T&T Clark.

Hartenstein, Friedhelm

1997: *Die Unzugänglichkeit Gottes im Heiligtum. Jesaja 6 und der Wohnort JHWHs in der Jerusalemer Kulttradition.* WMANT 75; Neukirchen-Vluyn: Neukirchener.

Hasel, G. F.

1991: *Understanding the Book of Amos: Basic Issues in Current Interpretations.* Grand Rapids, MI: Baker.

Hauan, Michael J.

1986: "The Background and Meaning of Amos 5:17b." *HTR* 79: 337–48.

Hayes, John H.
   1988: *Amos: The Eighth-Century Prophet: His Times and His Preaching*. Nashville: Abingdon.

Hermanson, Eric A.
   1998: "Biblical Hebrew: Conceptual Metaphor Categories in the Book of Amos." *OTE* 11: 438–51.

Hertzberg, H. W.
   1950: "Die prophetische Kritik am Kult." *Theologische Literaturzeitung* 75: 219–26.

Hesse, Franz
   1956: "Amos 5, 4–6, 14f." *ZAW* 68: 1–17.

Heyns, Dalene
   1997: "Space and Time in Amos 7: Reconsidering the Third Vision." *OTE* 10/1: 27–38.

Hillers, Delbert R.
   1964: "Amos 7, 4 and Ancient Parallels." *CBQ* 26: 221–25.
   1995: "Palmyrene Aramaic Inscriptions and the Old Testament, especially Amos 2:8." *ZAH* 8: 55–62.

Hobbs, T. R.
   1969: "Amos 3, 1b and 2, 10." *ZAW* 81: 384–87.

Höffken, Peter
   1982: "Eine Bemerkung zum 'Haus Hasaels' in Amos 1, 4." *ZAW* 94: 413–15.

Hoffmann, Hans Werner
   1970: "Zur Echtheitsfrage von Amos 9, 9f." *ZAW* 82: 121–22.

Hoffmann, Y.
   1977: "Did Amos Regard Himself as a *nābī*?" *VT* 27/2: 209–12.
   1981: "The Day of the Lord as a Concept and a Term in the Prophetic Literature." *ZAW* 93: 37–50.

Hoftijzer, J., and G. van der Kooij (eds.)
   1976: *Aramaic Texts from Deir 'Alla*. Leiden: Brill.

Holladay, W. L.
   1970: "Once more, *ᵃnak* = 'Tin,' Amos vii 7–8." *VT* 20: 492–94.
   1972: "Amos VI 1bβ: A Suggested Solution." *VT* 22: 107–10.

Holter, Knut
   2000: *Yahweh in Africa: Essays on Africa and the Old Testament*. New York: Peter Lang.

Homan, Michael M.
   1999: "Booths or Succoth? A Response to Yigael Yadin." *JBL* 118/4: 691–97.

Horst, F.
   1929: "Die Doxologien im Amosbuch." *ZAW* 47: 45–54.

Houston, W. J.
    2009: "Exit the Oppressed Peasant? Rethinking the Background of Social Criticism in the Prophets." Pp. 101–16 in: J. Day (ed.), *Prophecy and the Prophets in Ancient Israel: Proceedings of the Oxford Old Testament Seminar*, New York: T&T Clark.

Hübner, Ulrich
    1992: *Die Ammoniter: Untersuchungen zur Kultur, Geschichte und Religion eines transjordanisches Volkes im 1. Jahrtausend v. Chr.* ADPV 16; Wiesbaden: Harrassowitz.

Huffmon, H. B.
    1983: "The Social Role of Amos' Message." Pp. 109–16 in: H. B. Huffmon, F. A. Spina, and A. R. W. Green (eds.), *The Quest for the Kingdom of God: Studies in Honor of George E. Mendenhall*, Winona Lake, IN: Eisenbrauns.

Hutton, Jeremy M.
    2014: "Amos 1:3–2:8 and the International Economy of Iron Age II Israel." *HTR* 107: 81–113.

Hyatt, J. Philip
    1956: "The Translation and Meaning of Amos 5, 23–24." *ZAW* 68: 17–24.

Irsigler, Hubert
    2004: "Keine Flucht vor Gott. Zur Verwendung mythischer Motive in der Rede vom richterlichen Gott in Amos 9,1–4 und Psalm 139." Pp. 184–233 in: Hubert Irsigler (ed.), *Mythisches in biblischer Bildsprache: Gestalt und Verwandlung in Prophetie und Psalmen*, Quaestiones Disputatae 209; Freiburg im Breisgau: Herder.

Irwin, Brian
    2012: "Amos 4:1 and the Cows of Bashan on Mount Samaria: A Reappraisal." *CBQ* 74: 231–46.

Isbell, Charles D.
    1977: "A Note on Amos 1:1." *JNES* 36: 213–14.
    1978: "Another Look at Amos 5:26." *JBL* 97: 97–99.

Jackson, Jared J.
    1986: "Amos 5,13 Contextually Understood." *ZAW* 98: 434–35.

Jacobs, Paul
    1985: "'Cows of Bashan': A Note on the Interpretation of Amos 4:1." *JBL* 104: 109–10.

Jaruzelska, Izabela
    1992–93: "Social Structure in the Kingdom of Israel in the Eighth Century B.C. as Reflected in the Book of Amos." *Folia Orientale* 29: 91–117.
    1998: *Amos and the Officialdom in the Kingdom of Israel: The Socio-Economic Position of the Officials in the Light of the Biblical, the Epigraphic and Archaeological Evidence.* Seria Sociologica 25; Poznan: Adam Mickiewicz University.

Jepsen, A.
    1980: "חָזָה chāzāh." *TDOT*, vol. IV, 280–90.

Jeremias, Jörg

    1996: *Hosea und Amos: Studien zu den Anfängen des Dodekapropheton.* FAT 13;
    Tübingen: Mohr Siebeck.

    1997: "Rezeptionsprozesse in der prophetischen Überlieferung—am Beispiel der
    Visionsberichte des Amos." Pp. 29–44 in: R. G. Kratz and T. Krüger (eds.),
    Rezeption und Auslegung im Alten Testament und in seinem Umfeld, Freiburg:
    Universitätsverlag.

    1998: *The Book of Amos: A Commentary.* Trans. D. W. Stott. OTL; Louisville, KY:
    Westminster John Knox [1995].

    2013: "Das Rätsel der Schriftprofetie." *ZAW* 125: 93–117.

Jong, Matthijs de

    2007: *Isaiah among the Ancient Near Eastern Prophets: A Comparative Study of the
    Earliest Stages of the Isaiah Tradition and the Neo-Assyrian Prophecies.* VTSup
    117; Leiden: Brill.

Joyce, Paul

    2011: "The Book of Amos and Psychological Interpretation." Pp. 105–16 in:
    A. C. Hagedorn and A. Mein (eds.), *Aspects of Amos: Exegesis and Interpreta-
    tion,* LHBOTS 536; New York: T&T Clark.

Junker, Hubert

    1950: "Leo rugiit, quis non timebit? Deus locutus est, quis non prophetabit? Eine
    textkritische und exegetische Untersuchung über Amos 3,3–8." *TTZ* 59:
    4–13.

Kaiser, Otto

    1998: "Kult und Kultkritik im Alten Testament." Pp. 401–26 in: M. Dietrich and
    I. Kottsieper (eds.), *"Und Mose schrieb dieses Lied auf": Studien zum Alten Testa-
    ment und zum Alten Orient,* AOAT 250; Münster: Ugarit-Verlag.

Kallner-Amiran, D. H.

    1950–51: "A Revised Earthquake-Catalogue of Palestine." *Israel Exploration Journal*
    1: 223–46.

Kapelrud, Arvid S.

    1956: *Central Ideas in Amos.* Oslo: Det Norske Videnskabs-Akademi.

    1958: "Profeten Amos og hans yrke." *NTT* 59: 76–79.

Keimer, Ludwig

    1927: "Eine Bemerkung zu Amos 7,14." *Biblica* 8: 441–44.

Kellermann, Ulrich

    1969: "Der Amosschluß als Stimme deuteronomistischer Heilshoffnung." *EvT* 29:
    169–83.

Kelly, J. G.

    1977: "The Interpretation of Amos 4:13 in the Early Christian Community."
    Pp. 60–77 in: R. McNamara (ed.), *Essays in Honor of Joseph P. Brennan,* Roch-
    ester, NY: Saint Bernard's Seminary.

Kennedy, D. F.

    1997: "'It Shall Not Be': Divine Forgiveness in the Intercessory Prayers of Amos
    (Am 7:1–6)." *OTE* 10/1: 92–108.

Kessler, Rainer
   1989: "Die angeblichen Kornhändler von Amos viii 4–7." *VT* 39/1: 13–22.
   2015: "Amos und die Weisheit." Pp. 51–57 in: V. K. Nagy and L. Egeresi (eds.), *Propheten der Epochen/Prophets during the Epochs,* AOAT 426; Münster: Ugarit-Verlag.

King, Philip J.
   1988: *Amos, Hosea, Micah—An Archaeological Commentary.* Philadelphia: Westminster.

Kleven, Terence
   1996: "The Cows of Bashan: A Single Metaphor at Amos 4:1–3." *CBQ* 58: 215–27.

Knierim, Rolf P.
   1977: "'I Will Not Cause It to Return' in Amos 1 and 2." Pp. 163–75 in: G. W. Coats and B. O. Long (eds.), *Canon and Authority: Essays in Old Testament Religion and Theology,* Philadelphia: Fortress.

Koch, Klaus
   1974: "Die Rolle der hymnischen Abschnitte in der Komposition des Amos-Buches." *ZAW* 86: 504–37.
   2007: "Jahwäs wachsame Augen im Geschick der Völker. Erwägungen zu Amos 9,7–10." Pp. 193–212 in: F. Hartenstein and M. Pietsch (eds.), *"Sieben Augen auf einem Stein" (Sach 3,9). Studien zur Literatur des zweiten Tempels* (FS Ina Willi-Plein), Neukirchen-Vluyn: Neukirchener.

Koch, Klaus, et al.
   1976a: *Amos: Untersucht mit den Methoden einer strukturalen Formgeschichte. Teil 1: Programm und Analyse.* AOAT 30; Kevelaer: Butzon & Bercker.
   1976b: *Amos: Untersucht mit den Methoden einer strukturalen Formgeschichte. Teil 2: Synthese.* AOAT 30; Kevelaer: Butzon & Bercker.
   1976c: *Amos: Untersucht mit den Methoden einer strukturalen Formgeschichte. Teil 3: Schlüssel.* AOAT 30; Kevelaer: Butzon & Bercker.

Köckert, Matthias
   1993: "Das Gesetz und die Propheten in Amos 1–2." Pp. 145–54 in: J. Hausmann and H.-J. Zobel (eds.), *Alttestamentliche Glaube und biblische Theologie* (FS Preuss), Stuttgart: Kohlhammer.

Köhlmoos, Melanie
   2001: "Der Tod als Zeichen: Die Inszenierung des Todes in Am 5." *BN* 107/108: 65–77.
   2004: "Amos 9,1–4, Jerusalem und Beth-El: Ein Beitrag zur Gerichtsverkündigung am Kultort in der Prophetie des 8. Jhs." Pp. 169–78 in: M. Augustin and H. M. Niemann (eds.), *Basel und Bibel: Collected Communications to the XVIIth Congress of the International Organization for the Study of the Old Testament, Basel 2001,* BEATAJ 51; Frankfurt am Main: Peter Lang.

Kratz, Reinhard G.
   1998: "Die Kultpolemik der Propheten im Rahmen der israelitischen Kultgeschichte." Pp. 101–16 in: B. Köhler (ed.), *Religion und Wahrheit: Religionsgeschichtliche Studien.* Wiesbaden: Harrassowitz.

2003: "Die Worte des Amos von Tekoa." Pp. 54–89 in: M. Köckert and M. Nissinen, (eds.), *Propheten in Mari, Assyrien und Israel,* FRLANT 201; Göttingen: Vandenhoeck & Ruprecht.

2011: *Prophetenstudien. Kleine Schriften II.* FAT 74; Tübingen: Mohr Siebeck.

2013: "Das Rätsel der Schriftprofetie: Eine Replik." *ZAW* 125: 635–39.

Krause, H.-H.

1932: "Der Gerichtsprophet Amos, ein Vorläufer des Deuteronomisten." *ZAW* 50: 221–39.

Krause, M.

1972: "Das Verhältnis von sozialer Kritik und kommender Katastrophe in den Unheilsprophezeiungen des Amos." Dissertation, Hamburg Universität.

Krüger, Thomas

2006: "Erwägungen zur prophetischen Kultkritik." Pp. 37–55 in: R. Lux and E.-J. Waschke (eds.), *Die unwiderstehliche Wahrheit* (FS Meinhold), Arbeiten zur Bibel und ihrer Geschichte 23; Leipzig: Evangelische Verlagsanstalt.

Kutscher, Eduard Y.

1977: *Hebrew and Aramaic Studies.* Jerusalem: Magnes.

Lafferty, Theresa V.

2012: *The Prophetic Critique of the Priority of the Cult: A Study of Amos 5:21–24 and Isaiah 1:10–17.* Eugene, OR: Pickwick.

Landsberger, Benno

1965: "Tin and Lead: The Adventures of Two Vocables." *JNES* 24: 285–96.

Landy, Francis

1987: "Vision and Poetic Speech in Amos." *HAR* 11: 223–46.

Lang, Bernhard

1981: "Sklaven und Unfreie im Buch Amos (II 6, VIII 6)." *VT* 31: 482–88.

1983: *Monotheism and the Prophetic Minority.* SWBA 1; Sheffield: Almond.

Lang, Martin

2003: "Amos und Exodus: Einige Überlegungen zu Am 3–6." *BN* 119/120: 27–29.

2004: *Gott und Gewalt in der Amosschrift.* Würzburg: Echter.

Lang, Martin, and Reinhard Messner

2001: "'Gott erbaut sein himmlisches Heiligtum': Zur Bedeutung von אֲגֻדָּתוֹ in Am 9:6." *Biblica* 82: 93–98.

Law, David R.

2012: *The Historical-Critical Method: A Guide for the Perplexed.* London: T&T Clark.

Leeuwen, C. van

1974: "The Prophecy of the *yōm yhwh* in Amos v 18–20." *OtSt* 19: 113–34.

Lehmann, Reinhard G., and Marcus Reichel

1995: "DOD und ASIMA in Tell Dan." *BN* 77: 29–31.

Lehming, S.

1958: "Erwägungen zu Amos." *ZTK* 55: 145–70.

Lemaire, André
2008: "Une guerre 'pour rien' (Amos 6,13)." Pp. 97–101 in: M. Augustin and H. M. Niemann (eds.), *Thinking Towards New Horizons: Collected Communications to the XIXth Congress of the International Organization for the Study of the Old Testament, Ljubljana 2007.* Frankfurt am Main: Peter Lang.
2011: "Le 'brûlement des os': Amos 2:1 et 2 Rois 23:16.20." Pp. 223–28 in: H. M. Niemann and M. Augustin (eds.), *"My Spirit at Rest in the North Country" (Zechariah 6.8): Collected Communications to the XXth Congress of the International Organization for the Study of the Old Testament, Helsinki 2010,* BEATAJ 57; Frankfurt am Main: Peter Lang.

Lescow, T.
1998: "Das vorexilische Amosbuch: Erwägungen zu seiner Kompositionsgeschichte." *BN* 93: 23–55.
1999: "Das nachexilische Amosbuch: Erwägungen zu seiner Kompositionsgeschichte." *BN* 99: 66–101.

Levin, Christoph
1995: "Amos und Jeroboam I." *VT* 45: 307–17.
2003: "Das Amosbuch der Anawim." Pp. 265–90 in: C. Levin, *Fortschreibungen: Gesammelte Studien zum Alten Testament,* BZAW 316; Berlin: De Gruyter.

Lieth, Albrecht von der
2007: "Sieben oder Worfeln? Eine neue Deutung von Am 9.9." *BN* 134: 49–62.

Limburg, James
1973: "Amos 7:4: A Judgment with Fire?" *CBQ* 35: 346–49.
1987: "Sevenfold Structures in the Book of Amos." *JBL* 106: 217–22.
1988: *Hosea—Micah.* Interpretation; Atlanta: John Knox.

Linder, Sven
1922: "Utsikten från Tekoa." Pp. 338–40 in: *Teologiska studier* (FS Erik Stave), Uppsala: Almqvist & Wiksell.

Lindström, Fredrik
1983: *God and the Origin of Evil: A Contextual Analysis of Alleged Monistic Evidence in the Old Testament.* ConBOT 21; Lund: Gleerup.

Linville, James R.
1999: "Visions and Voices: Amos 7–9." *Biblica* 80: 22–42.
2000a: "What Does 'It' Mean? Interpretation at the Point of No Return." *Biblical Interpretation* 8: 400–424.
2000b: "Amos among the 'Dead Prophets Society': Re-reading the Lion's Roar." *JSOT* 90: 55–77.
2008: *Amos and the Cosmic Imagination.* SOTSMS; Burlington, VT: Ashgate.

Löhr, M.
1901: *Untersuchungen zum Buche Amos.* BZAW 4; Giessen: Rickert.

Loretz, Oswald
1974: "Die Berufung des Propheten Amos (7,14–15)." *UF* 6: 487–88.
1981: "Ugaritische und hebräische Lexikographie (II)." *UF* 13: 127–35.

1982: "Ugaritisch-biblisch *mrzḥ*. 'Kultmahl, Kultverein' in Jer 16,5 und Am 6,7. Bemerkungen zur Geschichte des Totenkultes in Israel." Pp. 87–93 in: L. Ruppert, P. Weimar, and E. Zenger (eds.), *Künder des Wortes: Beiträge zur Theologie der Propheten,* Würzburg: Echter.

1989a: "Die babylonischen Gottesnamen Sukkut und Kajjamānu in Amos 5,26. Ein Beitrag zur jüdischen Astrologie." *ZAW* 101: 286–89.

1989b: "Amos vi 12." *VT* 39: 240–42.

1992: "Die Entstehung des Amos-Buches im Licht der Prophetien aus Māri, Ischchali und der Ugarit-Texte. Paradigmenwechsel in der Prophetenbuchforschung." *UF* 24: 179–211.

1993: "*Marziḫu* im ugaritischen und biblischen Ahnenkult." Pp. 93–144 in: M. Dietrich and O. Loretz (eds.), *Mesopotamica—Ugaritica—Biblica* (FS Bergerhof), AOAT 232; Kevelaer: Butzon & Bercker; Neukirchen-Vluyn: Neukirchener.

Lössl, Josef
2002: "Amos 6:1: Notes on Its Text and Ancient Translations." *Journal of Northwest Semitic Languages* 28: 43–61.

Lundbom, Jack R.
2007: "The Lion Has Roared: Rhetorical Structure in Amos 1:2–3:8." Pp. 65–75 in: S. Malena and D. Miano (eds.), *Milk and Honey: Essays on Ancient Israel and the Bible,* Winona Lake, IN: Eisenbrauns.

Lust, J.
1981: "Remarks on the Redaction of Amos v 4–6, 14–15." *OtSt* 21: 129–54.

Maag, Victor
1951: *Text, Wortschatz und Begriffswelt des Buches Amos.* Leiden: Brill.

MacDonald, Nathan
2008: *Not Bread Alone: The Uses of Food in the Old Testament.* Oxford: Oxford University Press.

Maier, Christl, and Ernst M. Dörrfuss
1999: "'Um mit ihnen zu sitzen, zu essen und zu trinken'. Am 6,7; Jer 16,5 und die Bedeutung von *marze*ᵃ*ḥ*." *ZAW* 111: 45–57.

Malamat, Abraham
1953: "Amos 1:5 in the Light of the Til Barsip Inscriptions." *BASOR* 129: 25–26.

Markert, Ludwig
1977: *Struktur und Bezeichnung des Scheltworts: Eine gattungskritische Studie anhand des Amosbuches.* BZAW 140; Berlin: De Gruyter.
1978: "Amos, Amosbuch." *Theologische Realenzyklopädie,* vol. 2, 471–87. Berlin: De Gruyter.

Marsh, John
1959: *Amos and Micah.* Torch Bible Commentaries; London: SCM.

Marti, Karl
1904: *Das Dodekapropheton.* KHC XIII; Tübingen: Mohr.

1918: "Zur Komposition von Amos 1, 3–2, 3." Pp. 323–30 in: W. Frankenberger and F. Küchler (eds.), *Abhandlungen zur semitischen Religionskunde und Sprachwissenschaft* (FS Baudissin), BZAW 33; Giessen: Alfred Töpelmann.

Martin-Achard, Robert
1984a: *Amos: l'homme, le message, l'influence.* Geneva: Labor et Fides.
1984b: "The End of the People of God: A Commentary on the Book of Amos." Pp. 1–74 in: R. Martin-Achard and S. Paul Re'emi, *God's People in Crisis,* International Theological Commentary; Edinburgh: Handsel.

Marx, Alfred
1994: *Les offrandes végétales dans l'Ancien Testament.* VTSup 57; Leiden: Brill.
2005: *Les systèmes sacrificiels de l'Ancien Testament.* VTSup 105; Leiden: Brill.

Mathias, Dietmar
1999: "Beobachtungen zur fünften Vision des Amos (9,1–4)." Pp. 150–74 in: C. Kähler, M. Böhm, and C. Böttrich (eds.), *Gedenkt an das Wort* (FS W. Vogler), Leipzig: Evangelische Verlagsanstalt.

Mays, James Luther
1969: *Amos: A Commentary.* OTL; London: SCM.

McComiskey, Thomas E.
1987: "The Hymnic Elements of the Prophecy of Amos: A Study of Form-Critical Methodology." *JETS* 30: 139–57.

McConville, J. Gordon
2006: "'How Can Jacob Stand? He Is So Small!' (Amos 7:2): The Prophetic Word and the Re-imagining of Israel." Pp. 132–51 in: B. E. Kelle and M. B. Moore (eds.), *Israel's Prophets and Israel's Past* (FS J. H. Hayes), LHBOTS 446; London: T&T Clark.

McKeating, H. M.
1971: *The Books of Amos, Hosea, and Micah.* CBC; Cambridge: Cambridge University Press.

McLaughlin, John
2001: *The* Marzēaḥ *in the Prophetic Literature: References and Allusions in Light of the Extra-Biblical Evidence.* VTSup 86; Leiden: Brill.
2014: "Is Amos (Still) among the Wise?" *JBL* 133: 281–303.

Meek, Theophile J.
1941: "Again the Accusative of Time in Amos 1:1." *JAOS* 61: 190–91.

Mein, Andrew
2011: "The Radical Amos in Savonarola's Florence." Pp. 117–40 in: A. C. Hagedorn and A. Mein (eds.), *Aspects of Amos: Exegesis and Interpretation,* LHBOTS 536; New York: T&T Clark.

Melugin, Roy F.
1992: "Amos." Pp. 735–49 in: E. Carpenter and W. McCown (eds.), *Asbury Bible Commentary,* Grand Rapids, MI: Zondervan.
1998: "Amos in Recent Research." *Currents in Research: Biblical Studies* 6: 65–101.

Metzger, Martin
1960: "Lodebar und der tell el-mghannije." *ZDPV* 76: 97–102.

Miller, Patrick D.
1970: "Animal Names as Designations in Ugaritic and Hebrew." *UF* 2: 177–86.
1986: "The Prophetic Critique of Kings." *ExAud* 2: 82–95.

Mills, Mary
2010: "Divine Violence in the Book of Amos." Pp. 153–79 in: J. M. O'Brien and C. Franke (eds.), *The Aesthetics of Violence in the Prophets,* LHBOTS 517; New York: T&T Clark.

Milstein, Sara J.
2013: "'Who Would Not Write?' The Prophet as Yhwh's Prey in Amos 3:3–8." *CBQ* 75: 429–45.

Mittmann, Siegfried
1971: "Gestalt und Gehalt einer prophetischen Selbstrechtfertigung (Am 3, 3–8)." *TQ* 151: 134–45.
1976: "Amos 3,12–15 und das Bett der Samarier." *ZDPV* 92: 149–67.

Moeller, Henry
1964: "Ambiguity at Amos 3:12." *Bible Translator* 15: 31–34.

Möller, Karl
2000: "'Hear This Word against You': A Fresh Look at the Arrangement and the Rhetorical Strategy of the Book of Amos." *VT* 50: 499–518.
2003a: *A Prophet in Debate: The Rhetoric of Persuasion in the Book of Amos.* JSOT-Sup 372; Sheffield: Sheffield Academic Press.
2003b: "Reconstructing and Interpreting Amos's Literary Prehistory: A Dialogue with Redaction Criticism." Pp. 397–441 in: C. Bartholomew et al. (eds.), *'Behind' the Text: History and Biblical Interpretation,* Carlisle: Paternoster.
2012: "Amos, Book of." Pp. 5–16 in: M. J. Boda and J. G. McConville (eds.), *Dictionary of the Old Testament: Prophets,* Downers Grove, IL: InterVarsity.
2014: *Reading Amos as a Book.* Cambridge: Grove Books.

Montgomery, James A.
1904: "Notes on Amos." *JBL* 23: 94–96.
1906: "Notes from the Samaritan." *JBL* 25: 49–54.
1912: "Notes on the Old Testament." *JBL* 31: 140–46.

Morgenstern, Julius
1936: "Amos Studies I." *HUCA* 11: 19–140.
1937–38: "Amos Studies II." *HUCA* 12–13: 1–53.

Moughtin-Mumby, Sharon
2011: "'A Man and His Father Go to Naarah in Order to Defile My Holy Name!' Rereading Amos 2.6–8." Pp. 59–82 in: A. C. Hagedorn and A. Mein (eds.), *Aspects of Amos: Exegesis and Interpretation,* LHBOTS 536; New York: T&T Clark.

Mulder, Martin J.
1984: "Ein Vorschlag zur Übersetzung von Amos iii 6b." *VT* 34: 106–8.
1995: "כַּרְמֶל karmel." *TDOT,* vol. VII, 325–36.

Müller, Hans-Peter
1971: "Die Wurzeln עִיק, יָעַק und עוּק." *VT* 21: 556–64.

Müller, Reinhard
2010: "Der finstere Tag Jahwes. Zum kultischen Hintergrund von Am 5,18–20."
ZAW 122: 576–92.

Mulzer, Martin
1996: "Amos 8,14 in der LXX. Ein Einwurf in die Tel Dan-Text Debatte." *BN* 84:
54–58.

Murtonen, A.
1952: "Amos: A Hepatoscoper?" *VT* 2: 170–71.

Nägele, S.
1995: *Laubhütte Davids und Wolkensohn: Eine auslegungsgeschichtliche Studie zu*
Amos 9,11 in der jüdischen und christlichen Exegese. AGJU 24; Leiden: Brill.

Nahkola, Aulikki
2011: "Amos Animalizing: Lion, Bear and Snake in Amos 5.19." Pp. 83–104 in:
A. C. Hagedorn and A. Mein (eds.), *Aspects of Amos: Exegesis and Interpretation,*
LHBOTS 536; New York: T&T Clark.

Naiden, Fred S.
2006: "Rejected Sacrifice in Greek and Hebrew Religion." *JANER* 6: 189–223.

Neher, André
1950: *Amos: Contribution à l'étude du prophétisme.* Paris: Vrin.

Neubauer, Karl Wilhelm
1966: "Erwägungen zu Amos 5, 4–15." *ZAW* 78: 292–316.

Neusner, Jacob
2007: *Amos in Talmud and Midrash.* Lanham, MD: University Press of America.

Niditch, Susan
1980: "The Composition of Isaiah 1." *Biblica* 61: 509–29.
1983: *The Symbolic Vision in Biblical Tradition.* Harvard Semitic Monographs 30;
Chico, CA: Scholars Press.

Niehaus, J.
1992: "Amos." Pp. 315–494 in: T. E. McComiskey (ed.), *The Minor Prophets, vol. 1,*
Grand Rapids, MI: Baker.

Niemann, H. Michael
1994: "Theologie in geographischem Gewand. Zum Wachstumsprozess der Völker-
spruchsammlung Amos 1–2." Pp. 177–96 in: H. M. Niemann, M. Augustin,
and W. H. Schmidt (eds.), *Nachdenken über Israel: Bibel und Theologie* (FS
Schunck), BEATAJ 37; Frankfurt: Peter Lang.

Nissinen, Martti
2003: *Prophets and Prophecy in the Ancient Near East.* With Contribution by
Choon-Leong Seow and Robert K. Ritner. WAW 12; Atlanta: SBL.
2010: "Biblical Prophecy from a Near Eastern Perspective: The Cases of Kingship
and Divine Possession." Pp. 441–68 in: A. Lemaire (ed.), *Congress Volume*
Ljubljana 2007, VTSup 133; Leiden: Brill.

Noble, Paul R.

1995a: "The Literary Structure of Amos: A Thematic Analysis." *JBL* 114: 209–26.

1995b: "'I Will Not Bring "It" Back' (Amos 1:3): A Deliberately Ambiguous Oracle?" *ExpTim* 106: 105–9.

1997: "Amos' Absolute 'No.'" *VT* 47: 329–40.

1998: "Amos and Amaziah in Context: Synchronic and Diachronic Approaches to Amos 7–8." *CBQ* 60: 423–39.

1999: "A Note on *ûnᵉśāʾô dôdô ûmᵉśārᵉpô* (Amos 6,10)." *ZAW* 111: 419–22.

Nogalski, James D.

1993a: *Literary Precursors to the Book of the Twelve.* BZAW 217; Berlin: De Gruyter.

1993b: *Redactional Processes in the Book of the Twelve.* BZAW 218; Berlin: De Gruyter.

1993c: "The Problematic Suffixes of Amos ix 11." *VT* 43: 411–17.

2003: "The Day(s) of YHWH in the Book of the Twelve." Pp. 192–213 in: P. L. Redditt and A. Schart (eds.), *Thematic Threads in the Book of the Twelve,* BZAW 325; Berlin: De Gruyter.

2007: "Recurring Themes in the Book of the Twelve: Creating Points of Contact for a Theological Reading." *Interpretation* 61: 125–36.

Nogalski, James D., and Marvin A. Sweeney (eds.)

2000: *Reading and Hearing the Book of the Twelve.* SBL Symposium Series 15; Atlanta: SBL.

Noonan, Benjamin

2013: "There and Back Again: 'Tin' or 'Lead' in Amos 7:7–9?" *VT* 63: 299–307.

Norin, Stig

2009: "Der Tag Gottes im Alten Testament. Jenseits der Spekulationen—Was ist übrig?" Pp. 33–42 in: A. Hultgård and S. Norin (eds.), *Le Jour de Dieu/Der Tag Gottes,* WUNT 245; Tübingen: Mohr Siebeck.

Novick, Tzvi

2008: "Duping the Prophet: On אֲנָךְ (Amos 7.8b) and Amos's Visions." *JSOT* 33: 115–28.

Nowack, W.

1922: *Die kleinen Propheten.* HKAT III:4; Göttingen: Vandenhoeck & Ruprecht.

Nwaoru, Emmanuel

2009: "A Fresh Look at Amos 4:1–3 and Its Imagery." *VT* 59: 460–74.

O'Connell, R. H.

1996: "Telescoping N + 1 Patterns in the Book of Amos." *VT* 46: 56–73.

Oestreich, Bernhard

1998: *Metaphors and Similes for Yahweh in Hosea 14:2–9 (1–8).* Frankfurt am Main: Peter Lang.

Ogden, Kelly

1992: "The Earthquake Motif in the Book of Amos." Pp. 69–80 in: K.-D. Schunck and M. Augustin (eds.), *Goldene Äpfel in silbernen Schalen. Collected*

Communications to the XIIIth Congress of the International Organization for the Study of the Old Testament, Leuven 1989, BEATAJ 20; Frankfurt am Main: Peter Lang.

O'Kennedy, D. F.
1997: "'It Shall Not Be': Divine Forgiveness in the Intercessory Prayers of Amos (Am 7:1–6)." *OTE* 10: 92–108.

Olyan, Saul M.
1991: "The Oaths in Amos 8:14." Pp. 121–49 in: G. A. Anderson and S. M. Olyan (eds.), *Priesthood and Cult in Ancient Israel,* JSOTSup 125; Sheffield: Sheffield Academic Press.
2015: "Ritual Inversion in Biblical Representation of Punitive Rites." Pp. 235–43 in: J. J. Collins, T. M. Lemos, and S. M. Olyan (eds.), *Worship, Women, and War: Essays in Honor of Susan Niditch,* Brown Judaic Studies; Providence, RI: Brown University.

Osten-Sacken, Peter von der
1979: "Die Bücher der Tora als Hütte der Gemeinde. Amos 5, 26f. in der Damaskusschrift." *ZAW* 91: 423–35.

Oswald, Wolfgang
2009: "Zukunftserwartung und Gerichtsankündigung. Zur Pragmatik der prophetischen Rede vom Tag Jhwhs." Pp. 19–31 in: A. Hultgård and S. Norin (eds.), *Le Jour de Dieu/Der Tag Gottes,* WUNT 245; Tübingen: Mohr Siebeck.

Ouellette, Jean
1972: "The Shaking of the Thresholds in Amos 9:1." *HUCA* 43: 23–27.
1973: "Le mur d'étain dans Amos vii, 7–9." *RB* 80: 321–31.

Overholt, Thomas A.
1979: "Commanding the Prophets: Amos and the Problem of Prophetic Authority." *CBQ* 41: 517–32.

Paas, Stefan
1993: "'He Who Builds His Stairs into Heaven . . .' (Amos 9:6a)." *UF* 25: 319–25.
2002: "Seeing and Singing: Visions and Hymns in the Book of Amos." *VT* 52: 253–74.

Pakkala, Juha
2010: "Why the Cult Reforms in Judah Probably Did Not Happen." Pp. 201–35 in: R. G. Kratz and H. Spieckermann (eds.), *One God—One Cult—One Nation,* BZAW 405; Berlin: De Gruyter.

Park, Aaron W.
2001: *The Book of Amos as Composed and Read in Antiquity.* Studies in Biblical Literature 37; New York: Peter Lang.

Paul, Shalom M.
1971: "Amos 1:3–2:3: A Concatenous Literary Pattern." *JBL* 90: 397–403.
1978: "Fishing Imagery in Amos 4:2." *JBL* 97: 183–90.
1991: *Amos.* Hermeneia; Philadelphia: Fortress.

Pfeifer, Gerhard

1976: "Denkformenanalyse als exegetische Methode, erläutert an Am 1, 2–2, 16." *ZAW* 88: 56–71.

1983: "Unausweichliche Konsequenzen. Denkformenanalyse von Amos iii 3–8." *VT* 33: 341–47.

1984: "Die Denkform des Propheten Amos (iii 9–11)." *VT* 34: 476–80.

1987: "'Ich bin in tiefe Wasser geraten, und die Flut will mich ersäufen' (Psalm LXIX 3)—Anregungen und Vorschläge zur Aufarbeitung wissenschaftlicher Sekundärliteratur." *VT* 37: 327–39.

1988a: "Die Fremdvölkersprüche des Amos—Spätere *vaticinia ex eventu?*" *VT* 38: 230–33.

1988b: "'Rettung' als Beweis der Vernichtung (Amos 3,12)." *ZAW* 100: 269–77.

1989: "Das Ja des Amos." *VT* 39: 497–503.

1991: "Jahwe als Schöpfer der Welt und Herr ihrer Mächte in der Verkündigung des Propheten Amos." *VT* 41: 475–81.

1995: *Die Theologie des Propheten Amos.* Frankfurt am Main: Peter Lang.

1996: "Amos 1:1: Worte des Amos?" Pp. 165–68 in: M. Augustin and K.-D. Schunck (eds.), *"Dort ziehen Schiffe dahin . . ." Collected Communications to the XIVth Congress of the International Organization for the Study of the Old Testament, Paris 1992,* Frankfurt am Main: Peter Lang.

Pietsch, Michael

2013: *Die Kultreform Josias: Studien zur Religionsgeschichte Israels in der späten Königszeit.* FAT 86; Tübingen: Mohr Siebeck.

Pinker, Aron

2003: "Reconstruction of the Destruction in Amos 6,10." *ZAW* 115: 423–27.

Pitard, Wayne T.

1992: "Aram (Place)." *ABD,* vol. 1, 338–41.

Polley, M. E.

1989: *Amos and the Davidic Empire: A Socio-Historical Approach.* New York: Oxford University Press.

Pope, Marvin H.

1981: "The Cult of the Dead at Ugarit." Pp. 159–79 in: G. D. Young (ed.), *Ugarit in Retrospect,* Winona Lake, IN: Eisenbrauns.

Power, E.

1927: "Note to Amos 7,1." *Biblica* 8: 87–92.

Praetorius, F.

1915: "Bemerkungen zu Amos." *ZAW* 35: 12–25.

Priest, John

1965: "The Covenant of Brothers." *JBL* 84: 400–406.

Pschibille, J.

2001: *Hat der Löwe erneut gebrüllt? Sprachliche, formale und inhaltliche Gemeinsamkeiten in der Verkündigung Jeremias und Amos.* Biblisch-theologische Studien 41; Neukirchen-Vluyn: Neukirchener.

Puech, Émile
    1977: "Milkom, le dieu ammonite, en Amos i 15." *VT* 27: 117–25.

Rabinowitz, Isaac
    1961: "The Crux at Amos iii 12." *VT* 11: 228–31.

Radine, Jason
    2010: *The Book of Amos in Emergent Judah.* FAT 45; Tübingen: Mohr Siebeck.
    2014: "Vision and Curse Aversion in the Book of Amos." Pp. 84–100 in: E. R. Hayes and L.-S. Tiemeyer (eds.), *"I Lifted My Eyes and Saw": Reading Dream and Vision Reports in the Hebrew Bible,* LHBOTS 584; London: Blooms-bury.

Rahtjen, Bruce D.
    1964: "A Critical Note on Amos 8:1–2." *JBL* 83: 416–17.

Ramírez, Guillermo
    1996: "The Social Location of the Prophet Amos in Light of the Group/Grid Cultural Anthropological Model." Pp. 112–24 in: S. B. Reid (ed.), *Prophets and Paradigms* (FS G. Tucker), JSOTSup 229; Sheffield: Sheffield Academic Press.

Ramsey, George W.
    1970: "Amos 4:12: A New Perspective." *JBL* 89: 187–91.

Rector, Larry J.
    1978: "Israel's Rejected Worship: An Exegesis of Amos 5." *ResQ* 21: 162–75.

Redditt, Paul L., and Aaron Schart (eds.)
    2003: *Thematic Threads in the Book of the Twelve.* BZAW 325; Berlin: De Gruyter.

Reider, Joseph
    1954: "Etymological Studies in Biblical Hebrew." *VT* 4: 276–95.

Reimer, Haroldo
    1992: *Richtet auf das Recht! Studien zur Botschaft des Amos.* SBS 149; Stuttgart: Katholisches Bibelwerk.
    2000: "Amós, profeta de juicio y justicia." *RIBLA* 35/36: 153–68.

Rendtorff, Rolf
    1973: "Zu Amos 2, 14–16." *ZAW* 85: 226–27.

Reventlow, Henning Graf
    1962: *Das Amt des Propheten bei Amos.* FRLANT 80; Göttingen: Vandenhoeck & Ruprecht.

Rice, Gene
    1978: "Was Amos a Racist?" *JRT* 35: 35–44.

Richard, E.
    1982: "The Creative Use of Amos by the Author of Acts." *NovT* 24: 37–53.

Richardson, H. Neil
    1966: "A Critical Note on Amos 7:14." *JBL* 85: 89.
    1973: "Skt (Amos 9:11): 'Booth' or 'Succoth'?" *JBL* 92: 375–81.

Riede, Peter

2008: *Vom Erbarmen zum Gericht. Die Visionen des Amosbuches (Am 7–9*) und ihre literatur- und traditionsgeschichtliche Zusammenhang.* WMANT 120; Neukirchen-Vluyn: Neukirchener.

Rilett Wood, Joyce

1998: "Tragic and Comic Forms in Amos." *Biblical Interpretation* 6: 20–48.

2002: *Amos in Song and Book Culture.* JSOTSup 337; Sheffield: Sheffield Academic Press.

Roberts, H. C.

1993: "La época de Amós y la justicia social." *Bible Translator* 50: 95–106.

Roberts, J. J. M.

1965: "A Note on Amos 7:14 and Its Context." *ResQ* 8: 175–78.

1970: "Recent Trends in Amos Studies." *ResQ* 13: 1–16.

1985: "Amos 6:1–7." Pp. 155–66 in: J. T. Butler, E. W. Conrad, and B. C. Ollenburger (eds.), *Understanding the Word,* JSOTSup 37; Sheffield: JSOT.

Robinson, Theodore H.

1954: "Amos." Pp. 70–108 in: T. H. Robinson and F. Horst, *Die zwölf kleinen Propheten,* 2nd ed., HAT 14; Tübingen: Mohr.

Rösel, H. N.

1993: "Kleine Studien zur Entwicklung des Amosbuches." *VT* 43: 88–101.

Rosenbaum, S. N.

1990: *Amos of Israel: A New Interpretation.* Macon, GA: Mercer University Press.

Rottzoll, Dirk U.

1988: "II Sam 14,5—eine Parallele zu Am 7,14f." *ZAW* 100: 413–15.

1996: *Studien zur Redaktion und Komposition des Amosbuchs.* BZAW 243; Berlin: De Gruyter.

Rowley, H. H.

1947: "Was Amos a Nabi?" Pp. 191–98 in: J. Fück (ed.), *Festschrift Otto Eissfeldt,* Halle: Max Niemeyer.

Rudolph, Wilhelm

1970: "Amos 4,6–13." Pp. 27–38 in: H. J. Stoebe (ed.), *Wort—Gebot—Glaube. Beiträge zur Theologie des Alten Testaments* (FS W. Eichrodt). Zürich: Zwingli.

1971: *Joel—Amos—Obadja—Jona.* KAT XIII/2; Gütersloh: Gerd Mohn.

Ruiz González, G.

1987: *Comentarios hebreos medievales al libro di Amós.* Madrid: UPCM.

Rüterswörden, Udo

2010: "'Rosen und Lavendel statt Blut und Eisen.' Zum Abschluss des Amosbuches." Pp. 211–21 in: P. Mommer and A. Scherer (eds.), *Geschichte Israels und deuteronomistisches Geschichtsdenken* (FS W. Thiel), AOAT 380; Münster: Ugarit-Verlag.

Sæbø, Magne

2004: "Die Gemeinde als Individuum. Bemerkungen zur kollektiven Du-Anrede bei Amos und anderen vorexilischen Propheten." Pp. 307–20 in:

F. Hartenstein (ed.), *Schriftprophetie* (FS Jeremias), Neukirchen-Vluyn: Neukirchener.

Sanderson, Judith

1998: "Amos." Pp. 218–23 in: C. Newsom and S. Ringe (eds.), *The Women's Bible Commentary,* Louisville, KY: Westminster John Knox.

Schart, Aaron

1998: *Die Entstehung des Zwölfprophetenbuchs: Neubearbeitungen von Amos im Rahmen schriftenübergreifender Redaktionsprozesse.* BZAW 260; Berlin: De Gruyter.

2003: "The Fifth Vision of Amos in Context." Pp. 46–69 in: P. L. Redditt and A. Schart (eds.), *Thematic Threads in the Book of the Twelve,* BZAW 325; Berlin: De Gruyter.

2004: "Die Jeremiavisionen als Fortführung der Amos-visionen." Pp. 185–202 in: F. Hartenstein (ed.), *Schriftprophetie* (FS Jeremias), Neukirchen-Vluyn: Neukirchener.

2007: "The First Section of the Book of the Twelve Prophets: Hosea—Joel—Amos." *Interpretation* 61: 138–52.

2009: "Totenstille und Endknall. Ein Beitrag zur Analyse der Soundscape des Zwölfprophetenbuchs." Pp. 257–74 in: C. Karrer-Grube et al. (eds.), *Sprachen—Bilder—Klänge* (FS R. Bartelmus), AOAT 359; Münster: Ugarit-Verlag.

Schenker, A.

1986: "Steht der Prophet unter dem Zwang zu weissagen, oder steht Israel vor der Evidenz der Weisung Gottes in der Weissagung des Propheten? Zur Interpretation von Amos 3,3–8." *BZ* 30: 250–56.

Scherer, Andreas

2005: "Vom Sinn prophetischer Gerichtsverkündigung bei Amos und Hosea." *Biblica* 86: 1–19.

Schmid, Herbert

1967: "'Nicht Prophet bin ich, noch bin ich Prophetensohn.' Zur Erklärung von Amos 7,14a." *Judaica* 23/2: 68–74.

Schmidt, B. B.

1996: *Israel's Beneficent Dead: Ancestor Cult and Necromancy in Ancient Israelite Religion and Tradition.* Winona Lake, IN: Eisenbrauns.

Schmidt, Ludwig

2007: "Die Amazja-Erzählung (Am 7,10–17) und der historische Amos." *ZAW* 119: 221–35.

Schmidt, W. H.

1965: "Die deuteronomistische Redaktion des Amosbuches: Zu den theologischen Unterschieden zwischen dem Prophetenwort und seinem Sammler." *ZAW* 77: 168–93.

1973: *Zukunftsgewißheit und Gegenwartskritik: Grundzüge prophetischer Verkündigung.* Biblische Studien 64; Neukirchen-Vluyn: Neukirchener.

Schmitt, John J.

1991: "The Virgin of Israel: Referent and Use of the Phrase in Amos and Jeremiah." *CBQ* 53: 365–87.

Schorch, Stefan
  2010: "'A Young Goat in Its Mother's Milk'? Understanding an Ancient Prohibition." *VT* 60: 116–30.
  2012: "'Vielleicht wird der Herr doch gnädig sein!' Das Konzept der Unverfügbarkeit Jhwhs in der alttestamentlichen Prophetie." Pp. 457–68 in: A. Berlejung and R. Heckl (eds.), *Ex oriente Lux: Studien zur Theologie des Alten Testaments* (FS R. Lux), Leipzig: Evangelische Verlagsanstalt.

Schullerus, Konrad
  1996: "Überlegungen zur Redaktionsgeschichte des Amosbuches anhand von Am 9,7–10." *BN* 85: 56–69.

Schult, Hermann
  1971: "Amos 7, 15a und die Legitimation des Aussenseiters." Pp. 462–78 in: H. W. Wolff (ed.), *Probleme biblischer Theologie* (FS von Rad), Munich: Chr. Kaiser.

Schüngel-Straumann, Helen
  1972: *Gottesbild und Kultkritik vorexilischer Propheten.* SBS 60; Stuttgart: Katholisches Bibelwerk.

Schütte, Wolfgang
  2011: "Israels Exil in Juda und die Völkersprüche in Am 1–2." *Biblica* 92: 528–53.
  2012: "Wie wurde Juda israelitisiert?" *ZAW* 124: 52–72.

Schwantes, Milton
  1991: *Das Land kan seine Worte nicht ertragen: Meditationen zu Amos.* Trans. I. Kayser. Munich: Chr. Kaiser.

Schwantes, S. J.
  1967: "Notes on Amos 4:2b." *ZAW* 79: 82–83.

Segert, S.
  1967: "Zur Bedeutung des Wortes nōqēd." Pp. 279–83 in: B. Hartmann et al. (eds.), *Hebräische Wortforschung* (FS W. Baumgartner), VTSup 16, Leiden: Brill.
  1984: "A Controlling Device for Copying Stereotype Passages? (Amos i 3–II 8, vi 1–6)." *VT* 34: 481–82.

Seidel, Theodor
  1987: "Heuschreckenschwarm und Prophetenintervention. Textkritische und syntaktische Erwägungen zu Am 7,2." *BN* 37: 129–38.

Seierstad, Ivar P.
  1934: "Erlebnis und Gehorsam beim Propheten Amos." *ZAW* 52: 22–41.

Seifert, Brigitte
  1996: *Metaphorisches Reden von Gott im Hoseabuch.* FRLANT 166; Göttingen: Vandenhoeck & Ruprecht.

Seleznev, Michael
  2004: "Amos 7:14 and the Prophetic Rhetoric." Pp. 251–58 in: L. Kogan, N. Koslova, S. Loesov, and S. Tischchenko (eds.), *Babel und Bibel 1: Ancient Near Eastern, Old Testament and Semitic Studies,* Orientalia et Classica 5; Moscow: Russian State University of the Humanities.

Sellin, Ernst

    1929a: *Das Zwölfprophetenbuch.* 2nd and 3rd rev. ed. KAT XII:1; Leipzig: A. Deichertsche Verlagsbuchhandlung.

    1929b: "Drei umstrittene Stelle des Amosbuches." *ZDPV* 52: 141–48.

Seybold, Klaus

    1998: "מָשַׁח *māšaḥ*." *TDOT,* vol. IX, 43–54.

Sherwood, Yvonne

    2001: "Of Fruit and Corpses and Wordplay Visions: Picturing Amos 8:1–3." *JSOT* 92: 5–27.

Shveka, Avi

    2012: "'For a Pair of Shoes': A New Light on an Obscure Verse in Amos' Prophecy." *VT* 62: 95–114.

Sibinga, J. M.

    2012: "The Composition of Amos 1–2 LXX." *VT* 62: 216–32.

Smelik, K. A.

    1986: "The Meaning of Amos v 18–20." *VT* 36: 246–48.

Smelik, Willem F.

    1999: "The Use of הזכיר בשם in Classical Hebrew: Josh 23:7; Isa 48:1; Amos 6:10; Ps 20:8; 4Q504 III 4; 1Qs 6:27." *JBL* 118: 321–32.

Smend, Rudolf

    1986a: "Das Nein des Amos." Pp. 85–103 in: Rudolf Smend, *Die Mitte des Alten Testaments.* BEvT 99; Munich: Christian Kaiser.

    1986b: "'Das Ende ist gekommen.' Ein Amoswort in der Priesterschrift." Pp. 154–59 in: Rudolf Smend, *Die Mitte des Alten Testaments,* BEvT 99; Munich: Christian Kaiser.

Smith, Gary V.

    1988: "The Deadly Silence of the Prosperous." *JBL* 107: 289–91.

    1989: *Amos: A Commentary.* Grand Rapids, MI: Zondervan.

Smith, George Adam

    1906: *The Book of the Twelve Prophets. Vol. 1: Amos, Hosea, and Micah.* 12th ed. The Expositor's Bible; London: Hodder and Stoughton.

Smith, Mark S., and Wayne T. Pitard

    2009: *The Ugaritic Baal Cycle.* Vol. 2. Leiden: Brill.

Smith, Regina

    1994: "A New Perspective on Amos 9:7a: 'To Me, O Israel, You Are Just Like the Kushites.'" *Journal of the Interdenominational Theological Center* 22: 36–47.

Smith-Christopher, Daniel L.

    2011: "Engendered Warfare and the Ammonites in Amos 1.13." Pp. 15–40 in: A. C. Hagedorn and A. Mein (eds.), *Aspects of Amos: Exegesis and Interpretation,* LHBOTS 536; New York: T&T Clark.

Snijders, L. A.

    1998: "נַחַל *naḥal*; אֵיתָן *'ētān*." *TDOT,* vol. IX, 335–40.

Snyman, S. D.
1994: "A Note on Ashdod and Egypt in Amos iii 9." *VT* 44: 559–62.
1995: "'Violence' in Amos 3,10 and 6,3." *ETL* 71: 30–47.
1996: "Towards a Theological Interpretation of HMS in Amos 6:1–7." Pp. 201–9 in: M. Augustin and K.-D. Schunck (eds.), *"Dort ziehen Schiffe dahin . . ." Collected Communications to the XIVth Congress of the International Organization for the Study of the Old Testament, Paris 1992,* Frankfurt am Main: Peter Lang.
2006: "Eretz and Adama in Amos." Pp. 137–46 in: H. M. Niemann and M. Augustin (eds.), *Stimulation from Leiden. Collected Communications to the XVIIIth Congress of the International Organization for the Study of the Old Testament, Leiden 2004,* Frankfurt am Main: Peter Lang.

Soden, Wolfram von
1990: "Zu einigen Ortsbenennungen bei Amos und Micha." *ZAH* 3: 214–20.

Soggin, J. Alberto
1970: "Das Erdbeben von Amos 1, 1 und die Chronologie der Könige Ussia und Jotham von Juda." *ZAW* 82: 117–21.
1971: "Amos VI:13–14 und I:3 auf dem Hintergrund der Beziehungen zwischen Israel und Damaskus im 9. und 8. Jahrhundert." Pp. 433–41 in: H. Goedicke (ed.), *Near Eastern Studies in Honor of William Foxwell Albright,* Baltimore: Johns Hopkins University Press.
1987: *The Prophet Amos.* Trans. J. Bowden. London: SCM [1982].
1995: "Amos and Wisdom." Pp. 119–23 in: J. Day et al. (eds.), *Wisdom in Ancient Israel* (FS Emerton), Cambridge: Cambridge University Press.

Soper, B. Kingston
1959: "For Three Transgressions and for Four: A New Interpretation of Amos i. 3, etc." *ExpTim* 71: 86–87.

Speiser, E. A.
1947: "Note on Amos 5:26." *BASOR* 198: 5–6.

Spieckermann, Hermann
1989: "Dies irae: der alttestamentliche Befund und seine Vorgeschichte." *VT* 39: 194–208.
1997: "Konzeption und Vorgeschichte des Stellvertretungsgedankens im Alten Testament." Pp. 281–95 in: J. A. Emerton (ed.), *Congress Volume Cambridge 1995,* VTSup 66; Leiden: Brill.

Stamm, Johann Jakob
1980: "Der Name des Propheten Amos und sein sprachlicher Hintergrund." Pp. 137–42 in: J. A. Emerton (ed.), *Prophecy* (FS Fohrer), BZAW 150; Berlin: De Gruyter.

Steiner, Richard C.
2003: *Stockmen from Tekoa, Sycomores from Sheba: A Study of Amos' Occupations.* CBQMS 36; Washington, DC: Catholic Biblical Association of America.

Steinmann, Andrew E.
1992: "The Order of Amos' Oracles against the Nations: 1:3–2:16." *JBL* 111: 683–89.

Steins, Georg
    2004: "Das Chaos kehrt zurück! Aufbau und Theologie von Amos 3–6." *BN* 122: 35–43.
    2010: *Gericht und Vergebung. Re-Visionen zum Amosbuch.* SBS 221; Stuttgart: Katholisches Bibelwerk.

Stoebe, Hans Joachim
    1957: "Der Prophet Amos und sein bürgerlicher Beruf." *Wort und Dienst* 5: 160–81.
    1989: "Noch einmal zu Amos VII 10–17." *VT* 39: 341–54.

Story, Cullen I. K.
    1980: "Amos—Prophet of Praise." *VT* 30: 67–80.

Strawn, Brent A.
    2005: *What Is Stronger than a Lion? Leonine Image and Metaphor in the Hebrew Bible and the Ancient Near East.* OBO 212; Fribourg: Academic Press; Göttingen: Vandenhoeck & Ruprecht.
    2013: "What Is Cush Doing in Amos 9:7? The Poetics of Exodus in the Plural." *VT* 63: 99–123.

Strijdom, Petrus D. F.
    1996: "What Tekoa Did to Amos!" *OTE* 9: 273–93.
    2011: "Reappraising the Historical Context of Amos." *OTE* 24: 221–54.

Stuart, Douglas K.
    1987: *Hosea—Jonah.* Word Biblical Commentary 31; Waco, TX: Word.

Sweeney, Marvin A.
    1995: "Formation and Form in the Prophetic Literature." Pp. 113–26 in: J. L. Mays et al. (eds.), *Old Testament Interpretation: Past, Present, and Future: Essays in Honour of Gene M. Tucker,* Edinburgh: T&T Clark.
    2000: *The Twelve Prophets. Vol. 1. Hosea, Joel, Amos, Obadiah, Jonah.* Berit Olam; Collegeville, MN: Michael Glazier.
    2009: "Amos (Book and Person): Hebrew Bible/Old Testament." *EBR,* vol. 1, 1029–35.

Szabó, Andor
    1975: "Textual Problems in Amos and Hosea." *VT* 25: 500–524.

Tadmor, Hayim
    1958: "The Campaigns of Sargon II of Assur: A Chronological-Historical Study." *JCS* 12: 77–100.

Tawil, Hayim
    1976: "Hebrew צלח/הצלח, Akkadian *ešēru/šūšuru:* A Lexicographical Note." *JBL* 95: 405–13.

Terrien, Samuel
    1962: "Amos and Wisdom." Pp. 108–15 in: B. W. Anderson and W. J. Harrelson (eds.), *Israel's Prophetic Heritage: Essays in Honor of James Muilenburg,* New York: Harper.

Thompson, Henry O.
  1992: "Kir." *ABD*, vol. 4, 83–84.
  1997: *The Book of Amos: An Annotated Bibliography.* American Theological Library Association Bibliography Series 42; Lanham, MD: Scarecrow.

Thompson, Michael E. W.
  1992: "Amos—A Prophet of Hope?" *ExpTim* 104: 71–76.

Timmer, Daniel
  2014: "The Use and Abuse of Power in Amos: Identity and Ideology." *JSOT* 39: 101–18.

Torczyner, H.
  1936: "Presidential Address." *JPOS* 16: 6–7.

Tov, Emanuel
  2014: "New Fragments of Amos." *DSD* 21: 3–13.

Tromp, N. J.
  1984: "Amos v 1–17: Towards a Stylistic and Rhetorical Analysis." *OtSt* 23: 56–84.

Troxel, Ronald
  2012: *The Prophetic Literature: From Oracles to Books.* Malden, MA: Wiley-Blackwell.

Tsumura, D. T.
  1988: "'Inserted Bicolon,' the AXYB Pattern, in Amos i 5 and Psalm ix 7." *VT* 38: 234–36.

Tucker, Gene M.
  1973: "Prophetic Authenticity: A Form-Critical Study of Amos 7:10–17." *Interpretation* 27: 423–34.
  1977: "Prophetic Superscriptions and the Growth of a Canon." Pp. 56–70 in: G. W. Coats and B. O. Long (eds.), *Canon and Authority: Essays in Old Testament Religion and Theology,* Philadelphia: Fortress.
  1997: "The Futile Quest for the Historical Prophet." Pp. 144–52 in: E. E. Carpenter (ed.), *A Biblical Itinerary: In Search of Method, Form, and Content* (FS Coats), JSOTSup 240; Sheffield: Sheffield Academic Press.
  2006: "Amos the Prophet and Amos the Book: Historical Framework." Pp. 85–102 in: B. E. Kelle and M. B. Moore (eds.), *Israel's Prophets and Israel's Past* (FS J. H. Hayes), LHBOTS 446; London: T&T Clark.
  2009: "The Social Location of Amos: Amos 1:3–2:16." Pp. 273–84 in: J. J. Ahn and S. L. Cook (eds.), *Thus Says the Lord: Essays on the Former and Latter Prophets in Honor of Robert R. Wilson,* LHBOTS 502; London: T&T Clark International.

Uehlinger, Christoph
  1989: "Der Herr auf der Zinnmauer. Zur dritten Amos-Vision (Am. vii 7–8)." *BN* 48: 89–104.

Ullucci, Daniel
  2012: *The Christian Rejection of Animal Sacrifice.* Oxford: Oxford University Press.

Ulrichsen, Jarl Henning
1992–93: "Der Einschub Amos 4,7b-8a. Sprachliche Erwägungen zu einem umstrittenen Text." *Orientalia Suecana* 41–42: 284–98.

Utzschneider, Helmut
1988: "Die Amazjaerzählung (Am 7,10–17) zwischen Literatur und Historie." *BN* 41: 76–101.

Viberg, Åke
1992: *Symbols of Law: A Contextual Analysis of Legal Symbolic Acts in the Old Testament.* ConBOT 34; Stockholm: Almqvist & Wiksell.
1996: "Amos 7:14: A Case of Subtle Irony." *TynBul* 47/1: 91–114.

Vieweger, Dieter
1994: "Zur Herkunft der Völkerworte im Amosbuch unter besonderer Berücksichtigung des Aramäerspruchs." Pp. 103–19 in: P. Mommer and W. Thiel (eds.), *Altes Testament: Forschung und Wirkung* (FS Reventlow), Frankfurt am Main: Peter Lang.

Vincent, Jean Marcel
2000: "'Visionnaire, va t'en!' Interprétation d'Amos 7,10–17 dans son contexte." *ETR* 75: 229–50.

Vogels, Walter
1972: "Invitation à revenir à l'alliance et universalisme en Amos ix 7." *VT* 22: 223–39.

Vogt, Ernest
1956: "Waw Explicative in Amos vii 14." *ExpTim* 68: 301–2.

Vollmer, Jochen
1971: *Geschichtliche Rückblicke und Motive in der Prophetie des Amos, Hosea und Jesaja.* BZAW 119; Berlin: De Gruyter.

Vriezen, Theodorus C.
1970: "Erwägungen zu Amos 3, 2." Pp. 255–58 in: A. Kuschke and E. Kutsch (eds.), *Archäologie und Altes Testament* (FS Kurt Galling), Tübingen: Mohr (Siebeck).

Vuilleumier, René
1960: *La tradition cultuelle d'Israël dans la prophétie d'Amos et d'Osée.* Cahiers théologiques 45; Neuchâtel: Delachaux & Niestlé.

Waard, J. de
1977: "The Chiastic Structure of Amos v 1–17." *VT* 27: 170–77.

Wafawanaka, Robert
2003: "Amos' Attitude toward Poverty: An African Perspective." *African Journal of Biblical Studies* 19: 97–109.

Wainwright, G. A.
1956: "Caphtor—Cappadocia." *VT* 6: 199–210.

Wal, A. van der
1983a: *Amos: A Classified Bibliography.* 2nd ed. Amsterdam: Vu Boekhandel.
1983b: "The Structure of Amos." *JSOT* 26: 107–13.

Waltke, Bruce K., and Michael O'Connor
1990: *An Introduction to Biblical Hebrew Syntax*. Winona Lake, IN: Eisenbrauns.

Ward, James M.
1969: *Amos & Isaiah: Prophets of the Word of God*. Nashville: Abingdon.

Waschke, Ernst-Joachim
1994: "Die fünfte Vision des Amosbuches (9,1–4)—Eine Nachinterpretation." *ZAW* 106: 434–45.
2012: "Anmerkungen zu den ersten vier Visionen des Amos (Am 7,1–8; 8,1.2)." Pp. 419–34 in: A. Berleijung and R. Heckl (eds.), *Ex oriente Lux: Studien zur Theologie des Alten Testaments* (FS R. Lux), Leipzig: Evangelische Verlagsanstalt.
2015: "Die Visionen des Amosbuches." Pp. 59–70 in: V. K. Nagy and L. Egeresi (eds.), *Propheten der Epochen/Prophets during the Epochs,* AOAT 426; Münster: Ugarit-Verlag.

Watts, John D. W.
1954: "Note on the Text of Amos v 7." *VT* 4: 215–16.
1997: *Vision and Prophecy in Amos,* Expanded Anniversary ed., Macon, GA: Mercer University Press [1958].

Wei, Tom F.
1992: "Hamath, entrance of." *ABD,* vol. 3, 36–37.

Weigl, Michael
1995: "Eine 'unendliche Geschichte': אֲנָךְ (Am 7,7–8)." *Biblica* 76: 343–87.

Weimar, Peter
1981: "Der Schluss des Amos-Buches. Ein Beitrag zur Redaktionsgeschichte des Amos-Buches." *BN* 16: 60–100.

Weinstein, D.
1970: *Savonarola and Florence: Prophecy and Patriotism in the Renaissance*. Princeton, NJ: Princeton University Press.

Weippert, Helga
1985: "Amos: Seine Bilder und ihr Milieu." Pp. 1–29 in: H. Weippert, K. Seybold, and M. Weippert, *Beiträge zur prophetischen Bildsprache in Israel und Assyrien,* OBO 64; Freiburg: Universitätsverlag.

Weiser, Artur
1929: *Die Profetie des Amos*. BZAW 53; Giessen: A. Töpelmann.
1956: "Amos." Pp. 127–205 in: A. Weiser and K. Elliger, *Das Buch der zwölf kleinen Propheten,* 2nd ed., ATD 24/25; Göttingen: Vandenhoeck & Ruprecht.

Weiss, Meir
1966: "The Origin of the 'Day of the Lord'—Reconsidered." *HUCA* 37: 29–60.
1967a: "Methodologisches über die Behandlung der Metapher dargelegt an Am. 1,2." *TZ* 23: 1–25.
1967b: "The Pattern of Numerical Sequence in Amos 1–2: A Re-examination." *JBL* 86: 416–23.
1995: "Concerning Amos' Repudiation of the Cult." Pp. 199–214 in: D. P. Wright et al. (eds.), *Pomegranates and Golden Bells* (FS J. Milgrom), Winona Lake, IN: Eisenbrauns.

Weissenberg, Hanne von
2012: "The Twelve Minor Prophets at Qumran and the Canonical Process."
Pp. 357–75 in: N. Dávid et al. (eds.), *The Hebrew Bible in Light of the Dead Sea Scrolls*, FRLANT 239; Göttingen: Vandenhoeck & Ruprecht.

Wellhausen, Julius
1893: *Skizzen und Vorarbeiten 5. Die kleinen Propheten übersetzt, mit Noten*. 2nd ed. Berlin: Georg Reimer.

Werlitz, Jürgen
2000: "Amos und sein Biograph: Zur Entstehung und Intention der Prophetenerzählung." *BZ* 44: 233–51.
2001: "Was hat der Gottesmann aus Juda mit dem Propheten Amos zu tun? Überlegungen zu 1 Kön 13 und den Beziehungen des Textes zu Am 7,10–17." Pp. 109–23 in: J. Frühwald-König et al. (eds.), *Steht nicht geschrieben? Studien zur Bibel und ihrer Wirkungsgeschichte* (FS Schmuttenmayr), Regensburg: Pustet.

Werner, Herbert
1969: *Amos*. Exempla Biblica 4; Göttingen: Vandenhoeck & Ruprecht.

Widbin, R. B.
1996: "Center Structure in the Center Oracles of Amos." Pp. 177–92 in: J. E. Coleson and V. H. Matthews (eds.), *Go to the Land I Will Show You* (FS D. W. Young), Winona Lake, IN: Eisenbrauns.

Williams, A. J.
1979: "A Further Suggestion about Amos iv 1–3." *VT* 29: 206–11.

Williamson, Hugh G. M.
1990: "The Prophet and the Plumbline: A Redaction-Critical Study of Amos vii." Pp. 101–21 in: A. S. van der Woude (ed.), *In Quest of the Past: Studies on Israelite Religion, Literature and Prophetism*, OTS 26; Leiden: Brill.

Willi-Plein, Ina
1971: *Vorformen der Schriftexegese innerhalb des Alten Testaments: Untersuchungen zum literarischen Werden der auf Amos, Hosea und Micha zurückgehenden Bücher im hebräischen Zwölfprophetenbuch*. BZAW 123; Berlin: De Gruyter.
1999: "Das geschaute Wort. Die prophetische Wortverkündigung und der Schriftprophet Amos." *Jahrbuch für Biblische Theologie* 14: 37–52.

Wittenberg, G. H.
1987: "'They Dismiss the Day of Disaster but You Bring Near the Rule of Violence.'" *Journal of Theology for Southern Africa* 58: 57–69.
1991: "A Fresh Look at Amos and Wisdom." *OTE* 4: 7–18.

Wöhrle, Jakob
2006: *Die frühen Sammlungen des Zwölfprophetenbuches: Entstehung und Komposition*. BZAW 360; Berlin: De Gruyter.
2008a: *Der Abschluss des Zwölfprophetenbuches: Buchübergreifende Redaktionsprozesse in den späten Sammlungen*. BZAW 389; Berlin: De Gruyter.
2008b: "'No Future for the Proud Exultant Ones': The Exilic Book of the Four Prophets (Hos., Am., Mic., Zeph.) as a Concept Opposed to the Deuteronomistic History." *VT* 58: 608–27.

Wolff, H. W.
:   1964: *Amos' geistige Heimat.* WMANT 18; Neukirchen-Vluyn: Neukirchener.

    1971: *Die Stunde des Amos: Prophetie und Protest.* 2nd ed. Munich: Chr. Kaiser.

    1973: *Amos the Prophet: The Man and His Background.* Trans. F. R. McCurley. Philadelphia: Fortress [1964].

    1977: *Joel and Amos.* Trans. W. Janzen, S. D. McBride, Jr., and C. A. Muenchow. Hermeneia; Philadelphia: Fortress [1969, 1975].

Wolters, Al
:   1988: "Wordplay and Dialect in Amos 8:1–2." *JETS* 31/4: 407–10.

Woude, A. S. van der
:   1981: "Bemerkungen zu einigen umstrittenen Stellen im Zwölfprophetenbuch." Pp. 483–99 in: A. Caquot and M. Delcor (eds.), *Mélanges bibliques et orientaux en l'honneur de M. Henri Cazelles,* AOAT 212; Kevelaer: Butzon & Bercker; Neukirchen-Vluyn: Neukirchener.

    1982: "Three Classical Prophets: Amos, Hosea and Micah." Pp. 32–57 in: R. Coggins, A. Phillips, and M. Knibb (eds.), *Israel's Prophetic Tradition* (FS Ackroyd), Cambridge: Cambridge University Press.

Wright, T. J.
:   1976: "Amos and the 'Sycomore Fig.'" *VT* 26: 362–68.

Würthwein, Ernst
:   1950: "Amos-Studien." *ZAW* 62: 10–52.

    1963: "Kultpolemik oder Kultbescheid?" Pp. 115–31 in: E. Würthwein and O. Kaiser (eds.), *Tradition und Situation: Studien zur alttestamentlichen Prophetie* (FS Weiser), Göttingen: Vandenhoeck & Ruprecht.

Yadin, Yigael, et al.
:   1960: *Hazor II: An Account of the Second Season of Excavations, 1956.* Jerusalem: Magnes.

Youngblood, Ronald
:   1971: "לקראת in Amos 4:12." *JBL* 90: 98.

Zalcman, Lawrence
:   1980: "Piercing the Darkness at *bôqēr.*" *VT* 30: 252–55.

    1981: "Astronomical Illusions in Amos." *JBL* 100: 53–58.

    2002: "Laying *dmśq 'rś* to Rest." *VT* 52: 557–59.

    2003: "Philistines on the Threshold at Amos 9:1?" *RB* 110: 481–86.

Zevit, Ziony
:   1975: "A Misunderstanding at Bethel: Amos vii 12–17." *VT* 25: 783–90.

    1979: "Expressing Denial in Biblical Hebrew and Mishnaic Hebrew, and in Amos." *VT* 29: 505–9.

Zwickel, Wolfgang
:   2015: "Amos 1,1 und die Stratigraphie der eisenzeitlichen Ortslagen in Galiläa." Pp. 31–49 in: V. K. Nagy and L. Egeresi (eds.), *Propheten der Epochen/Prophets during the Epochs,* AOAT 426; Münster: Ugarit-Verlag.

TRANSLATION

Introducing Amos: Superscription and Motto

1 ¹The words of Amos, who was among the sheep breeders from Tekoa—what he saw concerning Israel in the days of Uzziah, king of Judah, and in the days of Jeroboam son of Joash, king of Israel, two years before the earthquake.

²He said: YHWH roars from Zion, and from Jerusalem he utters his voice; the pastures of the shepherds dry up, and the top of Carmel withers.

Oracles against Neighboring Nations

³Thus says YHWH:
For three crimes of Damascus, or four, I will not hold it back.
Because they have crushed Gilead with threshing carts of iron,
⁴I will send fire against Hazael's house, and it will consume Ben-Hadad's fortresses.
⁵I will break the bar of Damascus and cut off the ruler from the valley of Aven and the scepter-bearer from Beth-Eden.
The people of Aram will be exiled to Kir, says YHWH.
⁶Thus says YHWH:
For three crimes of Gaza, or four, I will not hold it back.
Because they have deported entire populations, handing them over to Edom,
⁷I will send fire against the wall of Gaza, and it will consume its fortresses.
⁸I will cut off the ruler from Ashdod and the scepter-bearer from Ashkelon.
As I turn my hand against Ekron, the remaining Philistines will perish, says the Lord YHWH.
⁹Thus says YHWH:
For three crimes of Tyre, or four, I will not hold it back.
Because they delivered entire populations to Edom
and did not remember the treaty of brothers,
¹⁰I will send fire against the wall of Tyre, and it will consume its fortresses.
¹¹Thus says YHWH:
For three crimes of Edom, or four, I will not hold it back.
Because he pursued his brother with the sword and stifled his compassion.

His anger tore ceaselessly, and his fury—he kept it forever.
¹²I will send fire against Teman, and it will consume the fortresses of Bozrah.
¹³Thus says YHWH:
For three crimes of the Ammonites, or four, I will not hold it back.
Because they have cut open pregnant women
in Gilead, in order to expand their territory,
¹⁴I will kindle a fire in the wall of Rabbah, and it will consume its fortresses,
with shouting on the day of battle, with gale on the day of whirlwind.
¹⁵Their king will go into exile, he and his officials together, says YHWH.
2 ¹Thus says YHWH:
For three crimes of Moab, or four, I will not hold it back.
Because he burned to lime the bones of the king of Edom,
²I will send fire against Moab, and it will consume the fortresses of Kerioth.
Moab will perish in tumult, amid shouting and trumpet blasts.
³I will cut off the ruler from its midst, and all its officials I will kill with him,
says YHWH.

The Oracle against Judah

⁴Thus says YHWH:
For three crimes of Judah, or four, I will not hold it back.
Because they have rejected the law of YHWH and have not kept his statutes
—and their lies, after which their fathers walked, have led them astray—
⁵I will send fire against Judah, and it will consume the fortresses of Jerusalem.

The Oracle against Israel

⁶Thus says YHWH:
For three crimes of Israel, or four, I will not hold it back;
because they sell the innocent for silver, and the poor for a pair of sandals;
⁷they who trample the heads of the weak into the dust of the earth
and pervert the way of the needy.
A man and his father go to the same girl, thus profaning my holy name.
⁸They stretch themselves out beside every altar, on garments taken in pledge,
and they drink the wine of those who have been fined, in the house of their god.
⁹But I was the one who destroyed the Amorite before them,
although he was as tall as the cedars and as strong as the oak trees;
I destroyed his fruit above and his roots below.
¹⁰I was the one who brought you up from the land of Egypt;
I led you through the wilderness for forty years,
to take possession of the land of the Amorite.
¹¹And I raised up some of your children as prophets,
and some of your young men as Nazirites.
Is it really not so, Israelites? says YHWH.
¹²But you gave the Nazirites wine to drink,
and you commanded the prophets: "Do not prophesy!"
¹³Look! I will make it sway under you,

just like a wagon sways when it is full of grain.
¹⁴The swift will find no refuge, the strong will not retain his force,
the warrior will not save his life.
¹⁵The bowman will not stand his ground, the fast runners will not escape,
nor will the horseman save his life.
¹⁶The bravest among the warriors
will flee away naked on that day, says YHWH.

A Call to Listen

3 ¹Listen to this word that YHWH speaks concerning you, Israelites,
concerning the whole clan that I brought up from the land of Egypt:
²You alone have I cared for among all the clans of the earth;
therefore, I will call you to account for all your misdeeds.

Lions and Traps: A Discourse on Prophecy and Disaster

³Do two walk together if they have not made an appointment?
⁴Does a lion roar in the thickets when it has no prey?
Does a young lion growl from its lair if it has not caught something?
⁵Does a bird fall into a trap on the ground if there is no bait for it?
Does a trap spring up from the earth when it captures nothing at all?
⁶If the trumpet is blown in a town, will the people not tremble?
If disaster befalls a town, has not YHWH caused it?
⁷Indeed the Lord, YHWH, does nothing without disclosing his plan to his
servants the prophets.
⁸The lion has roared. Who is not frightened?
The Lord YHWH has spoken. Who can but prophesy?

Oracles against Samaria and Bethel

⁹Proclaim over the fortresses in Ashdod, and the fortresses in the land of Egypt,
saying: "Gather on the mountains of Samaria!
See the great tumult inside the city and the oppression in its midst!"
¹⁰For they do not know how to do what is right, says YHWH,
those who store up violence and devastation in their fortresses.
¹¹Therefore, thus says the Lord YHWH:
An enemy will surround the land.
He will tear down your strongholds, and your fortresses will be plundered.
¹²Thus says YHWH:
Just as a shepherd rescues from the lion's mouth
only a couple of bones or a piece of an ear,
so will the Israelites living in Samaria be rescued:
only a corner of a bed, and a piece of a couch.
¹³Listen and warn the house of Jacob,
says the Lord, YHWH, the God of hosts:

[14]When I deal with the misdeeds of Israel,
I will deal with the altars of Bethel.
The horns of the altar will be cut off and fall to the ground.
[15]I will demolish the winter house along with the summer house.
The ivory houses will be ruined, and many houses will come to an end, says YHWH.

Concerning the Wealthy Women in Samaria

4   [1]Listen to this word, O cows of Bashan on Mount Samaria,
who oppress the poor and crush the needy,
while saying to their masters: "Bring us something to drink!"
[2]The Lord YHWH swears by his holiness:
Behold, days are coming upon you
when they will carry you away with hooks,
and the remainder of you with harpoons.
[3]Through the breaches you will depart, every woman straight ahead,
and you will be thrown out toward Hermon, says YHWH.

A Sarcastic Call to Transgress through Worship

[4]Come to Bethel and transgress, go to Gilgal and add to your transgressions!
Bring your sacrifices in the morning, your tithes on the third day;
[5]burn a thank-offering of leavened bread
and proclaim freewill offerings, make them known!
For you Israelites love to do so, says the Lord YHWH.

Disasters with Didactic Dimensions

[6]I, for my part, gave you empty mouths in all your towns
and shortage of food in all your dwelling places.
Yet you did not return to me, says YHWH.
[7]I also held back the rain from you, three months before the harvest.
I would let it rain on one town, but not on another.
One field would get rain, but another field that received no rain would dry up.
[8]Two or three towns would then stagger into another town to drink water,
without being able to quench their thirst.
Yet you did not return to me, says YHWH.
[9]I struck you with scorching and plant rust, repeatedly;
your gardens and vineyards, your fig trees and olive trees were devoured by locusts.
Yet you did not return to me, says YHWH.
[10]I sent pestilence against you, like that of Egypt,
I killed your elite soldiers with the sword, your horses were taken as booty,
and I made the stench from your camps rise even into your nostrils.
Yet you did not return to me, says YHWH.
[11]I overthrew some of you, like God overthrew Sodom and Gomorrah,
you became like a firebrand rescued from the flames.
Yet you did not return to me, says YHWH.

¹²Therefore, thus I will do to you, Israel
—and because I will do this to you, prepare to meet your God, O Israel!

Interlude: The First Doxology

¹³See, the one who forms mountains and creates wind,
who announces his thoughts to humans,
the one who makes dawn into darkness and treads on the heights of the world—
YHWH, the God of hosts, is his name!

A Concentric Centerpiece

5 ¹Listen to this word that I deliver against you as a dirge, O house of Israel!
²She is fallen, to rise no more, virgin Israel,
abandoned on her land, with no one to raise her up.
³For thus says the Lord YHWH:
The city that marches out with a thousand shall have a hundred left,
and the one that marches out with a hundred shall have ten left,
for the house of Israel.
⁴Thus says YHWH to the house of Israel:
Seek me and live!
⁵Do not seek Bethel, do not enter into Gilgal, and do not cross over to Beer-
Sheba! For Gilgal will go into captivity, and Bethel will come to nothing.
⁶Seek YHWH and live!
Otherwise he will attack the house of Joseph like fire.
It will devour, and there will be no one to quench it for Bethel.
⁷They who turn justice into wormwood
and throw righteousness to the ground
—⁸The one who made the Pleiades and Orion,
who turns deep darkness into morning, and darkens day into night,
who calls for the waters of the sea and pours them out on the surface of the earth,
YHWH is his name!
⁹It is he who flashes destruction on the stronghold,
so that destruction comes upon the fortified city—
¹⁰they hate the one who reproves in the gate,
they detest the one who speaks the truth.
¹¹Therefore, because you impose taxes on the poor one, and take levies of grain
from him: You have built houses of hewn stone but you shall not live in them.
You have planted pleasant vineyards but you shall not drink their wine.
¹²For I know that your crimes are many and that your sins are numerous,
you opponents of the innocent, receivers of bribes,
who turn aside the needy in the gate.
¹³Therefore, at such a time the wise one keeps quiet, for it is an evil time.
¹⁴Seek good and not evil, so that you may live,
and YHWH the God of hosts may be with you, just as you claim that he is.
¹⁵Hate evil and love good! Maintain justice in the gate!

Perhaps YHWH the God of hosts will be gracious to the remnant of Joseph.
¹⁶Therefore, thus says YHWH the God of hosts, the Lord:
In all open squares there will be wailing,
and in all streets they will say, "Woe! Woe!"
They will call the peasant to mourning,
and those skilled in lamentation to wailing.
¹⁷In all vineyards there will be wailing,
for I am going to pass through the midst of you, says YHWH.

Beware of the Day of YHWH

¹⁸Woe to those who long for the day of YHWH!
What will the day of YHWH be for you?
It will be darkness, not light!
¹⁹As if someone flees from a lion, only to be confronted by a bear; and then, as
he comes home and leans his hand against the wall, he is bitten by a snake.
²⁰Truly, it is darkness, the day of YHWH, rather than light,
gloom without any brightness in it!

Rejected Sacrifice

²¹I hate, I reject your festivals,
and I do not delight in your assemblies.
²²Even if you bring me burnt offerings,
and your grain offerings, I will not accept them.
I will not even look at the communion sacrifices of your fatlings.
²³Take away from me the noise of your songs!
I do not want to hear the music of your harps.
²⁴But let justice roll down like waters,
righteousness like an ever-flowing stream.

Desert Wandering and Deportation

²⁵Did you bring me sacrifices and grain offerings for forty years in the desert,
O house of Israel?
²⁶Or did you carry around Sakkuth, your king, and Kaiwan, your images, your
astral gods, which you made for yourselves?
    ²⁷I will drive you into exile beyond Damascus, says YHWH—God of hosts is
his name.

The Party Is Over

6   ¹Woe to the carefree in Zion, and the confident on Mount Samaria,
the distinguished men of the foremost nation, to whom the house of Israel comes.
    —²Cross over to Calneh and see,
go from there to Hamath-Rabbah,

then go down to Gath of the Philistines!
Are you better than these kingdoms? Or is their territory greater than yours?—
    ³You who want to ward off the day of disaster,
yet you bring near a reign of violence.
    ⁴Woe to those who recline on beds of ivory and lounge on their couches,
those who eat lambs from the flock and calves from the feeding stall,
⁵who intone to the lyre
and improvise on musical instruments, like David,
⁶who drink wine from bowls and anoint themselves with the finest oil
but do not worry over the injury of Joseph.
    ⁷Therefore, they shall now be among the first to go into exile;
the banquet of the loungers shall cease.

Death, Destruction, and Deception

⁸YHWH the Lord has sworn by himself (says YHWH the God of hosts):
I abhor Jacob's arrogance, I hate his fortresses,
I will hand over the city and everything in it.
    ⁹And if ten men are left in one house, they shall die. ¹⁰When one's relative and
embalmer carries his remains out of the house, and he asks someone at the rear of the
house, "Is anyone with you?," he will reply, "No one." Then he will say, "Hush!," for
the name of YHWH must not be invoked.
    ¹¹See, YHWH commands,
and he will knock the great house to pieces, and the small house to rubble.
    ¹²Can horses run on rocks? Can one plow the sea with oxen?
But you have turned justice into poison
and the fruit of righteousness into wormwood!
    ¹³You who rejoice over Lo-Dabar,
saying: "Did we not capture Karnaim for ourselves by our own strength?"
¹⁴For I am raising up a nation against you, O house of Israel,
says YHWH the God of hosts,
and they will oppress you from Lebo-Hamath to Wadi Arabah.

The First Pair of Visions: Canceled Calamities

7   ¹This is what the Lord YHWH showed me:
He was forming locusts when the late crops began to sprout—
the late crops, that is: after the king's mowing.
²And when they had finished devouring the vegetation of the land, I said:
"O Lord YHWH, please forgive! How can Jacob survive? He is so small."
³Then YHWH relented concerning this: "It will not happen," said YHWH.
    ⁴This is what the Lord YHWH showed me:
The Lord YHWH was summoning a judgment by fire.
It consumed the great deep and it devoured the land.
⁵And I said: "O Lord YHWH, please stop! How can Jacob survive?
He is so small."

⁶Then YHWH relented concerning this:
"This will not happen either," said YHWH.

The Third Vision: A Riddle Made of Metal

⁷This is what he showed me:
The Lord was standing on a tin wall, holding tin in his hand.
⁸YHWH asked me: "What do you see, Amos?" and I answered: "Tin."
Then the Lord said: "See, I am about to set tin in the midst of my people Israel.
I will no longer spare them."

A Bridge between Two Passages

⁹The high places of Isaac will become desolate,
and the sanctuaries of Israel will become ruins.
I will attack the house of Jeroboam with the sword.

A Narrative Interlude: Amos versus Amaziah

¹⁰Then Amaziah, priest in Bethel, sent word to Jeroboam, king of Israel:
"Amos has conspired against you in the midst of the house of Israel.
The land cannot bear all his words.
¹¹For this is what Amos has said:
'Jeroboam will die by the sword, and Israel will surely be exiled from its land.'"
¹²And Amaziah said to Amos:
"Go away, seer! Flee to the land of Judah! Eat your bread there, and prophesy there!
¹³But do not prophesy in Bethel again,
for it is a royal sanctuary, a state temple."
¹⁴Amos answered Amaziah:
"I (am/was) not a prophet, nor a prophet's son.
I (am/was) a herdsman and a tender of sycamore trees.
¹⁵But YHWH took me from behind the flock.
YHWH said to me: 'Go! Prophesy to my people Israel!'
¹⁶Now then, listen to the word of YHWH!
You say: 'Do not prophesy against Israel and do not preach against the house of Isaac!'
¹⁷Therefore, thus says YHWH:
'Your wife will prostitute herself in the city,
your sons and your daughters will fall by the sword,
and your land will be divided up by a measuring line.
You yourself will die in an unclean land,
and Israel will surely be exiled from its land.'"

The Fourth Vision: A Basketful of Bad News

8 ¹This is what the Lord YHWH showed me: A basket of summer fruit.
²He asked me: "What do you see, Amos?" and I answered:
"A basket of summer fruit."
Then YHWH said to me: "The end has come for my people Israel.
I will no longer spare them."

³The songstresses of the palace will wail on that day, says the Lord YHWH.
Many corpses, cast out everywhere. Hush!

Reinterpretations of the Words of Amos

⁴Hear this, you who trample on the poor
and do away with the afflicted of the land,
⁵saying: "When will the new moon be over, that we may sell grain,
and when will the Sabbath end, that we may market wheat?"
—making the ephah smaller and the shekel bigger,
dealing deceitfully with false scales,
⁶buying the poor for silver and the needy for a pair of sandals—
"and that we may sell the sweepings of the wheat."
⁷YHWH has sworn by the pride of Jacob:
"Never will I forget any of their deeds."
⁸Shall not the earth quake because of this, and all its inhabitants mourn?
Shall not all of it rise like the Nile, be stirred up and then sink like the Nile in Egypt?
⁹On that day, says the Lord YHWH, I will make the sun go down at noon
and thus darken the earth in broad daylight.
¹⁰I will turn your feasts into mourning and all your songs into dirges.
I will put sackcloth on everyone's loins and baldness on every head.
I will make it like the mourning for an only son,
the end of it will be like a day of bitterness.
¹¹Yes, the days are coming, says the Lord YHWH,
when I will send a famine over the land:
not hunger for bread, or thirst for water,
but for hearing the words of YHWH.
¹²They shall stagger from sea to sea, from north to east,
they shall roam around seeking the word of YHWH, but they shall not find it.
¹³In that day, the beautiful young women and the young men shall faint from
thirst.
¹⁴Those who swear by the guilt of Samaria
or say, "As your god lives, O Dan," or, "As the way of Beer-Sheba lives,"
they will fall to rise no more.

A Vision of Inescapable Destruction

9   ¹I saw the Lord standing by the altar, and he said:
Strike the capitals so that the thresholds shake!
Cut them off—on the heads of them all!
The remainder of them I will kill with the sword.
Not one of them shall be able to escape, not one fugitive shall survive.
²Though they dig down to Sheol, from there my hand will take them,
and though they climb up to heaven, from there I will bring them down.
³Though they hide on the top of Carmel, there I will search them out and seize
them, and though they conceal themselves from my sight at the bottom of the sea,

there I will command the serpent and it will bite them.
⁴Even if they go into captivity in front of their enemies,
there I will command the sword to slay them.
I will fix my eye upon them, for harm and not for good.

The Last Doxology

⁵The Lord YHWH of hosts,
the one who touches the earth so that it trembles, and all who live in it mourn,
and all of it rises like the Nile and sinks again like the Nile in Egypt,
⁶who builds his stairs in the heavens and founds his vault on the earth,
who calls for the waters of the sea and pours them out on the surface of the earth,
YHWH is his name!

The Turning Point

⁷Are you not like the Cushites to me, you Israelites? says YHWH.
True, I brought Israel up from the land of Egypt,
but also the Philistines from Caphtor, and Aram from Kir.
⁸Behold, the Lord YHWH's eyes are set upon the sinful kingdom.
I will destroy it from the face of the earth,
except that I will not completely destroy the house of Jacob, says YHWH.
⁹For I am about to give the order
and shake the house of Israel among all the nations,
as one shakes with the sieve and not a pebble falls to the ground.
¹⁰They shall die by the sword, all the sinners among my people,
those who say: "Disaster will never come near us or confront us."

A Hopeful Epilogue

¹¹On that day I will restore David's fallen hut.
I will repair its breaches, restore its ruins,
and build it up as in the days of old,
¹²so that they may possess the remnant of Edom
and all the nations over whom my name has been called,
says YHWH who will do this.
¹³Yes, days are coming, says YHWH,
when the plowman will catch up with the reaper,
and the one who treads grapes will catch up with the planter,
when the mountains will drip grape juice, and all the hills will flow.
¹⁴I will restore the fortunes of my people Israel:
They shall rebuild deserted cities and inhabit them,
they shall plant vineyards and drink their wine,
they shall grow gardens and eat their fruit.
¹⁵I will plant them on their own land,
and they shall never again be uprooted from the land that I have given them,
says YHWH your God.

NOTES AND COMMENTS

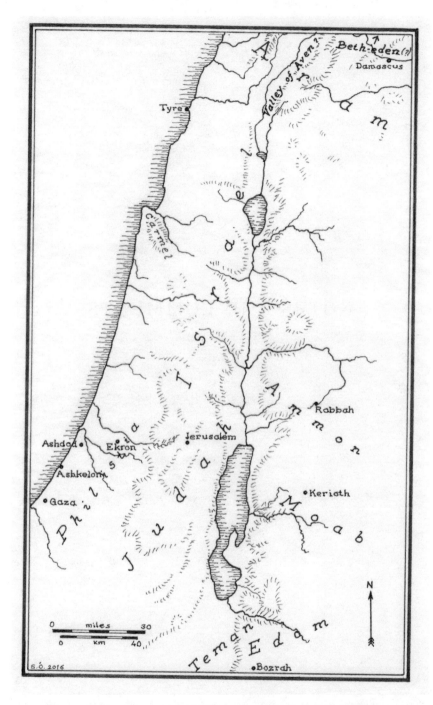

Map showing nations and places mentioned in Amos 1:3–2:16.
Drawing by Sverrir Ólafsson, published with permission of the artist.

Oracles against the Nations (1–2)

_____

Introducing Amos: Superscription and Motto (1:1–2)

1 ¹The words of Amos, who was among the sheep breeders from Tekoa—what he saw concerning Israel in the days of Uzziah, king of Judah, and in the days of Jeroboam son of Joash, king of Israel, two years before the earthquake.

²He said: YHWH roars from Zion, and from Jerusalem he utters his voice; the pastures of the shepherds dry up, and the top of Carmel withers.

INTRODUCTION TO 1:1–2

In the extant exegetical commentaries on Amos, the passage 1:1–2 is commonly regarded as the book's first unit (see, e.g., Paul 1991: 33–42 and Jeremias 1998: 11–14). However, it needs to be emphasized that this is a composite rhetorical unit, consisting of two verses that have very little in common in terms of form or genre. Whereas v. 1 can be categorized as a superscription, which is part of the editorial framework but not part of the book itself, the oracle in v. 2 would seem to constitute the beginning of the book's actual contents. Moreover, the superscription is written in prose, with an overloaded syntax, whereas v. 2 is a piece of well-balanced poetry. One might thus argue that these two utterances should not be read in conjunction, since they belong to different genres, as well as to different levels of redaction and composition.

Nevertheless, there are good reasons to treat 1:2 as part of the book's editorial framework. Because of its solemn tone and its wide scope, this saying is often called a "motto" (thus, e.g., Wolff 1977: 119 and Paul 1991: 36). In other words, this oracle would seem to serve as a programmatic prologue of sorts to the ensuing collection of oracles in its entirety. Moreover, there are also good reasons to read 1:2 as a continuation of the superscription. There is in fact a syntactical connection between these two utterances. Clearly, the first word of v. 2, the verbal form _wayyōʾmar_, "(and) he said," refers back to v. 1. In order to answer the question "Who is speaking?" the reader must consult the superscription, which provides the desired information. In other words, as the text now stands, the reader is prompted to combine 1:1 and 1:2, despite the formal differences between these two verses.

In a recent study, Karl Möller has made some insightful remarks about Amos 1:1–2 as a literary introduction with the function of "drawing the reader or hearer in" (2003a: 165). Among other things, Möller points out that the book of Amos contains a "narrative frame" that starts in 1:2 ("and he said") and is continued in chapter 7 (vv. 10, 12, 14) (2003a: 159). I agree with Möller that the existence of such a fragmentary narrative structure may, at least to some extent, inform the reading of this prophetic book in its entirety. Arguably, however, this is not the most important aspect of Amos 1:1–2 in its capacity as a literary introduction.

If the book of Amos is viewed as a literary and theological work, and if such a work can be seen as in some respects analogous to a musical composition, I suggest that the complex unit 1:1–2 constitutes its overture. Several themes and metaphors that contribute to the distinct character of this prophetic book are introduced already in the two opening verses. The following list of recurring motifs and/or thematic threads that begin in either 1:1 or 1:2 is not exhaustive, but it illustrates the role played by the introduction (1:1–2) vis-à-vis the book in its entirety:

> Visions (1:1; 7:1–8; 8:1–2; 9:1)
> Shepherding (1:1, 2; 3:12; 7:14–15)
> Earthquake (1:1; cf. 2:13–16; 3:14–15; 6:11; 8:8; 9:1)
> Jerusalem/Zion (1:2; 6:1; 9:11)
> Mount Carmel (1:2; 9:3)
> Roaring lion (1:2; 3:4, 8, 12; 5:19)
> Drought (1:2; 4:7–8; 8:11–12)[1]

As will be demonstrated below, the superscription in 1:1 appears to have grown in several stages, beginning with the first version of the book of Amos. The motto-like oracle in 1:2 was probably appended to the superscription in the exilic or the early postexilic period, during the process that resulted in the second major version of this book.

NOTES

1:1. *sheep breeders.* The LXX (εν νακκαριμ) apparently misrepresents בנקדים (*bnqdym*) as a toponym, Nakkarim.

Israel. The LXX has "concerning Jerusalem" (ὑπὲρ Ιερουσαλημ) instead of the MT's "concerning Israel" (*ʿal yiśrāʾēl*). This is clearly a scribal mistake, to a certain extent understandable in light of the reference to Jerusalem in 1:2.

1:2. *dry up.* Considering the immediate context, this is probably an instance of the verb *ʾbl* II, "to be dry" (cf. the Targum: wyṣdwn), rather than *ʾbl* I, "to mourn" (cf. LXX: ἐπένθησαν). This is the position taken by most modern commentaries, translations, and dictionaries (with reference to Akkadian *abālu* B, see *CAD* s.v.). Even Clines, who argues that there was only one *ʾbl* stem in classical Hebrew (with "to mourn" as its lexical sense), would seem to agree that the expression in Amos 1:2 refers to drought (1992: 9).

COMMENTS

1:1. Since 1:1 is the superscription of this prophetic book, it follows (to state the obvious) that it is not part of the book's actual contents. This verse belongs, almost by definition, to the editorial framework (Tucker 1977: 56–59). Such superscriptions were probably produced in scribal circles (Tucker 1977: 67); hence, it is unlikely that Amos 1:1 contains information deriving directly from the eponymous prophet.

The overloaded syntax, which creates great problems for the translator, indicates that the superscription has gone through several stages of editorial activity.[2] It is impossible to reconstruct this process in all its details; however, on the basis of previous research the following outline can be offered. The original superscription was, simply, "the words of Amos from Tekoa" (cf. Jer 1:1; Prov 30:1; 31:1). This heading was attached to a collection of oracles, probably consisting of the oldest core of chapters 3–6 (Fuhs 1977: 276–77).

In the next stage, corresponding to what I call the "first version" of the book (see Table 2), the superscription was expanded. According to a tentative reconstruction, this version was introduced as follows: "The words of Amos from Tekoa, what he saw concerning Israel, two years before the earthquake" (Wolff 1977: 117–18).

Subsequently, further details were added. It is uncertain whether the information that Amos "was among the sheep breeders" was derived from the legend in 7:10–17 (Wolff 1977: 117; Jeremias 1998: 11–12) or whether, conversely, the author of the legend (especially 7:15) was inspired by this part of the superscription (Tucker 1973: 429). What can be said with certainty is that the synchronistic reference to the reigns of two kings, one in Israel and one in Judah, bears the hallmark of Deuteronomistic editorship (Tucker 1977: 69; Rottzoll 1996: 9). Thus, it is likely that the phrases "in the days of Uzziah, king of Judah, and in the days of Jeroboam son of Joash, king of Israel" were added as the book went through a revision influenced by Deuteronomistic ideology. This corresponds to what I have chosen to call "the second version," which appeared after 587 B.C.E. (see Table 2).

It is instructive to make a systematic comparison between Amos 1:1 and other superscriptions in the prophetic books in the Hebrew Bible. The phrase in v. 1aα, "the words of (*dibrê*)" + PN (the name of the prophet), is found also in Jer 1:1. Arguably, though, this construction is more typical of the wisdom tradition (Prov 30:1; 31:1; Qoh 1:1; cf. Wolff 1977: 119–20). In prophetic literature one would rather expect that the utterances collected are presented as the word(s) of YHWH (Hos 1:1; Mic 1:1; Joel 1:1; Zeph 1:1; Hag 1:1; Zech 1:1; see also Jer 1:2 and Ezek 1:3).

The next clause provides information about the prophet's location (or place of origin) and vocation (at least, before the prophetic call experience): "who was among the sheep breeders (*bannōqĕdîm*) from Tekoa" (v. 1aβ). Once again, the closest parallel is found in Jer 1:1, which has "one of the priests who (were) in Anathoth" (cf. also Ezek 1:3 and Mic 1:1). For a discussion of the implications of the designation *nōqēd* ("sheep breeder"), see below.

What makes Amos 1:1 difficult to translate is the fact that the object of the ensuing relative clause, "what/which he saw (*'ăšer ḥāzâ*)" (v. 1bα), would seem to be the "words" mentioned earlier. This somewhat surprising syntactic juxtaposition may, as suggested by Jeremias, be the result of two originally separate superscriptions—one referring to a collection of words (chapters 1–6*) and the other to a collection of visions (chapters 7–9*)—"having been fused together" (1998: 12). However, the notion that "words" (of divine origin) could be the object of visual perception is not unparalleled in the prophetic literature. It is attested also in Isa 2:1 and Mic 1:1. Since the lexeme *dābār* can denote things or matters as well as spoken words, it would be possible to translate "the matters . . . which Amos saw concerning Israel" (see Andersen and Freedman 1989: 184–85). Notably, although the superscription does not present Amos as a prophet (*nābîʾ*), the occurrence of the verb *ḥzh* might imply that he was considered to be a "seer" (*ḥōzeh*).

The superscription ends with a truly unique feature: the statement that Amos's activity occurred "two years before the earthquake" (more on that below). However, this intriguing piece of information is preceded by another kind of chronological reference: "in the days of Uzziah, king of Judah, and Jeroboam son of Joash, king of Israel" (v. 1bβ). Three other books within the book of the Twelve contain similarly phrased references to the reign(s) of one or several kings (Hos 1:1; Mic 1:1; Zeph 1:1). This feature would seem to betray Deuteronomistic influence (W. H. Schmidt 1965: 168, 170; Tucker 1977: 69). On the basis of these and other observations, scholars have elaborated a theory according to which an exilic or a postexilic version of the book of Amos was part of a collection of four prophetic books comprising Hosea, Amos, Micah, and Zephaniah.[3] This hypothetical collection, sometimes called "the book of the Four" (so Albertz 2003), can be seen as an important stage in the gradual growth of the book of the Twelve.

It is highly unlikely that the superscription, or any part of it, was composed by Amos himself. In previous scholarship, the biographical and chronological data provided by 1:1 (and 7:14) were nevertheless often taken, uncritically, as a point of departure for the reconstruction of the prophet's life and career.[4] However, because of the absence of other sources that might corroborate the information given in the superscription, all such reconstructions must be regarded as speculative.[5] In the following, I offer a summary of the scholarly debate, as well as some cautious remarks concerning the possibility of extracting reliable biographical, geographical, and/or historical information from Amos 1:1.

To begin with, the name of the eponymous prophet, Amos, deserves some comment. It can be derived from the verbal stem *ʿms*, "to carry (a load)" (see further Stamm 1980). The meaning was probably something like "carried/protected (by YHWH)" (cf. Isa 46:3 and Ps 68:20 [Eng. v. 19]). Personal names consisting of *ʿms* and the name of a deity are attested in Phoenician sources.[6]

According to the superscription, Amos was a "sheep breeder (*nōqēd*)" (1:1a). In the light of 2 Kgs 3:4, where this designation is used of (the allegedly very rich) King Mesha of Moab, "sheep breeder" would seem to be the most adequate translation of *nōqēd* (so all modern dictionaries). Clearly, such a person had a higher status than an ordinary shepherd. This supposition is confirmed by the texts from Ugarit, where the lexeme *nqd* refers to "sheep managers" linked to the royal court or to a temple (Craigie 1982: 30–33). In a passage in the Baal cycle (*KTU/CTU* 1.6.VI: 54–56), one person is said to be both *rb nqdm* and *rb khnm*, that is, overseer of "sheep managers," as well as of priests (see Dietrich and Loretz 1977: 337). However, it does not follow that such sheep managers, or chief shepherds, always belonged to the staff of a temple, as claimed by Haldar (1945: 79, n. 5).[7] The speculative hypothesis that the term *nōqēd* denoted a specialized cultic functionary who inspected the livers of animals in order to obtain omens has likewise been refuted.[8] To sum up, the information that Amos was one of the "sheep breeders" in the region of Tekoa implies (whether historically correct or not) that he had a relatively high social status. In addition, one may regard this as a literary motif, connected to the literary theme of shepherding, which recurs already in 1:2 (see also 3:12 and 7:14–15).

Amos's hometown, the reader is told, was Tekoa, situated about eighteen kilometers south of Jerusalem (see further Wolff 1977: 123). Even Rosenbaum (1990), who defends the thesis that Amos was an Israelite (that is, not a Judean) prophet, concedes that 1:1a most likely refers to a place in Judah, Amos's alleged residence in exile (cf. also 7:10–16).[9] Tekoa is mentioned in a dozen texts in the Hebrew Bible (see, e.g., 2 Sam 14:2, 9; 2 Chr 11:6; Neh 3:5, 27). It occurs twice in other prophetic texts, but mainly due to the assonance between Tekoa (*tĕqôaʿ*) and the verb *tqʿ*, "to blow (a trumpet)" (Jer 6:1; Ezek 7:14). In an episode narrated in 2 Samuel, Joab brings a "wise woman" from Tekoa to King David (2 Sam 14:2); however, this does not warrant the conclusion that this village in the Judean mountains was known as a center for traditional wisdom (thus Wolff 1977: 123). In earlier scholarship, Amos's alleged background, including his experiences of the dramatic landscape surrounding Tekoa, was sometimes used as a key to the interpretation of his prophetic messages.[10] By contrast, I suggest that the significance of this geographical detail in 1:1 is that it says something about the perspective of the book of Amos, through all its versions: It deals mainly with Israel, the Northern Kingdom, but from a Judean point of view.

As argued above, the synchronistic dating in v. 1b was probably added by a Deuteronomistic redaction, with the aim of creating a chronological framework for a collection of prophetic writings containing Hosea, Amos, Micah, and Zephaniah (see Nogalski 1993a: 84–89). The reference to the reigns of Uzziah in Judah (ca. 783–742 B.C.E.) and Jeroboam II in Israel (ca. 786–746) leaves a span of several decades. Scholars have often placed Amos's prophetic activity somewhere between 760 and 750 B.C.E.[11] But it must be kept in mind that the editor(s) responsible for this addition to the superscription probably lacked reliable information regarding the date of the oldest layer of oracles. The association between Amos and Jeroboam may in fact depend on the legend in 7:10–17 (Levin 1995: 307, 314).

Because of the absence of explicit references to Assyria, commentators have often excluded the possibility that the original "words of Amos" derive from the turbulent years in the 730s (thus, e.g., Paul 1991: 1 and Jeremias 1998: 1–2). However, a date during or after the so-called Syro-Ephraimite crisis (734–732 B.C.E.) would make excellent sense for those oracles that belong to the core of chapters 3–6 (with Kratz 2003: 81 and Levin 1995: 315–17). Such a date of origin would explain the strong element of (implicitly) pro-Judean critique of the kingdom of Israel and of the ruling elite in Samaria. In my opinion, the similarities to some prophecies in the book of Isaiah (8:1–4; 17:1–3; 28:1–4) imply a common setting. As regards the conspicuous silence in the book of Amos regarding Assyria (and other empires), I suggest that it might have theological and/or rhetorical motivations.

Despite its apparent exactness, the concluding phrase of the superscription, "two years before the earthquake," cannot be used in support of a fixed date for Amos's activity (Jeremias 1998: 13). Such disasters have occurred rather frequently in Palestine throughout history (see Kallner-Amiran 1950–51). The mention in Zech 14:5 of an earthquake during the reign of Uzziah does not prove much, since it could be based on Amos 1:1. Owing to the fact that the mention of the earthquake comes immediately after the synchronistic reference to kings in Israel and Judah, both ancient and modern readers have quite naturally assumed that an event during the era of Jeroboam and Uzziah is meant. However, this juxtaposition is the result of editorial reworking. In view of the archaeological evidence, it is indeed likely that a devastating quake occurred in Israel around the middle of the eighth century (Austin, Franz, and Frost 2000). Some scholars even maintain that it can be dated more precisely to 760 B.C.E. (thus Soggin 1970 and Wolff 1977: 124). This is, above all, based on the excavation report from Hazor. On closer examination, however, the calculation in this report, as well as the interpretation of the destruction layer in question, is explicitly based upon a conventional interpretation of Amos 1:1 (Yadin et al. 1960: 36). This is a classic case of circular argumentation (Levin 1995: 314–15; Jeremias 1996: 184). It is, of course, possible that a natural catastrophe in the eighth century B.C.E. (or later?) was interpreted as a (partial) fulfillment of some oracles (e.g., 3:14–15) and hence as a validation of Amos as a "true" prophet (Paul 1991: 36; Freedman and Welch 1994: 190–96). However, it needs to be stressed that the original referent of the intriguing phrase "two years before the earthquake" cannot be reconstructed with any certainty.

On a different note, it is important to study the literary and theological aspects of the earthquake motif. From this perspective, the last words of the superscription introduce a "thematic thread" that runs through the entire book of Amos (T. Collins 2001: 96–98). Images of tremor and convulsion or of collapsing buildings surface in several subsequent passages (2:13–16; 3:14–15; 4:11; 6:11; 8:8; 9:1, 5).[12]

1:2. Because of its position and programmatic character, the saying in v. 2 has often been called the book's "motto."[13] One might also classify it as a preface (Cripps 1929: 115). Regardless of which label one prefers, it is essential to recognize that this utterance belongs to the editorial framework of the book of Amos. Syntactically, it is connected to the superscription (1:1) but not to the ensuing cycle of oracles against various nations (Nogalski 1993a: 82–83; Schart 1998: 54). This short poem, with its hymnic style, is not one of the oracles in the collection; rather, it constitutes, together with 1:1, an introduction to the collection of oracles in its entirety (see Möller 2003a: 165–71).

Most probably representing the ideological interests of an exilic or postexilic redaction, this "motto" invites the reader to study the prophecies in the book through a special lens, which focuses on theophany and eschatology (cf. Jeremias 1998: 13–14). At the same time, this utterance appears to have been inserted at the beginning of Amos in order to create a catchword link to the end of Joel. At any rate, Amos 1:2a looks like a verbatim quotation from Joel 4:16a (Eng. 3:16a), or vice versa (see Nogalski 1993a: 24–27 and 1993b: 36–37).

Instead of a messenger formula, "thus says YHWH" (cf. 1:3, 6, 9, etc.), there is a simple "he said (*wayyōʾmar*)" at the beginning of 1:2. In order to answer the question "Who is speaking?" the reader must consult v. 1, which provides the sought-after information: Amos. Thus, v. 2 is presented as a summary of "the words of Amos" (v. 1a). Remarkably enough, however, this summary does not even allude to a number of topics in the book that are often thought to be of central importance: corruption in the courts, critique of the rich, or condemnation of cultic sites. It describes divinely decreed destruction, but not in terms of punishment for unethical behavior. Nevertheless, 1:2 does serve as a motto or preface by introducing several themes that recur in subsequent passages.

The main topic of v. 2 is the manifestation of YHWH's awe-inspiring power and glory and "the resultant catastrophic effects upon the cosmos and nature" (Paul 1991: 38). In terms of intertextuality, this utterance belongs to a web of theophany depictions (see Pss 29:3–9; 50:2–4; Jer 25:30; Joel 4:16 [Eng. 3:16]).[14] It is important to note that, in the case of Amos 1:2, the dramatic demonstrations of divine power are said to emanate from Zion, the temple mount in Jerusalem. A location situated within the borders of Israel, Mount Carmel, is also mentioned, but as a target of divine destructiveness (v. 2b). Thus, the motto verse confirms and reinforces the Judah-oriented perspective of this prophetic book (Schart 1998: 166–67).

Because of their metaphorical character, several formulations in v. 2 are susceptible to more than one interpretation (cf. Weiss 1967a). In the opening clause, it is declared that "YHWH roars (*yiš²āg*) from Zion" (v. 2aα). The verb *š²g* ("to roar") would seem to imply that the deity is depicted as a lion. This hypothesis is strengthened by the observation that the parallel clause, "and from Jerusalem he utters his voice (*yittēn qôlô*)" (v. 2aβ), contains an expression, *ntn qôl* (literally, "give voice"), which may denote the sound made by a lion (Jer 2:15; Amos 3:4). Such a lion metaphor might suggest a range of notions, including majestic power, strength, and frightening rapaciousness.[15] However, the formulations in v. 2a are ambiguous. As indicated by 2 Sam 22:14, the phrase *yittēn qôlô* ("he utters his voice/thunders") may also refer to the sound of thunder. Thus, the first half of 1:2 evokes two images, in a kind of double exposure: The image of a roaring lion is merged with the image of a thundering storm-god. The thematic thread of the (roaring) lion reappears later in the book, in 3:3–8 (vv. 4 and 8), in a discourse on the role of prophecy in the face of calamities, as well as in 3:12 and 5:19.

According to v. 2b, the theophany somehow brings about a severe drought, which affects "the pastures of the shepherds" (2bα), as well as "the top of Carmel" (2bβ). As several scholars have pointed out, it is impossible to construct a causal connection between this depiction of withering grass and plants and a preceding thunderstorm (accompanied by rain!) or a lion's roar (see Weiss 1967a: 6–9). However, the relation between vv. 2a and 2b need not be understood in terms of cause and effect. In my opinion, this is rather a case of the juxtaposition of two motifs that are both associated with theophany: thunder (v. 2a) and drought (v. 2b; cf. Isa 19:5–7; 42:15; Hos 13:15; Hag 1:11; Nah 1:4). These two manifestations of divine power and dangerousness represent different types of perception: on one hand, audible phenomena (the lion's roar, the "voice" of the thunder), and on the other hand, visible effects in the landscape (drought, wilting vegetation).

On the literary level, v. 2b introduces several thematic threads. The topic of drought (and thirst), which is also linked to Carmel elsewhere in the Hebrew Bible (see 1 Kings 18; Nah 1:4), recurs in 4:7–8 (literally) and 8:12–13 (metaphorically). Since the verbal form *wĕʾābĕlû* (in 2bα) could be taken to mean that the pastures "mourn" rather than "dry up" (Clines 1992), it is also possible to find an allusion to the theme of mourning and lamentation (see 5:1–2, 16–17; 8:3, 10).

Further, the ensuing expression, "pastures of the shepherds" (a unique variation of "pastures of the wilderness," see Ps 65:13 [Eng. v. 12]; Jer 9:9; 23:10; Joel 1:19, 20; 2:22), evokes the image of a group of shepherds. One might thus detect an associative link to the mention of "sheep breeders" in v. 1. At any rate, the theme of shepherding, which is connected to the lion theme, resurfaces in 3:12 and 7:14–15. On the level of composition, finally, the recurrence of the phrase "the top of Carmel" (v. 2bβ) in 9:6 may indicate that 1:2 and 9:1–6 are part of an editorial framework constructed around the collections of words and visions in 1:3–8:14 (cf. similarly Jeremias 1998: 14).

Read in conjunction, the superscription (v. 1) and the motto (v. 2) foreground the notion of a theophany that brings about destruction in the form of an earthquake and/or a severe drought. Moreover, the verbal form *wayyōʾmar* ("he said"), which ties vv. 1 and 2 together, introduces a quasi-narrative dimension (cf. Möller 2003a: 159). It enables the reader to envision the entire book as a kind of drama. This is the opening scene: The prophet has spoken, and (or, because) the divine lion has roared (cf. 3:8). The shepherds, one may infer, have fled. The vegetation is withering. The drama may begin.

Oracles against Neighboring Nations (1:3–2:3)

1 ³Thus says YHWH:
For three crimes of Damascus, or four, I will not hold it back.
Because they have crushed Gilead with threshing carts of iron,
⁴I will send fire against Hazael's house, and it will consume Ben-Hadad's fortresses.
⁵I will break the bar of Damascus and cut off the ruler from the valley of Aven and the scepter-bearer from Beth-Eden.
The people of Aram will be exiled to Kir, says YHWH.
        ⁶Thus says YHWH:
For three crimes of Gaza, or four, I will not hold it back.
Because they have deported entire populations, handing them over to Edom,
⁷I will send fire against the wall of Gaza, and it will consume its fortresses.
⁸I will cut off the ruler from Ashdod and the scepter-bearer from Ashkelon.
As I turn my hand against Ekron, the remaining Philistines will perish,
says the Lord YHWH.
        ⁹Thus says YHWH:
For three crimes of Tyre, or four, I will not hold it back.
Because they delivered entire populations to Edom
and did not remember the treaty of brothers,
¹⁰I will send fire against the wall of Tyre, and it will consume its fortresses.
        ¹¹Thus says YHWH:
For three crimes of Edom, or four, I will not hold it back.
Because he pursued his brother with the sword and stifled his compassion.
His anger tore ceaselessly, and his fury—he kept it forever.
¹²I will send fire against Teman, and it will consume the fortresses of Bozrah.
        ¹³Thus says YHWH:
For three crimes of the Ammonites, or four, I will not hold it back.

Because they have cut open pregnant women
in Gilead, in order to expand their territory,
¹⁴I will kindle a fire in the wall of Rabbah, and it will consume its fortresses,
with shouting on the day of battle, with gale on the day of whirlwind.
¹⁵Their king will go into exile, he and his officials together, says YHWH.
2 ¹Thus says YHWH:
For three crimes of Moab, or four, I will not hold it back.
Because he burned to lime the bones of the king of Edom,
²I will send fire against Moab, and it will consume the fortresses of Kerioth.
Moab will perish in tumult, amid shouting and trumpet blasts.
³I will cut off the ruler from its midst, and all its officials I will kill with him,
says YHWH.

INTRODUCTION TO THE CYCLE OF
ORACLES AGAINST THE NATIONS

The first major section of the book of Amos, comprising 1:3–2:16, contains a number
of prophecies belonging to a genre that is commonly labeled "oracles against nations"
(henceforth, OAN). Several prophetic books contain a section with OAN, albeit not
placed at the beginning (see, e.g., Isaiah 13–23; Jeremiah 46–51; Ezekiel 25–32). What
makes the collection in Amos 1–2 unique is its character as a well-structured composition. As shown by Paul (1971), repeated motifs and catchword connections contribute
to a sense of literary cohesion. The OAN cycle consists of eight oracles, which are commonly divided into four pairs:

1. 1:3–5 Aram + 1:6–8 Philistia
2. 1:9–10 Tyre + 1:11–12 Edom
3. 1:13–15 Ammon + 2:1–3 Moab
4. 2:4–5 Judah + 2:6–16 Israel

Several attempts have been made to find an underlying logic governing the sequence
of nations. Whereas Bentzen (1950: 87–93) has suggested a rather farfetched analogy
with the geographical pattern found in Egyptian execration texts, Paul (1971) has maintained that the pattern (which he describes as "concatenous") is primarily based on a
catchword principle. Possibly, the present structure is the result of a combination of
several ordering principles (see Steinmann 1992). However, if one makes a subdivision into four *pairs* (as above), it is possible to detect a rather straightforward logic.
The key is provided by the last pair, which consists of Judah and Israel. The preceding
pairs are made up of neighboring nations of this couple, according to a north-south
pattern. Consistently, one of Israel's neighbors is placed together with one of Judah's
(cf. Steinmann 1992: 687; Jeremias 1998: 23–25): Aram (Israel) + Philistia (Judah) //
Tyre (Israel) + Edom (Judah) // Ammon (Israel) + Moab (Judah).

This structural arrangement, where Judah and Israel are not addressed until the
end of the cycle, would seem to imply the use of a strategy that has been described as a
"rhetoric of entrapment."[16] In the words of John Barton, the aim of the prophet appears
to have been "to startle his hearers by suddenly turning on them after lulling them into
a false sense of their own security by denouncing their neighbours" (1980: 36). Leaving

speculations concerning an original oral performance aside, one may nevertheless observe such a rhetorical strategy at work in the OAN cycle, viewed as a literary composition. At first, the addressees are invited to give their consent to the words of judgment against old archenemies (the Arameans and the Philistines) and other neighboring (and rival) nations. Then, unexpectedly, the series continues with equally grave accusations and severe pronouncements of punishment directed against Judah and Israel.

It is worth noticing that YHWH judges all nations according to certain ethical demands. Barton has argued that the accusations in 1:3–2:3 are based on ancient international warfare conventions (1980: 39–61; see also Hutton 2014: 101–2), but the existence of such conventions remains hypothetical. In some cases, Barton concedes, it is possible that the prophet appeals "to principles of conduct which he believes all nations *ought* to accept" (1980: 59, emphasis in the original). At any rate, one may speak of a certain "universalist" tendency in the OAN cycle. Arguably, all of the eight nations mentioned in Amos 1:3–2:16 are treated in a similar way. The underlying idea would seem to be that the jurisdiction of YHWH has a universal scope. As a consequence, those nations that worship YHWH as their patron deity—Judah and Israel—are not thought to enjoy special privileges (see also Amos 3:1–2; 9:7). They will be judged according to the same rules as their neighbors. This point is underscored by the fact that all eight oracles follow a similar pattern:

a. Messenger formula: "Thus says YHWH."
b. Introductory phrase: "For three crimes . . . or four, I will not hold it back."
c. Accusation: "Because . . ."
d. Proclamation of punishment: "I will send fire . . ." (or a similar formulation).

The structural symmetry in this series of eight oracles is not perfect, however. On closer examination it becomes evident that two similar, yet different patterns have been applied. In the following I refer to them as patterns A and B. The main differences between them concern the elements (c) and (d) above. Whereas pattern A involves one short accusation (c) and a rather elaborate pronouncement of punishment (d), where further consequences are added to the destruction of buildings/walls by fire, pattern B features an extended section dealing with accusations (c) and a short pronouncement of punishment, restricted to punishment by fire. A further difference is that pattern A includes a concluding formula, "says (the Lord) YHWH," which lacks a counterpart in pattern B. Four oracles adhere to pattern A, and three follow pattern B. Interestingly, the distribution of these two patterns coincides to a large extent with the division of the series into four pairs:

1. 1:3–5 against Aram (A) + 1:6–8 against Philistia (A)
2. 1:9–10 against Tyre (B) + 1:11–12 against Edom (B)
3. 1:13–15 against Ammon (A) + 2:1–3 against Moab (A)
4. 2:4–5 against Judah (B) + 2:6–16 (or 2:6–8) against Israel (modified; see below)

Considerations of both content and historical context support the hypothesis that the oracles that correspond to pattern A represent the oldest layer.[17] Hence, the original OAN cycle probably consisted of two pairs and a concluding climax, namely, the oracle against Israel. Within each pair, the oracle against the northern neighbor mentions Gilead, whereas Edom is mentioned in the oracle against the southern neighbor: Aram (Gilead)—Philistia (Edom) // Ammon (Gilead)—Moab (Edom) // (climax:) Israel.

At a later stage, according to this hypothesis, the three pattern B oracles were added. It has been suggested that this happened toward the end of the eighth century B.C.E. (Schütte 2011). For reasons stated below, I find it more likely that the pattern B prophecies originated during the postmonarchic era. Possibly, however, the additions were made in two successive steps. The oracles against Tyre and Edom are clearly connected to the prophecy against Philistia. Together, these three form a sub-group within the cycle, centering on trade with prisoners of war—an observation which has been taken as an indication that the Philistia oracle is a later addition, too, despite its adherence to pattern A (see Steins 2010: 40–47).

When it comes to the Judah oracle, the picture is very different. It is not closely connected to any other oracle in the series. In fact, the indictments against Judah differ from the others in a conspicuous way. Whereas the previously mentioned nations are accused of various crimes of war, the charges against Judah are of a distinctly religious nature, centering on Torah (dis)obedience (2:4b). The language used has an unmistakable Deuteronomistic flavor.[18]

In the oracle against Israel, which constitutes the climax of the series, the section containing accusations has been expanded (2:6–8, cf. also vv. 11–12). At the same time, the topic has shifted, from international warfare (or, in 2:4, Torah obedience) to social and economic oppression. Most likely, the disaster depicted in 2:13–16 should be understood as a divinely decreed punishment for the crimes enumerated earlier. However, the phrase that introduces the punishment in the seven preceding oracles, "I will send fire," is missing here. Given this deviation from the structural pattern, the Israel oracle can be described as open-ended. In this way, the transition to the next part of the book, comprising chapters 3–6, which develops the theme of Israel's alleged crimes in more detail, becomes rather smooth.

To sum up, the original OAN cycle focused on the fate of the Northern Kingdom, Israel. Concisely formulated judgments over neighboring nations (Aram, Philistia, Ammon, and Moab) were followed by a more elaborate diatribe against Israel. The main purpose seems to have been to explain and justify the downfall of Israel in 722 B.C.E., from a Judah-centered perspective (see Fritz 1987: 37–38). According to the original OAN cycle, the Northern Kingdom, Judah's mighty rival, had incurred the wrath of YHWH, just like some neighboring nations. Possibly, this was meant to serve as a warning to the people in Judah (Fritz 1987: 38). After 587 B.C.E., the cycle was expanded and updated. In order to provide a theological explanation for the disaster that had struck Jerusalem, the Judah oracle was included. At the same time (or, perhaps, in a separate move), further oracles against other nations in the region (Tyre and Edom) were added. In this editorial layer, the anti-Edomite bias is unmistakable, as will be shown below.

THE FUNCTION AND MEANING OF
THE INTRODUCTORY REFRAIN

All eight oracles in the OAN cycle in Amos 1–2 begin in exactly the same way, with the messenger formula, followed by an introductory sentence, into which the name of a city or a nation (X) has been inserted: ʿal šĕlōšâ pišʿê [X] wĕʿal ʾarbāʿâ lōʾ ʾăšîbennû, "for three crimes of X, or four, I will not hold it back" (1:3, 6, 9, etc.). Within the composition as a whole, this sentence serves as a refrain that ties the oracles together. Even more important, the verbatim repetition of this refrain has the effect of placing all the addressees on the same level.

Despite the fact that the introductory sentence consists of well-known Hebrew words, it is difficult to interpret. The scholarly literature is replete with more or less ingenious suggestions as to its contextual meaning and function. The first part of the refrain, literally "for three crimes of X, and/or for four," displays a kind of staircase parallelism that recalls the so-called graded numerical sayings attested in the wisdom literature (see Möller 2003a: 180–85), as well as in Ugarit (*KTU/CTU* 1.4.III: 17–18). Sayings of this type are usually constructed according to the principle $x // x + 1$, for instance, "Three things are too wonderful for me, four I do not understand" (Prov 30:18, NRSV). As a rule, the introduction of such a saying is followed by exactly $x + 1$ (in the example cited: $3 + 1 = 4$) illustrations of the phenomenon in question (Prov 30:18–19, 21–23, 29–31). In the series of oracles in Amos 1–2, however, this is not the case.

The oracles that adhere to pattern A (Aram, Philistia, Ammon, and Moab) mention only one crime, instead of the expected four. Apparently, the traditional formulaic language is here being reused in a less strict fashion. Rather than trying to figure out alternative ways of doing the arithmetic (Weiss 1967b), the task of the interpreter is to assess the rhetorical function. In my opinion, it is twofold. On one hand, the initial mention of the numbers three and four emphasizes that the ensuing accusation concerns an outrageous incident that is part of a pattern of repeated unethical conduct. On the other hand, the numerical mismatch within the immediate context creates a sense of suspense (see similarly Möller 2003a: 183–84).

Interestingly, the editor(s) responsible for the pattern B oracles would seem to have interpreted the numerical formula more literally, yet without any transparent consistency. Whereas the Tyre oracle contains two allegations (1:9), it is possible to find a complete set of four accusations in the Edom oracle (1:11). Possibly, this was meant to indicate that Edom was the worst perpetrator among the neighboring nations (Chisholm 1990: 196), a notion that would be in line with the strong anti-Edomite tendency in exilic and postexilic Judean prophecy.[19] Within the concluding pair, the Judah oracle, with its three accusations, is outnumbered by the prophecy against Israel, which lists at least four allegations. In his analysis of the Israel pericope, Chisholm finds four "conceptual" crimes but as many as nine or ten "formal" accusations (1990: 192–94).

The concluding clause within the introductory refrain, *lō' 'ăšîbennû*, literally "I will not let it/him return," has been subject to several different interpretations (see Linville 2000a). This is due to the fact that the masculine pronominal suffix (*-ennû*) lacks a clear referent. Since the gender of cities and countries is usually feminine, one may rule out the theory (advanced by Barré 1986) that the pronoun refers back to the city/state mentioned (Damascus, Gaza, Tyre, etc.). Hence, it is more likely that the clause points forward, in anticipation (Rudolph 1971: 130). However, the destructive fire (mentioned in all oracles except the one directed against Israel) is a rather unlikely candidate, because *'ēš* ("fire") is a predominantly feminine noun. Further suggestions, based on the premise that "it" must refer to a specific word or concept, include YHWH's anger (Knierim 1977), as well as the "day of battle," mentioned in 1:14 and 2:2 (Rilett Wood 2002: 24).

The translation given above, "I will not hold it back," is based upon the alternative hypothesis that "it" refers, in a general sense, either to the ensuing pronouncement of judgment or to the divine act of punishment itself.[20] Arguably, such an interpretation makes excellent sense within both the immediate and the somewhat wider context. An interesting parallel is provided by Num 23:20, where Balaam says, "he (YHWH) has blessed, and I cannot revoke it (*wĕlōʾ ʾăšîbennâ*)" (NRSV). Common to this passage and the refrain in Amos 1–2 is the idea that certain divine decisions (concerning blessing or punishment) are irreversible (cf. Rilett Wood 2002: 144). There is, however, no reason to assume that the phrase in the OAN cycle is ambiguous, referring simultaneously to the irrevocability of both judgment and salvation (as argued by Noble 1995b).

NOTES

1:5. *the ruler.* Hebrew *yôšēb* can also mean "inhabitant"—thus the LXX and the Vulgate. However, "ruler" makes a much better parallel to "scepter-bearer" (*tômēk šēbeṭ*). The same applies to 1:8.

1:11. *stifled his compassion.* The expression *wĕšiḥēt raḥămāyw* is a *crux interpretum.* Since no exact parallels have been found, it is uncertain whether the verb *šḥt* (Piel, "to destroy") really can denote the act of suppressing an emotion, as presupposed by my translation. Hence, scholars have sought alternative solutions. If one reads a form of *reḥem* ("womb") instead of *raḥămîm* ("compassion"), with support from the Septuagint, the clause could be rendered "he destroyed his/its womb" and taken as an allusion to Esau's birth (Barton 1980: 21, with reference to *Pesiqta Rabbati* 48a). This is worth considering. It has further been argued by Paul, in an attempt to find a literary link between the Edom oracle and the ensuing Ammon oracle, that v. 11bβ refers to violence against "its/his women" (*raḥămāyw*) in warfare (see 1971: 402–3; 1991: 14–15, 64–65). Although the reference to Judg 5:30 (where *raḥam* undoubtedly means "young woman") may at first seem intriguing, this hypothesis lacks a solid lexicographic foundation. The same holds for the suggestion that *raḥămāyw* in Amos 1:11 means "his allies" (Fishbane 1970, 1972). It is a fact that elsewhere in the Hebrew Bible the plural form *raḥămîm* (with or without a suffix) always denotes compassion. Moreover, the idea that someone might be able to withhold or stifle compassion is attested in other biblical texts. See Pss 40:12 (Eng. v. 11) and 77:10 (Eng. v. 9).

he kept it forever. I am taking שְׁמָרָה as a perfect (third-person singular masculine) with an object suffix (singular feminine), *šĕmārāh,* despite the absence of a *mappîq* (cf. Isa 23:17). Alternatively, *šĕmārâ* may be understood as a feminine singular perfect, which is vocalized according to the principle of *nĕsîgâ* (retracted accent)—thus Wolff (1977: 131), Andersen and Freedman (1989: 268), and Jeremias (1998: 18). This solution has the advantage that a shift of grammatical subject is avoided: "His anger tore ceaselessly, and his fury kept forever." However, such an intransitive use of the verb *šāmar* is not attested elsewhere in the Hebrew Bible.

1:14. *the day of battle.* Or "the day of the battle." A small, but perhaps significant, difference between the MT (*bĕyôm milḥāmâ*) and the text in 4XII^g is that the latter has the definite article.

1:15. *Their king.* Because the immediate context mentions "his officials" (*wĕšārāyw*), I find no reason to follow the lead of the Vulgate and read *mlkm* (here rendered "their king") as Milkom, that is, as a reference to the Ammonite patron deity (as argued by Puech 1977).

COMMENTS

1:3–5. *The Aram oracle.* In verse 3a, Damascus, the capital of the Aramean kingdom, stands metonymically for the entire nation. For the interpretation of the remainder of v. 3a, see "The Function and Meaning of the Introductory Refrain." Aram might be called the archenemy of the Northern Kingdom (see Axskjöld 1998), so it is fitting that this oracle comes first in the series. Two kings of Aram are mentioned. During the reign of Hazael (842–ca. 800 B.C.E.) and his successor, Ben-Hadad (or Bir-Hadad, often referred to as Ben-Hadad III), Israel and the Arameans fought many battles over territories. Clearly, Amos 1:3–5 draws on memories of those conflicts (see Vieweger 1994). For both parties, control over the Transjordanian region called Gilead was of prime importance. It is therefore not surprising that the accusation directed against Aram-Damascus concerns atrocities committed in Gilead.

1:3. The expression "because they have crushed (ʿal-dûšām) Gilead with threshing carts of iron" (v. 3b) should probably be understood as a metaphor for military acts of violence against a defeated population. Since threshing sledges of this type had teeth of iron underneath, the notion of brutality is foregrounded. Similar imagery is attested in Assyrian annals and treaties (Fritz 1987: 29; Paul 1991: 47–48), as well as in a few biblical texts. Of special interest is 2 Kgs 13:7, where victorious Aramean warfare against Israel is metaphorically described as an act of crushing (dûš). Mention should also be made of Isa 41:15, where a threshing sledge metaphor occurs in a depiction of restored military power and greatness for Judah.[21] It is not possible to determine whether Amos 1:3 refers to (the memory of) a specific historic event, such as Hazael's conquest of Gilead (2 Kgs 10:32–33). The early interpretative tradition that the victims were pregnant women, attested in the form of textual expansion both in a Qumran manuscript (5QAmos) and in the Septuagint, can be explained as a harmonizing interpretation influenced by 1:13 (with, e.g., Paul 1991: 47, n. 32).

1:4. The punishments for Aram's crime(s), decreed by YHWH, are pronounced in vv. 4 and 5. The clause occurring in v. 4, wěšillaḥtî ʾēš bě [X] wěʾākělâ ʾarmĕnôt [Y], "I will send fire against X and it will consume the fortresses of Y," is going to be repeated, as a second refrain, in all the ensuing oracles, except for the last one, the Israel pericope (see 1:7, 10, 12, 14; 2:2, 5). Fire is a ubiquitous metaphor for anger in the Hebrew Bible (see, e.g., Deut 19:6; 32:22; Isa 5:25; 66:15; Jer 4:4; 15:14; Ps 89:47). In this case, however, a literal interpretation, destruction by fire, is equally possible. According to 1:4 the primary targets of the divine rage/fire are "Hazael's house" and "Ben-Hadad's fortresses." As noted above, memories of intense wars were associated with these two rulers. Arguably, the expression bêt ḥāzāʾēl, "Hazael's house," is intentionally ambiguous. It could, of course, refer to a royal building in Damascus, or it could signify the entire Aramean kingdom (Höffken 1982). However, there is another possibility. Hazael was a usurper who founded a new dynasty (see 2 Kgs 8:7–15 and Pitard 1992: 340). Hence, this prophecy would seem to proclaim both an imminent attack on Damascus and, as a consequence, the end of the "house" (= dynasty) of Hazael (cf. bêt dāwīd, "the house/dynasty of David," in 1 Kgs 12:20 and 2 Kgs 17:21).

1:5. In close conjunction with v. 4, the opening clause in v. 5 announces that YHWH will "break the bar of Damascus" (v. 5aα). This is another way of saying that an attacking army will break through the city gate of the capital in order to capture the city. Thereafter the focus of attention shifts to other parts of the Aramean kingdom. More precisely, the following threats concern some kind of local rulers referred to as "the ruler" in "the valley of Aven" and "the scepter-bearer" in a place called "Beth-Eden" (v. 5aβγ).

Unfortunately, it is not possible to determine the geographical location of *bīqʿat ʾāwen*, mentioned in v. 5aβ. Possibly, reference is made to "the fertile valley between the Lebanon and Anti-Lebanon ranges, called el-Beqaʾ today" (Jeremias 1998: 27). Since elsewhere the Hebrew lexeme *ʾāwen*, carrying such senses as "sin" and "evil," may serve as a substitute for an original divine name (see Hos 4:15; 5:8), one cannot rule out the possibility that this peculiar toponym is the result of ideologically motivated editorial distortion (see Paul 1991: 52–53).

As regards Beth-Eden in v. 5aγ (a name that in Hebrew might evoke notions of paradisiac delight), an identification with *bīt adini,* attested in Akkadian sources, is now widely accepted. During large parts of the eighth century B.C.E. this Aramean city-state northeast of Damascus, with Tel Barsip as its administrative center, was ruled by a relatively autonomous Assyrian governor (Malamat 1953; Schütte 2011: 532). However, a thorough survey of the political history of *bīt adini* would hardly throw further light on Amos 1:5. I suggest that the main function of these two examples, Beth-Eden and the valley of Aven, is to underscore that YHWH's judgment concerns the entire Aramean territory: all its cities and districts and all its rulers.

According to the concluding clause of verse 5, the survivors among the Aramean people will be exiled. The destination of these deportees is said to be a place called Kir (cf. similarly 2 Kgs 16:9). Kir is also mentioned in Amos 9:7, where it appears to refer to the original Aramean homeland. Rather than reflecting an authentic tradition, this could be a literary device, conveying the idea that YHWH, as the lord of history, is capable of bringing peoples back and forth. On the basis of Isa 22:6, one may guess that the province of Kir was situated to the east, not far from Elam.[22] It is worth noting that 1:5b introduces a theme that pervades all sections of the book of Amos: forced migration (deportation and exile).

Commentators have often dated the Aram oracle to around 760 B.C.E., allegedly the time of Amos's prophetic activity (see, e.g., Wolff 1977: 149–51 and Barton 1980: 30–31). Admittedly, several details in 1:3–5, such as the mention of Hazael and Ben-Hadad and (memories of) war in Gilead, are consistent with this supposition (Vieweger 1994). However, for the following reasons I find it more likely that this prophecy originated in the 730s or later: (1) During the so-called Syro-Ephraimite crisis, 734–732 B.C.E., Aram-Damascus became an ally of Israel and, concomitantly, a powerful enemy of Judah, a situation that gave rise to anti-Aramean prophecies in prophetic circles in Jerusalem (see Isa 7:4–9; 17:1–6);[23] (2) the motif of deportation implies a date of origin during or subsequent to the reign of Tiglath-Pileser III, who introduced mass deportation (deployed only sporadically by some of his predecessors) as a systematic strategy of the Assyrian empire (see Paul 1991: 54–55). Because of the definitive character of this prophecy of doom I agree with Wolfgang Schütte (2011: 531) that it should probably be regarded as a *vaticinium ex eventu,* composed during the decades following the Assyrian conquest of Damascus and adjacent territories in 732 B.C.E. and the ensuing deportations (so also Fritz 1987: 37–38).

1:6–8. *The Philistia oracle.* The next addressee is Philistia, for which the city of Gaza stands as a representative in vv. 6–7 (with Mays 1969: 32). Three other Philistine cities—Ashdod, Ashkelon, and Ekron—are mentioned in v. 8. Since Aram could be called Israel's archenemy, it is logical that the second oracle in the first pair concerns Philistia, Judah's long-standing rival in the west. However, as indicated by Isa 9:11 (Eng. v. 12), the Philistines belonged to Israel's traditional enemies, as well.

According to the accusation in v. 6b, the Philistines had been involved in large-scale deportations, apparently affecting whole villages (Wolff 1977: 157). This is usually taken as a reference to the slave trade. Nothing is said about the identity of the victims, but we are told that they were delivered (that is, sold) to Edom. Possibly, the historical background is that prisoners of war sometimes ended up as workers in the Edomite copper mines at Feinan (Paul 1991: 57; Schütte 2011: 540–44). Gaza's punishment, targeting its city wall and fortresses, is announced by means of the stereotypical "I will send fire" refrain (v. 7). This could refer to Tiglath-Pileser's campaign in 738 B.C.E.

On the whole, however, the statements made in this prophecy regarding the fate of Philistine cities do not yield much information that can be tied to specific historical events. In the threats against the local rulers in Ashdod and Ashkelon (v. 8a), some key formulations from v. 5αβγ (*yôšēb,* "ruler," and *tômēk šēbeṭ,* "scepter-bearer") are reused. This observation indicates that stylistic concerns may have been more important to the author than an aspiration for historical accuracy. Yet it is perhaps possible to find an allusion to the frequent shifts on Ashdod's throne around 712 B.C.E. (see Tadmor 1958: 79–80). The clause "I turn my hand against Ekron" (v. 8bα) would seem to refer to some kind of punitive action against that city. Ekron was captured by the Assyrian army during Sargon II's campaign in Philistia in 712 B.C.E. (Tadmor 1958: 83). Finally, it is declared that "the remaining Philistines will perish" (v. 8bβ). This could refer either to some unmentioned Philistine cities, for instance Gath (Rudolph 1971: 132), or (perhaps more likely) to the survivors of a major catastrophe (cf., e.g., Isa 46:9 and Mic 2:12).

Because the Philistia oracle adheres to pattern A (see above), I suggest that it originated around the end of the eighth or the beginning of the seventh century B.C.E. It is likely that it served as a source of inspiration for the anti-Philistine oracle in Ezek 25:15–17 (note the striking similarities between Amos 1:8 and Ezek 25:16). However, the central role assigned to Edom might indicate a later date for Amos 1:6–8 (Steins 2010: 40–45, 49–50). An alternative explanation would be that the Philistia prophecy underwent an anti-Edomite revision, in order to link it more firmly to the next pair of oracles (Schütte 2011: 533).

1:9–10. *The Tyre oracle.* In 1:9–10, the discourse makes a move to the north again: to Tyre, a city-state on the Phoenician littoral. Like the next one (1:11–12), this oracle follows pattern B (see above). Nonetheless, the similarities between the Tyre pericope and the preceding (pattern A) prophecy against Philistia are striking. To begin with, and far from surprisingly, the refrains are repeated verbatim (v. 9a = v. 6a; v. 10 = v. 7), the only difference being that Gaza has been replaced by Tyre. Much more remarkable is the fact that the first accusation against the Phoenician city seems to have been copied from the Philistia oracle.

Despite slight differences in wording between 1:9bα and 1:6b, the content is the same. Like Gaza, Tyre is accused of participating in the slave trade, where "entire populations" (gālût šĕlēmâ, v. 9, exactly as in v. 6) are being handed over to Edom (destined for the copper mines?). The only detail in 1:9–10 that lacks a close counterpart in the Philistia oracle is the allegation that "they" (that is, the leaders and people of Tyre) had failed to observe (or, remember, zkr) "the treaty of brothers" (bĕrît ʾaḥîm, v. 9bβ). This expression, which echoes the diplomatic language used throughout the ancient Near East (see Paul 1991: 61–62), might allude to the legendary treaty between Solomon and Hiram, king of Tyre (1 Kings 5; 9). One may especially note the address "my brother" within a dialog between these two kings, in 1 Kgs 9:13 (see further Priest 1965: 400–405).

Oracles against Tyre, which was famous for its wealth built on trade, are a prominent feature in some prophetic texts from the exilic and postexilic periods (Isaiah 23; Ezekiel 26–27; Zech 9:3–4). Possibly, one or several of these prophecies were occasioned by the lengthy Babylonian siege of this harbor city (585–573 B.C.E.). Several factors indicate that Amos 1:9–10 likewise originated in the postmonarchic era. Because it adheres to pattern B, and because it consists almost entirely of quotations, the Tyre oracle should most certainly be regarded as a secondary addition to the series (with, e.g., Mays 1969: 34). To this, one may add further observations. By means of the strong verbal and thematic links between the prophecies against Philistia and Phoenicia (Tyre), these two nations are pictured as partners in crime. In a postexilic text, Joel 4:4–6 (= Eng. 3:4–6), similar accusations are directed against Tyre (in tandem with its neighbor, Sidon) and Philistia. According to the Joel passage (v. 6), the Phoenicians and the Philistines (in cooperation?) had sold people from Jerusalem and Judah as slaves to Greeks. Although the final destination is a different one, Greece instead of Edom, the basic idea is the same (see Steins 2010: 48–49). One may add that Philistia-Phoenicia-Edom occurs as a hostile triad, from Judah's perspective, also in Obad 1:18–20.

Against this background, I find it likely that Amos 1:9–10 was composed after 587 B.C.E., in a situation when neighboring nations were accused of profiting from Judah's misfortunes. In this context, it is also worth noting that a new theme, betrayal between brothers, is introduced by the Tyre pericope (v. 9b; cf. v. 11b). This leads to the next oracle, which is directed against the third participant in the slave-trade triangle, Edom.

1:11–12. *The Edom oracle.* As expected, the prophecy against Edom, Judah's neighbor and rival in the southeast, resembles the preceding oracles in several respects; but in some respects it stands out. Thus, instead of listing just one or two crimes (which would seem to be the norm within the series), this prophecy lists four (in v. 11). Notably, this is in line with a strictly literal interpretation of the stereotypical introductory refrain. Furthermore, whereas the preceding oracles use the plural when describing the atrocities (presumably) committed by the nation in question, the Edom oracle consistently uses the third-person singular. In v. 11b one may thus speak of a personification metaphor.

Despite some interpretative difficulties (see the Notes), the general drift of v. 11b is conveyed quite clearly. Notably, the first link in this chain of accusations against the Edomites would seem to describe a scene involving two individuals, or to be more precise, two brothers: "he pursued his brother with the sword" (v. 11bα). The reader is reminded of the fraternity language used for diplomatic relations in 1:9.[24] In addition, I suggest, this depiction of two brothers contains an unmistakable allusion to the traditional tale about the (twin) brothers Jacob and Esau, representing Israel/Judah and Edom (with Jeremias 1998: 30 and Hagedorn 2011: 52).

In the version of the story preserved in Genesis, Esau is, remarkably, the one who takes the initiative of reconciliation between the brothers (Gen 33:1–11), despite the hatred he had harbored because of Jacob's deceitful behavior (Gen 27:41). By contrast, the miniature narrative in Amos 1:11 portrays Esau/Edom as unrelentingly and incessantly aggressive: "he pursued his brother with the sword and stifled his compassion. His anger (*'appô*) tore (*wayyiṭrōp*) ceaselessly, and his fury (*wĕʿebrātô*)—he kept it forever" (v. 1bβγδ). Personified Edom appears to be driven by his emotions. This aspect is underscored through the sudden shift of grammatical subject in v. 11bγ. Here, the anger of Esau/Edom is metaphorically depicted as a wild animal tearing (*ṭrp*) its prey. In v. 12 it is announced that YHWH will send punitive fire against the region of Teman (note that no walls are mentioned), as well as against Edom's fortified capital, Bozrah.

Several factors indicate that the Edom oracle belongs to a secondary editorial layer. To begin with, it follows the B pattern. Further, the uncompromisingly negative portrayal of Edom in v. 11 is consistent with a post-587 B.C.E. date of origin. The hatred against Edom is a prominent theme in exilic and postexilic prophecy.[25] Judging from such texts as Obad 1:10–14 and Ps 137:7, the main reason for this animosity would seem to have been the (alleged) Edomite participation in the plundering of Jerusalem. It is likely that the gradual infiltration of Edomites into the Negev provided additional fuel to the anti-Edom sentiments among prophetic circles in Jerusalem (see Bartlett 1989: 140–74 and Eidevall 2009: 154).

The biblical picture of this neighbor, or "brother," is not entirely negative (Bartlett 1977), however. Thus, Deut 23:8 (Eng. v. 7) admonishes the reader not to "abhor" any Edomite, adding the motivation "for he is your brother." Interestingly, a certain ambivalence toward Edom is reflected in the OAN cycle as a whole, where this nation features in the role of perpetrator (1:11–12) and accomplice (1:6, 9), but also in the role of victim, namely, in 2:1 (see further Hagedorn 2011: 46–56).

1:13–15. The Ammon oracle. The third and last pair among the "other" nations (that is, the neighbors of Israel and/or Judah) consists of a traditional Transjordanian couple: Ammon (referred to as "the Ammonites") and Moab (cf. Gen 19:36–38; Deut 23:4–7 [Eng. vv. 3–6]). Since both oracles (comprising 1:13–15 and 2:1–3) follow pattern A, it is likely that they formed part of the original OAN cycle.

One may note some striking similarities between the Aram oracle (1:3–5) and the prophecy against Ammon. Both nations are accused of war atrocities carried out against the population of Gilead. In 1:13b, the Ammonites are charged with a particularly gruesome crime. We are told that they had ripped open pregnant women, thus killing both the mother and the unborn child. Sadly enough, this practice appears to have been a not uncommon element of ancient warfare, as indicated by both biblical (2 Kgs 8:12; 15:16; Hos 14:1 [Eng. 13:16]) and extrabiblical texts.[26]

Could the slaughter of defenseless women and unborn children be understood in terms of military strategy? An immediate effect would be panic and despair among the enemies. Another aim is indicated by v. 13bβ, where we are told that the Ammonites did this "in order to expand their territory." One may infer that the underlying rationale was to prevent the birth of potential freedom fighters among the defeated population. Further possible aspects have been discussed by Daniel Smith-Christopher (2011: 23–26, 33–39), who concludes that "Amos 1.13 portrays a violent attempt to not only change borders but change cultural and sexual identities as well" (2011: 40).

At the opening of v. 14, the occurrence of the expression *wĕhiṣṣattî*, "I will kindle," instead of the expected *wĕšillaḥtî*, "I will send" (1:4, 7, 10, 12; 2:2, 5) should probably be seen merely as a case of stylistic variation using established phraseology (cf. Jer 49:27). Once again, the main target of the divine fire is said to be the capital city—in this case Rabbah, located on the same site as today's Amman. In accordance with what I have called pattern A, the stereotypical fire formula (v. 14a) is followed by further announcements of consequences for the condemned nation. In v. 14b an imminent (or recent?) military attack is pictured in a vivid way.[27] First, the sound of "shouting" (*tĕrûʿâ*) evokes the image of an approaching army. In the next move, the battle itself is metaphorically depicted as a devastating storm. By means of the expressions *bĕyôm milḥāmâ* ("on the day of battle," 14bα) and *bĕyôm sûpâ* ("on the day of whirlwind," 14bβ), a forceful parallelism is crafted. This language evokes the notion of a day of divine intervention, when YHWH acts against his foes (cf. 5:18–20).

Like the Aram oracle, the prophecy against the Ammonites ends with a prediction of deportation (v. 15). In the latter case, though, the focus is the fate of the king and the ruling elite. It is unlikely that in v. 15b *mlkm* ("their king") originally referred to the Ammonite god Milkom (thus the Vulgate), as has been suggested (see the Notes). One might, at most, speak of a possible allusion or double entendre. In the light of the surrounding passages it is safe to assume that, in this cycle of oracles against neighboring nations, "Yahweh's war is not against gods" (Wolff 1977: 161).

As a result of the aggressively expansive politics of Tiglath-Pileser III in the 730s B.C.E., the Ammonite kingdom became an Assyrian vassal state, as evidenced by tribute lists (Hübner 1992: 188–89). One may infer that a military attack (or, threat) against Rabbah preceded this development. The deportation of an Ammonite king is not recorded in the extant sources; nevertheless, it is conceivable that Amos 1:13–15 was composed during the era of Assyrian dominance, in the last decades of the eighth century or at the beginning of the seventh century B.C.E.

2:1–3. *The Moab oracle.* As regards the decreed punishments, the prophecy against Moab shows great affinities with the preceding oracle against Ammon. Subsequent to the fire formula (2:2a), which mentions the land (Moab) and one city, Kerioth, it is announced that the ruler and other leaders will fall victim to a devastating military attack (2:2b–3; cf. 1:14b–15).

Some details differ, however. In 2:2b, a further war signal, the sound of the trumpet, has been added to the intense shouting, and the storm metaphor (1:14b) has been replaced by the motif of "tumult (*šāʾôn*)" (2:2bα). A further difference concerns the fate of the ruling elite. Whereas the Ammon oracle speaks of deportation (1:15), the utterance in 2:3 states that the Moabite king and his officials will be killed by YHWH (or perhaps on YHWH's order?).

The most distinct feature of the Moab oracle is the accusation. According to v. 1b, the Moabites had "burned to lime (*laśśîd*) the bones of the king of Edom." What kind of crime is implied? What is the significance of the enigmatic expression *laśśîd* (commonly rendered "to lime")? In the absence of contextual clues or helpful literary parallels, one has to resort to guesswork. Apparently, the act of burning occurred subsequent to the death and burial of the anonymous Edomite ruler. Thus, it would seem to be a case of the desecration of remains in a royal grave, "an act of hostility both to the dead themselves and their survivors" (Olyan 2015: 136). As shown by inscriptions in Phoenician graves as well as in a burial cave in Jerusalem, tomb invasion was in itself seen as a heinous crime.[28]

Arguably, the irreversible act of burning the disinterred remains would have made the offense even worse. As indicated by the account of Josiah's destruction of the sanctuary in Bethel (2 Kgs 23:16–18), bone burning was also a means of desecrating a holy place. Possibly, the expression used in Amos 2:1, "to lime," refers to the fact that only white ashes (white as lime) remained after the destruction of the bones (thus apparently the Vulgate, which renders *laśśîd* with *ad cinerem*, "to ashes"). Alternatively, as indicated by Targum Jonathan, the aim of the incineration was literally (and horribly) to produce lime, which was used to plaster and whitewash buildings (thus Paul 1991: 72; cf. Deut 27:2, for such use of lime). On either interpretation, the Assyrian practice of forcing defeated enemies to grind up the bones of their ancestors would seem to provide an illuminating parallel.[29]

It should be noted that the alleged crime (whatever its exact nature) was committed against Edom. Here, in contrast to several preceding accusations in the cycle (1:6, 9, 11), Edom is the victim, not the perpetrator. Moreover, the observation that only Moab and Edom are mentioned is a clear indication that the OAN cycle concerns violations of laws of international conduct and that the perspective is not confined to offenses against Israelites or Judeans (with Rudolph 1971: 136 and Barton 1980: 21, 43–45). It is not possible to pinpoint the historical context. In the scholarly literature references are often made to the account in 2 Kings 3 and to the Mesha stele, which likewise appears to allude to enmity between Moab and Edom in the ninth century B.C.E. It is reasonable to assume, however, that conflicts between Edom and Moab, two neighboring nations, may have arisen at several other occasions as well.

The Moab oracle was probably composed at the same time as the prophecy against the Ammonites, namely, toward the end of the eighth or at the beginning of the seventh century B.C.E. According to Assyrian records, Moab was subjugated and forced to pay tribute during the reign of Tiglath-Pileser III (Gass 2009: 116–18). In a text from this period (Nimrod letter 14), an assault on a Moabite city by an unidentified tribe (from "Gidir") is also mentioned (Gass 2009: 118–21). Thus, the formal predictions in 2:2–3 could refer to a contemporary crisis, or even, if understood as rhetorically exaggerated *vaticinia ex eventu*, to past events.

The Oracle against Judah (2:4–5)

2   [4]Thus says YHWH:
For three crimes of Judah, or four, I will not hold it back.
Because they have rejected the law of YHWH and have not kept his statutes
—and their lies, after which their fathers walked, have led them astray—
[5]I will send fire against Judah, and it will consume the fortresses of Jerusalem.

INTRODUCTION TO THE JUDAH ORACLE

As the text moves on to Judah, which most likely was the homeland of the editor(s) responsible for Amos 2:4–5, the character of the discourse changes abruptly. The center of attention moves away from the scene of international politics (1:3–2:3) to the field of inner-Judean ideological debate—from crimes against fellow human beings to disobedience toward the national deity. While the six preceding nations were charged with war atrocities and/or complicity in the slave trade (see the Comments on 1:3–2:3), the accusations against the people and leaders of Judah concern, above all, the failure to observe religious rules.

As demonstrated below, the Judah oracle makes excellent sense in a postmonarchic setting as it seems to provide a theological explanation for the disaster that occurred in 587 B.C.E. To this one may add the observation that this oracle follows the so-called B pattern, just like the (exilic or postexilic) oracles against Tyre and Edom. (See further "Introduction to the Cycle of Oracles against the Nations" above.)

COMMENTS

2:4. According to v. 4bβ, the chief crime of the Judeans was related to YHWH's Torah: "they have rejected (*m's*) the law (or, the teaching) of YHWH (*'et-tôrat yhwh*), and have not kept his statutes (*ḥuqqāyw*)." In view of such formulations, there can be no doubt that this oracle originated in circles influenced by "Deuteronomistic" ideas (W. H. Schmidt 1965: 177 and Jeremias 1998: 44). Although no exact parallels occur in Deuteronomy or in the Deuteronomistic History, a thorough examination of the intertextual ramifications of the Judah pericope reveals its similarity to Deuteronomistic language.[30]

Arguably, the closest counterparts to Amos 2:4bβ are found in 2 Kgs 17:13–15 (especially v. 15) and Jer 6:19 (cf. also Isa 5:24). In the former case, the theological statement "they rejected (*m's*) his statutes (*ḥuqqāyw*)" (2 Kgs 17:15) serves as an explanation for the demise of the Northern Kingdom. In the latter case, the allegation "as for my teaching/law (*tôrātî*), they have rejected (*m's*) it" (Jer 6:19) provides a religious justification for the downfall of Judah. In my opinion, Amos 2:4b needs to be interpreted along similar lines. The disaster in 587 B.C.E. is here described as a well-deserved punishment for the people's disloyalty to their divine overlord, YHWH.

The ensuing indictment, in v. 4bγ, is more obscure. It is stated that the Judeans have been led astray by "their lies (*kizbêhem*), after which their fathers walked (*'ăšer hālĕkû 'ăbôtām 'aḥărêhem*)." In Deuteronom(ist)ic texts, the phrase *hlk 'aḥărê*, "walk after," is a technical term for "idolatry" (Deut 4:3; 6:14; 8:19, etc.). The problem is that the lexeme *kāzāb*, "lie," is not attested elsewhere as a designation of other (or, "false") gods. Eberhard Bons (1996) has argued that the combination of the two motifs of leading astray and telling lies is better understood as referring to the activity of "false" prophets (cf. Isa 28:15; Mic 3:5). This suggestion, which goes back to the medieval Jewish commentator Kimchi, is entirely plausible (see Brettler 2006: 108–9); however, contrary to what Bons claims (1996: 210–11), it is certainly possible that the phrase "walk after" here alludes to worship of "foreign" deities. In a condensed form, v. 4bγ appears to denounce those who listen to prophetic messages that entice them to trust "false" gods.

2:5. In accordance with pattern B, which would seem to characterize later additions to the OAN cycle (see "Introduction to the Cycle of Oracles against the Nations" above), the Judah oracle concludes with the stereotypical punishment by fire formula (cf. 1:10, 12). It is worth noting, however, that v. 5 focuses on the fortresses of Jerusalem. Arguably, this prophecy makes excellent sense in a postmonarchic context as an attempt to deal with the theological problems created by the defeat of Jerusalem and the destruction of the temple in 587 B.C.E. (with Jeremias 1998: 44).

The Oracle against Israel (2:6–16)

2   ⁶Thus says YHWH:
For three crimes of Israel, or four, I will not hold it back;
because they sell the innocent for silver, and the poor for a pair of sandals;
⁷they who trample the heads of the weak into the dust of the earth
and pervert the way of the needy.
A man and his father go to the same girl, thus profaning my holy name.
⁸They stretch themselves out beside every altar, on garments taken in pledge,
and they drink the wine of those who have been fined, in the house of their god.
⁹But I was the one who destroyed the Amorite before them,
although he was as tall as the cedars and as strong as the oak trees;
I destroyed his fruit above and his roots below.
¹⁰I was the one who brought you up from the land of Egypt;
I led you through the wilderness for forty years,
to take possession of the land of the Amorite.
¹¹And I raised up some of your children as prophets,
and some of your young men as Nazirites.
Is it really not so, Israelites? says YHWH.
¹²But you gave the Nazirites wine to drink,
and you commanded the prophets: "Do not prophesy!"
¹³Look! I will make it sway under you,
just like a wagon sways when it is full of grain.
¹⁴The swift will find no refuge, the strong will not retain his force,
the warrior will not save his life.
¹⁵The bowman will not stand his ground, the fast runners will not escape,
nor will the horseman save his life.
¹⁶The bravest among the warriors
will flee away naked on that day, says YHWH.

INTRODUCTION TO THE ISRAEL ORACLE

The prophecy in 2:6–16 against Israel, the Northern Kingdom, constitutes the climax of the OAN cycle. A comparison with the other seven oracles in the series reveals that this prophecy has been extensively reshaped and expanded, most probably during the course of several successive redactions.

The opening verse, 2:6, stays within the structural pattern established by the preceding prophecies (see "Introduction to the Cycle of Oracles against the Nations"). The messenger formula ("Thus says YHWH") is followed by an exact repetition of the introductory numerical refrain: "For three crimes of Israel, or four, I will not hold it back" (v. 6a; cf. 1:3, 6, 9, 11, 13; 2:1, 4). As might be expected, the ensuing clauses (vv. 6–8) contain an enumeration of indictments, introduced by the preposition ʿal (here, "because"). Interestingly, the number of sins would seem to be precisely four, in accordance with a literal interpretation of the refrain (cf. Prov 30:18–23). From that point and onward, however, the Israel pericope deviates radically from the structural pattern. A historical retrospect, vv. 9–11, leads into further accusations (v. 12). Perhaps most conspicuously, the stereotypical "I will send fire" refrain (1:4, 7, 10, etc.) is missing. Although the concluding section, comprising vv. 13–16, can be categorized as a prophecy of disaster, it hardly serves as a close counterpart to the proclamations of punishment that constitute the last section of all the previous oracles.

Despite the existence of a concluding "says YHWH (nĕʾūm yhwh)" formula (2:16a), the absence of a proclamation of punishment gives an open-ended character to the Israel pericope. I suggest that this is a deliberate editorial arrangement. As a result, the reader is encouraged to read chapters 3–6 as a direct continuation of 2:6–16. According to this perspective, the pronouncement of certain punishments would seem to have been postponed, rather than omitted. Later on, the palaces and fortresses of Samaria are indeed threatened with destruction (3:11; cf. 6:8) and the population of Israel is threatened with deportation (4:3; 5:5, 27; 6:7).

According to my tentative reconstruction, the bulk of 2:6–16 (vv. 6–8, 9, 13–16) formed part of the first version of the book of Amos; however, one should not exclude the possibility that passages such as 2:6–8 and 2:13–16 have been subject to later expansions or revisions. As regards the utterances in 2:10–12, observations regarding the terminology would seem to indicate that they are influenced by Deuteronomistic theology. Therefore, I find it likely that vv. 10–12 were added by the editors responsible for the second (exilic or early postexilic) version of the book.

NOTES

2:7. *they who trample*. The participial construction *haššōʾăpîm* is difficult to interpret. It looks like a form of the verb *šʾp*, with the lexical sense "to gasp, pant" (including "to pant after" something), but this would be a strange way of describing oppression of the poor. With the majority of modern commentators, I prefer taking this apparent attestation of *šʾp* as a by-form of *šûp*, "to trample" (so also, e.g., Paul 1991: 79 and Jeremias 1998: 32). As shown by Gen 3:15, these two verbal stems were perceived as near homonyms. One may add that this analysis of the verbal form, and the translation "trample," is supported by the LXX, τὰ πατοῦντα ("treading").

2:13. *sway*. The translation of the otherwise unattested verb ʿwq/ʿyq, which occurs twice in v. 13, is extremely uncertain. Scholars have propounded several other suggestions. The ancient versions, which may represent qualified guesswork on the part of the translators, point in different directions. Whereas the LXX (ἐγὼ κυλίω) refers to the rolling movement of a wagon (creating the strange image of a deity who is rolling below the addressees), the Vulgate (*ego stridebo*) focuses on the creaking sound made by the wheels. The Targum uses a similar (but perhaps not cognate) Aramaic verbal stem, with the sense "(bring) distress." The modern translator's decision (or, guess) has to be based primarily on contextual considerations. See further the Comments on v. 13.

2:15. *stand his ground.* In this idiomatic English translation, the words "his ground" lack a counterpart in the Hebrew text.

2:16. *The bravest.* The rather strange rendering in the LXX, εὑρήσει τὴν καρδίαν αὐτοῦ ("he who finds his heart"), may in fact be based on a different (but most likely secondary) Hebrew *Vorlage,* since 4QXII^c has ומוצא (*wmwṣ'*). This reading may have arisen through metathesis of ואמיץ (*w'myṣ*).

COMMENTS

2:6–8. *Israel's four crimes.* Using an analogy from filmmaking, one could say that the discourse is zooming in as it approaches its final target, Israel. While the accusations in the preceding oracles (with the exception of the Judah pericope) concerned the sphere of international politics, the charges against Israel concern domestic politics and interpersonal relations. Still, there are various interconnections between the critique of Israel, in 2:6–8, and the indictments of the other nations, in 1:3–2:3 (see Hutton 2014: 111–12).

2:6. The first charge against the Israelites is found in 2:6b. By means of the topic, human trade, this utterance is connected to a couple of the preceding oracles, but the perspective is different. Whereas the Philistines and the Phoenicians were accused of delivering groups of slaves to their new masters in a foreign country (1:6, 9), 2:6b focuses on the beginning of the process, when individuals are being sold: "they sell the innocent for silver (*bakkesep*), and the poor for a pair of sandals (*ba'ăbûr na'ălāyim*)." This is usually, and probably correctly, taken as referring to the institution of debt slavery.[31]

According to several texts in the Hebrew Bible, people who were unable to pay their debts were forced to become slaves (or, sometimes, to sell their own children), but ideally for a limited period of six years (Exod 21:2–11; Deut 15:12–18; 2 Kgs 4:1; Neh 5:1–5). Rather than criticizing the system of debt slavery as such, the utterance in Amos v. 2:6b would seem to describe a situation in which the system was abused (Wolff 1977: 165–66; Bohlen 1986: 285). Because of the terseness of the language, however, it is difficult to reconstruct the details.

In v. 6bα, the expression *bakkesep,* "for silver (or, for money)," could refer to the payment. However, since it would be absurd to assume that the market price of an adult human being was as low as that of a pair of shoes, the parallel expression *ba'ăbûr na'ălāyim* ("for a pair of sandals") would seem to call for another kind of explanation. Nothing in the immediate context suggests that reference is made to the symbolic juridical act of removing a sandal (as in Ruth 4:8).[32] In Sir 46:19 a pair of shoes is mentioned as an example of something of little value.[33] Therefore, the point made is probably that unscrupulous creditors were prepared to sell impoverished fellow Israelites, even on account of relatively small debts.[34] In addition, it is emphasized that this was done to "the innocent (*ṣaddîq*)," as opposed to a thief who might be sentenced to pay the debt by becoming a slave (see Exod 22:2 [Eng. v. 3]).[35]

2:7. The second charge against Israel in v. 7 continues the theme introduced by v. 6b, namely, oppression of the poor. According to a plausible interpretation of v. 7aα, the rich are said to "trample the heads of the weak into the dust of the earth" (see the Notes). In the next clause, this conventional image of subjugation and cruelty (cf. Isa 3:15) is replaced by another metaphor. The reader is told that the oppressors "pervert (*nṭh*) the way of the needy" (v. 7aβ). In the light of the intertextual evidence, and especially Prov 17:23, where the wicked are said to pervert (*nṭh*) "the paths of justice" (see also Exod 23:6), it is reasonable to assume that the specific topic of Amos 2:7a is corruption in the Israelite courts.[36]

The third charge is more difficult to interpret. Although the lexical sense of each word in 2:7b is well known, the referent of this utterance remains somewhat obscure. It is stated that two people, father and son, "go to (*yēlĕkû ʾel*)" a third person, called "the girl (*hannaʿărâ*)" (v. 7bα). Is that a crime, on par with those previously mentioned? Why would YHWH, through the prophet, denounce such a trivial act as a way of "profaning my holy name" (v. 7bβ)? Scholars have come up with a number of creative solutions, including the proposals that this particular *naʿărâ* was in fact a money-lending "alewife" (Coote 1981: 35) or a "hostess" at a banquet that involved a syncretistic cult (Barstad 1984: 35). It has even been suggested that *naʿărâ* was the name of a (hitherto unknown) village, Naarah, where such a banquet was held (Moughtin-Mumby 2011).

It seems preferable to assume that *naʿărâ*, in accordance with its established lexical sense, denotes either a (free) young woman or a maid. Clearly, the utterance focuses on the relations between these three people: the (young) man, his father, and the *naʿărâ*. Further, it appears to be emphasized, as an oddity, that father and son visit the *same* girl (cf. the LXX). Since the expression "to go/come into (*bôʾ ʾel*)" frequently refers to sexual intercourse (Gen 6:4; 16:2; 30:3, 4, etc.), the phrase *hlk ʾl*, "to go to," might be taken as a near equivalent, or at least as an allusion to sexual intent (thus *HALOT*, s.v.).[37]

On the basis of these observations it is likely that v. 7b describes some kind of illicit sexual behavior that was considered to be incestuous. According to the regulations in Leviticus 18 and 20, intercourse between a father and his daughter-in-law was prohibited (Lev 18:15; 20:12), as was intercourse between a son and his father's wife (who need not be his mother; Lev 18:8; 20:11; cf. 18:7). As noted by Levin (2003: 277), the phrase used in 2:7bβ, "profane my holy name" (*hll* in Piel + *ʾet šēm qodšî*), occurs also in Lev 20:3, in proximity to one of the passages containing incest laws (cf. also Stuart 1987: 317). It remains to explain why Amos 2:7b speaks of a *naʿărâ* rather than a wife (*ʾiššâ*). Possibly, reference is made to sexual intercourse with (or, rape of) a female servant who belonged to the family (Fendler 1973: 42–43; Fleischer 1989: 61–72; Jeremias 1998: 37). In the words of Paul, this young woman was "just one more member of the defenseless and exploited human beings in northern Israel" (1991: 82–83). Thus interpreted, the third charge continues the theme of oppression of the poor.

2:8. It is difficult to determine whether v. 8 contains one or two charges. I suggest that this utterance describes two different aspects of one scenario: feasting in a sanctuary. What made this revelry morally repulsive to the first readers is probably the fact that the participants were, shamelessly and repeatedly, utilizing expropriated goods for their own pleasure. Furthermore, they were apparently doing this in places dedicated to the cult of YHWH, "beside every altar" (v. 8aβ). The group of participants appears to include both ruthless usurers, sprawling on confiscated garments (v. 8a), and corrupt judges, enjoying wine obtained through fines (v. 8b). In this way, the fourth charge against Israel is connected to the first charge (v. 6b), concerning debt slavery, as well as to the second (v. 7a), which condemned corruption in the courts (see Jeremias 1998: 37).

According to the legislation in Exod 22:25–26 (Eng. vv. 26–27) and Deut 24:12–13, a creditor was, on certain occasions, allowed to take a debtor's clothes in pledge. This may have applied only when the loan was due (Paul 1991: 83–85). Regarding the cloak, however, it is specifically stated that it has to be returned to the owner before sunset, with the following justification: "because it is his only covering" (Exod 22: 26 [Eng. v. 27]).[38] Against that background the behavior of the revelers described in Amos 2:8a must have been seen as outrageous. Instead of returning the cloak to the poor person who needed it as covering for the night, they would recline on it, rather than using (and soiling) their own.

The second part of the charge, in v. 8b, is likewise about abuse of the legal system. The wine served at the feast(s) had apparently been received as payment from fined criminals (or, bought for money paid to the court).[39] Clearly, the sin denounced in v. 8b is indulgence at public expense. Fines were exacted in cases of theft or injury, for instance if a pregnant woman had been beaten so badly that she miscarried (Exod 21:22). The aim of such a system was, of course, primarily to recompense the injured party, not to sponsor the judges' luxury consumption. It should be noted that the motifs of wine-drinking and oppression of the poor are combined also in other passages in the book of Amos, which describe (and denounce) the lifestyle of the rich (4:1; 5:11; 6:6).

Most likely in order to present the behavior as even more abhorrent, the final clause adds the information that the wine-drinking took place in "the house of their god" (v. 8bβ). I find it unlikely that the expression *bêt ʾĕlōhêhem* (which, admittedly, might be translated "house of their gods") alludes to the worship of other deities (thus Barstad 1984: 33–34). Such a grave accusation as "idolatry" would hardly be mentioned just as a note in the margin. It may seem odd that YHWH speaks about himself in the third person, but this creates an ironic distance from the perpetrators (Paul 1991: 86) and perhaps from the sanctuary (in Bethel?), as well (thus Jeremias 1998: 38). The corrupt revelers are reminded, above all, that they have offended not only their fellow Israelites, but YHWH himself. As a consequence, they are told, "their god" (presumably, their patron god) has become their prosecutor and judge.

If the passage 2:6–8 is read as one complex argument, its main purpose seems to be to demonstrate that the judicial system in the Northern Kingdom was completely corrupt. The king of Israel is not mentioned, but it is implied that he had failed in his capacity as guarantor of justice. On a theological level, this political critique may serve as an explanation for the catastrophe of 722 B.C.E. Clearly, the reader is led to conclude, YHWH would have to abandon such a corrupt society. Interestingly, oppression of the poor is regarded as Israel's major fault, not worship of other gods. However, since the name "Israel" eventually became a designation also for the people of Judah, this passage was probably also read as a critique of mistreatment of the poor in Judah (during the monarchic era) or in Yehud (during the Persian period).

2:9–12. YHWH's deeds in the past and Israel's ingratitude. The historical retrospect in 2:9–11, which takes the form of divine self-praise, leads over to an accusation centering on the Israelites' alleged lack of appreciation (v. 12). This speech has three parts, dealing with (1) the conquest of Canaan (v. 9), (2) the exodus from Egypt (v. 10), and (3) the appointment of prophets and Nazirites (v. 11). The first two parts, which recount divine deeds in the past, are introduced by an emphatic first-person pronoun, "but I (wĕʾānōkî)" (vv. 9aα, 10aα), which signals a contrast to the preceding descriptions of what "they" (the Israelites, or groups among them) had done (vv. 6–8). In addition, this repeated "I" emphasizes that the great events mentioned were made possible by YHWH alone. One may further note that, probably in order to create a rhetorical effect, the chronological order has been reversed in vv. 9–10: the conquest comes before the exodus.

2:9. In v. 9 all the original inhabitants of Canaan/Palestine are called Amorites, as in some late passages in Genesis (Gen 15:16; 48:22). In accordance with a tradition that has left traces elsewhere in the Hebrew Bible (Num 13:31–34; Deut 1:28; 9:1–3; 2 Sam 21:15–22), these aborigines are depicted as (superhuman?) giants.

The rhetorical device of personification is combined with a tree metaphor, as the reader is told that the Amorite "was as tall as the cedars and as strong as the oak trees" (v. 9aβ). In this way, it is underlined that the Israelites could not possibly have conquered Canaan without divine assistance. YHWH boasts that he was the one who "destroyed" (Hiphil of *šmd*) the Amorites (v. 9aα). Developing the tree metaphor further, the deity proclaims: "I destroyed his fruit above and his roots below" (v. 9b). This is an image of total annihilation, emphasizing the impossibility of producing "fruit," a metaphor for new generations (see 2 Kgs 19:30; Isa 14:29; Hos 9:16).

The theme of divine violence pervades the book of Amos, but in most cases the underlying idea is that YHWH, as universal judge, had to punish human acts of injustice and violence (see Mills 2010). Here in 2:9, however, nothing is said about any sins that might have justified YHWH's decision to destroy the Amorites (in sharp contrast to 1:3–2:3). The genocide (allegedly) carried out against the original population is not presented as a punishment, but as a necessary precondition for the conquest. YHWH did this in order to be able to give the land to the people of Israel, as implied by v. 9aα, where the Israelites are referred to in the third-person plural: "I was the one who destroyed the Amorite before them (*mippĕnêhem*)." This motive is stated more explicitly at the end of v. 10: "to take possession of (or, inherit, *lārešet*) the land of the Amorite" (v. 10bβ).

2:10. In v. 10, there is a sudden shift to direct address. This utterance is about what the divine "I" has done to "you," the Israelites. The concise account of the exodus provided by this oracle consists of conventional formulations belonging to the Deuteronomistic repertoire: "I was the one who brought you up (Hiphil of *ʿlh*) from the land of Egypt" (v. 10a; see Judg 2:1; 6:8; 1 Sam 10:18; cf. also the numerous attestations in Deuteronomy and elsewhere of a similar phrase with the verb *yṣʾ* instead of *ʿlh*); "I led you through the wilderness for forty years" (v. 10bα; see especially Deut 29:4; cf. also Num 14:33; 32:13; Deut 2:7; Josh 5:6; Jer 2:6). There are thus good reasons to assume that v. 10 should be ascribed to an exilic or postexilic redaction informed by Deuteronomistic ideology (W. H. Schmidt 1965: 179–80; Jeremias 1998: 39–41). Arguably, the same applies also to those passages in Amos that contain similar phrases, namely, 3:1, 5:25, and 9:7 (see the Comments on these verses).

2:11. In v. 11 the focus of attention moves from wanderings in the wilderness (v. 10b) to life in the land of Canaan/Israel. Arguably, the main rhetorical purpose of v. 11 is to exonerate YHWH. The underlying idea is, I suggest, that the deity could not be blamed for the prevailing situation, and its fatal consequences, because he had continually "raised up" (Hiphil of *qûm*) prophets who could teach and warn the people (cf. Deut 18:15–19). Somewhat surprisingly, nothing is said about judges, kings, or priests. Instead, the Nazirites are mentioned together with the prophets.

This collocation (prophets—Nazirites) is unique within the Hebrew Bible. Whereas a prophet was defined primarily by his or her role as intermediary, the defining characteristic of a Nazirite was the vow to abstain from certain things, such as drinking wine, shaving the head, or touching corpses (Num 6:1–8). Possibly, the author had Samuel in mind (Andersen and Freedman 1989: 331–32).[40] According to the traditions collected in the Deuteronomistic History, Samuel combined the two functions of Nazirite and prophet in one person, besides his role as judge (1 Sam 1:22; 3:20). It is stated that the Nazirites were selected from "your young men (*mibbaḥûrêkem*)" (v. 11aβ). In subsequent parts of the book, the category of young men, *baḥûrîm* (literally, "chosen ones") will recur in more sinister contexts (4:10; 8:13). The concluding words, in v. 11b, underscore that the Israelites have been forgetful and ungrateful.

2:12. The ensuing allegation, in v. 12, looks like a direct rejoinder to v. 11; hence, it is often ascribed to the same editorial layer as v. 11 (thus, e.g., Jeremias 1998: 41–42 and Förg 2007). However, the fact that v. 11 ends with a concluding formula (*nĕʾum yhwh*, "says YHWH") might indicate that v. 12 is an even later addition (cf. Rudolph 1971: 147).

Using hyperbole, this utterance states that the Israelites have purposefully prevented YHWH's messengers from fulfilling their mission. They have made the Nazirites break their vows, by offering them wine (v. 12a), and they have tried to prohibit the prophets from speaking (v. 12b). The quoted words of prohibition, "Do not prophesy!" (v. 11bβ), which are ascribed to the addressees, anticipate the debate between Amos and Amaziah in chapter 7. According to that narrative, Amaziah sealed his own fate as he attempted to silence Amos (see 7:16–17). A similar point is made here. Because the Israelites, unwilling to listen and take warning, have attempted to silence the prophets commissioned by YHWH (vv. 11–12), nothing can stop the impending disaster (see vv. 13–16).

2:13–16. *Announcement of an inescapable disaster.* Unlike the seven preceding oracles against various nations, the Israel oracle does not contain a formal pronouncement of punishment, introduced by the fire formula (cf. 1:4, 7, 10, 12, 14; 2:2, 5). Still, the concluding part of the Israel pericope, comprising vv. 13–16, serves a similar function. This passage can be classified as a prediction of disaster. Unfortunately, the utterance that appears to describe the event itself, v. 13, is difficult to interpret (see below). The ensuing verses (vv. 14–16) focus entirely on the effects of the disaster among the population.

Hence, it is uncertain to what kind of catastrophe this passage refers. On the basis of clues provided by the wider context, some scholars have assumed that 2:13–16 describes an earthquake (so, e.g., Rudolph 1971: 148–49 and Wolff 1977: 171). Mention of a memorable (and probably major) quake is made already in the book's superscription, which states that Amos received words and visions concerning Israel "two years before the earthquake" (1:1). To this, one may add the observation that the vision of an earthquake in 9:1 is followed by an utterance (9:1b) that recalls 2:14–16.

However, contextual considerations may also speak in favor of another alternative. In the previous oracles against other nations war is a prominent theme, whereas references to earthquakes are absent. Therefore, it has been suggested that the entire passage depicts a military attack, first metaphorically in terms of an earthquake, in v. 13, and then literally in vv. 14–16 (Mays 1969: 53; Jeremias 1998: 42–44). As will be shown below, however, v. 13 cannot be taken as a metaphor for a military attack, so it seems preferable to read the passage in its entirety as referring to an earthquake and its consequences. As pointed out by Möller (2003a: 209–10), the depiction of helpless soldiers (vv. 14–16) creates an ironic effect.

2:13. The opening utterance of v. 13 contains an interpretative crux (see the Notes). In order to understand the actions described, one needs to know (or figure out) the sense of the otherwise unattested verb *ʿûq* (or *ʿîq*), which occurs twice (!) in this utterance. Apparently, an advanced wordplay is involved. To begin with, some kind of divine activity is denoted by means of a Hiphil participle of *ʿûq* (*mēʿîq*), as YHWH declares that he is going to cause something (the earth?) to *ʿûq* under (the feet of?) the addressees (v. 13a). In the next part of the image, the same verb, but now possibly in Qal, describes something relating to (the course or movement of) a wagon "when it is full of grain" (v. 13b).

The translation offered here is based upon the supposition that the verb *ʿûq* means "to sway" or the like (see *HALOT*, s.v.). Arguably, this hypothesis makes good sense in both parts of the utterance. The trembling of the ground, under the feet of the Israelites, is then metaphorically likened to the swaying movement of an overloaded cart. Alternatively, one might translate "split open."[41] In that case, the idea would be that the tracks made by a heavy wagon resemble fissures opened by an earthquake (Jeremias 1998: 43). Other suggestions based on the lexical senses of similar words in cognate languages, including "to hamper" (Paul 1991: 94) and "to creak" (Müller 1971: 556–59, cf. the Vulgate), are less attractive, because they fail to account for the actual formulations used in the first clause.[42] In the light of the wagon motif in v. 13b, it is hard to see the point in a declaration that YHWH is about to hinder or (cause something to) creak "under you" (v. 13a).

Leaving the crux connected to the verb *ʿûq* aside, the wagon metaphor deserves some attention. As shown above, it may reasonably depict the effects of a major quake. However, it would be unduly far-fetched to take v. 13b as a metaphor for an earthquake, which in its turn serves as a metaphor for the invasion of a hostile army (against Mays 1969: 53 and Jeremias 1998: 42–44). Finally, one may perceive a note of fine irony in this utterance. The image of a cart filled with food, which could be seen as a graphic illustration of abundance, is here used as a metaphor for a terrible disaster (thus also Paul 1991: 95 and Möller 2003a: 210).

2:14–16. In vv. 14–16 one single point is being made, over and over again, in a sevenfold repetition (cf. Paul 1991: 95): There will be no escape from the impending disaster. No one will be able to flee, not even the swiftest (vv. 14aα, 15aβ) or the strongest (v. 14aβ) among the Israelites. Apparently, neither arrows nor chariots (drawn by horses) will be of any use (v. 15)—an indication that the author did not have a regular military attack in mind. Unable to fight this particular danger, even the bravest warriors will panic and try to flee (v. 16), but in vain (v. 14b).

A sense of utter hopelessness is conveyed by the refrain-like phrase *lōʾ yĕmallēṭ napšô*, "will not save his life," which concludes vv. 14 ("the warrior will not save his life") and 15 ("nor will the horseman save his life"). The only interpretative problem in this passage is found in v. 16, where it is stated that "the brave (*wĕʾammîṣ libbô,* literally, "the one with a strong heart") among the warriors (*baggibbôrîm*)" will be "naked" (*ʿārôm*) as he attempts to run away. Should the nudity of the warrior be taken literally or metaphorically? It is hard to tell. Because he is running away rather than parading, he cannot be depicted as a stripped and disarmed prisoner of war. As argued above, the scene is probably a major natural disaster, not a military defeat. Possibly, what is meant by the expression in v. 16 is that even strong heroes will be forced to flee (hastily) without weapons, as indicated by the Targum.[43] At any rate, notions of shame and helplessness are foregrounded by the motif of nakedness. Finally, it should be noted that the theme of no escape (from YHWH's judgment) recurs in 9:1–4.

The Words of Amos (3–6)

Ivory fragment featuring a sphinx, from Samaria, dating to the ninth or the eighth century B.C.E. (Israel Museum, Jerusalem). Drawing by Sverrir Ólafsson, published with permission of the artist.

A Call to Listen (3:1–2)

3 ¹Listen to this word that YHWH speaks concerning you, Israelites,
concerning the whole clan that I brought up from the land of Egypt:
²You alone have I cared for among all the clans of the earth;
therefore, I will call you to account for all your misdeeds.

INTRODUCTION TO 3:1–2

With its call to listen to the prophetic message, the unit 3:1–2 can be seen as a prologue to the central part of the book, comprising chapters 3–6. On another level, the imperative "Listen to this word (*šimʿû ʾet haddābār hazzeh*)" (3:1a), which is repeated in 4:1 and 5:1, functions as an important structuring device *within* chapters 3–6 (see, e.g., Nogalski 1993a: 74–75).¹ Hence, the primary function of 3:1–2 arguably is to serve as an introduction to a section consisting of 3:1–15 (Möller 2003a: 217–22; cf. also Gitay 1980: 293–96).

From a rhetorical point of view, v. 1 evokes what appears to have been one of the most cherished topoi within the national ideology of the kingdom of Israel, the exodus as an event of divine election, in order to turn it against this nation (v. 2). With its announcement of impending divine retribution against Israel (v. 2), the passage 3:1–2 (and, by extension, the entire section comprising chapters 3–6) is linked to the Israel oracle in 2:6–16 (and, by extension, to the entire section comprising chapters 1–2). Whereas 3:1a probably should be ascribed to the first version of the book (in the eighth or the seventh century B.C.E.), observations regarding the use of typically Deuteronomistic vocabulary (v. 1b) and echoes of Hoseanic theology (v. 2) suggest that the remainder of the passage (vv. 1b–2) represents a somewhat later addition. More detailed arguments are provided in the Comments.

NOTES

3:1. *speaks.* The verb form used, *dibber,* can also be rendered "has spoken."

3:2. *I cared for.* This translation represents an attempt to capture the specific nuances of the verb *ydʿ,* "to know," in this context.

COMMENTS

3:1. The opening call, "Listen to this word that YHWH speaks concerning you" (v. 1a), is addressed to all Israelites, literally "the sons/children of Israel" (*běnê yiśrā'ēl*). It is followed by a reference to the exodus from Egypt (v. 1b). The combination of the exodus motif and the address *běnê yiśrā'ēl* recalls the passage 2:9–12. In both cases, the rhetorical device of a retrospective look at the glorious past serves as a foil to accusations concerning the actions and attitudes of the addressees.

Because of the abrupt switch to divine speech in the first person, v. 1b is often regarded as a later addition (thus, e.g., Paul 1991: 100 and Jeremias 1998: 49). I find this likely. Notably, the vocabulary used in v. 1bβ is distinctly Deuteronomistic: "that I brought up (Hiphil of *'lh*) from the land of Egypt" (see Judg 2:1; 6:8; 1 Sam 10:18). Thus, while v. 1a may belong to the book's oldest editorial layer, it is reasonable to assume that v. 1b (as well as v. 2, see below) is the product of an exilic or postexilic redaction (cf. W. H. Schmidt 1965: 172–73 and Wolff 1977: 175).

Furthermore, the vocabulary used in v. 1b is noteworthy from a rhetorical point of view. For example, the occurrence of the lexeme *mišpāḥâ,* which denotes an extended family group or a clan, might imply a notion of intimacy between YHWH and Israel. This aspect of intimacy is developed further in v. 2a.

3:2. In v. 2a it is stated that, "among all the clans (*mišpěḥôt*) of the earth," YHWH has entered into a personal "family" relationship only with the clan/people of the Israelites. The same idea is expressed in Deut 10:15 (with a similar use of *raq,* "only"). Yet another illuminating intertext is provided by Gen 12:3, featuring the phrase "all the clans of the earth" in the context of election and commission (cf. also Gen 28:14). A distinct feature of the utterance in Amos 3:2 is that it employs the verb *yd',* "to know," in order to describe the deity's caring attitude toward the elected. A close parallel is found in Hos 13:5 (see also Gen 18:19 and Deut 9:24). Further affinities with Hoseanic theology are displayed by v. 2b (Jeremias 1998: 49–51), where it is emphasized that the status of being selected entails increased responsibility and accountability. Playing on the polysemous and ambiguous character of the verb *pqd,* which can mean (among other things) "to take care of" as well as "to punish," the concluding clause of v. 2 asserts that YHWH will take care of his family in an unexpectedly harsh way: "I will call you to account (*'epqōd 'ălêkem*) for all your misdeeds" (cf. similarly Paul 1991: 100, 102).

Lions and Traps: A Discourse on Prophecy and Disaster (3:3–8)

3 ³Do two walk together if they have not made an appointment?
⁴Does a lion roar in the thickets when it has no prey?
Does a young lion growl from its lair if it has not caught something?
⁵Does a bird fall into a trap on the ground if there is no bait for it?
Does a trap spring up from the earth when it captures nothing at all?
⁶If the trumpet is blown in a town, will the people not tremble?
If disaster befalls a town, has not YHWH caused it?

⁷Indeed the Lord, YHWH, does nothing without disclosing his plan to his servants the prophets.

⁸The lion has roared. Who is not frightened?
The Lord YHWH has spoken. Who can but prophesy?

INTRODUCTION TO 3:3–8

Positioned between the prologue in 3:1–2 and the ensuing oracles of judgment in 3:9–15, the passage 3:3–8 seems to serve as an additional prologue that introduces two topics of significance for the ensuing discourse, namely, divinely decreed disasters and divinely inspired prophecy. With the exception of v. 7, which is best explained as a later insertion (see the Comments on v. 7), this passage constitutes a neatly and intricately composed unit, most probably belonging to the first version of the book of Amos.

The original composition (without v. 7) consists of a series of rhetorical (or, didactic) questions (vv. 3–6) and a concluding utterance (v. 8) featuring additional questions (juxtaposed with statements). One may speak of a process of intensification, in more than one respect (with Lindström 1983: 204–5 and Jeremias 1998: 51–52). To begin with, the images become gradually more threatening (Gese 1962: 426). The initial image of a peaceful walk (v. 3) is followed by depictions of hunting and hunted animals (vv. 4–5) and, finally, scenes of fear and panic (vv. 6a, 8a). On the level of content, there is a development from diverse observations concerning cause and effect (in a wide sense, vv. 3–5) to more specific topics, such as disasters in cities (v. 6a), divine agency (v. 6b), and prophecy (v. 8; see also v. 7).

Interestingly, this development in terms of content corresponds to a formal progression: from five questions that are marked by the interrogative particle *hă-* (vv. 3–5), via two conditional questions construed with *ʾim* ("if," v. 6), to a final pair of questions introduced by *mî lōʾ* ("who [will/would] not?" v. 8). Hence, the structure might be outlined as follows: vv. 3–5 // vv. 6–8 (with v. 7 as an insertion). However, as Table 3 shows, such simple divisions fail to account for the complexity of the passage 3:3–8*. Containing more than one climax (vv. 6b and 8b), it probably conveys more than one single message.

Each rhetorical question in the series indicates that two (or more) events are strongly (perhaps even inevitably) interrelated. As a rule, this connection can be de-

Table 3. Patterns and Variations within the Series of Rhetorical Questions in 3:3–6, 8

Verse	Event, motif	Observation	Domain	Implied event
3	Road, walking	Visual	Society	Preceding (mutual) decision
4a	Lion, roaring	Auditive	Nature	Capture of prey
4b	Lion, roaring	Auditive	Nature	Capture of prey
5a	Bird, trap, falling	Visual	Nature	Preparation of trap, with bait
5b	Trap, springing up	Visual	Nature	Capture of bird
6a	City, trumpet blown	Auditive	Society	Fear among the city's population
6b	City, disaster	Visual?	Society	(Preceding?) divine activity
8a	Lion, roaring	Auditive	Nature/society	Fear among human beings
8b	YHWH, speaking	Auditive	Society	Prophetic activity

scribed in terms of cause and effect (or, effect and likely cause). Possibly, one of the points made is that "nothing is accidental" (Paul 1991: 104). Arguably, though, it is more accurate to speak of the relation between observation and implication (cf. similarly Pfeifer 1983: 343 and Schenker 1986: 252–53). On the basis of one event that is observed, the occurrence of another event is being inferred. Within this series of nine didactic questions, the examples cited are drawn from different domains, yet according to a recognizable pattern. Finally, one may note that visual experiences alternate with auditory perceptions (see Paul 1991: 108).

NOTES

3:3. *made an appointment.* Cf. the LXX: εἰ πορεύσονται δύο ἐπὶ τὸ αὐτὸ καθόλου ἐὰν μὴ γνωρίσωσιν ἑαυτούς ("Will two travel together at all, unless they know each other?"). Evidently, the Greek translator has read a form of *ydʿ*, "to know," instead of the less common verb *yʿd*, "to make an appointment" (in Niphal, cf. Exod 25:22; 30:6). As pointed out by others, the MT should be given precedence, since it represents the *lectio difficilior* (see Junker 1950: 4–5; Wolff 1977: 179–80).

3:6. *has not YHWH caused it?* Since the MT lacks an object or suffix corresponding to "it," one might consider an alternative translation: "If disaster befalls a town, does not YHWH (re)act?" (cf. similarly Mulder 1984: 107 and NEB; see also Linville 2000b: 71). However, the ancient versions support the traditional interpretation, which is reflected in the translation above.

COMMENTS

3:3. Within its literary context, the utterance in v. 3 serves as a bridge between the preceding historical retrospect (vv. 1–2) and the ensuing series of rhetorical questions; however, this need not indicate that v. 3 is an editorial addition (as argued by Mittman 1971: 135–36). Although YHWH and Israel are not mentioned in v. 3, readers almost inevitably think of their relationship as they are confronted with this image of two people who have agreed to travel together (Hayes 1988: 124; Linville 2008: 71–72). Indeed, the Septuagint seems to reflect such an understanding. Thus interpreted, v. 3 may inspire attempts to read 3:3–8 in its entirety as an allegory, but the primary function of the ensuing series of rhetorical questions is not to tell a story. Therefore, although the interpreter needs to be attentive to metaphorical meanings attached to some motifs within this passage, excessive allegorizing should be avoided.

Read more plainly, v. 3 uses the image of an everyday experience, two people who are seen walking together, to introduce the principle of observation and implication. It is argued, by means of a rhetorical question, that such a joint walk is always preceded by a mutual decision. Although this is not an instance of logical necessity, the reader is led to infer that these two people must have made an appointment (*yʿd*) on a previous occasion.[2] Evidently, this discourse is characterized by persuasive rhetoric, rather than by pure logic.

3:4. Read in isolation, vv. 4–5 could be taken as a small compilation of traditional proverbial sayings intended to elucidate the ubiquitous phenomenon of cause and effect (or, observation and implication), with the help of examples drawn from the domains of animal life and hunting. However, within their literary context, these sayings take on further nuances of meaning. In v. 4, it is stated twice that a lion's roar, sounding from the forest or from the lion's den, indicates that it has caught (*lkd*) prey. On one level, this refers to observations made concerning the behavior of this predator. On another level, the lion motif and the verbal expressions used, *yišʾag* (v. 4a, "roars") and *yittēn qôlô* (v. 4b, "growls" or, more literally, "gives its sound" or "utters its voice"), recall YHWH's roar, as described in the book's motto: "YHWH roars (*yišʾag*) from Zion, and from Jerusalem he utters his voice (*yittēn qôlô*)" (1:2a). In this way, a sense of threat emanating from YHWH is evoked. To a certain extent, therefore, v. 4 would seem to anticipate the ensuing utterances concerning the deity's words and actions (in vv. 6b and 8b).

3:5. In this utterance, a scene from the sphere of fowling is viewed from two different perspectives. At first, in v. 5a, the bird is in view. Because it swoops down on the ground and gets ensnared, one may conclude that someone has set up a *môqēš*, that is, a bait or decoy (Paul 1991: 111; *DCH*, s.v.). In v. 5b, the focus of attention shifts from the downward movement of the bird to the upward movement of the trap (*pah*). Most likely, the word *pah* denotes a clapnet (Junker 1950: 6; Wolff 1977: 185). When it suddenly springs up and shuts, one may infer that a bird has been caught (*lkd*). By means of the trap motif, and the reappearance of the verb *lākad* ("to catch," cf. 4b), v. 5 evokes notions of inescapability (cf. 2:14–16) and entrapment (Jeremias 1998: 52; Milstein 2013: 438). In the Psalms, situations of human distress are often depicted with the help of bird-fowler-trap imagery (Pss 91:3; 119:110; 124:7; 140:6 [Eng. v. 5]; 141:9). Hence, informed listeners/readers might identify with the bird and ask whether they are themselves about to be trapped by some enemy—perhaps even by YHWH and/or by this piece of prophetic rhetoric.

3:6. On the syntactic level, one may note that v. 6 contains conditional questions introduced by *ʾim* ("if"), in contrast to the preceding series of questions marked by *hă* (vv. 3–5). This formal switch coincides with a change in topic and tone. Here in v. 6, this series of didactic questions reaches its first climax (Wolff 1977: 186; Möller 2003a: 229–30). The vague sense of threat associated with the lion and trap motifs (vv. 4–5) is heightened, as v. 6a depicts a scene closer to home, from the point of view of the addressees. The shofar, an instrument made of a ram's horn, was used as an alarm signal in various situations of acute danger. Hence, it is not possible to decide whether this utterance refers to a particular kind of "evil" (*rāʿâ*) or catastrophe that might befall a city. Also in this case (cf. v. 5), one and the same event appears to be viewed from two different angles. Whereas v. 6a focuses on the immediate effect of the disaster, namely, panic among the population, v. 6b concentrates on the ultimate cause of the calamity.

If the rhetorical question in v. 6b is transformed into a statement, it appears to say that each time a city is struck by a disaster one may infer that YHWH has been actively involved—that he "has caused it (or, has acted)" (*ʿāśâ*, v. 6bβ). In some respects, though, the interpretation of v. 6b is a matter of dispute. It is thus uncertain how the first addressees were expected to react to the underlying idea that YHWH was the instigator of all catastrophes. Until recently, commentators have often assumed that v. 6b merely expresses an opinion that was widely accepted at the text's time of origin (see the examples cited by Lindström 1983: 201). However, as shown by Lindström, it is a misconception that the biblical authors and their audience shared a strong belief in divine "pancausality" (1983: 208–9). According to other passages in the book of Amos

(5:18–20; 6:1–7, 13–14), the main problem (from the prophet's/author's point of view) seems rather to have been the unfounded optimism of the people and their leaders, which made them unwilling or unable to understand that their national patron deity might turn against them and destroy them. Therefore, I find it unlikely that it was regarded as an indisputable truth that all disasters were caused by YHWH.

Against that background, I suggest that v. 6b should be read as a bold affirmation of a "truth" that was far from self-evident, namely, that calamity in a city cannot occur unless it has somehow been caused (or condoned) by YHWH. Indeed, the rhetorical question in v. 6b seems to have been designed to persuade the addressees to accept a provocative and unsettling perspective. It leaves listeners/readers with only two options: (1) to accept the implied statement or (2) to deny the notion of divine agency in the context of disasters altogether. Whereas the second option would indicate that YHWH was aloof and inactive, the first might imply that the deity had destructive intentions.

Within its literary context, v. 6 foreshadows all the ensuing announcements of impending disasters that will befall the cities of Israel (see, e.g., 3:9–15; 4:1–3; 5:3; 6:8–11). In a narrower sense, it prepares the reader for 3:9–13, a passage containing threats against one specific city, Samaria.

3:7. The utterance in v. 7 is commonly, and probably correctly, regarded as a secondary insertion into the rhetorical unit encompassing 3:3–8.[3] There are several reasons for this scholarly supposition (see Auld 1986: 30–31). First, v. 7 is written in prose, whereas the remainder of 3:3–8 consists of poetic utterances. Second, and more specifically, this prosaic saying abruptly interrupts the chain of rhetorical questions. Third, v. 7 discontinues the otherwise consistent focus on matters relating to cause and effect, or observation and implication. Finally, and perhaps most important, there is a strong tension between the message conveyed by this utterance and the implicit statements made by the immediately surrounding verses. Auld describes the rather awkward position of v. 7 within 3:3–8 thus: "Far from offering a rhetorical enhancement, it actually appears to do violence to the argument of the whole section" (1986: 31). Nonetheless, this utterance is part of the text as we now have it; hence, it is necessary to determine its function within its immediate literary context.

I find it likely that v. 7 was inserted for theological reasons, in order to correct or modify certain views expressed in (or, implied by) vv. 6 and 8. According to v. 6, calamities sent by YHWH may occur in a city, apparently without any previous notice. In v. 7, on the other hand, we learn that the deity "does nothing without disclosing his plan (sôdô) to his servants the prophets ('ăbādāyw hannĕbî'îm)." Having been informed in advance, the prophets would, in their turn, be able to inform the people, thus giving them a chance to repent. Arguably, v. 7 was inserted in order to make the portrayal of YHWH less harsh and capricious. Emphasizing that YHWH would never send disasters without warning his people through prophetic messages, this utterance manages to exonerate the deity. Joseph Blenkinsopp has suggested that "the stricken city is Jerusalem" and that v. 7 "places the blame [for that disaster] where it belongs: with the people and their rulers" (2014: 131).

In addition, v. 7 apparently seeks to prevent a possible interpretation of v. 8: that (given the right circumstances) anyone could act as a prophet (with Auld 1991: 3). According to v. 8 (see below), a person is compelled to prophesy when YHWH speaks to him or her. This stands in sharp contrast to v. 7, which speaks of "the prophets" as a confined and elevated group endowed with an honorary title ("servants" of YHWH) and enjoying privileged access to YHWH's council (*sôd*, cf. Jer 23:18, 22). Here, the ancient idea that prophets may overhear the deliberations in the heavenly council (1 Kgs 22:19–23; Isa 6:1–8) has been fused with terminology linked to the ideal that true prophets ought to be like Moses. Since the prophetic designation "servant(s)" is unique within the book of Amos, but common in the book of Jeremiah (7:25; 25:4; 26:5; 29:19; 35:15; 44:4) and in 2 Kings (17:13, 23; 21:10; 24:2), it is reasonable to assume that 3:7 was added by an editor who was inspired by Deuteronomistic theology (W. H. Schmidt 1965: 183–85; Jeremias 1998: 54).

3:8. In v. 8, the passage reaches its final focal point, which can be described as a second climax. If one allows for the possibility that a text such as this, which is characterized by gradually heightened intensity, may contain more than one rhetorical peak, there is no compelling reason, as far as I can see, to regard v. 8 as a secondary addition (so Lindström 1983: 203–4 and Aurelius 2006: 329–30, n. 4). Again, a change on the level of content is signaled by a syntactic shift (cf. Wolff 1977: 183). In this utterance, two short statements are followed by questions starting with *mî lōʾ*, "who (will/ would) not?" In v. 8a, central aspects of the preceding argumentation, in vv. 4–6, have been concentrated in a few words: "The lion has roared. Who is not frightened?" Here the motif of the roaring lion recurs (v. 4), but it merges with the depiction of the fear aroused by the sound of the trumpet (v. 6a). Because v. 8b is formally constructed as an exact parallel to v. 8a, an intuitive analogy is created. It is suggested that the two processes described are similar in some significant way: the effect of the lion's roar, which induces fear among humans (v. 8a), and the effect of YHWH's speech, which is said to incite (or compel) humans to prophesy (v. 8b).

This analogy evokes a number of potentially disturbing associations. To begin with, prophecy would seem to be linked to fear. Further, the reader may be inclined to interpret the roaring lion as a metaphorical portrayal of YHWH. In that case, since a lion would not roar unless it had taken prey (v. 4), the question arises: Who is the victim? In the light of the exodus theme in 3:1–2, as well as the possibility of reading 3:3 allegorically, Israel is a likely candidate. Alternatively, YHWH's partner/prey could be the one mentioned in v. 8b, namely, the prophet (Milstein 2013: 437–38, 440). Indeed, the very juxtaposition of vv. 8a and 8b appears to link the role of the prophet to the destructive and terrifying aspects of the deity (Jeremias 1998: 54). It is important to keep in mind, however, that such meanings and messages are, at the most, suggested by the text.

What v. 8 actually implies (by means of rhetorical questions) is that one may speak of an adequate human response in both situations described. When a lion roars, one should be afraid. Likewise, when YHWH speaks, one should prophesy. To a certain extent, the utterance in 3:8 seems to serve the same legitimizing function as a prophetic call narrative (Milstein 2013: 432–33; see also Möller 2003a: 231–33). One may further note that whereas v. 8b is clearly at odds with v. 7 (see above), its depiction of prophetic experience is perfectly consistent with the way authentic prophetic activity is understood in 7:10–17 (cf. Mittmann 1971: 145). What matters, according to this perspective, is a personal call experience (7:15), not membership in a certain guild (7:14). One may add the observation that the extended series of rhetorical questions ends on a self-referential note, since the concluding example (in v. 8b) illustrates the process that allegedly preceded the prophetic messages recorded in the book of Amos (see further Linville 2008: 75).

Oracles against Samaria and Bethel (3:9–15)

3 ⁹Proclaim over the fortresses in Ashdod, and the fortresses in the land of Egypt, saying: "Gather on the mountains of Samaria!
See the great tumult inside the city and the oppression in its midst!"
¹⁰For they do not know how to do what is right, says YHWH,
those who store up violence and devastation in their fortresses.
¹¹Therefore, thus says the Lord YHWH:
An enemy will surround the land.
He will tear down your strongholds, and your fortresses will be plundered.
   ¹²Thus says YHWH:
Just as a shepherd rescues from the lion's mouth
only a couple of bones or a piece of an ear,
so will the Israelites living in Samaria be rescued:
only a corner of a bed, and a piece of a couch.
   ¹³Listen and warn the house of Jacob,
says the Lord, YHWH, the God of hosts:
¹⁴When I deal with the misdeeds of Israel,
I will deal with the altars of Bethel.
The horns of the altar will be cut off and fall to the ground.
¹⁵I will demolish the winter house along with the summer house.
The ivory houses will be ruined, and many houses will come to an end, says YHWH.

INTRODUCTION TO 3:9–15

Within the section 3:9–15, which contains oracles of doom concerning two cities of major political and religious significance, Samaria and Bethel, it is possible to make the following subdivisions: vv. 9–11 // v. 12 // vv. 13–15 (thus also, e.g., Mays 1969: 62–71, Wolff 1977: 189–202, and Sweeney 2000: 221–24).

   Arguably, 3:9–11 constitutes a clearly demarcated unit. This passage is opened by an imperative form of the verb *šāmaʿ*, "Proclaim!" (Hiphil; cf. Qal of the same verb in 3:1; 4:1; 5:1), and it is concluded by an announcement of judgment (v. 11) introduced by *lākēn,* "therefore" (cf. 4:12; 6:7; see further Snyman 1995: 32). On the macro level, I suggest, 3:9–11 can be read as a postponed divine verdict against the cities and fortifications of Israel. In the cycle of oracles against the nations (1:3–2:16), the refrain-like formula "I will send fire . . . and it will consume the/its fortresses (*ʾarmĕnôt/ĕhā*)" (1:4, 7, 10, 14; 2:2, 5) was missing only in one instance, namely, in the Israel pericope (2:6–16). Notably, one of the most conspicuous features of 3:9–11 is the fourfold repetition of the motif of "fortresses," or "palaces" (*ʾarmĕnôt*). However, a subtle shift has occurred. Destruction by fire is not explicitly mentioned in 3:9–11. Concerning the fate of the fortresses in Samaria, it is declared that they are going to be plundered (3:11).

   Because of its focus on the destruction of Samaria as an event sanctioned by YHWH, the prophecy in 3:9–11 probably formed part of the first version of the book of Amos, in the late eighth or the early seventh century B.C.E. The same holds for the oracle that has been preserved in 3:12. I find it likely that this satirical simile goes back to an oral performance by a prophet (perhaps named Amos) in the 730s or 720s.

Although 3:13–15 now seems to constitute the last unit within 3:9–15, it is unlikely that this passage should be regarded as an originally unified prophecy of disaster. I argue below that vv. 13–14 should be ascribed to a postmonarchic redaction (with Jeremias 1998: 61–63 and Fleischer 2001: 174–76). Whereas v. 15 seems to continue the depiction of demolition occurring in Samaria (3:11, 12), as if nothing had happened in between, the insertion in 3:13–14 shifts the focus from Samaria to Bethel and from political-economic issues to the cultic-religious sphere. In addition, it is possible to discern a shift of perspective in vv. 13–14. Rather than being the central topic of the discourse, the fate of the Northern Kingdom is here used as a warning example for a later generation, presumably in Judah.

NOTES

3:9. *fortresses.* Or "palaces" (*ʾarmĕnôt*). This alternative is applicable in vv. 10 and 11, as well.

Ashdod. According to the LXX, the message should be proclaimed among the Assyrians (ἐν Ἀσσυρίοις), not to the (Philistine) population in Ashdod. The LXX version can be explained as an attempt to create a better balance in the text, since both Assyria and Egypt were great empires and were mentioned in parallel in other prophetic texts (e.g., Hos 9:3). The difference between בְּאַשְׁדּוֹד (*bᵉʾšdwd*) and בְּאַשּׁוּר (*bᵉʾšwr*) is not great, especially considering the well-attested d/r (ד/ ר) confusion in the history of textual transmission. For the following reasons, I suggest that the MT's *bᵉʾšdwd* ("in Ashdod") should be given precedence. This reading can, to begin with, be regarded as *lectio difficilior;* moreover, it is supported by the Targum. Finally, as argued in the Comments on 3:9, a reference to Ashdod makes excellent sense in the literary context.

3:11. *An enemy.* With most modern interpreters I find it likely that the Hebrew lexeme *ṣar* here carries the sense of "adversary, enemy." Evidently, this utterance describes a military invasion. Several ancient translations reflect an alternative lexical sense, namely, "distress" (see Wolff 1977: 190–91 and Paul 1991: 118). Through a deviating (and obviously erroneous) vocalization of צר (*ṣr*), the LXX managed to transform v. 11 into yet another oracle against Tyre (*ṣōr,* cf. 1:9–10).

will surround. It would have been possible to retain the MT's noun phrase, *ṣar ûsābîb,* and render it by "an enemy, and (he will be) surrounding," or the like. However, with several other commentators (e.g., Stuart 1987: 328 and Paul 1991: 118), I prefer making a slight emendation, reading יְסוֹבֵב ("he will surround") instead of וּסְבִיב, with support from the Vulgate (*circumietur*) (cf. also the Peshitta). Since the consonants ו (waw) and י (yod) were easily confused in the transmission of Hebrew manuscripts, the MT might be the result of a scribal mistake.

3:12. *a piece.* The interpretation of *ûbidmešeq* is a famous crux. It has to be admitted that the translation "a piece (of a couch)" is based on guesswork. However, in light of the parallel phrase, *bipʾat miṭṭâ,* "the corner of a bed," such a rendering fits the context much better than a reference to Damascus (thus the LXX, which locates the event described in Damascus, and the Vulgate, which imagines a Damascene bed). Possibly, there once existed a noun *dĕmešeq* that denoted some part of a couch (see *DCH*, s.v.). Alternatively, the text is corrupt. Several emendations have been suggested. According to Gese, the text originally contained the word pair *ʾmšt—pʾh* (Hebrew equivalents of the Akkadian word pair *pūtu—amartu/amaštu*), designating the two opposite ends of a bed (1962: 427–32; see also Mittmann 1976: 152–58, who advocates the conjecture *dabbešet*). In my opinion, the most promising attempts to address the crux have been made by Rabinowitz (1961) and Zalcman (2002). What they have in common is the idea that the first three consonants of the MT ובדמשק are to be read as *ûbad*, "and a part." Whereas Rabinowitz reconstructed the phrase *ûbad miššōq ʿāreš* ("a piece out of the leg of a bed"), Zalcman presented the following emendation, *ûbad mešî qārûaʿ* ("and torn fine fabric"), which he hoped would settle the issue. However, the scholarly debate will probably continue.

3:15. *many houses.* The Hebrew *bāttîm rabbîm* could also be taken to mean "great houses" (so Paul 1991: 126–27). The translation here ("many houses"), which would seem to make even better sense in a climactic statement such as this (thus also Wolff 1977: 199), is supported by the LXX and the Vulgate.

come to an end. I am reading *wĕsāpû* as a form of the verb סוף (*swp*, "to come to an end, perish"), rather than ספה (*sph*, usually with an active sense in Qal, "to sweep away").

COMMENTS

3:9. This passage begins with a small mystery. Who are the addressees in v. 9a? Apparently, a completely fictive scenario has been constructed for rhetorical purposes (Fleischer 2001: 171). Anonymous and unidentified heralds are given instructions (cf. Isa 40:1–2 and Jer 50:2) to proclaim their message so that it is heard in the fortresses of foreign countries: in Ashdod and in Egypt.

A single Philistine city, Ashdod, is here mentioned together with an entire nation, Egypt. Apparently, such an asymmetrical combination was seen as problematic by the Septuagint translator (who read Assyria instead of Ashdod); however, the reference to Ashdod makes excellent sense both within 3:9–11 and in relation to the wider context. Several scholars have noted the assonance between *ʾašdôd* and *šōd* ("violence") in v. 10b (see, e.g., Harper 1905: 76). Indeed, as noted by Paul (1991: 116–17), the author's choice of precisely these two locations was probably dictated by a desire to create an effect of paronomasia, because there is also a striking resemblance between *miṣrāyim* (Egypt, v. 9a) and the expression *hāʾ ōṣěrîm* ("those who store up") in v. 10b. One may add the observation that these two geographical names create connections between 3:9–11 and preceding passages. Whereas Ashdod provides a link to the OAN cycle (1:8), the mention of Egypt recalls the references to the exodus tradition in 2:10 and 3:1–2.

According to v. 9b, the mission of the heralds is to deliver a peculiar invitation to the Ashdodites (that is, the Philistines) and the Egyptians. They shall be summoned to gather as spectators on the mountains surrounding Samaria in order to witness "the great tumult (*mĕhûmōt*) inside the city and the oppression (*waʿăšûqîm*) in its midst" (v. 9bβγ). Clearly, Samaria is depicted as the very opposite of an ideal and idyllic city: Instead of order, there is tumult; instead of justice, oppression has prevailed. But why are these two foreign nations called as witnesses? It has been suggested that *two* nations are invited, because the law required (at least) two witnesses in a case of capital offense (Hayes 1988: 127–28; see Deut 17:6; 1 Kgs 21:10). This might be part of the answer, but it remains to explain why two *nations* are summoned—and why exactly these two: Philistia and Egypt.

Previously, in chapters 1–2, the structural arrangement of the series of oracles indicated that Israel was as culpable and worthy of condemnation as the neighboring nations. Here, in 3:9, a similar point is made, as international guests are invited to witness the crimes committed in Samaria. I suggest that the Egyptians and the Philistines were picked out because they were regarded as Israel's archenemies par excellence. According to the narratives in the Pentateuch and the Deuteronomistic History, these two nations enslaved and/or tyrannized the ancestors of the Israelites (see Exodus 1–15; Judges 13–16; 1 Samuel 4–18). It is likely that the author and the first readers of Amos 3:9–11 were acquainted with these traditions (in some version or other). Thus, the irony is unmistakable, as the utterance in v. 9 implies that observers coming from Ashdod and Egypt will be shocked by the violence and corruption displayed in Israel's capital. Apparently, the point made is that the Israelites had become just like (or, even worse than) their worst enemies. With regard to the exodus tradition, it would seem as though "the oppressed were redeemed from oppression only to become oppressors themselves" (Snyman 1995: 35).

3:10. According to v. 10a, the inhabitants in Samaria are (without exception?) incapable of ethical conduct. This situation is described in terms of a lack of knowledge, perhaps implying that basic moral principles were not being taught: "they do not know how to do what is right" (v. 10a; cf. similarly Hos 4:6). This accusation sounds rather vague and sweeping, but it is followed, in v. 10b, by a charge that appears to target the ruling classes. Only they would be able to store things in fortresses (ʾarmĕnôt). Processes of corruption and economic exploitation are here described with the help of a rhetorically efficient metonymy. Thus, it is stated that the rich in Samaria "store up violence and devastation (ḥāmās wāšōd) in their fortresses" (v. 10b). I suggest that this should be interpreted as a reference to the violent methods used in order to expropriate money and goods from the poor (with Jeremias 1998: 58). At the same time, this highly condensed expression implies that treasures collected by such means are of no avail. In the end, they may bring "violence and devastation" on their (illegitimate) owners (cf. Möller 2003a: 237).

3:11. In v. 11 it is announced that the divine punishment for these crimes will be carried out by a foreign army, in a military operation with three discernible stages (with Mays 1969: 65). A large-scale invasion of the country (v. 11aβ) is followed by massive destruction of vital fortifications (v. 11bα), and then the successful attack culminates in plundering (v. 11bβ). Notably, poetic justice is achieved, as the treasuries in the fortresses (ʾarmĕnôt), allegedly filled with goods acquired through robbery (see v. 10b), are robbed by the invaders.

Although Assyria is not mentioned by name, it is reasonable to assume that this utterance refers to the Assyrian siege, conquest, and looting of Samaria in 722 B.C.E.— either in anticipation or (perhaps more likely) in retrospect.

3:12. As noted above, the section 3:9–15 contains a cluster of oracles that are held together by a common focus on divinely decreed destruction of the political and cultic centers of Israel: Samaria and Bethel. In its present position, the prophecy recorded in

3:12 appears to elaborate further on the hostile (Assyrian?) attack on Samaria, which was prefigured by v. 11. Originally, however, this utterance may have referred to some other kind of catastrophe, such as an earthquake. On the literary level, the lion theme recurs in v. 12a (cf. 3:4, 8), in combination with the shepherd theme (cf. 1:2).

Using subtle irony, v. 12 describes an almost total destruction in terms of rescue (albeit of minimal proportions). The first part of the utterance consists of a simile drawn from the domain of shepherding (v. 12a). An animal has been torn by a lion, but the shepherd manages to rescue (Hiphil of *nṣl*) some parts of it by snatching them from the lion's mouth. According to v. 12bα, this simile indicates how the inhabitants of Samaria are going to "be rescued" (Niphal of *nṣl*).

It would be misguided to interpret this as a hopeful prophecy, promising that a minority among the population will actually be saved. On closer examination, the point made by the simile is a sinister one. Clearly, one has to infer that the lion's prey died. Despite the heroic deed of the shepherd (cf. 1 Sam 17:34–35), the life of the lamb could not be saved. But why risk one's own life for a couple of bones from a dead animal? Most likely, the shepherd intended to use the remains that he could "rescue" from the lion, "a couple of bones or a piece of an ear" (12aβ), as proof of what had happened (with, e.g., Pfeifer 1988b: 271). If an animal in a flock was lost, the shepherd was held economically responsible. Hence, in a case such as this, when a sheep had been killed by a lion, the shepherd would need to produce evidence in support of the story (see Exod 22:9–12). A parallel is provided by one of the episodes in the Joseph story, recounted in Gen 37:29–36. In order to substantiate their claim that Joseph had been devoured by an animal, the brothers took his mantle, which they had dipped in blood, to his father. Confronted with this (alleged) piece of evidence, Jacob was struck by grief. Arguably, then, 3:12 depicts a tragedy.

Unfortunately, the interpretation of the concluding part of this utterance, v. 12bβ, is hampered by the occurrence of an obscure word, *děmešeq* (see the Notes). In addition, the syntactic connection between 12bα and 12bβ is somewhat opaque. The translation here is based on two presuppositions: (1) that the last clause of this utterance contains two parallel phrases, both referring to parts of furniture, and (2) that this is a case of *bě essentiae*, where the preposition indicates the nature or extent of the activity described (Rabinowitz 1961: 229). Arguably, this reading is the one that makes best sense in the context.

The interpretive key lies in recognizing that one and the same scenario is depicted twice, in two structurally symmetrical statements—metaphorically first, in v. 12a, and then literally, in v. 12b.[4] Since it is stated that the inhabitants of Samaria will be "rescued" in the same way as the sheep that was attacked (and killed!) by a lion, it is reasonable to assume that the pieces of furniture mentioned in v. 12bβ correspond precisely to the pieces of the killed animal (v. 12aβ) with regard to their function (with Pfeifer 1988: 271–73 and Möller 2003a: 239).

Thus interpreted, 3:12 conveys the message that whatever remains of the city of Samaria after the impending catastrophe will primarily serve as proof of the massive destruction (with Mays 1969: 67). To this one may add the observation that the lexemes *miṭṭâ*, "bed," and *ʿereś*, "couch, divan," occur also in 6:4, in the context of a description of the extravagant life of the rich and powerful elite in Samaria. Interestingly, extant archaeological and iconographic remains from the ancient Near East show that luxurious beds were sometimes decorated with ornamentation featuring lions and other animals (see Mittmann 1976: 159–67).

3:13. Evidently, a new unit begins in v. 13. This utterance is introduced by the imperative *šimʿû* ("Listen"), which elsewhere serves to mark the beginning of a new section (3.1; 4:1; 5:1). Moreover, v. 13 contains a renewed assurance that this is an oracle from YHWH (cf. vv. 11 and 12, which have the messenger formula *kōh ʾāmar yhwh*, "thus says YHWH"). Notably, the expanded authentication formula employed, *nĕʾum ʾădōnāy yhwh ʾĕlōhê haṣṣĕbāʾôt*, "says the Lord, YHWH, the God of hosts" (v. 13b), is unique within the Hebrew Bible (but cf. Amos 6:14).

In v. 13a, the unspecified addressees are admonished to listen as well as to "warn the house of Jacob (*wĕhāʿîdû bĕbêt yaʿăqōb*)."[5] The terminology used is typical of the Deuteronomistic History. As regards the connotations of the expression *ʿwd* (Hiphil) + *bĕ* ("to warn"), a text such as 2 Kgs 17:13 is revealing (cf. also 17:15). It explains that the fall of the Northern Kingdom had been preceded by warnings (Hiphil of *ʿwd* + *bĕ*) issued by the prophets (addressing both Israel and Judah). When it comes to the use of the designation "house of Jacob" in v. 13, the fact that it occurs frequently in exilic or postexilic texts (e.g., Isa 2:5; 14:1; 46:3; 48:1; Obad 1:17–18; see also Amos 9:8!) is a strong indication that it does not refer to the kingdom of Israel, which ceased to exist in 722 B.C.E. Rather, it denotes the postmonarchic (largely Judean) community of YHWH worshipers (see Jeremias 1998: 62). They are the ones who should take warning from the event described in v. 14, the destruction of the sanctuary in Bethel.

3:14. The opening words of v. 14, *kî bĕyôm poqdî* ("when I deal with" or, "on the day when I call to account"), recall 3:2, where the verb *pqd* is used in a similar way (see the Comments on 3:2). Hence, it is possible to read v. 14 as a description of the (partial?) fulfillment of something that was hinted at in 3:2, namely, a coming day of reckoning, when YHWH will punish the Israelites for all their sins and crimes. This impression is strengthened by the fact that *pqd* recurs in v. 14bα, where it is declared that "the altars (plural!) of Bethel" will become the primary target of YHWH's punitive actions.[6]

In the next clause, one particular and significant aspect of the demolition is foregrounded: "The horns of the altar will be cut off" (v. 14bβ). Breaking off the four "horns" at the corners would certainly have a desecrating effect (King 1988: 103–4). Evidently, the sacrificial cult would have to be discontinued. As a further consequence of this act of destruction, the temple in Bethel would lose its function of asylum because it would not be possible to grasp the horns of the altar in order to escape one's persecutors (cf. 1 Kgs 1:50–53; 2:28–29). To sum up, the destructive act described in v. 14b would be of great symbolic and practical significance, since it would mean that the sanctuary no longer could provide "immunity, and expiation for the people" (Paul 1991: 124).

According to the well-known account in 2 Kings 23 (vv. 15–18), King Josiah demolished the main altar at Bethel, as he desecrated this cultic site in the 620s B.C.E. For the addressees of Amos 3:13–14, I suggest, this event (or, this legendary account) belonged to the past. Judging from the introductory exhortation in v. 13 ("Listen and warn"), they are encouraged to learn from Bethel's fate. Arguably, this would mean avoiding involvement in (allegedly) illegitimate cultic practices. It is worth noting that Bethel appears to have regained importance as a cultic site in the sixth century B.C.E., subsequent to the destruction of the temple in Jerusalem (see Blenkinsopp 2003). In that historical context, the words of Amos 3:13–14 could have served as a concrete warning (together with the utterances in 4:4–5 and 5:4–5): Do not favor Bethel over against Jerusalem!

3:15. As argued above, several factors indicate that vv. 13–14 were inserted at a relatively late stage. Hence it is possible, but far from certain, that v. 15 originally followed directly after v. 12 (thus Jeremias 1998: 59–60 and Fleischer 2001: 173–74). Within the text as we now have it, the transition from v. 14 to v. 15 is characterized by both continuity and discontinuity. Generally speaking, the passage 3:13–15 is held together by the topic "destruction of edifices"; however, the focus of attention has suddenly changed from cultic installations (v. 14) to private mansions.

Notably, the lexeme *bayit* ("house") is used in divergent ways in these two utterances. In v. 14, this word refers to groups and places, such as "the house of Jacob" and Beth-El ("the house of El"). In v. 15, on the other hand, where *bayit* occurs four times, it consistently denotes concrete buildings, which are destined for destruction. Some of these houses are described as luxurious (see below). Furthermore, the phrase "many houses" in v. 15b implies that this demolition would happen in a city with a large population. Most likely, then, this utterance refers to the capital of Israel, Samaria (cf. v. 12). However, it is not possible to determine whether the author had an earthquake or a military attack in mind.

According to the opening clause, YHWH will "demolish the winter house along with the summer house" (v. 15a). Clearly, only the upper classes could afford the luxury of owning two houses—one for the summer and another for the winter. For the interpretation of the text it matters less whether this refers to two adjacent buildings (Hayes 1988: 136) or to two dwellings in different locations, for instance in Samaria and in the Jordan valley (Sweeney 2000: 224). Given the extant textual evidence, including the Hebrew Bible (1 Kgs 21:1, 18; Jer 36:22) and inscriptions from the ancient Near East, it was above all a royal privilege to possess separate summer and winter houses (or, palaces; see King 1988: 64–65). The impression that this utterance primarily targets the rich elite in Samaria is confirmed by the reference to "ivory houses (*bāttê haššēn*)" in 15bα. Arguably, only the richest among the population would have the means to decorate their homes with ivory (cf. 6:4). It is worth noting that some exquisite ivory plaques and hundreds of ivory fragments have been unearthed during the archaeological excavations conducted at Samaria (see King 1988: 145 and Jaruzelska 1998: 79–82).

A final note on v. 15 may be added. Although it might be a coincidence, this observation still deserves some attention. The word *qayiṣ* ("summer") recurs in 8:1–2, in the context of a vision report that revolves around a wordplay: *qayiṣ* "summer/harvest"—*qēṣ* "end." I suggest that such an assonance-association might be intended also here, in 3:15, indicating that the end (*qēṣ*) has come for the summer (*qayiṣ*) houses (with Linville 2008: 79).

Concerning the Wealthy Women in Samaria (4:1–3)

4   ¹Listen to this word, O cows of Bashan on Mount Samaria,
who oppress the poor and crush the needy,
while saying to their masters: "Bring us something to drink!"
²The Lord YHWH swears by his holiness:
Behold, days are coming upon you

when they will carry you away with hooks,
and the remainder of you with harpoons.
³Through the breaches you will depart, every woman straight ahead,
and you will be thrown out toward Hermon, says YHWH.

INTRODUCTION TO 4:1–3

Despite the fact that the formulaic exhortation "Listen to this word (*šimʿû haddābār hazzeh*)" in 4:1a would seem to signal the beginning of a new major section (cf. 3:1 and 5:1), it is possible to read the unit 4:1–3 as a direct continuation of the preceding passage, 3:9–15. The topic of divine judgment over Samaria is developed, as the focus shifts from the houses (3:15) to their inhabitants. In 4:1 we are allowed a glimpse of daily life in Samaria before 722 B.C.E., as the prophet/author imagined it. The remainder of this prophecy, 4:2–3, depicts the deportation of Samaria's population. Hence, there can be no doubt that the imminent disaster is envisioned as a military attack. According to 4:1, the crimes that (allegedly) motivated such punishment were related to systematic oppression of the poor (see 2:6–8; 3:9–10; 5:10–12). Since this text is devoid of unambiguously cultic references or allusions, I see no reason to interpret the bovine imagery (in v. 1a) as indicating that it also (or primarily) denounces participation in an "idolatrous" fertility cult (so Barstad 1975; 1984: 37–47; see also Jacobs 1985).

In one respect at least, the passage 4:1–3 is unique, not only within the book of Amos, but within the entire corpus of prophetic literature in the Hebrew Bible: The addressees of this oracle are female. To be more precise, these words appear to be directed against women belonging to the wealthy and powerful elite in Samaria. In terms of content and perspective, the oracles in Isa 3:16–4:1 may provide a parallel, but there, the women in Jerusalem are not addressed directly. I suggest that it is because of the exceptional character of Amos 4:1–3 that some commentators have denied the obvious, namely, that women are being addressed. According to an interpretive tradition going back to Jerome, this prophecy is instead about men who are metaphorically (and pejoratively) portrayed as women (see further Irwin 2012: 232).

With the majority of modern scholars, I treat 4:1–3 as an oracle concerning primarily (albeit not exclusively) the wealthy women in Samaria. As regards the time of origin, I suggest the final decades of the eighth century B.C.E. Nothing in the content or the phraseology of this prophecy indicates a later date.

NOTES

4:1. *their masters.* The masculine plural suffix in לאדניהם (*laʾădōnêhem*, "to their masters") has often been seen as problematic. On the assumption that this expression refers to the women's husbands, one might have expected a feminine suffix (so BHSapp), and preferably in the second-person plural (thus the Vulgate). However, such irregular (or, inclusive) use of masculine pronouns for feminine nouns is not uncommon in biblical Hebrew (see *GKC* §135o and McLaughlin 2001: 111). One may add the observation that if the MT is retained, *ʾădōnêhem* can be interpreted either as "their husbands" or as "their lords"—that is, the masters of the poor and needy (Fleischer 1989: 82). In other words, the referent of the suffix ("their") changes with the nuance. I chose the rendering "their masters" in order to reflect this interesting ambiguity.

4:2. *upon you.* The MT has a second-person masculine plural suffix (-*kem*), implying that the punishment will affect both men and women. In the LXX, on the other hand, the pronouns in 2aβ and 2b are consistently feminine.

with hooks. The interpretation of *běṣinnôt* is a matter of dispute. What kind of instrument is being used in order to carry away the addressees? The main options are: (1) "shields" (plural of *ṣinnâ;* thus the Targum and Aquila; cf. also the LXX, ἐν ὅπλοις, and the Vulgate, *in contis*); (2) "baskets" (cf. Aramaic *ṣnʾ*), as argued by Paul (1978: 185–90 and 1991: 132–35); (3) "ropes," a suggestion made by S. J. Schwantes (1967) with reference to Akkadian *ṣinnatu* and *ṣerretu* (thus also Wolff 1977: 206–7); and (4) "hooks," analyzing *ṣinnôt* as an unusual plural form of *ṣēn,* "thorn" (cf. Prov 22:5; so already Ibn Ezra; see Paul 1991: 131). The third alternative seems to be based on weak arguments (see Paul 1978: 184–85; 1991: 131). It is more difficult to choose between the remaining three on purely linguistic grounds. With regard to the literary context, I prefer the rendering "hooks" (with, e.g., Maag 1951: 190, Rudolph 1971: 161, Williams 1979: 208, and Jeremias 1998: 65, n. 31).

with harpoons. The expression *běsîrôt dûgâ* can be interpreted in two different ways, depending on whether *sîrôt* is taken as a plural form of *sîr,* "pot," or a plural form of a homonym with the sense "thorn" (see, e.g., Isa 34:13). In the scholarly literature, the following translations have been suggested: "fisherman's pots" (Paul 1978: 188–90, 1991: 133–35; cf. the LXX), "fish hooks" (Harper 1905: 87; Williams 1979: 208–9), and "harpoons" (Wolff 1977: 207; Jeremias 1998: 56, 65). I chose the latter here because it seems to provide a fitting parallel to *ṣinnôt,* "hooks."

4:3. *Through the breaches.* Although the English preposition "through" lacks a correspondence in the MT, it is necessary to include it in the translation (see, e.g., the Vulgate).

every woman straight ahead. Or, more idiomatically, "each one straight ahead" (NRSV). Such a translation, however, would conceal the fact that *ʾiššâ negdāh* represents a distinctly feminine variant of the phrase *ʾîš negdô* (Josh 6:5, 20).

you will be thrown. I am reading a Hophal form, instead of the MT's Hiphil, which requires a change of vowels in והשלכתנה. This slight emendation, which is supported by the LXX, has been adopted by most modern commentators.

Hermon. It is not possible to link ההרמונה in the MT to any known geographical location spelled *hrmwn* and pronounced "Harmon" (despite the attempt made by Freedman and Andersen 1970). Hence, this might be a case of textual corruption. Some of the ancient versions reflect a different word division, with הר (*har* = "mountain") followed by a place name. Whereas Remman (LXX) is otherwise unknown and a reference to Armenia (Symmachos) is unlikely, it is intriguing that Aquila (ἕρμωνα) and the Vulgate (*Armon*) may point in the direction of Hermon. Possibly, an alternative *Vorlage* had ח, not ה, as its second consonant (cf. the Targum חורמני). Such a Hebrew text, החרמונה ("toward Hermon"), is in fact attested by three Kennicott and de Rossi manuscripts (see Gelston 2010: 81–82). Hence, the hypothesis that 4:3 originally referred to Hermon rests on a rather solid foundation. In addition, this reading makes excellent sense in the context (so also Koch et al. 1976b: 23, Wolff 1977: 207, and Jeremias 1998: 65).

COMMENTS

4:1. I find it likely that this oracle originally addressed rich and powerful women. Even so, it is evident that the text as we now have it is directed to a wider readership. Thus, it is introduced by a gender-inclusive (formally masculine) imperative, "Listen! (*šimʿû*)" (v. 1aα). In this way, the editor(s) underlined that the ensuing words were thought to convey a message of relevance for both men and women. Thereafter, the primary addressees are called "cows of Bashan on Mount Samaria" (v. 1aβ). Because the immediately following clause uses feminine participles as it accuses these addressees of oppressing the poor (v. 1aγ), one may safely deduce that "cows of Bashan" is a metaphorical expression used about women residing in Samaria.

Given other biblical references to cattle from Bashan, the cultural associations linked to this metaphor were predominantly positive. The Transjordan region named Bashan appears to have been renowned for its well-fed livestock (Deut 32:14; Jer 50:19; Ezek 39:18). According to a plausible interpretation of Ps 22:13 (Eng. v. 12), bulls of the Bashan breed were considered more impressive, and therefore more frightening, than other bulls. To this one may add the observation that animal names (such as *ʾabbîr*, "bull") are frequently used metaphorically in the Hebrew Bible as titles for political leaders (see, e.g., 1 Sam 21:8; Job 24:22) and in the texts from Ugarit (see Miller 1970). Hence, it is reasonable to assume that the designation "cows of Bashan" conveyed notions of wealth, strength, and power. Possibly, as indicated by the iconography of the Egyptian goddess Hathor, the use of cow imagery implied that these rich women were seen as beautiful, as well (see Irwin 2012: 236). To sum up, the metaphor in v. 1aβ would seem to be free from pejorative connotations.[7] Admittedly, the notion of cows from the plains grazing in the mountains is slightly ironic (Fleischer 2001: 176–77). Only in retrospect, however, in the light of the ensuing indictment (in v. 1aγ + 1b) and announcement of punishment (vv. 2–3), does this metaphor take on a satirical and ominous character.

According to v. 1aγ, these upper-class women were actively involved in oppressing impoverished people (see further Fleischer 1989: 88–92). But instead of offering any details concerning their methods, such as economic exploitation or other forms of repression, the concluding line of v. 1 illustrates their attitude, by reporting what they (allegedly) used to say to their masters (*laʾădōnêhem*): "Bring us something to drink!" (v. 1b).

It is important to notice that *ʾādôn* means "lord" or "superior," rather than only "husband," although this word could be used by a woman addressing her husband (see 1 Kgs 1:17). By means of this word choice, the utterance gains additional nuances of meaning. Thus, it is possible to interpret the expression *laʾădōnêhem* ("to their masters") as referring to the double role of the men addressed: They are the women's spouses, but they are also the masters or employers of the poor and oppressed (Fleischer 1989: 82; cf. Jeremias 1998: 64; see also the Notes). Apparently, these women are in the position to give orders to their husbands, but—presumably because they lack empathy with the needy—they use their influence for egotistic purposes only.

So far, scholarly attempts to find a deeper sense in this request have not yielded any convincing results. Barstad (1984: 42) has claimed that this is an allusion to syncretistic banquets, and Irwin has suggested that the women's disrespectful behavior toward their men threatened "to overturn the prevailing social structure that in ancient Israel was the primary means by which the vulnerable were protected" (Irwin 2012: 241, see further 239–46). In my opinion, it is preferable to take the request for drinks (of wine?) as an allusion to the lifestyle of the rich.

There are several points of contact between 4:1 and 6:4–7. Both passages condemn the habits and attitudes of the elite. Arguably, though, the fact that 4:1 highlights the role of the rich women in Samaria does not make this utterance misogynistic. Rather, it shows that the prophet/author "believed that women were accountable for ethical obligations similar to those incumbent upon men" (Sanderson 1998: 222). It is worth noting that the passage 4:1–3 does not include a depiction of public exposure, sexual violence, or any other motif associated with so-called prophetic pornography (cf. Isa 3:17, 24; 47:2–3; Ezek 16:35–40; Hos 2:4–5 [Eng. vv. 2–3]); therefore, it is deplorable that some scholarly comments on Amos 4:1 have male chauvinist overtones. A couple of examples may suffice.[8] Wolff refers to the wealthy women in Samaria as "an elegant lot of tyrannical and drink-happy ladies" (1977: 205), and Mays describes them as "pampered darlings of society," exerting their power "with sweet petulant nagging" (1969: 72). Such paraphrases are far removed from the Hebrew text, which describes these women as wealthy and powerful. They are not accused of nagging or excessive drinking, but of complicity in oppressing the poor.

4:2. The proclamation of punishment (in v. 2b) is preceded by a solemn divine oath (v. 2aα, cf. similarly 6:8) and the formula "days are coming" (v. 2aβ, cf. 8:11; 9:13), which is otherwise typical of the book of Jeremiah. I suggest that v. 2a can be seen as part of an editorial framework that spells out the general and gender-inclusive relevance of this oracle, with its emphasis on the role of the elite women in Samaria. A similar effect is created by the occurrence of a masculine pronominal suffix in v. 2bα, which implies that both men and women will be carried into exile (but cf. the LXX). In the remainder of the passage, however, comprising vv. 2bβ and 3, the grammatical forms are feminine.

There can be no doubt that v. 2b depicts deportation of Samaria's inhabitants: "they will carry you away" (2bα). When it comes to the details of this description, however, scholarly opinions differ widely. This is a corollary of the fact that it is impossible to identify with any certainty the instruments referred to by the expressions *běṣinnôt* and *běṣîrôt dûgâ* (see the Notes). It is sometimes assumed that the metaphor in v. 1a ("cows of Bashan") continues into v. 2 and that the inhabitants of Samaria are portrayed as cattle that are led away with the help of hooks and/or ropes (thus, e.g., Kleven 1996 and Jeremias 1998: 64–65). Arguably, however, the bovine imagery is dropped already in v. 1b. According to an alternative theory, the deportees are pictured as fish that have been caught and are carried in baskets and pots (thus Paul 1978: 188–90; 1991: 133–35).[9] It is indeed likely that the noun *dûgâ* belongs to the semantic field of fishing; nevertheless, such a transport of (dead or dying) fish strikes me as a rather awkward metaphor for the departure of the survivors in the city, "the remainder of you (*'aḥărîtken*)" (v. 2bβ).

In a case such as this it is probably prudent to abstain from interpretations based on speculations concerning implicit imagery of one type or another (see similarly Möller 2003a: 258–59). Granting that the disputed words in v. 2b denote hooks of some kind, this utterance can be read as a quite literal account of a deportation. As noted by Kleven, "the Assyrians would drive hooks into the faces of their captives and would drag them along by a rope" (1996: 225).

4:3. In v. 3a, the text again focuses on the fate of Samaria's women. Apparently, they are forced to depart in a straight line, one behind the other, through breaches in the city walls, presumably made by the invaders (with Möller 2003a: 259 and Garrett 2008: 113). In the ensuing clause the brutality of the deportation is foregrounded: "you will be thrown out" (v. 3bα).

Unfortunately, the geographical destination indicated by the MT's *haharmônâ* cannot be determined with certainty. In my opinion, the most likely candidate is Mount Hermon (thus also Wolff 1977: 207 and Jeremias 1998: 65). The reading "toward Hermon (*haḥermônâ*)" is supported by several textual witnesses (see the Notes). If this is correct, the passage 4:1–3 begins and ends with references to mountains. The wealthy women will, along with other survivors, be brought from "Mount Samaria" (v. 1a) to Hermon (v. 3b). Interestingly, Hermon is situated at the northern edge of the Bashan region. This might add an ironic twist (Mays 1969: 73). Finally, it is worth noting that the utterance in 4:3 seems to be in agreement with 5:27 ("beyond Damascus"), as regards the geographical direction. The deportees will be taken to the north, to Syria, and possibly even farther, to Assyria.

A Sarcastic Call to Transgress through Worship (4:4–5)

4 ⁴Come to Bethel and transgress, go to Gilgal and add to your transgressions!
Bring your sacrifices in the morning, your tithes on the third day;
⁵burn a thank-offering of leavened bread
and proclaim freewill offerings, make them known!
For you Israelites love to do so, says the Lord YHWH.

INTRODUCTION TO 4:4–5

Clearly, 4:4–5 constitutes a rhetorical unit (with Wolff 1977: 211 and Paul 1991: 138). A change of addressees seems to occur in v. 4, and a concluding formula appears at the end of v. 5. This passage is artistically composed, containing a series of seven imperatives (see Möller 2003a: 263). In terms of topic, the discourse returns to cultic issues. In terms of genre, 4:4–5 can be described as a parody of a priestly invitation to sacrificial worship (see below). As a consequence, this passage, with its implicit accusations, would seem to provide a kind of background to the proclamation in 3:14 concerning the destruction of altars in Bethel. Here, however, both Gilgal and Bethel are mentioned.

In the introduction to this commentary, the passage 4:4–5 was tentatively incorporated in my reconstruction of the book's first editorial stage; however, it is difficult to pinpoint the date of origin. As argued in more detail in the Comments below, such a vehement verbal attack on these two cultic sites, Bethel and Gilgal, would make sense both shortly before and a long time after the disaster of 722 B.C.E.

NOTES

4:5. *thank-offering.* The LXX translator read תורה (*tôrâ,* "law, instruction") instead of תודה (*tôdâ,* "thank-offering"). In this version, the topic of sacrifices is abruptly replaced by a depiction of public Torah reading: καὶ ἀνέγνωσαν ἔξω νόμον.

leavened bread. Literally, "of that which is leavened" (*mēḥāmēṣ*).
make them known! The MT lacks an object suffix, corresponding to "them."

COMMENTS

4:4–5. The passage 4:4–5 can be characterized as a parody of an address to a cultic congregation, or as a "sarcastic imitation of the priestly call to worship" (Andersen and Freedman 1989: 433; cf. similarly Stuart 1987: 337). However, the sarcasm is mainly evident in v. 4a. As noted by Mays, the bulk of this prophecy "sounds like a catalogue of normal cultic acts" (1969: 75). Arguably, the rest of this oracle (vv. 4b–5) would have passed as uncontroversial had it not been for the introduction, which must have been shocking to an ancient audience.

In v. 4a, the addressees are invited to come and sacrifice at Bethel and Gilgal in order to "multiply" (Hiphil of *rbh*) transgressions, not to atone for them! Employing the verb *pšᶜ* (cf. the use of the corresponding noun in Amos 1:3, 6, 9, etc.), this formulation may imply that the cult at these two sites was seen as an act of rebellion, or even, as suggested by Karl Möller, "as something akin to the horrible war crimes committed by Israel's enemies" (2003a: 267). However, no explicit motivation is given. Since it is highly unlikely that an ancient Hebrew prophetic text would express a radically anti-cultic attitude, according to which all ritual procedures involved in animal sacrifice are sinful in themselves (see Eidevall 2012a: 5–30, 49–55), another explanation must be sought out. Let us review the main options:

1. *Transgressions of cultic regulations.* When this passage is compared with the cultic regulations in the Pentateuch, it is possible to detect (in v. 5a) a deviation from the principle laid down in Lev 2:11, which prohibits the sacrificial burning of leaven (thus Stuart 1987: 338). However, it is unlikely that Amos 4:4–5 criticizes the Israelites merely for that kind of technical violation, even if one assumes that the author/prophet shared the view expressed in Leviticus 2. As pointed out by Paul (1991: 141), moreover, there need not be any contradiction between 4:5a and the rules in Leviticus, since Lev 7:13 permits leavened bread in the context of a thank-offering, whereas Lev 2:11 is concerned with the grain offering. This interpretation is far-fetched; it has weak support in the text and fails to make sense in the literary context.

2. *Worship of other gods.* According to Hans Barstad, the passage 4:4–5 denounces rites that were "non-Yahwistic or Yahwistic/syncretistic" (1984: 57). Reference is made to some other texts as well as to "the general attitude of the prophet" (1984: 56). On closer examination, however, this hypothesis cannot be corroborated by the actual formulations of the text. Moreover, it fails to make sense within the immediate literary context. No allusions to alleged "idolatry" occur elsewhere in chapters 3–4.

3. *Inadequate inner disposition.* According to most modern commentators, the fault lies in the attitude of the worshipers. In their egotism they care only about themselves, while disregarding YHWH and their fellow human beings (so, e.g., Martin-Achard 1984b: 35 and Möller 2003a: 264). It is admittedly difficult to see how egotism could be the main motive behind the paying of tithes (v. 4bβ), which can be described as a religious tax with social dimensions (see Deut 14:28–29; 26:12; cf. also Mal 3:8–12). Nonetheless, this interpretation may find support in v. 5, where it is implied that the worshipers indulge in cultic excesses merely to satisfy themselves, because they "love to

do so" (v. 5bα). Assuming, despite the use of the general phrase "you Israelites (*běnê yiśrā'ēl*)" in v. 5b, that the addressees are those belonging to the upper classes (cf. 4:1–3), one may construct an image of rich people oppressing the poor and trying to compensate for their unethical behavior with lavish sacrifices (vv. 4bα, 5aα) and widely publicized donations (v. 5aβ). Such a reading would fit the literary context. However, this line of interpretation needs to be supplemented, because it does not account for the formulations in v. 4a. It remains to be explained why the sanctuaries of Bethel and Gilgal are particularly associated with the notion of multiplying sin and guilt. Further, the idea that the proclamation of doom over an entire nation can be based primarily on perceptions regarding the inner disposition of some worshipers looks suspiciously modern (with Soggin 1987: 72). Why condemn participation in sacrificial cults at these two sites on such grounds?

4. *Fundamental lack of cultic legitimacy and efficacy.* According to the opening words of v. 4, it is precisely because the worshipers go to Bethel and Gilgal (rather than to some other sanctuary) that they run the risk of increasing their guilt. Possibly, visiting these two sites was regarded as sinful in itself (cf. Stuart 1987: 337–38). At any rate, the sacrificial cult there was clearly deemed to be inefficacious. The reasons for that need not be inner-cultic, however. In the book of Amos, the condemnation of cultic sites would rather seem to be part of the divine punishment. This is evident in 3:9–15. Both the invasion of a foreign army (3:11) and the destruction of the altars in Bethel (3:14) are presented as consequences of the economic and political crimes (allegedly) committed in Samaria (3:9–10). I suggest that 4:4a should be understood as an expression of the idea that YHWH had abandoned the main sanctuaries in the Northern Kingdom, including (or, above all) Bethel and Gilgal (cf. 5:4–5). As a consequence, all cultic activities at these sites had become meaningless from a certain prophetic point of view (cf. W. H. Schmidt 1973: 72–80). It was too late. The sites were already doomed. This is why the passage 4:4–5 ridicules the attempts made by the Israelites to appease YHWH. The deity is not there to receive their offerings. Because of a major disturbance in the reciprocal relationship between the patron deity and the nation, all sacrifices will be rejected, regardless of the individual worshiper's inner disposition (see the Comments on 5:21–24).[10] To these considerations one may add that the postmonarchic editors of the book of Amos probably condemned attendance at sacrificial worship in Bethel and Gilgal as a violation of the cult centralization command (Deuteronomy 12).

To sum up, the passage 4:4–5 is about worship performed in the wrong time and place, and with the wrong attitude. Its rhetorical force is a product of the clash between the perspective of the prophet/author and the perspective of the Israelites depicted in the text. The partakers in the cultic celebrations enjoy them, just as they enjoy banquets in the city (6:4–6), happily but foolishly unaware of the impending disaster that will make an end of their feasting (3:11–15; 4:2–3; 5:1–3; 6:7). Amos 4:4–5 does not denounce sacrifices in general. This prophecy derides futile acts (including the offering of sacrifices) at places that are destined for destruction.

Amos 4:4–5 may possibly preserve a pre-722 B.C.E. oracle, conveying the message that the major cult centers are doomed, along with all other institutions in Israel (thus W. H. Schmidt 1973: 71). Alternatively, if this prophecy is dated to the seventh century or later, it can be read as part of an explanation of the downfall of the Northern Kingdom. At the same time, its anti-Bethel (and anti-Gilgal) polemics could have served pro-Jerusalemite propagandistic purposes, since Bethel continued to be an important (or, rival) cultic site during the reign of Josiah (see 2 Kgs 23:15–16) and throughout the sixth century (see Blenkinsopp 2003 and Radine 2010: 184–87).

Disasters with Didactic Dimensions (4:6–12)

4   ⁶I, for my part, gave you empty mouths in all your towns
and shortage of food in all your dwelling places.
Yet you did not return to me, says YHWH.
⁷I also held back the rain from you, three months before the harvest.
I would let it rain on one town, but not on another.
One field would get rain, but another field that received no rain would dry up.
⁸Two or three towns would then stagger into another town to drink water,
without being able to quench their thirst.
Yet you did not return to me, says YHWH.
⁹I struck you with scorching and plant rust, repeatedly;
your gardens and vineyards, your fig trees and olive trees were devoured by locusts.
Yet you did not return to me, says YHWH.
¹⁰I sent pestilence against you, like that of Egypt,
I killed your elite soldiers with the sword, your horses were taken as booty,
and I made the stench from your camps rise even into your nostrils.
Yet you did not return to me, says YHWH.
¹¹I overthrew some of you, as when God overthrew Sodom and Gomorrah;
you became like a firebrand rescued from the flames.
Yet you did not return to me, says YHWH.
      ¹²Therefore, thus I will do to you, Israel
—and because I will do this to you, prepare to meet your God, O Israel!

INTRODUCTION TO 4:6–12

The unit 4:6–11, to which the utterance in 4:12 has been appended, constitutes a well-defined composition within the larger composition (cf. Rudolph 1970: 27–28, 31). With regard to its content, this passage has been aptly characterized as a "catalogue of calamity" (Mays 1969: 78; similarly also Rudolph 1970: 34). It consists of five strophes, each one of them ending with the refrain "yet you did not return to me (*wělōʾ šabtem ʿāday*)" (vv. 6, 8, 9, 10, 11).

A similar historical exposé is found in Isa 9:7–20, which likewise enumerates disasters that had stricken Israel (or, Ephraim) in the past. It is worth noting that the perspective of these two historical reviews differs sharply from several other retrospective passages in the prophetic literature, such as Amos 2:9–12 or Hos 11:1–5 (cf. also 13:4–6), where a contrast is set up between YHWH's kindness and the people's ingratitude. What we have in Isa 9:7–20 and Amos 4:6–11 are not stories of divine salvific acts in the past (*Heilsgeschichte*), but the very opposite—narratives that focus on past disasters orchestrated by YHWH (that is, *Unheilsgeschichte*; see Rudolph 1971: 174 and Paul 1991: 141). In both texts it is emphasized that the Israelites failed to respond adequately to these calamities.

The rhetorical strategy employed invites the reader to sympathize with YHWH, whose patience is challenged by his people's stubbornness. Interestingly, disasters are here regarded as pedagogical tools used by the deity. Within its present literary context, Amos 4:6–11 provides explicit accusations that might explain the preceding condemnation of cultic sites (4:4–5), as well as the ensuing lament over Israel (5:1–2).

Arguably, a passage such as Amos 4:6–12 makes sense only after 587 B.C.E., in an era when prophetic literature begins to serve as history lessons. In some respects, this text differs markedly from those passages in the book of Amos that are commonly dated to the monarchic period. Perhaps most important, the perspective on disasters has shifted. The theme of a coming catastrophe, of which the addressees seem to be unaware (3:9–12; 4:1–3; 5:18–20; 6:1–7), has been replaced by retrospective reflections on profound disasters that have occurred already. Evidently, 4:6–12 speaks to a very different situation than several other passages within chapters 3–6: a situation when the worst imaginable scenario belonged to the past, also for the people in Judah.

The hypothesis that 4:6–12 was composed in the postmonarchic era is, in my opinion, corroborated by the observation that this passage looks like a case of inner-biblical exegesis. It is generally acknowledged that the author has drawn on traditional lists of covenant curses (see, e.g., Reventlow 1962: 86 and Brueggemann 1965). As shown by Wolff, the conspicuous points of contact with Leviticus 26, Deuteronomy 28, and 1 Kings 8 (vv. 33–40) indicate literary dependence (Wolff 1977: 213–14).

Jeremias has argued that, among these three intertexts, it is especially Solomon's prayer in 1 Kings 8 that may throw light on Amos 4:6–12 (see Jeremias 1998: 70–72 and Rilett Wood 2002: 199–202). These two texts share the notion that disasters have a didactic dimension, the goal being the people's "return" (*šûb*) to YHWH. However, while Solomon's prayer envisions that each catastrophe will provoke ritual repentance and prayer for forgiveness, the Amos passage deplores the fact that the addressees (as well as previous generations) have failed to respond as expected. Table 4 lists thematic and lexical links among the three intertexts.

Table 4. Intertextual Links between Amos 4:6–12 and 1 Kgs 8:33–40, Deut 28, and Lev 26

Amos 4:6–12	1 Kgs 8:33–40	Deuteronomy 28	Leviticus 26
6, 8, 9, 10, 11: Return (*šûb*)	33, 35 (cf. 47–48)		(40–45)
6: Famine, shortage (*ḥōser*)	37	48 *ḥōser*	26
7: Drought, no rain	35	24	(19)
8: Thirst		48	(20)
9: Scorching and rust	37 *šiddāpôn, yērāqôn*	22 *šiddāpôn, yērāqôn*	
9: Locusts	37	38	
10: Pestilence (*deber*)	37 *deber*	21 *deber*	25 *deber*
10: Like plague of Egypt		27	
10: Defeat, by sword (*ḥereb*)	33, 37	25, 26	17, 25 *ḥereb*
12: "I will do this to you"			16

NOTES

4:6. *empty mouths.* Literally, "clean teeth."

4:7. *I would let it rain.* The verbal forms in vv. 7aβ, 7b, and 8a encode an iterative aspect (thus also Paul 1991: 144–45 and Jeremias 1998: 66, n. 4; cf. *GKC* §112e and §112h). With reference to the LXX (cf. also the Targum and Peshitta), some scholars have argued for a translation in the future tense, despite the accompanying interpretive difficulties (so, e.g., Ulrichsen 1992–93 and Grätz 1998: 230–31).

received no rain. There is no need to emend the MT's *tamṭîr* into *ʾamṭîr*, as suggested in BHSapp, since the third-person feminine singular could be used in impersonal statements of the type "it rains" (cf. Pss 50:3; 68:15; see further Wolff 1977: 209 and Paul 1991: 145, n. 50).

4:9. *repeatedly.* This is a tentative rendering of הרבות (*harbôt*), a rather awkwardly positioned Hiphil infinitive of the verb *rbh*, "to multiply" (see Paul 1991: 137, 147; cf. also Garrett 2008: 121). Other scholars, following the lead of Wellhausen (1893: 79), read החרבתי, "I have caused to wither" (thus Wolff 1977: 210 and Jeremias 1998: 66), but such an emendation lacks support from the extant textual witnesses.

4:10. *elite soldiers.* In this context I find it likely that *baḥûrêkem,* plural of *bāḥûr* (literally, "chosen one," but usually "young man"), denotes elite troops (cf. Akkadian *bērul beḥrum,* see *CAD* B, 211–12; thus also Paul 1991: 137, 148). One may further note the assonance created by the collocation *baḥereb baḥûrêkem.*

taken as booty. The somewhat surprising wording of the MT, *ʿim šĕbî sûsêkem* (literally, "with the captivity/capture of your horses") is confirmed by the LXX (μετὰ αἰχμαλωσίας ἵππων σου). Arguably, the proposed emendation of *šĕbî* ("captivity") into *ṣĕbî* ("beauty, pride") is unwarranted (with Paul 1991: 148; but cf. BHSapp and Wolff 1977: 210).

into your nostrils. The conjunction in *ûbĕʾappĕkem* should probably be taken as an explicative *waw* (see Garrett 2008: 123).

COMMENTS

4:6. In terms of topic, there is an abrupt transition from the preceding passage (vv. 4–5), with its critique of contemporary cult activity at certain sites, to the ensuing historical exposé centering on past disasters (vv. 6–11). However, the editorial linking of these two passages, which have little in common as regards themes or vocabulary, has been crafted with great skill (see Rudolph 1970: 31 and Wolff 1977: 212–13, 220). The opening words of v. 6, "I, for my part" (*wĕgam ʾănî*), indicate that the ensuing utterance should be read as a contrast to, and thereby as a continuation of, the scenery depicted in vv. 4–5.[11]

Famine, a recurrent menace for the population in ancient Israel and Judah (see MacDonald 2008: 66–67), is the topic of the first strophe in this macabre catalogue of catastrophes (v. 6). The phrase used in v. 6aβ, *niqyôn šinnayim,* which literally means "clean teeth" (or, "cleanness of teeth"), should probably be understood as an idiomatic expression for starvation (cf. Paul 1991: 144). The underlying logic is plain: If one has nothing to eat, there is no possibility of food particles getting stuck between one's teeth.

At the same time, the formulations used in v. 6a are profoundly ironic. The opening clause, "I, for my part, gave you (*nātattî*)," might at first give the impression that the patron deity is referring to his great generosity toward his people in the past (see the use of *nātattî* in divine speech in Gen 15:18; 48:22; Amos 9:15). Then, however, it dawns upon the reader that this paradoxical "gift" consisted of an acute shortage (*ḥōser*) of supplies, resulting in hunger: empty mouths and empty stomachs (cf., as a contrast, Ps 23:1, *lōʾ ʾeḥsār*, "I shall not lack/want"). Without specifying what that would have entailed in practice, v. 6b reproaches those afflicted for not repenting properly: "Yet you did not return to me, says YHWH." This reproach is repeated, as a refrain, at the end of each strophe (see also vv. 8, 9, 10, 11).

4:7–8. The second strophe in this composition, comprising vv. 7–8, is considerably longer than the other four. Together with observations regarding alleged tensions on the level of content, this has given rise to several hypotheses about textual expansion.[12] However, since it seems to be impossible to restore an original version with any certainty, it is preferable to abstain from such speculations (with Jeremias 1998: 70). If this text is read as a theological exposition, rather than as a weather report, its apparent inconsistencies become less significant.

The topic that holds vv. 7–8 together is lack of water caused by long periods without rain. Verse 7 describes a state of drought, with disastrous consequences for the crops, and v. 8 focuses on the human condition of thirst. According to v. 7aα, it was YHWH who, for some reason, withheld the precipitation (cf. 1 Kings 17–18). In v. 7aβ the reader is informed that the rains failed at a critical time with regard to the harvest (see Hayes 1988: 146 and Paul 1991: 144). This might evoke the notion of a unique national disaster of exceptional proportions; however, the verbal forms used in the ensuing clauses (vv. 7aγ, 7b, and 8) indicate that the text refers to a frequently occurring situation (see the Notes).

Moreover, it is stated that typically, only some parts of the country were affected by such a drought: "I would let it rain on one town, but not on another. One field would get rain, but another field that received no rain would dry up" (7aγ–b). I suggest that the main function of this tantalizingly detailed description, which appears to diminish the severity of the disaster(s), is to provide a background for the dramatic scenario pictured in v. 8. Groups of people from stricken places are here depicted as roaming (or, staggering) from town to town, driven by thirst and hoping to find (and to be allowed to drink from) cisterns filled with rainwater (v. 8a). According to the refrain in v. 8b, however, those suffering from the drought did not turn to YHWH in their distress, nor did their neighbors who were better off.

I find it likely that vv. 7–8 (and especially v. 8a) served as a source of inspiration for the author of 8:11–12, who transformed the motif of thirst into a metaphor for a situation in which prophetic messages (likened to life-sustaining water) have become scarce.

4:9. Throughout the first three strophes (vv. 6–9), there is a constant focus on motifs related to famine. Here, in the third strophe (v. 9), several phenomena that would cause failed harvests are enumerated (cf. v. 7). Verse 9aα states that YHWH has sent "scorching and plant rust," referring to diseases afflicting cereal crops, and v. 9aβ focuses on locust attacks (apparently also sent by YHWH) that would devastate orchards as well as vineyards and olive plantations (cf. Joel 1:4–7). In v. 9b, it is repeated that the

Israelites persisted in their recalcitrant attitude despite all these divinely orchestrated disasters.

4:10. As this composition approaches its climax, it changes character. While vv. 6–9 can be described as a conventional catalogue of misfortunes, modeled on stock treaty (or, covenant) curses, the two concluding utterances (vv. 10–11) refer explicitly to accounts of spectacular disasters in the (legendary) past. In this way, the exceptional quality of the events described is underscored.

In v. 10, YHWH declares that he has punished his people with disease as well as defeat in his attempts to persuade them to repent. The motifs that occur in v. 10a, "pestilence" (*deber*) and death by the sword (*baḥereb*), constitute a traditional pair of curses (Lev 26:25; Deut 28:21–22; Jer 14:12). However, by means of the phrase *běderek miṣrayim*, literally "the way of Egypt," the reader is invited to make a comparison with the exodus story (cf. the use of this phrase in Isa 10:24, 26).

Rather than Amos 4:10 referring to one specific plague mentioned in the account in Exodus, for instance the fifth plague (Paul 1991: 147) or the tenth (Rudolph 1970: 33), I suggest that this passage alludes to the narrative in its entirety: a long series of calamities (including pestilence), followed by a defeat that wiped out the Egyptian army (see Exodus 7–15). Likewise, one may infer, YHWH had afflicted his own people with a series of scourges (vv. 6–10aα), culminating in a devastating military defeat. Against that background, it is possible to make sense of the otherwise puzzling mention of both soldiers and horses in v. 10aβ (cf. Exod 15:1, 21: "the horse and its rider").

At the same time, however, it is evident that this disaster is not pictured as an exact repetition of the demise of Pharaoh's army. Judging from the formulations in v. 10, the soldiers were killed on the battlefield, whereas the horses were carried away as booty. According to v. 10bα, the camps of the Israelite (or Judean?) army were filled with stench, presumably arising from the corpses that had been left lying on the ground (rather than on the bottom of the sea).

4:11. The fifth and final strophe refers to a catastrophe comparable to the one that, according to the legend, annihilated the cities on the plain (Gen 18:16–19:29; see also Deut 29:22 [Eng. v. 23] and Hos 11:8). The phrase "as when God overthrew (*kěmahpēkat ʾělōhîm*) Sodom and Gomorrah" (v. 11aβ) seems to have been a stock expression for a huge national disaster (Isa 13:19; Jer 50:40). Hence, it is difficult to ascertain whether the author had a specific event in mind. It has been suggested that v. 11 describes the earthquake mentioned in the superscription (1:1). As argued above, however, the composition 4:6–11 should probably be dated to the exilic or postexilic period; therefore, I find it more likely that the text alludes to the catastrophe that occurred in Jerusalem in 587 B.C.E. (with Jeremias 1998: 73).

Interestingly, it is emphasized that parts of the population were spared: "I overthrew some of you" (or, "some among you," *bākem*) (v. 11aα). These survivors, metaphorically depicted as "a firebrand rescued from the flames" (v. 11bα), would seem to be identical with the addressees. To this group, most likely the (post)exilic community, that recent disaster is presented as the very last warning. The fifth strophe ends on an ambiguous note. Since the refrain is repeated, without any change, one might deduce that all hope is gone: "Yet you did not return to me" (v. 11bβ). Alternatively, this could be read as the final call to repentance.

4:12. The utterance in v. 12 serves as a bridge between the preceding catalogue of catastrophes (vv. 6–11) and the doxology in v. 13. It is easy to translate but difficult to interpret. It is stated twice that YHWH is going to do something to Israel, but the reader is not given any clue as to *what* the deity is planning. The formulations used, "thus (*kōh*) I will do to you" (v. 12a) and "I will do this (*zōʾt*) to you" (v. 12bα), are vague in a disquieting way. As indicated by the use of a similar phrase in Lev 26:16, this could be understood as a threat. One may add that *lākēn* ("therefore") often introduces announcements of punishment (see 3:11; 5:11; 6:7). Possibly, YHWH threatens to send more disasters like the ones mentioned in vv. 6–11 (so Jeremias 1998: 74–75 and Garrett 2008: 125; cf. Paul 1991: 150–51); however, a more hopeful reading would also seem to be possible (Brueggemann 1965: 7–8).

Since the *yiqtol* (or, imperfect) forms imply future tense, and since the referent of "this" (*zōʾt*) is left open, I suggest that v. 12 should be understood as intentionally ambiguous.[13] Arguably, the sense of (vaguely threatening) ambiguity is reinforced by the concluding exhortation: "prepare to meet your God, O Israel" (v. 12 bβ). An encounter with God could mean either life or death. This could be the end, or perhaps a new beginning in Israel's relationship with YHWH—as if the people were standing at the foot of Mount Sinai again, preparing themselves for a theophany (cf. Exod 19:9–15). To sum up, 4:12 is a truly pivotal statement, which "develops suspense by postponing definition" (Carroll R. 1992: 215; see also Möller 2003a: 281).

Interlude: The First Doxology (4:13)

4   [13]See, the one who forms mountains and creates wind,
who announces his thoughts to humans,
the one who makes dawn into darkness and treads on the heights of the world—
YHWH, the God of hosts, is his name!

INTRODUCTION TO 4:13 AND THE
DOXOLOGIES IN THE BOOK OF AMOS

The utterance in 4:13 is the first in a series of three doxologies, or hymn fragments, that have been inserted by an editor into three sections within the book: at 4:13, 5:8, and 9:5–6. These short poetic pieces have several features in common, such as a cosmological perspective and a particular style, characterized by the use of participles as divine epithets.[14] In addition, all three passages feature a concluding refrain: "YHWH (God of hosts) is his name (*yhwh* [*ʾĕlōhê ṣĕbāʾôt*] *šĕmô*)" (4:13b; 5:8b; 9:6b).

It is difficult, but perhaps not necessary, to decide whether these doxologies are cited from a preexisting hymn that has been split up (Horst 1929; Watts 1997: 9–27) or whether they were composed with their present positions in the book of Amos in mind (McComiskey 1987: 155–56; Pfeifer 1991: 475–81). In either case, it is evident that they have been inserted at strategic points within the composition: immediately before the concentric composition in 5:1–17 (4:13), at the very center of that composition (5:8), and at the turning point between judgment and salvation toward the end of the composition (9:5–6). It is furthermore important to note that the intertextual links to other biblical passages (e.g., Isa 45:7, 19; 46:10; Psalm 104; Job 9:5–10) indicate an exilic or postexilic date of composition (see Foresti 1981: 175–84 and Jeremias 1998: 76–77).

Together with the motto-like utterance in 1:2, these three doxologies constitute a hymnic framework for this prophetic book in its entirety (see, e.g., Koch 1974: 534–35). This arrangement would seem to suggest some kind of liturgical setting for the reading of the book, at some (late) stage of its history of composition and redaction.[15] From a theological point of view, finally, the hymnic fragments introduce or reinforce certain aspects of the portrayal of YHWH: on one hand, the universal scope of YHWH's dominion, and on the other, the dual nature of this deity. In the doxologies, YHWH is endowed with absolutely sovereign power to create, but also to destroy. These passages have probably facilitated eschatological readings of Amos that are more or less detached from the political realities that are reflected elsewhere in this prophetic book.

NOTES

4:13. *the one who forms mountains and creates wind.* For stylistic reasons, the Hebrew participles in v. 13 are rendered by finite present tense forms, as in most modern translations (thus also, e.g., Wolff 1977: 211 and Jeremias 1998: 66). The first two participles, *yôṣēr* ("former/shaper") and *bōrēʾ* ("creator"), are sometimes rendered as nouns (so, e.g., Stuart 1987: 335). Alternatively, one might consider using verbs in the past tense, since the author probably thought of the creation of the mountains and the wind as events belonging to a distant past (thus Paul 1991: 137). However, it is imperative to recognize that this is a hymnic enumeration of divine capacities. Distinguishing between chronological stages in YHWH's activity would detract from the rhetorical force of this utterance.

his thoughts. The expression *mâ śēḥô* constitutes a *crux interpretum*, mainly because the noun *śēaḥ* is not attested elsewhere. Judging from the immediate context, this *hapax legomenon* denotes something that can be announced to someone. It could be a by-form of *śîaḥ*, "concern, musing" (so, e.g., Jeremias 1998: 66 and Garrett 2008: 127–28). At any rate, most scholars agree that the lexical sense has to be "thought(s)" or something similar. But whose thoughts are being disclosed? Possibly, the point made is that YHWH is able to reveal the innermost secrets of human minds (thus, e.g., Rudolph 1971: 181–82). I find it more likely that reference is being made to divine plans (with Wolff 1977: 211, 223–24; cf. similarly Jeremias 1998: 79). The LXX translation ἀπαγγέλλων εἰς ἀνθρώπους τὸν χριστὸν αὐτοῦ, with its eschatological and messianic message, can be regarded as a creative solution to the problem posed by the collocation מה שחו (interpreted as "his Messiah"). Equally unlikely is the suggestion that v. 13aβ refers to YHWH's communication with the first human being, Adam (Andersen and Freedman 1989: 456).

the one who makes dawn into darkness. Arguably, this is the most natural interpretation of the clause *ʿōśēh šaḥar ʿêpâ* (with, e.g., Koch 1974: 508, n. 16; Wolff 1977: 211; and Garrett 2008: 128; see also the Vulgate). The idea that YHWH can turn light into darkness is also attested in Amos 5:8. However, some scholars maintain that the clause in 4:13 expresses the opposite idea, namely, that YHWH turns darkness into dawn (which is likewise attested in 5:8!). In support of such a translation, Andersen and Freedman (1989: 453–55) offer a rather strained syntactic analysis (but see Gen 2:7). Paul (1991: 155), on the other hand, proposes an alternative (but quite unconvincing) semantic analysis, according to which *šaḥar* here means "blackness" (instead of "dawn") and *ʿêpâ* "brightness" (in contrast to the accepted lexical senses "darkness" and "mist"). Interestingly, the LXX (ὄρθρον καὶ ὁμίχλην) seems to reflect a different Hebrew *Vorlage*, with a copula: *šaḥar wĕʿêpâ*, "dawn and darkness" (a reading attested in a few Hebrew manuscripts recorded by Kennicott and de Rossi). However, because the MT makes good sense and can be seen as *lectio difficilior*, I have refrained from this (admittedly attractive) emendation.

COMMENTS

4:13. Introduced by a *kî* ("for") with indeterminate point of reference, which is followed by the deictic particle *hinnēh* ("see"), the doxology in v. 13 presents itself as a theological comment on the concluding words of v. 12, "prepare to meet your God, O Israel!" This miniature hymn portrays and extols the god whom Israel is about to encounter. It contains a series of five participial clauses (v. 13a) concerning the deity whose name is "YHWH, the God of hosts" (v. 13b). To some degree, this assemblage of divine epithets has a balancing effect in relation to the consistent emphasis on YHWH's destructive potential in vv. 6–11. Far from being resolved, however, the sense of ambiguity created by v. 12 is reinforced by v. 13.

In the two first participial clauses (v. 13aα) the focus lies on YHWH's role as creator. Since mountain ranges and air streams do not belong to the same category, some commentators follow the Septuagint and read "the thunder (*hāraʿam*)" instead of "mountains (*hārîm*)" (so, e.g., Nowack 1922: 141 and Mays 1969: 77). Conversely, however, it is possible to interpret these two phenomena, "mountains" and "wind," as standing for creation in its entirety, precisely because they belong to different categories. Moreover, this collocation manages to cover a wide range of interactions between the creator and the world. The mountains represent durability, visibility, and stability, and the wind is associated with mobility, invisibility, and change (cf. similarly Harper 1905: 104 and Linville 2008: 94–95). In this way, the dynamic (and unpredictable) aspects of YHWH's agency are foregrounded.

According to the next clause, the master of the universe is inclined to communicate with human beings. It is even stated that he "announces his thoughts" to them (v. 13aβ). This could be understood as an allusion to the important role of the prophets, in the same vein as the utterance in 3:7 (with Wolff 1977: 224). In the present context, however, such an assertion is far from reassuring, since it might imply that the addressees will be held accountable. They had, after all, received warnings through the prophets (Jeremias 1998: 79).

Further allusions to divine judgment can be found in the ensuing clauses (with Möller 2003a: 288). If one opts for the Septuagint's reading in v. 13aγ, "the one who makes dawn and darkness" (or, mist), the depiction of the deity becomes profoundly ambiguous. However, there are good reasons to retain the MT (see the Notes). According to what I consider the most plausible translation of the Hebrew text, YHWH is portrayed as "the one who makes dawn into darkness" (v. 13aγ)—darkness when one would have expected daylight; this theme, which hints at the destructive side of the deity's power, will be developed in several ensuing passages (5:8, 18–20; 8:9).

Unfortunately, the significance of the last divine epithet, "(the one who) treads on the heights of the world" (v. 13aδ), is somewhat elusive. First of all, it can be noted that "mountains (*hārîm*)" and "heights of the earth (*bāmŏtê ʾāreṣ*)" form an *inclusio*. Further, the epithet "the one who treads (*dōrēk*)" might evoke the notion of a victorious god (see Paul 1991: 156; cf. Deut 33:29 and Job 9:8).[16] In addition, it would seem to be possible to read v. 13aδ as a deuteronomistically flavored statement directed against the allegedly illegitimate open-air sanctuaries in the land (*ʾereṣ*), the so-called "high places (*bāmôt*)" (cf. Mic 1:3, 5; see Jeremias 1989: 79). Thus interpreted, the utterance in 4:13 would point forward to 7:9; however, it is important to keep in mind that this doxology does not contain any palpable references to history. Its perspective is cosmic, completely detached from human affairs (with an interesting exception: the idea that YHWH communicates his thoughts to humans). Allusions to cultic or political matters may nevertheless be perceived, as a result of the interaction between this hymnic piece and its present literary context.

A Concentric Centerpiece (5:1–17)

5 ¹Listen to this word that I deliver against you as a dirge, O house of Israel!
²She is fallen, to rise no more, virgin Israel,
abandoned on her land, with no one to raise her up.
³For thus says the Lord YHWH:
The city that marches out with a thousand shall have a hundred left,
and the one that marches out with a hundred shall have ten left,
for the house of Israel.
⁴Thus says YHWH to the house of Israel:
Seek me and live!
⁵Do not seek Bethel, do not enter into Gilgal, and do not cross over to Beer-
Sheba! For Gilgal will go into captivity, and Bethel will come to nothing.
⁶Seek YHWH and live!
Otherwise he will attack the house of Joseph like fire.
It will devour, and there will be no one to quench it for Bethel.
⁷They who turn justice into wormwood,
and throw righteousness to the ground
—⁸The one who made the Pleiades and Orion,
who turns deep darkness into morning, and darkens day into night,
who calls for the waters of the sea and pours them out on the surface of the earth,
YHWH is his name!
⁹It is he who flashes destruction on the stronghold,
so that destruction comes upon the fortified city—
¹⁰they hate the one who reproves in the gate,
they detest the one who speaks the truth.
¹¹Therefore, because you impose taxes on the poor one, and take levies of grain
from him: You have built houses of hewn stone but you shall not live in them.
You have planted pleasant vineyards but you shall not drink their wine.

¹²For I know that your crimes are many and that your sins are numerous,
you opponents of the innocent, receivers of bribes,
who turn aside the needy in the gate.
  ¹³Therefore, at such a time the wise one keeps quiet, for it is an evil time.
  ¹⁴Seek good and not evil, so that you may live,
and YHWH the God of hosts may be with you, just as you claim that he is.
¹⁵Hate evil and love good! Maintain justice in the gate!
Perhaps YHWH the God of hosts will be gracious to the remnant of Joseph.
  ¹⁶Therefore, thus says YHWH the God of hosts, the Lord:
In all open squares there will be wailing,
and in all streets they will say, "Woe! Woe!"
They will call the peasant to mourning,
and those skilled in lamentation to wailing.
¹⁷In all vineyards there will be wailing,
for I am going to pass through the midst of you, says YHWH.

INTRODUCTION TO 5:1–17

There is now a wide consensus that the section 5:1–17, which constitutes the center-piece of the book of Amos in its entirety, displays an artistically crafted concentric (or chiastic) structure. This was demonstrated by Jan de Waard (1977) in a groundbreaking study (see also Tromp 1984). The structure in Amos 5:1–17 displayed in Table 5 represents a slightly modified version of de Waard's analysis.

One of the most important conclusions to be drawn from the observations made by de Waard and others is that the section 5:1–17 (and, by extension, all sections of this prophetic book) needs to be read as literature, not as an exact transcript of a speech delivered at a certain time and place (with Tromp 1984: 71). While such a concentric arrangement might be detected and appreciated by attentive readers, it would probably be lost on attentive listeners (except for obvious verbal repetitions, such as *diršû*, "seek," in vv. 6 and 14).

Who created this neat symmetric structure? When and why? We will probably never know. Arguably, such a scribal exercise, which primarily involved rearranging existing prophecies, would make sense as a means to cope with a posttraumatic situation, for instance in the wake of the destruction of Jerusalem and its temple in 587 B.C.E. However, it seems possible to reconstruct several stages of development. In my

Table 5. The Concentric Structure in Amos 5:1–17

A. Lamentation (vv. 1–3)
          B. Exhortation to seek (vv. 4–6)
                    C. Critique of injustice (v. 7)
                              D. Doxology extolling YHWH's power (vv. 8–9)
                    C′. Critique of injustice (vv. 10–12 [13])
          B′. Exhortation to seek (vv. 14–15)
A′. Lamentation (vv. 16–17)

---

opinion, there are good reasons to assume that several of the oracles preserved in 5:1–17 were part of the first (preexilic) version of this prophetic book: vv. 1–3, 4–5, 7, 10, 12, 14–15 (?), and 16–17. For the purposes of the second (exilic or early postexilic) version, some additions were inserted: vv. 6 and 11 (as well as vv. 14–15?). At the same time, a concentric structure was created.

As shown below, it is likely that the central passage of the composition, vv. 8–9, should be seen as an even later addition. If this is correct, a first version of the concentric arrangement existed before the redactional activities through which the doxologies where inserted into the book.[17] Within that hypothetically reconstructed composition (5:1–17*), the central theme was a critique of social and economic injustice (vv. 7 + 10–13). These accusations were framed by exhortations (vv. 4–6 + 14–15) and lamentations (vv. 1–3 + 16–17).

Depending on the reader's perspective and strategy, the concentric structure in Amos 5:1–17 can be interpreted in two diametrically opposite ways. Because it begins and ends with depictions of death and lament, one might deduce that there is no hope for the addressees. But if the center of the composition is seen as more important than the periphery, it is perhaps possible to arrive at a more hopeful interpretation. In other words, the section 5:1–17 (like the rest of the book) is characterized by a double perspective. On one hand, it is definitely too late for Israel, the Northern Kingdom (vv. 1–3, 16–17). There can be little doubt that the text as we have it is written from a post-722 B.C.E. perspective. On the other hand, the exhortations in vv. 6 and 14 imply that there might still be time for the readers to reflect (on past disasters) and repent: "Perhaps YHWH the God of hosts will be gracious to the remnant of Joseph" (v. 15b).

NOTES

5:3. *for the house of Israel.* I see no compelling reason to move *lĕbêt yiśrāʾēl* ("for the house of Israel") to the first line (after *yhwh*), as advocated by Wolff (1977: 227). The word order of the MT is supported by the LXX and the Targum.

5:6. *he will attack.* The exact meaning of the verbal form *yṣlḥ* in this context is uncertain. In my opinion, it is preferable to take it as a form of *ṣlḥ* II, "rush (upon)" (so also Garrett 2008: 143). With reference to the semantic range of some other Semitic verbs, Tawil (1976) has maintained that *ṣlḥ* may carry the sense "burn" (cf. similarly Paul 1991: 165); however, this remains purely hypothetical.

5:8. *The one who made.* In this case it would be strange to render the Hebrew participle *ʿōśēh* with the present tense ("he who makes"). See, however, the discussion in the Notes to 4:13.

the Pleiades and Orion. The identification of *kîmâ ûkĕsîl* with the Pleiades and Orion is commonly accepted (so most commentaries; see especially Paul 1991: 168, with references). Among the ancient versions, this interpretation is attested in Theodotion. The LXX speaks freely of παντα ("everything"). In Job 38:31, however, the LXX identifies *kîmâ* with the Pleiades and *kĕsîl* with Orion. The Vulgate has Arcturus and Orion here in Amos 5:8.

5:9. *he who flashes.* This rendering of the Hebrew המבליג (*hammablîg*) has been adopted by several modern Bible translations (e.g., NIV and NET; see also RSV and NRSV). It is tentatively based on comparative philology. Referring to Arabic *blj* ("glänzen") and Syriac *blq* ("erscheinen"), Ges[18] lists "aufglänzen lassen" ("flash" or "let something flare up") as the primary lexical sense of the Hebrew *blg* in Hiphil. However, the remaining occurrences in the Hebrew Bible (Ps 39:14; Job 9:27; 10:20) attest to another (yet semantically related?) sense, namely, "smile" or "be cheerful" (cf. the Vulgate's translation in Amos 5:5: *subridet*). Alternatively, one might consider an emendation to המפליג, *hammaplîg,* as suggested by BHSapp, and translate "he who dispenses destruction," which comes close to the reading (and the *Vorlage*?) represented by the LXX: ὁ διαιρῶν συντριμμὸν. See further the discussion in Paul (1991: 169).

on the stronghold. I am reading ʿ*ōz,* "stronghold," instead of the MT's ʿ*āz,* "strong." This revocalization of עז finds some support in the LXX. In addition, it improves the poetic parallelism.

5:11. *impose taxes.* The strange-looking form בּוֹשַׁסְכֶם (*bôšaskem*) constitutes a *crux interpretum.* The pronominal suffix for the second-person plural is easily recognizable, but a verbal stem consisting of the consonants *bšs* is not attested elsewhere in biblical Hebrew. Several hypotheses have been put forward. In my opinion, the most attractive solution to this puzzle is to regard *bšs* as a metathesized form of the Akkadian verbal stem *šbš,* which denoted the activity of collecting agricultural taxes, *šibšu* (with Paul 1991: 172–73; cf. *CAD,* s.v. *šabāšu*). This suggestion was originally made by Torczyner (1936), also known as Tur-Sinai. Alternatively, but perhaps less likely, *bôšaskem* might be analyzed as a variant form of the verb *bûs,* "to trample." For a more detailed discussion, see Fleischer (1989: 164–69).

5:13. *keeps quiet.* I am taking *yiddōm* as a form of the verb *dmm* I, which means "to be(come) still," that is, to cease some kind of activity. The more specific meaning "to be silent" can be derived from this basic lexical sense (see Eidevall 2012b: 169–70). According to an alternative (but arguably less likely) interpretation, this is instead an instance of *dmm* II, "to mourn" (so Stuart 1987: 344 and Paul 1991: 175–76). See also Goff (2008).

5:15. *Hate evil and love good!* According to an alternative tradition, attested in 4QXII[g] (שנאנו) and the LXX (μεμισήκαμεν τὰ πονηρὰ καὶ ἠγαπήκαμεν τὰ καλά), v. 15aα contains an assertion in the first-person plural ("We [have] hate[d] evil and love[d] good"), rather than (as in the MT) an exhortation with imperatives.

5:16. *to wailing.* In the last clause of v. 16, it is preferable to read וְאֶל־מִסְפֵּד (*wěʾel-mispēd*) (cf. the Vulgate and Peshitta); however, this requires a transposition of the preposition ʾ*el.*

COMMENTS

5:1–3. The summons in 5:1, "Listen to this word" (*šimʿû ʾet-haddābār hazzeh*), serves more than one function. To begin with, it serves as a macrostructural marker that divides chapters 3–6 into two parts of roughly equal length: chapters 3–4 // 5–6. At the same time, it introduces the concentric section comprising 5:1–17. It does so in a very dramatic way, by means of intoning a dirge. Another conspicuous feature is the absence of a messenger formula, or any other hint that YHWH is speaking. According to Jeremias (1998: 85), 5:1 was composed in deliberate contrast to 3:1, indicating that the ensuing section contains the words of the prophet Amos, rather than the words of

YHWH (thus also Rilett Wood 2002: 132). On closer examination, such a distinction cannot be upheld. Arguably, the sayings in chapters 5–6 are oracles of the same type as those collected in chapters 3–4. Indeed, a messenger formula is cited shortly after the opening summons, in 5:3.

If one attempts to read the book of Amos as a drama, the passage 5:1–3 becomes a major turning point. After a series of serious accusations, interspersed with threats and proclamations of punishment, the discourse reaches a climax at the end of chapter 4: "prepare to meet your God, O Israel!" (4:12). The notion of an imminent theophany creates suspense (4:13). Will it entail judgment or rather a chance for repentance? Almost shockingly, 5:1–3 implies that the outcome of the theophany was disastrous (with Paul 1991: 159). The Israelites, it seems, are invited to partake in their own funeral. However, one should probably make a distinction between the addressees, called "house of Israel" (v. 1) on one hand, and "virgin Israel" in v. 2 on the other, the latter most likely referring to the Northern Kingdom. I suggest that the former is best understood as a reference to the Judeans.

5:1. In 5:1 the prophet Amos (or, the literary character Amos) is presented as speaking directly to an audience in the first person, for the first time since 1:2. As a consequence, this utterance contributes to the notion that this book portrays an eighth-century prophet debating with various groups in Bethel and Samaria (Möller 2003a: 122–47). In addition, this utterance seems to convey a certain view of the processes involved in prophetic revelation and performance. The prophet having received a message from the divine realm, one may infer, it was up to him to decide how this "word" was to be communicated. In this case, we are told that the prophet chose to deliver the divine message "as a dirge (*qînâ*)" (v. 1b).

5:2. The ensuing oracle, in v. 2, is indeed performed as a traditional dirge, marked by the characteristic 3 + 2 rhythm of the *qînâ* meter (see Jeremias 1998: 86 and Fleischer 2001: 190). In line with an ancient, cross-cultural metaphor, the nation of Israel (the Northern Kingdom) is personified as a woman (cf. Isa 23:12; 37:22; 47:1).[18]

The Hebrew lexeme used, *bĕtûlâ*, denotes a young, unmarried woman. In this context, arguably, the rendering "virgin" is quite apt, since it foregrounds the notion of unfulfilled hopes that would have been attached to the image of a young woman who died unmarried and childless. A strong sense of tragedy, and of premature death, is conveyed by this metaphorical depiction of the downfall of the Northern Kingdom: "She is fallen (*nāpĕlâ*), to rise no more, virgin Israel, abandoned on her land (*ʿal ʾadmātāh*), with no one to raise her up" (v. 2). The vocabulary used evokes associations with death in battle (*npl*), and perhaps also with the loss of land (*ʾădāmâ*), as noted by Carroll R. (1992: 224).

I find it likely that this utterance originated shortly after the disaster in 722 B.C.E., as a genuine dirge. Read on its own, it expresses collective grief, without the slightest nuance of satire. Inserted into its present literary context, however, this lament takes on an ironic character. According to the implied setting, these words were spoken by the prophet to a group of Israelites before the national catastrophe, inviting them to lament their own death, as if it had already happened. It is important, however, to keep in mind that the first readers of the book probably belonged to the educated elite in Judah. For these addressees, the downfall and "death" of the Northern Kingdom was an event of the past, in need of explanation, but it might also serve as a warning example.

5:3. In v. 3 the distinct 3 + 2 rhythm of the *qînâ* lament is abandoned, and so is the female personification of the nation. Using a rhetorical style based on arithmetic, but without recourse to metaphor, this oracle depicts a military defeat. It implies that the population of every town and city in the country is going to be decimated, in the literal sense of that English word: Only one-tenth of the soldiers sent out will survive. The concluding expression, "house of Israel" (*bêt yiśrāʾēl*), forms an *inclusio* together with v. 1b, demarcating vv. 1–3 as a unit within the larger section of 5:1–17.

5:4–6. Although the designation "house of Israel" serves as a catchword connection between vv. 3b and 4a, indicating continuity in terms of addressees, the transition from vv. 1–3 to vv. 4–6 is far from smooth. To begin with, the messenger formula marks some kind of break. Even more important, there is no continuity in terms of content. To put it simply, the exhortation in v. 4b, "Seek me and live!," does not follow logically from the preceding utterances. On the contrary, it would seem pointless to give this kind of advice to a nation that has already been declared dead.

One may of course conjecture that it was important for the author to demonstrate that the Israelites had received such admonitions in advance (admonitions that they did not heed). But the sequential order remains strangely illogical. Paul tries to resolve the tension, speaking of "a ray of hope" and suggesting that "the final death statement has not been signed" (1991: 161). Yet the tension is there, as long as one tries to make sense of this array of prophecies within a pre-722 perspective. As a consequence of the present textual arrangement (which is due to the concentric structure in 5:1–17), the dirge in 5:2 tends to lose some of its rhetorical force. The same can be said of the exhortation in v. 4. Whereas the lament in v. 2 runs the risk of being reduced to a rhetorical trick designed to induce repentance, the hope implied by the formulation "live (*wiḥyû*)" in v. 4 appears to be very frail, if not altogether unfounded. It has even been suggested that it is ironic (Weiser 1929: 191–94).[19]

Arguably, though, the utterances in 5:4–6 make perfect sense immediately after 5:1–3 if taken as exhortations and warnings directed to the first readers of (the first version of) the book. They knew that the end had come for Israel. For them, therefore, the past tense used in the dirge (v. 2) was not strange at all. But they were still alive (in Judah). Hence, they still had a choice. For them it was, according to the author, essential to act wisely in order to avoid a similar fate.

5:4. In v. 4 the addressees are encouraged to "seek" YHWH. Elsewhere in the Hebrew Bible, the phrase "seek (*drš*) YHWH" has cultic connotations (see Lust 1981: 138–40). It may denote an act of prayer to YHWH in a sanctuary (Deut 12:5; Ps 34:5, 11) or an act of inquiry concerning YHWH's will through the consultation of oracles (Gen 25:22; 1 Kgs 22:5). In 1–2 Chronicles and Ezra, to "seek (*drš*) YHWH" means to worship this deity. Against this background, I find it likely that this phrase carries cultic connotations in Amos 5:4, too (contra Paul 1991: 162). In other words, the first readers were admonished to pay attention to oracles from YHWH and to offer sacrificial gifts to him, preferably in Jerusalem.

5:5. In v. 5 it is explained why sacrificial worship was of no avail to the Israelites: They had sought YHWH in the wrong places (cf. Deut 12:5). This negated invitation to come and worship is in effect a prohibition: "Do not seek (*drš*) Bethel, do not enter into Gilgal" (v. 5aαβ). Apparently, these cultic sites were considered to be doomed. Bethel and Gilgal were condemned also in 4:4. Here Beer-Sheba, a pilgrimage site in the south, has been added. It is reasonable to assume that Amos 5:5 expresses a conviction that YHWH had abandoned these sanctuaries; therefore, the Israelites could not avert the catastrophe through cultic activities at these sites.[20] Within its present literary context this utterance is a warning to the Judeans: Do not go there! Do not repeat the mistakes of the Israelites! Thus, the first readers were instructed that they should seek YHWH in Jerusalem (cf. 1:2) and not in any rival sanctuary, such as Bethel.[21]

The oracle in 5:5 has been composed with artistry. First of all, the references to the three toponyms are arranged to form a chiastic structure: Bethel—Gilgal—Beer-Sheba—Gilgal—Bethel. The punch line (v. 5bβ), with its pun on Bethel, may have a specific background (see Harper 1905: 112 and Paul 1991: 164, n. 45). A place called Beth-Awen was apparently situated in the vicinity of Bethel (Josh 7:2; 18:12; 1 Sam 13:5; 14:23). The idea seems to be that instead of "God's dwelling" (*bêt ʾēl*), the site Bethel would become like its neighboring town, Beth-Awen, the name of which could be taken to mean "dwelling of nothingness" (see also Hos 4:15).

The preceding clause (v. 5bα), which deals with the fate of Gilgal, excels in alliterations: *haggilgāl gālōh yigleh* ("Gilgal will go into captivity"). The wordplay involved emphasizes that, instead of continuing to worship in Gilgal (or at other cultic sites), the population will be exiled. A corresponding pun on the remaining toponym, Beer-Sheba, is missing. However, this observation need not indicate that v. 5aγ represents a later addition (thus Jeremias 1998: 89).[22]

5:6. The opening line of v. 6 reiterates the message from 5:4b: "Seek YHWH and live!" (v. 6a); however, this *inclusio* does not signal closure. The exhortation is followed by a warning: "Otherwise he will attack the house of Joseph like fire" (v. 6bα). Since "the house of Joseph" usually refers to the tribes of Ephraim and Manasseh, this warning seems to be directed against the Northern Kingdom. Possibly, though, the utterance in v. 6 is a later addition, which makes the point that the inhabitants of the Northern Kingdom had received warnings before the catastrophe.[23] This warning is followed by a threat. If the Israelites fail to seek YHWH in the right way, the deity will "attack" or "rush upon" them (see the Notes).

Interestingly, this saying focuses especially on the destruction of one of the three sites mentioned in v. 5, namely, Bethel. In this respect, 5:6 recalls 3:13–14. Arguably, both passages allude to the (legendary?) destruction of the Bethel sanctuary during the reign of Josiah. According to 5:6, Bethel will be consumed by a fire that no one can put out (v. 6bβ). To a certain degree, this resembles the punishment by fire decreed against various nations and cities in chapters 1–2 (1:4, 7, 10, etc.); however, the terminology is different. Moreover, the fire mentioned in 5:6 is metaphorical. This oracle envisages, not that YHWH will send fire on the tribes of Ephraim, but that he will attack them "like fire (*kāʾēš*)" (v. 6bα). A similar expression occurs in Jer 4:4 (and in Jer 21:12), where the unquenchable fire is a metaphor for YHWH's wrath.

5:7. In v. 7, exhortations in the second-person plural (vv. 4–6) are, rather abruptly, replaced by accusations in the third-person plural. The introductory participial clause, "they who turn (*hahōpěkîm*) justice into wormwood" (v. 7a), looks like the continuation of a "woe" exclamation (see Maag 1951: 30 and Soggin 1987: 88–89). In terms of content, the discourse now switches from cultic issues to the topic of (lack of) justice.

Two rather unconventional metaphors are used. According to the first, in v. 7a, justice (*mišpāṭ*) has become a poisonous plant. Perverted justice in the courts is thus pictured as a poison that makes the societal body sick. This would seem to presuppose that ideally justice could be seen as something life-sustaining, perhaps as a salubrious plant of some kind. According to a likely interpretation of the second metaphor, in v. 7b, righteousness (ṣĕdāqâ)—the virtue which was supposed to guarantee that victimized people would be assisted—is here personified as a helpless victim of violence who has been left lying on the ground.

5:8–9. At this juncture an abrupt shift occurs. Clearly, vv. 8–9 have been inserted at a rather late stage (with, e.g., Fleischer 2001: 189–90 and Jeremias 1998: 85, 90) and interrupt the discourse on justice and corruption (which is resumed in v. 10) in a rather awkward way. It is worth noting that 5:1–17 would display a concentric structure also without the insertion of vv. 8–9. In that case, the central topic of the composition would have been (the lack of) justice. Now this strategic place, at the very center of this prophetic book, is occupied by a doxology (v. 8) and a transitional utterance (v. 9).

As noted above (see "Introduction to 4:13 and the Doxologies in the Book of Amos"), the three doxologies in 4:13, 5:8, and 9:5–6 exhibit strong similarities in terms of content and style, including a shared concluding refrain. Hence, they may look like fragments from one and the same hymn. In the following discussion, however, such questions will be left aside. The analysis focuses on the function of 5:8 within its literary context.

5:8. Whether composed with its present position in mind or not, the doxology in 5:8 has been deliberately placed in the midst of accusations (vv. 7 + 10–12), exhortations (vv. 4–6 + 14–15), and lamentations (vv. 1–3 + 16–17). It is possible to find some intriguing connections between this doxology and the surrounding utterances.

To begin with, the theme of transformation, expressed by the verb hpk, serves as a link to v. 7. Whereas in v. 7 the leaders in Israel are accused of turning (hahōpĕkîm) justice into wormwood (that is, into injustice), YHWH is here extolled because he is able to turn (hōpēk) "deep darkness into morning" and "day into night" (v. 8aβγ). Thus, the corrupt actions denounced in the surrounding verses (7, 10–12) are put in perspective. One may infer that YHWH has the capacity to undo all corrupting transformations made by the Israelites. But this could be a source of either hope (for justice) or fear (of divine judgment).

The portrayal of divine sovereignty in v. 8 is characterized by deep ambivalence. YHWH is depicted as both creator and destroyer. In the opening line (v. 8aα) the deity is said to be the maker of two constellations in the sky, kîmâ and kĕsîl, which are usually identified with the Pleiades and Orion. This epithet implies that he can bring about perfect order on a cosmic scale. In addition, as the creator of all the stars in heaven, YHWH can be regarded as the one who may bring brightness in the dark night. However, he may likewise turn daylight into darkness (v. 8aγ; cf. also 4:13). According to the concluding part of the depiction (v. 8baβ), YHWH may even let the earth be flooded by the waters of the ocean. In this way the reader is reminded that YHWH has the power to let the forces of chaos loose, undoing the order of creation and threatening all life on earth (cf. Genesis 6–8; see Steins 2004: 42).

5:9. This utterance serves as a bridge between the hymnic saying in v. 8 and the interrupted diatribe against those who have perverted justice (vv. 7 + 10–12). Arguably, the clause "YHWH is his name!" at the end of v. 8 marks the end of the doxology. Despite this, v. 9 adds a further clause, describing divine activity, in the hymnic style.

Unfortunately, the meaning of *mablîg* (Hiphil participle of *blg*), here rendered "he who flashes," is uncertain (see the Notes). However, there can be no doubt that this oracle highlights the destructive side of the deity's power. This is efficiently illustrated by the twofold use of the word *šōd* ("violence, destruction")—as the grammatical object of *mablîg* in v. 9a (that is, as something that YHWH brings about) and as the subject of the next clause, v. 9b (cf. Zalcman 1981: 57). Notably, the divine punitive actions described are directed against the fortifications of the cities. Variations on this motif constitute a prominent thematic thread in large parts of the book of Amos (see 1:4, 7, 10, 12, 14; 2:2, 5; 3:10–11; 6:8)

5:10. Here, the topic introduced in v. 7, lack of justice, continues, as though nothing had come in between vv. 7 and 10. The anonymous wrongdoers (presumably people belonging to the upper classes in Samaria) who were allegedly perverting justice (v. 7) are now accused of hating those who dare to speak the truth. Retaining the Hebrew word order, one might translate "they hate in the gate" (v. 10a). The open space near the city gate was a place for trade and cult activities. It was also the place where judicial disputes were settled. Quite possibly the lexeme *môkîaḥ* (here translated, literally, as "one who reproves") was used as a designation for a certain legal functionary, such as an arbiter or umpire (see Job 9:33) or a prosecutor (see Prov 28:23).

The second clause, "they detest the one who speaks the truth" (v. 10b), may perhaps refer specifically to disrespect for truthful witnesses (Jeremias 1998: 92). Such details cannot be reconstructed with certainty. Still, the picture that emerges is clear enough. This oracle describes a society in which the courts are corrupted, a society in which it might be dangerous to speak the truth, especially if it entails accusing powerful people of serious crimes. Sadly, this utterance could easily be applied to many modern societies.

5:11. As a rule, there is a link between legal corruption and the economic interests of certain influential groups; therefore, the accusations in v. 11aα seem to follow rather logically upon the allegations in v. 10. However, the switch from the third-person to the second-person plural signals some kind of discontinuity. Possibly, v. 11 has been inserted between vv. 10 and 12 at a later stage.[24] The topic is undoubtedly oppression of the poor and needy, but which specific acts are denounced? Interpretation is made difficult by the occurrence of syntactic incongruities and rare lexemes.

To begin with, in v. 11aα, the juxtaposition of *lākēn*, "therefore," and *yaʿan*, "because," is unparalleled. Apparently, cause and consequence are referred to at the same time. To make things even worse, the strange-looking verbal form in v. 11aβ, *bôšaskem*, constitutes a *crux interpretum*. I find it likely that *bšs* should be understood as a Hebrew equivalent of the Akkadian verb *šabāšu*, which denotes the activity of collecting grain taxes (with Paul 1991: 172–73). This solution would create an almost perfect parallelism, since the next clause protests against the imposition of heavy "levies of grain" (v. 11aβ; cf. Jaruzelska 1998: 146–52). One may infer that these levies made poor farmers even poorer, a process that might lead to debt slavery (see 2:6 and 8:4–6). After the indictment (v. 11aαβ) comes the verdict (v. 11aγδ + b). It is stated that the rich oppressors are going to lose their houses and their vineyards. Arguably, these curse-like threats (which constitute reversals of the promises formulated in Isa 65:21) allude to imminent (or, already implemented) deportation and exile.

5:12. Despite the absence of a messenger formula, it is evident that the "I" speaking in v. 12 is YHWH. The addressees are told that the deity is aware of all the crimes and transgressions that they have committed (v. 12a). Some of these crimes are enumerated in the ensuing clauses (v. 12b): persecuting innocent people, taking bribes, and (according to what I take to be the most likely interpretation of 12bβ, "who turn aside the needy in the gate") denying poor people a fair trial. Once again, the topic is corruption in the courts (cf. vv. 7 and 10). The declaration that YHWH knows about all this can be understood as an implicit threat. However, within the present literary arrangement, it serves above all to justify and reinforce the threat pronounced in v. 11.

It is worth noting that, according to the passage 5:10–12 (or, 5:7 + 10–12), the divine anger that brought about the downfall of the Northern Kingdom was mainly provoked by widespread corruption in the courts and systematic oppression of the poor, not by "idolatry" or any other cultic or religious offenses.

5:13. Somewhat unexpectedly, an admonition to keep quiet has been appended to the outspoken diatribe against injustice (vv. 10–12). According to v. 13, a wise one (*maśkîl*) must hold his tongue (*yiddōm*) in such an "evil time" (*ʿēt rāʿâ*). The idea that holding one's tongue may be a sign of wisdom is at home in sapiential literature (see, e.g., Prov 10:19). In the present context, however, it would be preposterous to conclude that the prophet speaking in the preceding passages (5:1–12) should not be counted among the wise. Indeed, the advice offered by v. 13 can hardly be reconciled with the remainder of the book, which expressly esteems prophetic *speech,* rather than silence (see 2:12; 3:8; 7:10–17; 8:11–12). With regard to its immediate literary context, this utterance falls outside the (otherwise) neat concentric structure of 5:1–17.[25]

Amos 5:13 is commonly, and as far as I can see, correctly, considered to be a late gloss.[26] I suggest that this utterance contains a reflection made by a reader in the Persian or Hellenistic era who was reminded of contemporary corruption and oppression and who identified himself (or herself) with the despised, and probably silenced, truth-teller mentioned in v. 10.[27] According to Jeremias, this postexilic reader wanted to "warn against inappropriate speech" in particular (1998: 94).[28] It is, finally, worth noting that this comment has been placed at the very center of the book of Amos (Andersen and Freedman 1989: 505; Dines 2001: 585).

5:14–15. Because of the concentric arrangement of 5:1–17, readers now experience a replay of its main topics and themes, but in reversed order. In v. 14 they encounter yet another variation on the theme of seeking. However, in the passage 5:14–15 the focus has shifted from cultic practice (vv. 4–6) to moral conduct. At the same time, the tension created by the juxtaposition of lamentations (implying that it is too late) and exhortations (implying that there is still hope) has been mitigated by means of cautionary and conditional formulations: "may be" (v. 14b) and "perhaps" (v. 15b).

5:14. The straightforward command in v. 14a, "Seek (*drš*) good (*tôb*) and not evil (*rāʿ*), so that you may live," can be seen as an ethical application of the exhortations to "seek (*drš*)" YHWH, which were pronounced in vv. 4 and 6. In both cases, the consequence of appropriate "seeking" is said to be survival. In v. 14b, a further comment is added: "and YHWH the God of hosts may be with you, just as you claim that he is." Possibly, this alludes to a conviction held by the addressees, or even to a popular liturgical phrase (cf. Mays 1969: 101–2).

If, as seems likely, the first readers addressed by this text were Judeans during the latter part of the monarchic era, one may detect an allusion to a key notion within Zion theology, "God (YHWH) is with us" (see Ps 46:6; Mic 3:10–11; Isa 7:14; 8:9–10).[29] In order to avert a disaster similar to the one that had ended the kingdom of Israel, the Judeans must avoid the false security that such phrases might induce and act in accordance with YHWH's commandments.

5:15. In v. 15aα the exhortation from v. 14a is rephrased, in a chiastic manner: "Hate evil (rāʿ) and love good (ṭôb)!" Interestingly, this is followed by an admonition to "maintain justice in the gate" (15aβ), which refers back to the section dealing with legal corruption (vv. 7, 10–12). This is, in my opinion, a clear indication that vv. 14–15 originated as written (as distinct from oral) prophecy. More precisely, I suggest that this passage was composed in order to serve as the continuation of a composition including 5:4–6 as well as 5:7 and 5:10–12*.[30]

In order to survive, the addressees are told, they must restore the judicial system; however, it seems to be uncertain whether any such reforms really would help. The concluding promise (v. 15b) is filled with reservations. It begins with a cautionary "perhaps" (ʾûlay), which stresses that YHWH's mercy should not be seen as a more or less automatic response to repentance.[31] A similar point is made in Zeph 2:3, with the help of similar expressions.

Further, in case the deity decides to show mercy, this will apparently apply to only a limited group, "the remnant (šĕʾērît) of Joseph" (v. 15b). This may sound harsh, but the message of 5:15 is consonant with the overall message of the book of Amos. Since the destruction of the kingdom of Israel, referred to as the "house of Joseph" in v. 6, had been decreed by YHWH (and, at the time of composition, already belonged to the past), the prophetic words could not contain any hope for that nation as a whole, only for those who survived the disaster in 722 B.C.E. Evidently, some of them took refuge in Jerusalem. While acknowledging (in retrospect) that in fact only a "remnant" from the Northern Kingdom was saved, 5:15 may also be read as directed to the people in Judah, either as a warning (if written before 587 B.C.E.) or as a vague promise (in a post-587 setting).

5:16–17. Following the logic of concentricity, we are back where this composition started. Once again, the theme is death and lamentation (cf. vv. 1–3). The all-encompassing, national scope of the imminent catastrophe and the accompanying lamentation is conveyed by the threefold repetition of the lexeme mispēd, "wailing," in vv. 16–17 (Paul 1991: 179).

5:16. Like several of the preceding prophecies (vv. 11, 13), v. 16 is introduced by lākēn, "therefore," in this case followed by the messenger formula (v. 16aα). According to the ensuing utterance, sounds of lamentation and sighing, hô-hô ("Woe! Woe!" or "Alas! Alas!"), will be heard in all public spaces (v. 16aβ).

Somewhat surprisingly, the reader is then informed that peasants from the countryside will be summoned to participate in the lamentations in the cities (v. 16bα). The main function of this unexpected motif is probably to underscore the magnitude of the presaged calamity (with Jeremias 1998: 96). Apparently, the entire nation will be involved. Guilds of more or less professional (mostly female) mourners are referred to in several biblical texts (Jer 9:16–17; Ezek 32:16; 2 Chr 35:25; see Paul 1991: 180). In the exceptional situation envisaged by Amos 5:16, one may infer, the expert wailers and dirge chanters, "those skilled in lamentation" (v. 16bβ), are going to need assistance even from agricultural workers.

Since the lexeme used in v. 16bα, *ʾikkār*, seems to have denoted ordinary farm-workers, as opposed to wealthy landowners, one may reconstruct the following scenario: The poor peasants will be forced to do their masters and oppressors (4:1; 5:10–12) a last service—to sing at their funerals (Gese 1962: 432–33).

5:17. According to v. 17a, even the vineyards will become locations for lamentation. This can be understood as a reversal of traditional cultural ideas, such as the link between vineyards and feasts (see, e.g., Judg 9:27; 21:20–21) or between wine and joy (see Ps 104:15). A similar prediction of disaster, concerning Moab, is found in Isa 16:10 (and in Jer 48:33). Vineyards were mentioned earlier, in v. 11. In order to avoid the impression that these two utterances are incompatible, one may perhaps imagine that the author/editor imagined that the vineyards were going to be filled with wailing (v. 17) before they were deserted and overtaken by others (v. 11). However, it is arguably preferable to abstain from attempts to create logical, or chronological, consistency within the concentric composition as a whole.

In the last clause of v. 17, the reader is told that the disaster occasioning the lamentation should be interpreted as the work of YHWH. All of this (vv. 16–17a) will apparently happen as a consequence of YHWH's arrival: "for I am going to pass through (ʿbr) the midst of you" (v. 17b). The verb ʿbr belongs to the stock vocabulary of the theophanic tradition (see Hauan 1986 and Fuhs 1999: 418–21). In this case, however, the notion of YHWH's coming is void of positive connotations. This theophany depiction cannot even be regarded as ambiguous, as was the case in some previous passages (4:12–13; 5:8). Here, YHWH's "passing through" means danger, destruction, and disaster.

It is instructive to compare Amos 5:17b with Exod 12:12, where a similar formulation is used: "For I will pass through (ʿbr) the land of Egypt that night, and I will strike down every firstborn." Even though it is difficult to establish a case of literary dependence between these passages, it is evident that Amos 5:17b suggests a drastic reversal of the exodus tradition (with Harper 1905: 127, Mays 1969: 99, and Fleischer 2001: 206). Israel has, shockingly, been assigned the role played by Egypt in that drama—the role of the detested oppressor, YHWH's arrogant enemy.

The utterance in v. 17b rounds out the composition comprising vv. 1–17. At the same time, it falls somewhat outside of the concentric pattern, since it leaves the theme of mourning (vv. 1–3 + 16–17a) and (re)introduces the topic of theophany. Thus, v. 17b serves as a bridge to the ensuing passage (vv. 18–20). However, there is a visible break between these two passages, since v. 17 ends with the formula "says YHWH" (*ʾāmar yhwh*).

Beware of the Day of YHWH (5:18–20)

5   [18]Woe to those who long for the day of YHWH!
What will the day of YHWH be for you?
It will be darkness, not light!
[19]As if someone flees from a lion, only to be confronted by a bear; and then, as
he comes home and leans his hand against the wall, he is bitten by a snake.
[20]Truly, it is darkness, the day of YHWH, rather than light,
gloom without any brightness in it!

INTRODUCTION TO 5:18–20

There can be no doubt that 5:18, introduced by a woe exclamation, begins a new section (cf. 6:1). Because of the *inclusio* created by vv. 18b and 20, it is reasonable to assume that another unit starts in v. 21 (see R. Müller 2010: 576–77). The rhetorical unit 5:18–20 is one of the most famous, and also one of the most hotly debated, passages in the book of Amos.

With most modern commentators I find it likely that a piece of oral prophecy from the eighth century B.C.E. has been preserved in Amos 5:18–20 (albeit with some redactional alterations). Arguably, if one searches for a suitable time of origin, the best candidate would be the last decade of the Northern Kingdom's existence as a (vassal) state, during the reign of Hoshea (731–722 B.C.E.) but before the Assyrian siege of Samaria (with R. Müller 2010: 591; see also Levin 1995: 316–17). Despite the military attack by Tiglath-Pileser III in 732, which decimated the territory of Israel, the leading circles decided to foment a renewed rebellion against Assyria. The rhetoric of 5:18–20, which is directed against exaggerated optimism and false security, would seem to presuppose such a situation.

An additional argument for a rather early dating is the fact that strikingly similar formulations occur in the oracular text from Deir 'Alla (commonly dated to the eighth century), in a passage that describes some kind of catastrophe brought about by the sun goddess. Reinhard Müller (2010: 588–90) has called attention to this illuminating parallel. Indeed, an utterance in the first part of this inscription, *šm ḥšk w'l ngh,* "there is darkness, not brightness," provides a close parallel to Amos 5:18bβ, "it will be darkness, not light" (*hû' ḥōšek wĕlō' 'ôr*), as well as to 5:20b, "gloom without any brightness in it" (*wĕ'āpēl wĕlō' nōgah lô*).[32] This proves beyond a reasonable doubt that the core expressions used in Amos 5:18–20 belonged to the repertoire of disaster prophecy in the eighth century B.C.E. in the region known as Canaan or Palestine.

Much of the exegetical discussion of Amos 5:18–20 has centered on the expression "the day of YHWH" (*yôm yhwh*). Interpretation is made difficult by the circumstance that all other biblical attestations (or near equivalents) of this phrase occur in texts that most likely are later than (and, possibly, dependent on) Amos 5:18–20 (see Oswald 2009 and R. Müller 2010: 582). Several competing theories concerning the original significance of the day of YHWH have been advanced, but no consensus is yet in sight.[33] In this case, however, I suspect that some scholars have exaggerated the difficulties (see, e.g., Andersen and Freedman 1989: 521). In the Comments, I show that rhetorical analysis, informed by comparative studies, may throw a considerable amount of light on the function of this phrase in Amos 5:18–20.

NOTES

5:19. *bitten by a snake.* Or, more literally, "the snake bites him."

5:20. *Truly, it is darkness.* Because v. 20 is introduced by the negated interrogative participle *hălō',* one might alternatively render this utterance as a composite question: "Is it not darkness, the day of YHWH, rather than light, gloom without any brightness in it?" In my opinion, however, it is sometimes preferable to take *hălō'* as an assertive participle. See, for example, 1 Sam 23:19; 1 Kgs 11:41; Isa 44:20; Jer 3:4; see also *GKC* §150e. Amos 9:7 presents a parallel case.

COMMENTS

5:18. Within its present literary context, the oracle preserved in v. 18 connects to the topic of the preceding passage (vv. 16–17a), lamentation, via its opening word: *hôy* ("woe"). Apart from specialized uses in prophetic discourse, this exclamation was primarily associated with mourning for the dead (see 1 Kgs 13:30; Jer 22:18).[34] Moreover, this utterance develops a theme that was intimated in v. 17b: the reversal of celebrated traditions and of great expectations. According to v. 17b, the impending theophany will entail disaster and defeat, not deliverance. According to v. 18b, the upcoming, and much-longed-for, "day of YHWH" will be characterized by "darkness, not light."

It is reasonable to interpret the motif of darkness as a metaphor rather than as a literal prediction of a solar eclipse (cf. Harper 1905: 132). With regard to prominent themes in the present context of the oracle, this imagery could stand for a military defeat or some other major catastrophe (cf. 5:3, 12, 16, 27). Alternatively, it might refer to a disastrous deterioration in divine-human relations, manifested in a rejected, nonfunctioning cult (cf. the interpretation of 5:21–24 below). In other words, the two standard theories concerning the day of YHWH, maintaining that it was connected either to holy war traditions (Gerhard von Rad) or to the cult (Sigmund Mowinckel), appear to fit equally well into the literary context.[35]

A rhetorical analysis can add some further insights. Because the addressees are said to "long for" (Hitpael of *'wh*) the day of YHWH (v. 18a), one may deduce that this key concept had predominantly positive connotations. Clearly, the primary aim of this oracle is to counteract the unfounded optimism entertained by the audience. In this perspective, the introductory "woe" would seem to serve as a wake-up call, signaling imminent danger (cf. similarly 6:1).

The opening address (v. 18a) is followed by a question (v. 18bα), in which it is of vital importance to notice the emphasis on *lākem*, "for you." The prophet/author does not ask, in general terms, "What will the day of YHWH be like?" The question is decidedly contextual and relational: "What will the day of YHWH be/entail *for you*?" The answer given in v. 18bβ, that "it will be darkness, not light," must be understood as reversing the audience's expectations; otherwise, it fails to make any sense, from a rhetorical point of view.

On the basis of this brief rhetorical analysis of v. 18 one may draw two important conclusions concerning the phrase *yôm yhwh* ("the day of YHWH"): (1) It was known by the addressees (with, e.g., R. Müller 2010: 582), and (2) it carried predominantly positive connotations among its primary addressees.[36]

It follows, I suggest, that the denotation of this phrase was not necessarily redefined by the prophet/author responsible for 5:18–20 from a positive concept ("light") to a negative one ("darkness"). Rather, the expression *yôm yhwh* was recontextualized to signify defeat and darkness for the addressees, in a certain situation—which does not preclude that it could still mean brightness and prosperity for others, or on other occasions (thus also Jeremias 1998: 100). As shown below, comparative evidence suggests that the audience's allegedly mistaken expectations were connected to a religious festival.

Reinhard Müller has recently demonstrated that the closest biblical and extrabiblical parallels speak strongly in favor of a cultic interpretation of *yôm yhwh*. In Mesopotamia, expressions constructed in exactly the same way, for instance, "the day of Enlil" (*ūm Enlil*) or "the day of the god" (*ūm ili*), were used as designations for major cultic celebrations (2010: 584–85).

Turning to the Hebrew Bible, two expressions, which denote cultic events, can arguably be regarded as close counterparts to *yôm yhwh* in Amos 5:18, 20: "the day that YHWH has made" (Ps 118:24) and "the days of the Baals" (Hos 2:15 [Eng. v. 13]). Of particular interest is Hos 9:5, where the phrase "the day of the festival of YHWH (*yôm ḥag yhwh*)" occurs in an oracle that discusses attitudes toward an upcoming religious feast. Thus, in the light of extant data, it is reasonable to assume that *yôm yhwh* in Amos 5:18 originally referred to a cultic event. Indeed, Amos 5:18–20 makes excellent sense in that type of setting, as a provocative prophecy uttered during or shortly before a festival at a major shrine, perhaps in Bethel (see similarly Hayes 1988: 171–72).

5:19. While the utterance in v. 18 undoubtedly addresses the (unwarranted) optimism of the addressees, v. 19 is open to more than one interpretation. This proverb-like saying is about someone who encounters one dangerous animal after another, first a lion and then (which might be even worse) a bear, and manages to escape from them, but who eventually falls victim to a snake hidden inside the house. This can be taken as an illustration of what it means to have extremely bad luck, but such a message would fit rather awkwardly into the context. The preceding prophecies have spoken about calamities as (allegedly well-deserved) divine punishments, rather than as misfortunes.

Alternatively, v. 19 might be read as a depiction of YHWH's (successive) punitive actions against Israel (so Linville 2008: 113). In support of such an interpretation one may refer to the fact that elsewhere in the Hebrew Bible YHWH is pictured, metaphorically, both as a lion (e.g., Hos 5:14; 13:7–8) and as a bear (Hos 13:8). But YHWH is in fact never depicted as a snake, and therefore I find such an interpretation relatively unlikely. But it is not necessary to regard the animals in v. 19 as metaphors. This saying is hardly an allegory. It is rather a story in miniature, designed to illustrate what the day of YHWH is going to be like.

According to a common interpretation, the point made by the short narrative in Amos 5:19 is that it will be impossible to flee from the imminent disasters orchestrated by YHWH (so, e.g., Paul 1991: 185–86 and Carroll R. 1992: 244). But other passages in the book of Amos, such as 2:14–16 and 9:2–4, convey much more clearly the message that no one will be able to escape. In my opinion, it is preferable to read v. 19 as a comment on the topic of v. 18: false security and unfounded optimism. Clearly, the climax of this brief narrative, which is characterized by a gradual "escalation in horror" (Nahkola 2011: 104), is the surprising attack by the snake. Notably, this happens in the moment when the protagonist begins to relax, since he feels secure in his home. Therefore, I suggest that 5:19 illustrates illusory reassurance in a situation of crisis, a theme that is developed further in 6:1–7 (see Wolff 1977: 256 and Fleischer 2001: 208).

5:20. Rather than adding any new perspective, v. 20 echoes the message of v. 18, but now rephrased as a rhetorical question (as in the NRSV: "Is not the day of the Lord darkness, not light, and gloom with no brightness in it?"). In fact, this short oracle says twice what was stated already in v. 18bβ, that the day of YHWH will be dark, not light. This twofold repetition serves more than one rhetorical purpose. To begin with, it creates an elegant *inclusio*. At the same time, the element of inevitability is reinforced. Since the negated interrogative particle *hălō'* often has an emphatic and assertive function, I have chosen to render this question as a statement in the English translation: "Truly, it is darkness, the day of YHWH, and not light, gloom without any brightness in it!"

Rejected Sacrifice (5:21–24)

5   ²¹I hate, I reject your festivals,
and I do not delight in your assemblies.
²²Even if you bring me burnt offerings,
and your grain offerings, I will not accept them.
I will not even look at the communion sacrifices of your fatlings.
²³Take away from me the noise of your songs!
I do not want to hear the music of your harps.
²⁴But let justice roll down like waters,
righteousness like an ever-flowing stream.

INTRODUCTION TO 5:21–24

The rhetorical unit comprising vv. 21–24 has often been seen as a paradigmatic instance of cult-critical prophecy. Within the Hebrew Bible, this vehement attack on the sacrificial cult is matched only by Isa 1:11–15 (see Eidevall 2013).[37] Contrary to a widespread opinion, however, Amos 5:21–24 does not denounce sacrifices as such (see, e.g., Berquist 1993: 61 and Lafferty 2012). As I argue in more detail below, rejection of sacrificial offerings was always situation-bound (see also the Comments on 4:4–5).

Divine rejection of sacrifices is a rather common motif in the Hebrew Bible (see Gen 4:4–5; Lev 10:1–2; Num 16:15; 1 Sam 15:13–23); however, this phenomenon was not restricted to the sphere of YHWH worship. It is, for instance, frequently attested in Greek sources (Naiden 2006). The risk of rejection (communicated by means of an oracle) can be seen as a corollary of the underlying principles that shaped the understanding of sacrificial cults in ancient societies. Offering sacrifices was regarded as analogous to giving gifts—that is, as a way of maintaining a reciprocal yet asymmetric relationship (see Ullucci 2012: 24–30 and Eidevall 2013: 34–38). From the deity's privileged position in the relationship, the deity would always have the possibility to either accept or refuse a sacrificial gift. The reason for rejection is not always stated (see Gen 4:4–5). In some cases it is about improper performance of the ritual (Lev 10:1–2); in others, the reason is (alleged) disloyalty toward the deity (1 Sam 15:13–23).

A particularly striking parallel to Amos 5:21–24 (especially v. 21) is found in the Ugaritic Baal epos (*KTU/CTU* 1.4.III: 17–21): "For two feasts (*dbḥm*) Baal hates / Three, the Cloud-Rider: A feast (*dbḥ*) of shame, a feast of strife, / And a feast of the whispering of servant-girls."[38] Despite differences in genre and context, these two passages have an interesting feature in common: the motif of a deity who dislikes certain feasts. In both cases, moreover, it is stated that the deity "hates" (*śn'* = Ugaritic *śn'a*) the feasts in question.[39] Whereas Baal complains of having been humiliated at a banquet for the members of the divine council (Smith and Pitard 2009: 475–80), YHWH addresses human worshipers in Amos 5:21–24. However, the lexeme *dbḥ*, which is used in the Ugaritic text, can denote either a feast or a sacrifice (cf. Hebrew *zebaḥ*). Hence, both passages can be related to the topic of rejected sacrifice.

The unit 5:21–24 consists of two parts, which have been juxtaposed rather abruptly: vv. 21–23, words of rejection // v. 24, concluding oracle. As observed by Meir Weiss, the first part, vv. 21–23, is a well-balanced composition that displays mathematical precision in its three-by-seven structure: These three verses consist of seven clauses, with seven verbs, and seven objects of divine rejection (1995: 201; see also Limburg 1987). One may add that the thematic structure of this section is tripartite: v. 21, festivals // v. 22, sacrifices // v. 23, music. Further, the expressions of divine dislike allude (anthropomorphically) to three different senses (Paul 1991: 192): smell (Hiphil of *ryḥ*, v. 21b), sight (Hiphil of *nbṭ*, v. 22b), and hearing (*šmʿ*, v. 23b). In the words of Jeremias, v. 21 starts with a forceful "bang," like a musical piece beginning with the sound of a drum (1998: 100). The majestic final chord of this rhetorical masterpiece is struck by the oft-quoted sentence in v. 24.

Most commentators advocate a date of origin in the eighth century B.C.E., before the fall of Samaria (thus, e.g., Wolff 1977: 262 and Jeremias 1998: 104). This is certainly plausible. Alternatively, this passage was composed shortly after that disaster. In either case, 5:21–24 was probably taken as an announcement that YHWH had abandoned the kingdom of Israel (cf. W. H. Schmidt 1973: 76). Because of the prevailing injustice, he had apparently decided to discontinue the reciprocal relationship with his people. This fatal decision, which entailed the patron deity preparing to withdraw his protection from the nation, was manifested by YHWH's refusal to accept the sacrificial gifts offered by the Israelites.

NOTES

5:22. *communion sacrifices.* The singular form *šelem* is exceptional. It appears to be used in a collective sense. The communion type of sacrifice is more commonly designated *zebaḥ šělāmîm.* Several exegetes advocate a slight emendation from שלם to the plural construct form שלמי (see BHSapp); however, this is not necessary. See Paul (1991: 191).

5:24. *ever-flowing stream.* Most dictionaries advocate this translation of *ʾêtān,* "ever-flowing." But according to Snijders (1998: 336–37) "flowing strongly" would be a more apt rendering. The phrase occurs also in Deut 21:4, where it appears to denote a wild brook (see Ges[18], with the proposed sense "Wildbachtal"). Against that background, Jan Dietrich suggests the following translation of Amos 5:24: "Aber das Recht wälze / flute wie Wasser, die Gerechtigkeit wie ein reißender Bach" (2010: 258). Clearly, a translation like "flowing strongly" would above all be consonant with an interpretation of this expression as referring to impending divine judgment (see Berquist 1993: 57, 61).

COMMENTS

5:21–23. In terms of genre, the first part of 5:21–24, comprising vv. 21–23, can be characterized as a negated form of the traditional cultic declaration, uttered by a priest, conveying the message that the deity had accepted the offerings (Rudolph 1971: 209, Wolff 1977: 261, and Jeremias 1998: 101–3). Since v. 21a refers to "your festivals" (*ḥaggêkem*), the setting seems to be one of the major annual festivals, possibly in Bethel. The two initial verb forms bring about an ominous reversal of the expectations attached to all sacrificial worship: "I hate, I reject (*śānēʾtî māʾastî*)" (v. 21a).

In v. 22a, the prophet/author uses priestly terminology of approval (cf. Lev 1:4; 7:18; 22:27), but with a preceding negation: "I will not accept (*lōʾ ʾerṣeh*)." Interestingly, this way of expressing rejection presupposes the possibility of divine acceptance. Three types of sacrifice are mentioned in v. 22: the burnt offering (*ʿōlâ*), the grain offering (*minḥâ*), and the communion sacrifice (*šelem*). These terms form a triad that covers the main types of sacrifice in ancient Israel and Judah.[40] Hence, this utterance seems to make a statement concerning the sacrificial cult in its entirety. But how should that statement be understood?

Scholars who defend the theory that Amos was an anti-cultic prophet have claimed that this prophecy rejects sacrifices as such (Krüger 2006: 47; Barton 2012: 84–92). These interpreters, however, neglect the fact that relational language is used throughout vv. 21–23 (see the Comments on v. 23). Moreover, they fail to account for the observation that v. 23 condemns musical performances with formulations as harsh as those employed in the denunciations of sacrificial offerings (in vv. 21–22).

5:23. Having already been informed that YHWH refuses to look at their offerings (v. 22), the addressees are now told that the deity refuses to listen to "the noise of your songs" and "the music of your harps" (v. 23). To the best of my knowledge, no commentator has ever maintained that Amos 5:21–24 renounces all kinds of music in the name of YHWH.

On a closer examination, the language used in vv. 21–23 is consistently relational. According to this prophecy, YHWH dislikes "*your* festivals (*ḥaggêkem*)" (21a), "*your* grain offerings (or, *your* gifts, *minḥōtêkem*)" (22a), and "*your* songs (*šîrêkā*)" (23a). Clearly, these formulations indicate that the words of rejection are directed against a specific group of addressees in a specific historical situation (with Vollmer 1971: 39 and Weiss 1995: 214). In view of the context, it is probably the sacrificial cult in the kingdom of Israel that is condemned.

5:24. The concluding words of this passage are often quoted: "But let justice (*mišpāṭ*) roll down like waters, righteousness (*ûṣĕdāqâ*) like an ever-flowing stream" (v. 24). Although the message seems to be straightforward, it is difficult to assess the function of this utterance in its present context, where it follows immediately after a negative cultic declaration (vv. 21–23). Some scholars interpret 5:21–24 in terms of an underlying opposition between cult and justice: YHWH demands justice, not sacrificial worship (Rudolph 1971: 208–12 and Ernst 1994: 120–26). However, the notion of a sharp division between cult and ethics looks suspiciously anachronistic. As pointed out by Soggin (1987: 99), "a society that was not founded on religion and the cult was inconceivable."

Possibly, the point made is that moral behavior should be seen as more important than sacrifice (Wolff 1977: 264 and Kaiser 1998: 418–19); however, the wording of the text hardly supports such a reading. No comparison is being made. Rather, v. 24 expresses a wish that justice should be allowed to prevail. I suggest that this utterance provides the reason why YHWH had decided to reject all sacrifices the Israelites offered. This happened, one may infer, because of the lack of justice in their society (see the use of *mišpāṭ* in 5:7, 15; see also 5:10–12). Since water can symbolize death as well as life, however, there appears to be yet another possibility. The utterance in v. 24, with its depiction of mighty streams of water, might perhaps also be read as a threat, which announces an impending disaster.[41]

As part of the emerging book of Amos, the passage 5:21–24 had the function of providing a theological perspective on the fate of the Northern Kingdom. The historical fact that Israel had been defeated by the Assyrians was explained as the consequence of another "fact," namely, that YHWH had rejected this nation and its worship.[42] For Judean readers, this prophecy could be seen as both reassuring and threatening at the same time. On one hand, it indicated that the reason why the disaster occurred was not that YHWH was unable to protect his own people. On the other hand, it could be read as a warning that the Judeans (and their sacrifices) might be rejected, too, if they failed to meet the divine demands for justice and righteousness.

Desert Wandering and Deportation
(5:25–27)

5   [25]Did you bring me sacrifices and grain offerings for forty years in the desert, O house of Israel?
[26]Or did you carry around Sakkuth, your king, and Kaiwan, your images, your astral gods, which you made for yourselves?
       [27]I will drive you into exile beyond Damascus, says YHWH—God of hosts is his name.

INTRODUCTION TO 5:25–27

Since the exclamation *hôy* ("Woe") in 6:1 clearly introduces another unit, it would follow that vv. 25–27 comprise a rhetorical unit (with Andersen and Freedman 1989: 530); however, this unit does not display much unity, since it is not held together by a common theme.

Subsequent to the finishing stroke in v. 24, all further argumentation concerning the cult would seem to be superfluous. Nevertheless, the utterance in v. 25 reverts to the topic of sacrifice, but from another angle altogether. Hence, it looks like a piece of *Fortschreibung,* which develops the theme of 5:21–24 in a new direction, in a later historical situation (see Wolff 1977: 264 and Jeremias 1998: 104–5). Within its present literary context, moreover, v. 25 can be seen as an editorial bridge between two different topics: the sacrificial cult (vv. 22–24) and exile (v. 27).

Since v. 26 rather abruptly introduces a topic that is otherwise conspicuously absent from the book of Amos, namely, worship of other gods, I agree with Jeremias (1998: 105) that it represents an even later addition than v. 25. Whereas v. 25 may stem from the exilic period, in the sixth century, I suggest that v. 26 is of postexilic origin.[43] The concluding utterance in v. 27 threatens the addressees with deportation and exile. For the ensuing discussion, it does not matter whether v. 27 is ascribed to the same layer as v. 25 or to an earlier one.

Despite, or perhaps because of, all interpretive difficulties involved, the passage 5:25–27 evidently attracted the interest of early Jewish and Christ-believing interpreters.[44]

NOTES

5:26. *Sakkuth, your king, and Kaiwan.* It is generally acknowledged that the names of the deities Sakkuth and Kaiwan have been vocalized in a polemical way in the MT, as *sikkût* and *kiyyûn* (so-called *šiqqûṣ* vocalization). See further Paul (1991: 196). According to an early line of interpretation, סכות should instead be read as *sukkôt* ("booths" or "shelters"). Whereas the LXX translates τὴν σκηνὴν τοῦ Μολοχ ("the tent of Moloch"), the *Damascus Document* (CD 7:14–16) interprets the expression "the booths of your king (סכות מלככם)" as referring to the books of the Torah. At the same time, a (messianic) connection is made between the king's tents in 5:26 and the promise concerning restoration of "the fallen booth (סוכת) of David" in 9:11. See further Osten-Sacken (1979).

your astral gods. This is a plausible interpretation of *kôkab ʾĕlôhêkem* (literally, "the star of your god[s]"). See Paul (1991: 188), Jeremias (1998: 98), and Garrett (2008: 175).

COMMENTS

5:25. The utterance in 5:25 has the form of a rhetorical question: "Did you bring me sacrifices and grain offerings for forty years in the desert, O house of Israel?" It has often been assumed that it alludes to an ideal period in the past without any sacrificial cult at all (thus, e.g., Wolff 1977: 264–65 and Linville 2008: 117). Thus understood, this oracle would imply that sacrificial worship is completely unnecessary. According to John Barton, the underlying logic of v. 25 is as follows: "Israel offered no sacrifices during the time in the wilderness, and that time was . . . the time of its honeymoon with Yahweh (Jer. 2.1–3), therefore sacrifice cannot be what Yahweh requires" (2005: 120). However, as I demonstrate below, this is not the most plausible interpretation of Amos 5:25.

To begin with, it is doubtful whether v. 25 depicts an ideal state. It is worth noting that, in contrast to some passages in the prophetic literature (Jer 2:2; Hos 2:16 [Eng. v. 14]; 9:10a), this utterance does not contain any positive image of the wilderness period. Since the phrase "forty years in the desert" (which does not occur in the idealizing texts mentioned above) is frequent in the Pentateuch, in Deuteronomy as well as priestly texts (see Num 14:33–34; 32:13; Deut 2:7; 8:2, 4, etc.), it is likely that Amos 5:25 alludes to traditions according to which the wilderness period was far from ideal. In the wilderness narratives of the Pentateuch, this is above all a time of grumbling and complaining and a period of repeated revolts against Moses and YHWH (Exod 16:1–12; 17:1–7; 32:1–29; Num 11:1–23; 16:1–17:5). However, the wilderness period is certainly not depicted as a time without sacrificial cult (see Leviticus 1–10; Num 7:1–88; 16:1–35). Hence, it is unlikely that the first readers of Amos 5:25 had such a view of the wilderness period (see Vollmer 1971: 38).

Next, it is necessary to examine the references to sacrificial cult in v. 25. Two types of offerings are mentioned. Whereas *zebaḥ* denotes an animal sacrifice that involved a communal meal, the lexeme *minḥâ* (which occurs also in v. 22) usually refers to a vegetal offering, consisting of flour mixed with oil (see Lev 6:7–8 [Eng. vv. 14–15];

23:13).[45] Together, these two terms would seem to constitute a kind of merism, standing for the entire sacrificial system (Wolff 1977: 265). Notably, the formulations used in v. 25 are not derogatory. This utterance does not explicitly denounce any type of sacrificial offering.

But which attitude toward sacrificial cult is expressed in v. 25? What is the function of this utterance? Everything depends on how the rhetorical question is understood. Which answer is implied? Several commentators presume, without further discussion, that the expected answer is an absolute "no," indicating that the Israelites did not bring any sacrificial gifts at all to YHWH during those forty years (thus, e.g., Schüngel-Straumann 1972: 33 and Paul 1991: 193). However, in the light of ancient notions of what we call religion—and, more specifically, in the light of the traditions recorded in the Pentateuch—it is more likely that the first readers would have answered something like, "Yes, our ancestors did probably offer sacrifices in the wilderness, but on a limited scale, not regularly or continuously during those forty years" (see similarly Dines 2001: 586).

With its reference to life in the desert, the scenery in v. 25 would seem to provide a contrast to the situation of abundance described and denounced in vv. 21–24 (with Andersen and Freedman 1989: 531). The argument made appears to be based on the presupposition that the wilderness period was characterized by limited resources. Cultic excesses would have been unthinkable in such a situation (Rudolph 1971: 212 and Paul 1991: 194); nonetheless, v. 25 points out, the ancestors were able to maintain contact with YHWH despite these circumstances.

On the basis of the discussion above, I suggest that the rhetorical question in Amos 5:25 comments on the situation after the destruction of the temple in Jerusalem in 587 B.C.E. For those in exile, the maintenance of a lavish cult would no longer be possible. The same would hold for those who remained in Judah. Thus, the "house of Israel" would have to endure another period of scarcity, like the legendary wandering through the desert in the mythic past. In that situation, v. 25 may have conveyed a glimpse of hope. Since there is no hint that the Israelites were cut off from communion and communication with their god during the forty years of desert trekking, a continued relationship with YHWH would seem to be possible also in exile. This utterance does not denounce the offering of sacrifices, but it would certainly seem to relativize the role of the sacrificial cult (cf. Jer 7:22).[46]

5:26. Because of the perplexing plurality of possible meanings conveyed by a *qatal* form preceded by the conjunction *wĕ* (ranging from past tense to future, including different kinds of modalities), and the scarcity of contextual clues, the relation between v. 26 and its immediate literary context can be construed in strongly divergent ways (see, e.g., Erlandsson 1968 and Gevirtz 1968). This utterance has thus been interpreted either as a predictive statement relating to v. 27, which likewise begins with a *weqatal* form, or as a continuation of the rhetorical question in v. 25 (Wolff 1977: 260, 265 and Jeremias 1998: 98, 105). In terms of content, the latter alternative makes better sense. A future-oriented interpretation would imply the strange notion that carrying around images of gods was part of the deported people's punishment. It is preferable to read v. 26 as a retrospective question, which supplements v. 25: "Or did you carry around Sakkuth, your king, and Kaiwan, your images, your astral gods, which you made for yourselves?"

Evidently, v. 26 is a late addition. This is indicated by the fact that it creates syntactic ambiguity and, above all, by the observation that it introduces a new topic, which does not occur anywhere else within chapters 3–6: "idolatry." With the notable exception of the Judah oracle in 2:4–5 (another addition), the book does not contain any accusations related to the cult of "foreign" deities and/or of images.[47] The downfall of the Northern Kingdom is not explained as a consequence of worship of other gods. In that respect, the book of Amos differs greatly from the Deuteronomistic History (see 2 Kgs 17:1–18). One may therefore conjecture that the postexilic reader who added v. 26 found the passage 5:21–27* somewhat puzzling. He might have asked, Why would YHWH reject the sacrificial cult so vehemently? And further, How could worship of YHWH (vv. 21–25), albeit deficient, incur the punishment of deportation (v. 27)? Sensing that something important was missing, this reader inserted a clarification: the rejected Israelite cult concerned other gods![48] The aberrant Israelites, we are told, even carried around statues of Assyrian astral deities in processions.

Through the addition of v. 26, the question in v. 25 takes on a new nuance. A sharp contrast is now being made between the wilderness generation and the addressees. It is implied that the sins of the latter are worse, since they include the worship of a diversity of foreign gods. But which deities did this postexilic author have in mind? According to a widely accepted hypothesis, the MT's *sikkût* and *kiyyûn* are pejoratively vocalized forms of the names of two Mesopotamian gods, namely "Sakkuth" and "Kaiwan" (see Paul 1991: 195–97). The astral character of these gods is emphasized. In this way, trust in omens based on astrology is added to the list of transgressions (cf. Isa 47:13). One may also trace a connection to 5:8, which declares that the constellations in the sky have been created by the one god, YHWH.[49] However, it is impossible to figure out precisely why these two gods are mentioned, out of all astral or celestial deities in the Assyrian-Babylonian pantheon. Whereas Kaiwan probably refers to the "star-god" Saturn, with the epithet *kaiamānu*, "the steady one," Sakkuth almost certainly corresponds to dSAG.KUD, a minor deity associated with Ninurta (Paul 1991: 195–96). Rather than assuming that these two gods were immensely popular in Israel or Judah at a certain time (for instance, in the eighth or seventh century B.C.E. or during the Persian era), I suggest that the interpolator used two names that he happened to know. Sakkuth may thus have been borrowed from 2 Kgs 17:30.[50]

5:27. This oracle, which concludes the unit 5:25–27, as well as chapter 5, states that "you" (presumably the population of the Northern Kingdom) will be driven into exile, "beyond Damascus." Interestingly, the Assyrians are not mentioned, but it is indicated that the captive Israelites will be taken in a certain direction, namely, to the north.[51] The motif of forced migration to or beyond Syria recalls Amos 4:3, which (according to my reconstruction) presaged deportation "toward Hermon." A similar threat concludes the ensuing passage, at 6:7.

The Party Is Over (6:1–7)

6 ¹Woe to the carefree in Zion, and the confident on Mount Samaria,
the distinguished men of the foremost nation, to whom the house of Israel comes.
    —²Cross over to Calneh and see,
go from there to Hamath-Rabbah,

then go down to Gath of the Philistines!
Are you better than these kingdoms? Or is their territory greater than yours?—

³You who want to ward off the day of disaster,
yet you bring near a reign of violence.
⁴Woe to those who recline on beds of ivory and lounge on their couches,
those who eat lambs from the flock and calves from the feeding stall,
⁵who intone to the lyre,
and improvise on musical instruments, like David,
⁶who drink wine from bowls and anoint themselves with the finest oil
but do not worry over the injury of Joseph.
⁷Therefore, they shall now be among the first to go into exile;
the banquet of the loungers shall cease.

INTRODUCTION TO 6:1–7 WITH A
DISCUSSION OF *MARZĒAḤ* BANQUETS

There is wide scholarly agreement that the passage 6:1–7 constitutes a coherent composition. Arguably, also v. 2 (which is often seen as a later addition) can be seen as part of the original rhetorical unit (see the Comments). This unit begins with a woe exclamation directed at those who are in a state of false security (v. 1; cf. 5:18), and it ends with a prediction of deportation (v. 7; cf. 4:2–3 and 5:27). There can be no doubt that 6:1–7 belongs to the oldest layer of the book of Amos; however, this is one of the instances in which the traditional dating of the prophetic activities of a certain Amos to the 760s or 750s B.C.E. has given rise to interpretive problems.

As explained in more detail below, several of these problems are solved if one posits a later date of origin, during the last two decades of the eighth century B.C.E., in the context of aggressive Assyrian expansion: first the Assyrian army captured Calneh and Hamath (6:2), then they took Samaria (6:1, 7), and, finally, even Jerusalem was threatened (see 2 Kgs 18:13–17). Against that backdrop, all features of this prophecy make perfect sense, including the reference to Zion in v. 1, the enumeration of cities in v. 2, and the mention of David in v. 5 (with Blum 1994).

Much of the exegetical discussion of Amos 6:1–7 has focused on the depiction of the extravagant habits of the upper classes in Samaria (and Jerusalem?) in vv. 4–6. Because the term *marzēaḥ* occurs in v. 7, several scholars have argued that Amos 6:4–6 describes, and denounces, a quite specific type of banquet that involved the worship of deities other than YHWH and/or various "syncretistic" ingredients. It is therefore necessary to discuss the influential hypothesis that Amos 6:4–6 polemicizes against "idolatrous" or "syncretistic" cult practices (propounded by Barstad 1984: 127–42; see also Greer 2007).

Because this lexeme occurs in the immediate context, in v. 7, it is indeed likely that vv. 4–6 describe a special kind of banquet, called *marzēaḥ*. However, it is questionable whether this implies that the passage condemns cultic and religious transgressions, such as the worship of other deities, as claimed by Barstad (1984: 140–41). The problem is that very little is known about the characteristic features of a *marzēaḥ* event in Israel or Judah in the eighth or seventh century B.C.E. As a consequence, it is difficult to find out in which ways (if any) such a banquet would have differed from a "regular" feast.

The lexeme *marzēaḥ* occurs only twice in the Hebrew Bible: here in Amos 6:7 and in Jer 16:5, where the expression *bêt marzēaḥ*, "house of *marzēaḥ*," appears within the context of mourning rituals. However, the Jeremiah text says nothing about any gatherings or banquets taking place in such a house. In order to find out more about the *marzēaḥ* institution, we need to turn to the extrabiblical evidence.

It is indeed remarkable that a Semitic word spelled *mrzḥ*, and denoting some kind of association, is attested in texts from a wide geographical area during a time period spanning more than two thousand years, from Ebla and Ugarit into the Hellenistic era.[52] Most likely, the practices connected to this institution varied over time and among cultures; nonetheless, having studied all relevant texts, John McLaughlin was able to find a few common denominators that could serve as defining characteristics (2001: 65–70). The constitutive elements of a *marzēaḥ* would seem to have been (1) upper-class membership, (2) some kind of religious affiliation, and (3) consumption of alcoholic beverages.

My own way of summarizing McLaughlin's findings would be to stress two aspects in particular: exclusivity and excess. A *mrzḥ* was something like a club for rich men, with a leader and a set of rules for membership and (at least, in some cases) with its own house and property. Further, heavy drinking would always be an important ingredient in such meetings (McLaughlin 2001: 69–70). The resemblances to a Greek *symposion* are rather striking.

As regards the religious or cultic aspects, it is important to notice that a *mrzḥ* association would always have a patron deity (McLaughlin 2001: 9–61, *passim*). Some texts mention sacrifices or other rituals, but it is uncertain whether this should be seen as a constitutive feature of a *marzēaḥ*.[53] Most likely, every banquet arranged in an ancient Near Eastern or Mediterranean society would include some kind of religious ritual.

To what extent can these perspectives on the *mrzḥ* institution throw light on Amos 6:4–6? I agree with McLaughlin that the description in this biblical passage "is consistent with what is known about the *marzēaḥ* from extra-biblical materials" (2001: 97). Notably, the upper-class connection is evident throughout, and the (probably excessive) drinking of wine is likewise mentioned (v. 6). Nevertheless, I believe McLaughlin overstates the case a little, as he concludes that "vv. 4–6b in particular describe an actual *marzēaḥ* feast" (2001: 97). In my opinion, Amos 6:4–6 does not necessarily provide an eyewitness account of what happened on a specific occasion, when the members of such an exclusive association were gathered in their house.[54] Rather, this passage uses the concept of a *marzēaḥ* in order to depict the lifestyle of the elite more broadly—a lifestyle that involved a lot of feasting and drinking, as well as exclusive banquets of the *marzēaḥ* type.

For the interpretation of Amos 6:4–6, however, it does not make any great difference whether we consider this passage to be an accurate description of such a banquet or not. As shown by McLaughlin (2001: 70–79), there is no reason to assume that funerary rites or ancestor cult were regular parts of such meetings. Further, since no other deity is mentioned in the text, nothing speaks against the assumption that the patron deity of the *marzēaḥ* association mentioned in v. 7 (and possibly described in vv. 4–6) was YHWH (with Polley 1989: 89).[55]

NOTES

6:1. *distinguished.* More literally, the passive participle of the verb *nqb* would seem to mean "pierced" or "perforated." However, one may reconstruct the following semantic development: "pierced"—"marked"—"distinguished." See Rudolph (1971: 215). See also *DCH* and *HALOT,* s.v.; and Num 1:17, where the phrase *niqbû běšēmôt* means "designated by name" (NRSV).

6:2. *Are you better.* Because of a certain syntactical ambiguity arising from the contextual position of this noun clause, one might also translate: "Are they better (off)." The choice depends on whether "these kingdoms" are thought to refer to Israel and Judah or to the neighboring nations mentioned in v. 2a (and v. 2bα). I find the latter alternative more likely. See the Comments on v. 2.

Or is their territory greater than yours? Several scholars, following the lead of Well-hausen (1893: 83), advocate a change of suffixes in v. 2bγ, reading *ʾim rab gěbûlkem miggěbûlām,* "or is your territory greater than theirs?" (thus, e.g., Rudolph 1971: 216 and Jeremias 1998: 108). However, such an emendation is unwarranted. The distribution of pronominal suffixes in the MT is confirmed by the LXX and Vulgate. See further the Comments on v. 2.

6:3. *reign of violence.* The collocation *šebet ḥāmās* is difficult to interpret. The uncertainty is primarily attached to the word *šebet,* which I have chosen to take as an infinitive of *yšb* and to translate "reign of violence" (thus also Wolff 1977: 272, "rule of violence"; and Jeremias 1998: 108). This rendering is based on the argument that the verb *yšb,* "to sit," can denote the act of sitting on a throne. Several emendations have been suggested, none of them convincing. See Wolff (1977: 272). The consonantal text of the MT, at least as regards שבת, is confirmed by the LXX; however, the Greek translator read this phrase as a reference to "false sabbaths" (σαββάτων ψευδῶν).

6:4. *Woe to those.* The opening words "woe to" have been added for the sake of structural clarity, since the verbal participles in vv. 4–6 appear to be connected to the woe (*hôy*) exclamation in v. 1. A similar solution has been adopted by the NRSV.

6:5. *intone to the lyre.* The verb *prṭ* is a *hapax legomenon;* hence, all translations of *happōrṭîm* are to some extent based on guesswork. As the ensuing phrase *ʿal-pî hannābel* seems to mean "to the tune of the lyre" (with Wolff 1977: 276 and Paul 1991: 199), it is likely that *prṭ* denotes singing of some kind. This line of interpretation is supported by the Vulgate, which has *canitis ad vocem psalterii.* Alternatively, but perhaps less likely, the verb *prṭ* describes the act of striking or plucking the strings of an instrument (Garrett 2008: 187); thus, apparently, the LXX (ἐπικροτοῦντες πρὸς τὴν φωνὴν τῶν ὀργάνων).

improvise. Alternatively, one might translate "they invent for themselves musical instruments, like David." See the Comments on v. 5.

6:7. *the banquet of the loungers shall cease.* According to the LXX translator, who seems to have read סוסים (*sûsîm,* "horses") instead of סרוחים (*sěrûḥîm,* "loungers"), there shall be no more "neighing of horses" (χρεμετισμὸς ἵππων).

COMMENTS

6:1. The opening words of 6:1, "Woe to the carefree in Zion" (6:1aα), have often been regarded as problematic, since no other references to Jerusalem are found within chapters

3–6. In order to solve the perceived problem, scholars have tended to resort to either emendation (see BHSapp and Soden 1990: 214–15) or excision, based on some kind of interpolation hypothesis (thus, e.g., Wolff 1977: 269–70 and Fleischer 1989: 226). However, the reading "in Zion (*běṣiyyôn*)" is attested by all textual witnesses. Further, if the mention of Zion is removed, the perfect poetic parallelism between "the carefree in Zion" (v. 1aα) and "the confident on Mount Samaria" (v. 1aβ) is destroyed (Jeremias 1998: 107, n. 1). In my opinion, all such operations are unwarranted.[56]

Once it is accepted that the first version of the book of Amos was composed in Judah, there is in fact no problem to be solved. Within a Judean setting, during the decade before the downfall of Samaria in 722 B.C.E., or the decades that followed that event, 6:1 makes excellent sense as we now have it (see Blum 1994: 33–36).[57] As will be shown below, the hypothesis that this passage was composed in Judah may contribute to clarifying some additional features in 6:1–7.

By means of its introductory interjection, *hôy*, "Woe" (or, "Alas"), the utterance in 6:1 recalls 5:18. As a consequence, it becomes possible to read 5:18–27 (especially vv. 18–20) and 6:1–7 together, as two successive woe oracles. In terms of topic, these passages exhibit a high degree of continuity. The theme of false security in the midst of crisis, which was introduced in 5:18–20, is developed further in 6:1–7, with additional emphasis on the arrogance of the wealthy. Apparently, judging from 6:1a, the members of the upper classes in Jerusalem were equally unaware of approaching danger (for instance, in the shape of the Assyrian army) and equally inclined to rely on unconditional divine protection, as were the ruling elite in Samaria. With regard to both form and content, it is instructive to compare Amos 6:1 with some woe oracles that were most certainly composed in Jerusalem (in the eighth century or later), namely, Isa 5:8–24 and 31:1–3.

The depiction in v. 1bα of a group of (self-appointed?) "distinguished men of the foremost nation" is usually read as referring to the leadership of Samaria, rather than Jerusalem (so, e.g., Mays 1969: 114–15 and Paul 1991: 200). This is reasonable from a syntactical point of view, since Samaria is the last word of v. 1a. However, on such an interpretation the formulation in v. 1bβ, "to whom the house of Israel comes," may seem perplexingly redundant. It is of course possible that "the house of Israel" here denotes the ordinary people of the Northern Kingdom, who would come to their leaders for consultation (Paul 1991: 200 and Garrett 2008: 179). But an alternative interpretation, proposed by Erhard Blum (1994), is worth considering. According to Blum, v. 1bβ refers to the arrival in Jerusalem of immigrants/refugees from the Northern Kingdom after 722 B.C.E. (1994: 33–34).[58] The issue cannot be settled with any certainty.

Even if the remainder of 6:1–7 should be read as primarily referring to the upper classes in Samaria, however, the mention of Zion in v. 1a remains significant for the interpretation. At that juncture, I suggest, something that has remained implicit throughout the preceding discourse becomes visible: the Zion-centered and Judah-oriented perspective of the editors (see also 1:2!). The opening clause of this utterance, which has caused so much debate, can be seen as a reminder to readers in Judah that all these prophecies had been collected (or composed) for their sake, as history lessons and as warning examples. In other words, the indictments in 6:1–7 and other passages against the ruling elite in the Northern Kingdom would seem to have served a twofold purpose. Besides providing explanations for the catastrophe in 722 B.C.E., they were also intended to be read as (re)directed against the leaders of Judah.

6:2. The utterance in v. 2 appears to interrupt the woe oracle comprising 6:1–7. There is an abrupt shift from a depiction in the third-person plural (v. 1) to a series of imperatives without any explicit addressee. Hence, 6:2 is often treated as a second-ary insertion (so, e.g., Wolff 1977: 274 and Jeremias 1998: 114–15). However, such a conclusion is not necessary, since the interruption may be understood as part of the prophet's/author's rhetorical strategy.

In v. 2, the anonymous addressees are commanded to travel to three cities in neigh-boring countries: to Calneh (= Kullani) and Hamath (here called Hamath-Rabbah, which means "the great Hamath"), both situated along the Orontes River, and to Gath, a city at the Philistine coast. Arguably, though, this instruction is a rhetorical device. Instead of actually making a journey to Calneh or any other place, the hearers/readers are asked to ponder the comparisons that are presented in v. 2b in the form of rhetorical questions. But who is speaking to whom, and what is the rhetorical purpose?

Possibly, v. 2 is a fictitious quotation, imitating political propaganda. It is conceiv-able that the rulers who were addressed in v. 1 would use such formulations in order to persuade their subjects that they need not worry—because their own nation is better and greater than the neighboring nations and cities mentioned (so, e.g., Carroll R. 1992: 256–57). One might translate v. 2bβγ as follows: "Are they (= the neighboring nations) better than these kingdoms? Or is their territory greater than yours?" In order to obtain coherence and logic in the rhetoric, one would then have to take "these king-doms" as referring to Israel and Judah, as though these two states were allies. However, it has proved difficult to find a matching historical situation or to reconstruct a fitting rhetorical situation.[59] Another interpretation must be sought.

It is worth noting that v. 2 is not marked as a quotation; therefore, it is probably preferable to assume that the prophetic voice uttering v. 1 continues to speak. Thus interpreted, the utterance in v. 2 invites the listeners/readers to make a comparison, which is far from reassuring. The point made by the rhetorical questions would seem to be that there is no significant difference in size or military strength between the nation of the addressees (Israel or Judah) and "these kingdoms" (v. 2bβ), that is, the cities/na-tions mentioned in v. 2abα. This understanding of the rhetorical function is reflected in the translation of v. 2bβ that was given above. The addressees are not "better than these kingdoms," but neither "is their territory greater than yours."

If, as seems likely, 6:2 was composed at the end of the eighth century, one may reconstruct the following scenario (with Blum 1994: 31–34; see also Jeremias 1998: 114–15): The cities (with surrounding territories) mentioned in v. 2abα had already been captured by the Assyrians. Calneh and Hamath were conquered by Tiglath-Pile-ser III in 738 B.C.E. and later were definitely subdued under Sargon II in 717 and 720, respectively (see Paul 1991: 201–3). The Philistine city of Gath was conquered by Sar-gon II in 711 B.C.E. (Blum 1994: 32–33). According to a likely interpretation of v. 2b, the point made is that there was hardly any reason to believe that Jerusalem would be able to resist the Assyrian army when those other cities of comparable strength (includ-ing, by that time, also Samaria!) had been defeated.

Interestingly, this oracle does not mention the possibility that YHWH might give protection. It sounds, in fact, almost like an echo of Assyrian propaganda. In Isa 10:9, a boastful Assyrian king asks rhetorical questions of a similar kind, implying that neither Samaria nor Jerusalem would withstand his invincible army: "Is not Calno (= Calneh) like Carchemish? Is not Hamath like Arpad, Samaria like Damascus?"[60]

Summing up, the carefree and confident attitude of the political leaders in Samaria and Jerusalem, which is described in v. 1, is revealed as unfounded in v. 2. In reality, and on their own (without the help of YHWH), this utterance points out, both Judah and Israel were small and insignificant when compared with Assyria—just like Calneh, Hamath, and Gath.

6:3. In v. 3 the woe oracle intoned in v. 1 continues, as if v. 2 had not come in between. The implicit accusations made, which are general and sweeping, are probably primarily directed against the leaders in Samaria, but they could easily be applied to the leading circles in Jerusalem as well. Employing irony and ambiguity, v. 3 describes the addressees as provoking or precipitating what they wished to ward off or postpone: the *yôm rāʿ*, which could be taken to mean "the day of disaster" or "the evil day," but also "the day of (moral) evil."

I find it likely that the phrase *yôm rāʿ*, "the day of disaster," should be understood against the background of hemerology, the widespread practice of differentiating (with the help of diverse divinatory techniques) between days of fortune and misfortune.[61] Above all, though, the expression *yôm rāʿ* evokes associations with the passage 5:18–20 and the motif of "the day of YHWH," which would turn out to be dark and destructive—in other words: a day of disaster. Both passages illustrate an ironic reversal of expectations.

In 6:3, however, the emphasis lies not primarily on the impossibility of escaping the coming catastrophe (as in 5:18–20), but rather on the active role of the addressees in making it happen: "you bring near a reign of violence" (v. 3b). Unfortunately, the translation of the phrase *šebet ḥāmās*, here rendered "a reign of violence," is uncertain (see the Notes). Alternative translations worth considering include "seat of violence" or "throne of violence"; however, there can be no doubt that v. 3b alludes to acts of oppressive violence (*ḥāmās;* cf. 3:9–10!) that are thought to "bring near" divine retaliation in the form of disaster.[62]

6:4–6. In v. 4 a new subunit begins, comprising vv. 4–6. Rather loosely attached to the woe exclamation in v. 1, but still attached, these verses describe the extravagant life of the rich in Samaria. As argued above, however, it is reasonable to assume that this text was written for a Judean readership. Hence, it might also address similar attitudes among the rich in Jerusalem. Judging from this passage, which probably should be seen as a caricature, the main ingredients in the lifestyle of the upper classes in Samaria were choice meals (v. 4b), music (v. 5), and plenty of wine and oil (v. 6a). One gets the impression of a never-ending party. Clearly, this passage condemns the lifestyle described. But on what grounds?

It is unlikely that Amos 6:4–6 is based on the idea that enjoying good food or fine wine, or being rich, should be regarded as a sin or a crime in itself (cf. Clines 1993: 144–46). In fact, it is difficult to find that kind of statement elsewhere in the Hebrew Bible, as noted by McLaughlin (2001: 87): "Since prosperity was considered a sign of divine blessing, that alone would not elicit the punishment of exile."[63] The indignation expressed in this text concerns not primarily what these privileged people are doing, but rather what they are *not* doing. The depiction of their luxurious banquets is framed by accusations targeting their passivity and indifference when action was called for. Judging from this text, and its context, the rich in Samaria (and/or Jerusalem), who were profiting from oppression (v. 3; see also 3:9–10 and 4:1–2), did not care about the suffering of other people (v. 6b). That was their sin (with McLaughlin 2001: 107).

One may add the observation that there is a structural similarity between the passages 6:4–6 and 5:21–24. In both cases, joyous and lavish feasting is denounced—either at communal sacrificial feasts (5:21–23) or at banquets of a more private nature (6:4–6). In terms of topics, there is a movement from meat consumption (5:22; 6:4b) to musical performance (5:23; 6:5; in both cases the lyre or harp, *nēbel,* is mentioned), followed by an accusation and/or a verdict (5:24; 6:6b–7).

6:4. In order to interpret v. 4 within its literary context (6:1–7) one has to assume that the participle *haššōkěbîm* ("those who recline") at the beginning of v. 4a is governed by the exclamation *hôy* ("woe!") in v. 1a. What follows is a typical banquet scene. Reclining on their couches (v. 4a), the participants are served food (v. 4b).

Some features in this description serve to underline the dimension of luxury. Thus, the mention of "beds of ivory" (4a) definitely indicates that those denounced belong to the very rich (King 1988: 139–42). Interestingly, several hundred pieces of exquisitely crafted ivory decorations, usually made in Phoenicia (and thus imported), have been unearthed in archaeological excavations at Samaria.[64] Even an eighth-century ivory bed—or, to be more precise, a couch richly decorated with inlay made of ivory—has been unearthed, at Salamis on Cyprus (King 1988: 147–48). It is further worth noting that those who recline on their couches are described as *sěrûḥîm* (here rendered by the verb "to lounge"). The adjective (or passive participle) *sārûaḥ,* implies a state of extreme relaxation. In Exod 26:12 it is used about a curtain that was hanging freely in the tabernacle.

As to the menu of this banquet, it is important to bear in mind that eating meat was in itself seen as a kind of luxury, connected to feasts rather than to ordinary everyday meals.[65] Lamb and veal were regarded as choice dishes. Arguably, the information that the lambs were taken directly "from the flock" (v. 4bα) and the calves "from the feeding stall (*mittôk marbēq*)" (v. 4bβ) was added merely to underline that these people could afford the very best and the most expensive meat.[66] In view of the poetic parallelism (it was hardly a crime to take lambs from the flock), as well as the rhetorical purpose of the passage as a whole, it is unlikely that the expression *mittôk marbēq* would imply any illicit procedure involved in the slaughter of the calves, as suggested by some scholars (Weippert 1985: 7–9 and Schorch 2010: 128–29).[67]

6:5. Besides eating (v. 4) and drinking (v. 6a), musical entertainment is described as an important ingredient in the banquet (v. 5). The lyre and other instruments are mentioned, but it is difficult to reconstruct the exact nature of the musical activities that are described. Because *ʿal-pî hannābel* in v. 5a would seem to mean "to the tune of the lyre" (Wolff 1977: 276), it is likely that the verb *prṭ,* a *hapax legomenon,* denotes singing of some kind (see the Notes). Some commentators believe that this unusual verb denotes howling or bawling rather than beautiful singing (Rudolph 1971: 217 and Jeremias 1998: 108). However, an identical verbal stem, *prṭ,* is attested in a Samaritan hymn, where it apparently carries the sense "sing" without any pejorative connotations (Montgomery 1906: 51–52).

In v. 5b, the participants in the banquet are, somewhat surprisingly, likened to David. Within this context, this is probably best interpreted as subtle irony (with Goswell 2011: 248–49). If original to the text, the expression *kĕdāwîd* ("like David") may, in addition, be understood as yet another hint that the author/editor had a Judean readership in mind (cf. the reference to Zion in v. 1). Alternatively, some scholars see the mention of David as a late gloss, mainly because it is lacking in the Septuagint and it disturbs the metrical balance (Jeremias 1998: 108, n. 6). In either case, the interpreter needs to search for a recognizable link between the figure of David and the activity described in v. 5b.[68] The verb *ḥšb* means "to think," but also "to devise" and the like.

Depending on how one understands the syntax and the semantics, v. 5b can be rendered in two different ways: (1) "they invent for themselves musical instruments, like David" (thus Paul 1991: 199, 206–7) or (2) "they improvise for themselves on musical instruments, like David" (see Andersen and Freedman 1989: 544, 563).[69] Interestingly, both interpretations can be linked to traditions about David. Whereas his skill in playing the lyre is a central motif in 1 Samuel 16 (see especially 16:23), the idea that David made musical instruments is attested only in rather late postexilic texts (1 Chr 23:5; 2 Chr 29:26–27; Neh 12:36; Ps 151:2).[70] I prefer the second alternative, albeit with a certain hesitation, mainly because it makes better sense in the context, which describes leisure and entertainment at a party (vv. 4–5a) rather than work, such as the construction of new devices.

6:6. In v. 6a, the depiction of the banquet scene is rounded out. Two additional commodities are mentioned, both of them associated with feasting and luxury: wine and oil. In some respects, the terminology used is conspicuous. Thus, in v. 6aα the reader is told that the revelers are drinking wine from "bowls" (*mizrāq*) rather than from ordinary cups (*kôs*). Since excessive drinking (and, one may infer, a high level of inebriety) was one of the hallmarks of a banquet of the *marzēaḥ* type, the point is perhaps primarily to indicate the large quantities of wine imbibed by the participants.

In addition, it is worth noting that the word *mizrāq* (etymologically, a vessel used for sprinkling) may have had overtly cultic connotations. A concordance search would seem to confirm this. In the Hebrew Bible, outside the book of Amos, the lexeme *mizrāq* in fact occurs "exclusively in cultic settings," as pointed out by Jonathan Greer (2007: 250).[71] This gives a further nuance to the picture, as it indicates the possibility of a ritual component in the feast (with Jeremias 1998: 113). However, the occurrence of this term is hardly sufficient evidence that the banquet described involved worship of deities other than YHWH, as claimed by some scholars (so, e.g., Greer 2007).[72] Still, there can be no doubt that the vocabulary employed in v. 6a hints at a certain religious dimension in the banquet described.

As part of the festivities, the reader is told, the guests would further pour out "the finest oils (*rēʾšît šĕmānîm*)" (v. 6aβ) and rub head and body with them (see Paul 208, n. 85.) According to the precise wording of the text, they would "anoint" (*yimšĕḥû*) themselves. The appearance of the verb *mšḥ* in this context is unexpected. Whereas other verbs, in particular *sûk*, were connected to the use of oil for hygienic or cosmetic purposes, *mšḥ* would seem to have been reserved for various kinds of ceremonial anointing (Greer 2007: 248–49.) As is well known, priests, prophets, and kings were inaugurated by means of such anointment. Clearly, then, *mšḥ* has cultic connotations; however, since the use of this verb in the Hebrew Bible is above all connected with the act of king-making, one should not overlook the possibility that the text here alludes to the political aspirations of the loungers.[73] I suggest that this conspicuous reference to the act of anointing, implying that these people regarded themselves as kings, may be linked to the equally conspicuous expression "like David" in v. 5.

On the whole, it seems safe to conclude, with Susan Ackerman, that the prophet/author "does not attack the religious aspects of the *marzēaḥ* of Samaria; rather he criticizes the *marzēaḥ* for what he perceives to be its social flaws" (1989: 279). At the same time, however, it is important to note that the portrayal of the allegedly condemnable social behavior and attitudes of the rich contains allusions to symbols and gestures of political and religious significance—the drinking from bowls and the anointing with oil (v. 6a)—gestures that apparently were not accompanied by acts of responsibility.

In v. 6b, this rather lengthy description of behavior at a banquet (vv. 4–6a) is followed by an unveiled accusation. The revelers are said to be totally indifferent to an acute crisis of one kind or other. Preoccupied with their own pleasures, they simply do not care about what is going on in the world around them. In the words of the text, they "do not worry over the injury (*šēber*) of Joseph."

Which historical event could this refer to? Because Joseph is mentioned, in what appears to be a case of metaphorical personification, Ephraim and Manasseh, the tribes of Joseph, come to mind. Arguably, the notion of an injury or breakdown (*šēber*) affecting these tribes or regions—that is, the heartland of the Northern Kingdom—points primarily to the Assyrian campaign in 733 B.C.E., which drastically reduced the territory of Israel (with Wolff 1977: 274, 277 and Jeremias 1998: 115). Since parts of the territory of Manasseh, such as the land around Megiddo, became an Assyrian province, whereas the territory of Ephraim around Samaria largely remained independent, one may perhaps describe this event as a separation between Ephraim and Manasseh, resulting in an injury (*šēber*) to the national body.

However, v. 6b can also be read as referring, in retrospect, to the final breakdown of the kingdom of Israel in 722 B.C.E. One may, at any rate, infer that the accusation in v. 6b, if originally directed against the elite in Samaria, was later reapplied to leading circles in Jerusalem ("the carefree in Zion," v. 1!), who allegedly displayed a similar attitude (see Fleischer 2001: 221).

6:7. The pronouncement of punishment (v. 7), which concludes the passage 6:1–7, is a piece of outstanding Hebrew poetry. If one disregards the opening words of this utterance, "Therefore, . . . now" (*lākēn ʿattâ*), what remains is a perfectly balanced bicolon. In the second colon, or clause (v. 7b), the reader/listener may delight in an elegant combination of alliteration (*sār, sĕrûḥîm*) and assonance (*mirzaḥ sĕrûḥîm*).

As regards its content, v. 7 is filled with irony, verging on satire (with Paul 1991: 210; see also J. J. M. Roberts 1985: 161). It is stated that the life of luxury, "the banquet of the loungers" (*mirzaḥ sĕrûḥîm*) will come to an abrupt end (v. 7b). The verb used, *sûr*, means both "to cease" and "to depart." This could be a metaphor, meaning that joy and festivity will vanish; however, the immediate context evokes a more literal interpretation. All the participants in the banquet will have to leave. According to v. 7a, they are going to be deported. Those who were in the habit of lounging (*srḥ*) during dinner (v. 4a; note that *srḥ* recurs in 7b!) will be forced to leave their luxurious couches and lead the march of the prisoners of war. Those who considered themselves "distinguished men of the foremost (*rēʾšît*) nation" (v. 1), and who gladly spent their money on "the finest (*rē'šît*) oil" (v. 6), will find themselves "among the first (*bĕrō'š*)" in line, as the people are forced to march into exile (v. 7a).

Death, Destruction, and Deception (6:8–14)

6   ⁸YHWH the Lord has sworn by himself (says YHWH the God of hosts):
I abhor Jacob's arrogance, I hate his fortresses,
I will hand over the city and everything in it.

⁹And if ten men are left in one house, they shall die. ¹⁰ When one's relative and embalmer carries his remains out of the house, and he asks someone at the rear of the house, "Is anyone with you?," he will reply, "No one." Then he will say, "Hush!," for the name of YHWH must not be invoked.

¹¹See, YHWH commands,
and he will knock the great house to pieces, and the small house to rubble.

¹²Can horses run on rocks? Can one plow the sea with oxen?
But you have turned justice into poison
and the fruit of righteousness into wormwood!

¹³You who rejoice over Lo-Dabar,
saying: "Did we not capture Karnaim for ourselves by our own strength?"
¹⁴For I am raising up a nation against you, O house of Israel,
says YHWH the God of hosts,
and they will oppress you from Lebo-Hamath to Wadi Arabah.

INTRODUCTION TO 6:8–14

The last section within chapters 3–6, comprising 6:8–14, hardly represents an original rhetorical unit, like 6:1–7. This passage is better described as a string of rather loosely connected oracles. The following subdivisions can be made: v. 8 // vv. 9–10 // v. 11 // v. 12 // vv. 13–14. However, these small units have been brought together to form an apt finale for Amos 3–6 (with Wolff 1977: 281). Several motifs from previous passages recur, such as unwarranted pride and security (vv. 8 and 13; cf. 5:18–20 and 6:1), corruption of justice in the courts (v. 12b; cf. 5:7, 10), military defeat (vv. 9–10 and 14; cf. 3:11 and 5:3), and the demolition of buildings (v. 11; cf. 3:15).

It is possible to discern an editorial framework, consisting of vv. 8 and 13–14, that ties the passage together. Notably, the formula "says YHWH the God of hosts" occurs in vv. 8 and 14. In terms of content, this framework highlights the theme that pride comes before a fall. It is indicated that chauvinistic attitudes among the leading circles in Israel were a major factor behind the downfall of this kingdom (in the form of Assyrian occupation and large-scale deportations). The leaders of the Northern Kingdom are depicted as trusting in their own military strength rather than in "the God of hosts." It is implied that this arrogance provoked YHWH's anger (v. 8). As a consequence, one may infer, it was possible for Assyria (the oppressor mentioned in v. 14) to conquer Israel and establish control over its territory.

Most of the prophetic utterances in 6:8–14 are included in my tentative reconstruction of the first version of the book of Amos (see Table 2); however, as demonstrated in the Comments below, vv. 9–10 appear to have been inserted at a later stage.

NOTES

6:8. *says YHWH the God of hosts.* Since the phrase *něʾûm-yhwh ʾělōhê ṣěbāʾôt* (which appears to be syntactically and semantically redundant) is missing in the LXX, it may represent a very late addition to the Hebrew text (see Jeremias 1998: 108, n. 9). Some scholars transpose this phrase to the end of v. 7 (thus, e.g., Rudolph 1971: 215, 218 and Wolff 1977: 273), but this operation lacks support in the extant textual witnesses. See further the Comments on v. 8.

6:10. *When one's relative and embalmer.* The first three words in the MT, *ûněśāʾû dôdô ûměsārěpô,* present great difficulties for the translator. A literal rendering, which leaves the *hapax legomenon* in the third word untranslated, might look like this: "he carries it/him, his uncle/relative and his *měsārēp*." The interpretive problems may to a certain extent be due to textual corruption (see BHSapp and Wolff 1977: 280). Interestingly, the LXX (καὶ ὑπολειφθήσονται) may reflect a Hebrew *Vorlage* that contained, at its beginning, ונשארו, *wěnišʾārû,* "and (some) remained." It is conceivable that ונשארו, standing immediately before ונשא, was lost due to the phenomenon of *homoioarcton* (a text-critical term referring to the similar beginning of two words), as suggested by Anthony Gelston (2010: 85) in his commentary on the critical apparatus in *BHQ* 13. However, the notion that some survived would seem to contradict v. 9. Therefore, I have made an attempt to make sense of the MT (thus also, e.g., Noble 1999). For a discussion of the possible meaning of the otherwise unattested participle *měsārēp* in this context, see the Comments on v. 10.

6:12. *plow the sea with oxen.* I am reading בבקר ים (*běbāqār yām,* "the sea with oxen") instead of the MT's בבקרים (*babběqārîm,* "with oxen"). This ingenious emendation, originally suggested by Michaelis in the eighteenth century, which retains the consonants of the MT, is accepted by almost all modern commentators (see, e.g., Wolff 1977: 284, Paul 1991: 218, and Jeremias 1998: 109; for a slightly different variant, see Loretz 1989b). The alternative, and more extensive, emendation proposed by Cooper (1988: 726), "Does a wild ox plow in the Valley?" (*ʾim yaḥărôš babbiq[ʿâ] rêm*), which has been endorsed by Allen (2008), fails to persuade me. A more traditional solution, advocated by the medieval Jewish commentator Kimchi, is to presuppose that the expression *basselaʿ,* "on the rock," does double duty in v. 12a, and to translate "Does one plow with oxen on the rocks" (or, "Does one plow with oxen there?"). See Stuart (1987: 361–62) and the translations offered by the JPS and KJV. In this case, the LXX offers little help. Obviously assuming that the overall topic in v. 12a is the behavior of (male) horses, the Greek translator created a most peculiar version of the second rhetorical question in v. 12: εἰ παρασιωπήσονται ἐν θηλείαις, "Will they be silent among females [that is, mares]?"

COMMENTS

6:8. In v. 8 a new unit starts, comprising vv. 8–14 (with, e.g., Fleischer 2001: 222). Remarkably enough, it is declared twice in the opening line (v. 8aαβ), by means of two different formulas, that the following oracle of doom (v. 8aγδ + b) contains the words of YHWH. Arguably, the second clause, "says YHWH the God of hosts (*něʾûm-yhwh ʾělōhê ṣěbāʾôt*)" (v. 8aβ), is redundant. For this reason, I have placed it in parentheses in the translation. This phrase may represent a late addition (see the Notes); nevertheless, it would seem to have a function within the larger structure of the text. I find it likely that this phrase was inserted in v. 8, as well as in v. 14, in order to form an *inclusio* that binds vv. 8–14 together (cf. similarly Paul 1991: 213 and Jeremias 1998: 115).

Verse 8 begins with a solemn divine oath, which underlines the severity of the matter. The reader is told that YHWH "has sworn by himself" (v. 8aα), that is, by his own *nepeš* (a lexeme that frequently denotes someone's soul, life, or "person"). This oath is followed by two expressions of divine resentment: "I abhor Jacob's arrogance, I hate his fortresses" (v. 8aγδ). Because Jacob often stands for Israel, and since the sinfulness or foolishness of human pride and arrogance is a topos in the wisdom literature (see, e.g., Prov 8:13; 16:18), it is likely that the phrase "Jacob's arrogance" (*gĕʾôn yaʿăqōb*) condemns chauvinist tendencies. It is worth noting that the Septuagint renders this phrase with "hubris" (ὕβρις). Thus interpreted, 6:8 recalls several utterances in the preceding sections of the book that denounce an attitude of (allegedly) unfounded self-confidence (5:14, 18; 6:1, 4–6).

The word *gāʾôn*, however, is semantically ambivalent, denoting both pride and arrogance. In addition, it can designate magnificence or exaltation (see the dictionaries). For the first hearers or readers, therefore, the expression *gĕʾôn yaʿăqōb*, "Jacob's pride" (or, arrogance), may have evoked positive associations (cf. Nah 2:3 [Eng. v. 2]). It is even possible that this phrase was used in the temple cult, as indicated by its occurrence in Ps 47:5 (Eng. v. 4), "the pride of Jacob (*gĕʾôn yaʿăqōb*) whom he loves." Interestingly, the formulation in Amos 6:8aγ, "I abhor Jacob's arrogance/pride," looks like a reversal of that cultic affirmation. Suddenly, and shockingly, it is thus declared that YHWH in effect detests what he was previously thought to love.

With regard to both tone and topic, there is a strong connection between 6:8 and 5:21–24. In both cases total rejection of the divine-human relationship is expressed in terms of abhorrence and hatred; however, in 6:8 the focus has shifted from the sacrificial cult to the nation's military defense. According to the statement in v. 8aδ, YHWH hates "his (Jacob's) fortresses" (*ʾarmĕnōtāyw*). Divinely decreed destruction of fortresses has been a prominent theme in the preceding parts of this prophetic book (see 1:4, 7, 10, 12, 14; 2:2, 5; 3:10–11; 5:9). In 6:8, the fortifications in Samaria are apparently seen as symbolizing the nation's arrogance and the illusory confidence of its leaders (with Paul 1991: 213). Because YHWH was the patron deity, the one who was expected to grant victory over attacking enemies, these words of rejection can be read as a threat. Divine protection will be withdrawn. As a consequence, the city runs the risk of being captured.

To make things even worse, the concluding clause of v. 8 asserts that YHWH will actively "hand over the city and everything in it" (v. 8b), literally "its fullness" (*ûmĕlōʾāh*), which must be taken to include both the population and all material goods. It is not said which city this concerns or to whom it was going to be delivered, but this "prediction" most probably refers to the Assyrian conquest of Samaria. In fact, v. 8 would seem to summarize the main message of the first version of the book of Amos, namely, that the downfall of the Northern Kingdom had been decreed by YHWH.

Apart from the reference to arrogance, no explicit motivation for the deity's rejection is given, but one may detect an allusion to the theme of oppression and corruption, via an intratextual link between v. 8aγδ and 5:10, where the two verbs *śnʾ* ("to hate") and *tᶜb* ("to abhor, detest") likewise stand in parallel position. Reading these two utterances together produces an image of poetic (or, prophetic) justice, which could be paraphrased as follows: Those who hate and detest justice in the courts will find out that they and their power structures are hated and detested by YHWH.

6:9. With its emphasis on the number ten, this prediction of a devastating military defeat may at first look like a continuation of 5:3, a prophecy presaging that a troop of one thousand soldiers would be decimated to one hundred, and a troop of one hundred men reduced to ten. That is where 6:9 picks up the theme. Taking it even further, it states that in case ten men were remaining in one house, they would also have to die, each and every one of them (see Wolff 1977: 282 and Schart 2009: 264).

On closer examination, however, one can see important differences between the utterances in 6:9 and 5:3. To begin with, the efficient rhetoric of 5:3 does not require any further elaboration. If the prophecy in 5:3 could be taken to imply that at least some (about one-tenth) would survive, the utterance in 6:9 seems to take away even that faint hope. At the same time, though, it switches the focus from the nation and its cities (a focus shared by 5:3 and 6:8) to the fate of one single house and its inhabitants.

As suggested by Jeremias (1998: 116–17), 6:9–10 can be regarded as an example of early Amos exegesis, which draws on 5:3 in an attempt to create a bridge between v. 8, which envisions the tragic end of a city's entire population, and v. 11, which depicts the massive destruction of houses. From a formal perspective, the secondary status of vv. 9–10, in relation to the surrounding poetic oracles, is clearly indicated by the fact that these two verses are written in prose.[74]

6:10. There can be no doubt that v. 10 constitutes a direct continuation of v. 9. In the words of Shalom Paul, this is a "closeup picture" that "zooms in" on the house mentioned in v. 9, showing the reader what is happening inside it shortly after the catastrophe (1991: 214). It has been suggested that the men in the house died of pestilence (Wolff 1977: 282), but I agree with Schart (2009: 264–65) that the focus on males in vv. 9–10, together with the stress on the number ten, indicates that this is about soldiers at war, just like 5:3. In a pestilence, surely, women and children would likewise be among the victims.

This verse contains a very short narrative, as well as a terse dialogue. As indicated by the verbal forms used (*wĕqatal*), this is not a narrative telling the listener or reader what actually happened (whether in fact or in fiction). Rather, the intention is to give an example that may illustrate the breadth of the announced disaster. Unfortunately, it is impossible to reconstruct exactly what happens in the brief narrative part, or exactly what is being said, and by whom, in the dialogue. In the very beginning of the verse, some difficulties may to be due to textual corruption (see the Notes to "When one's relative and embalmer").

Further uncertainty arises because of the occurrence of a *hapax legomenon*, the verbal participle *mĕsārēp*, here tentatively translated as "embalmer" (thus also Paul 1991: 213). Judging from the context, it is reasonable to assume that this word refers to someone who was "responsible for the burial being carried out correctly" (Noble 1999: 422). The form *mĕsārēp* can be analyzed in two different ways, but in either case it may denote a person who anoints the dead with aromatic spices. If it is taken as a variant spelling of *mĕśārēp*, "the one who burns," one may conjecture that he is burning spices (since the practice of burning dead bodies is poorly attested in ancient Israel and Judah; but see 1 Sam 31:12). Alternatively, this form could be analyzed as a participle of *srp*, a verb related to the noun *sĕrāp*, "resin," which is attested in Mishnaic Hebrew (Driver 1954 and Paul 1991: 215–16).

Above all, however, a reconstruction of the events recounted in v. 10 is made difficult by the extremely condensed style of narration. As far as I can see, the following can be said with certainty: A corpse is carried out from a house, by one or two people (as indicated in the translation above, the relative and the embalmer may theoretically be one and the same person). Yet another person, possibly a survivor, remains inside the building, in one of the inner rooms (with Schart 2009: 265).[75] Alternatively, this is another member of a rescue squad. When asked by the carrier(s) whether anyone else is there with him, this person replies, "No one," indicating that there are no (other) survivors. Then someone (either the one who asked the question or the one who answered it) says "Hush!" (*hās*). This is followed by a sinister concluding remark, added either by the speaker or by the narrator, which prohibits the invocation of YHWH's name (at least, in that specific situation).

Despite the many uncertainties involved in the interpretation, the outline is rather clear, and some intriguing details contribute to make a vivid impression. Indeed, v. 10 might even allow the modern reader a glimpse of how the search for survivors was conducted in the wake of a major catastrophe (cf. Andersen and Freedman 1989: 573–74). Nevertheless, it is a pity that some salient aspects of this description remain obscure. The singular pronoun in "one's (or, his) relative (*dôdô*)" suggests that there is a focus on the fate (and the bodily remains) of one individual among the ten. How is this to be understood? In addition, the identity of the person "at the rear of the house" is uncertain. If he is seen as a sole survivor, perhaps drawing his last breath, the short narrative becomes more dramatic and gripping (see Schart 2009: 265–66); however, it seems slightly more logical to conclude that this person is a member of a search team (Andersen and Freedman 1989: 573–74). With his answer, "No one," he confirms what the reader was told already in v. 9: All men in that house were dead. Arguably, the primary function of the male relative and the others is to serve as witnesses to the catastrophe.

The last words of v. 10 are enigmatic, despite the fact that they are easily translated. Who utters "for the name of YHWH must not be invoked" (v. 10b), and why? Starting with the latter question, it is likely that some kind of apotropaic thinking is involved. In a situation like that, one should avoid invoking the destructive power and presence of the deity who was thought to be responsible for the disaster (with Wolff 1977: 283 and Paul 1991: 216–17). Hence, lamenting or praying to YHWH could be seen as dangerous. But who is warning and silencing whom?

Assuming that there is logic in this short story, it seems preferable to take this as an explicative remark made by the narrator, intended to clarify the implication of the interjection *hās*, "Hush!" Otherwise, the person speaking would be represented, rather awkwardly, as violating his own prohibition by uttering the name YHWH.

6:11. In v. 11 the focus shifts once more, from the death of people inside an intact(?) building (v. 10) to the destruction of buildings. The latter constitutes one of the thematic threads that run through the book of Amos. Most frequently, the buildings mentioned in these oracles of destruction are fortresses or palaces (see the Comments on 6:8). Here, a related topic, the demolition of private houses, which was introduced in 3:15, resurfaces. In 6:11 it is emphasized that all buildings, large mansions along with smaller houses, will be turned into rubble. As a consequence, one may infer, the entire city will be made uninhabitable.

One might think of an earthquake (Wolff 1977: 283; cf. 1:1). Alternatively, and perhaps more likely, the point of reference is the destruction of Samaria in 722 B.C.E. The wording of v. 11 suggests that the destruction is carried out by an anonymous agent who is acting on YHWH's command (cf. Paul 1991: 217). I suggest that this anonymous destroyer should be identified with the Assyrian army. At any rate, this image of massive destruction concludes the first subsection within 6:8–14.

6:12. The saying in v. 12 would seem to begin a new subsection, comprising vv. 12–14, but it is in fact quite loosely connected to vv. 13–14 (see Jeremias 1998: 117–18). By means of rhetorical questions, a technique also employed elsewhere in the book of Amos (cf. 2:11; 3:3–6, 8; 5:18, 20, 25–26; 6:2; 8:8; 9:7), this utterance illustrates the alleged absurdity of the acts and attitudes of the addressees.[76] Evidently, horses are not able to run on rocks (v. 12aα).

In order to produce a suitable parallel to the first question, which stresses that certain things just cannot be done, one must make a small emendation of the Hebrew text in v. 12aβ (see the Notes to v. 12). This operation results in the rhetorically efficient formulation, "Can one plow the sea with oxen?" (*'im yaḥărôš bĕbāqār yām*). Because it heightens the notion of absurdity, this reconstructed reading is certainly superior to the MT's apparently pointless question, "Can one plow with oxen?" (*'im yaḥărôš babbĕqārîm*), which threatens to destroy the rhetoric of v. 12a.

It is implied in v. 12b that the behavior of the anonymous addressees is characterized by absurdity and therefore is comparable to the examples mentioned in the rhetorical questions (v. 12a). Most likely, the oracle recorded in v. 12 was originally directed against rich people, who (allegedly) used their influence to pervert the judicial system. Such an identification of the addressees is supported by the observation that the accusations in v. 12b concerning corruption, "you have turned (*hpk*) justice (*mišpāṭ*) into poison and the fruit of righteousness into wormwood (*lĕlaʿănâ*)," echo the indictments in 5:7 and 5:10–12. The resemblance with 5:7a, "they who turn (*hpk*) justice (*mišpāṭ*) into wormwood (*lĕlaʿănâ*)," is particularly striking.

6:13. In vv. 13–14, the topic of chauvinist arrogance, which was introduced in v. 8, is developed further.[77] The rhetoric in v. 13 revolves around two toponyms and their possible meanings. It excels, somewhat untypically for the book of Amos, in double entendre.[78]

At first, we are told that an anonymous group of people (probably the political elite in the Northern Kingdom) are rejoicing "over Lo-Dabar" (v. 13a). On one level, this can be interpreted as referring to a city in Transjordan named Lodevar (see Metzger 1960). This toponym is mentioned, with some variations in spelling, in Josh 13:26 (*ldbr*), 2 Sam 9:4–5 (*lw dbr*), and 2 Sam 17:27 (*lʾ dbr*). One may hypothesize that Lodevar had been (re)conquered by Israel at some point in the eighth century after a battle against the Ammonites (see Hayes 1988: 191–92 and Paul 1991: 219). On another level, however, v. 13a speaks about rejoicing over absolutely "nothing" (*lōʾ dābār*). Hence, the point made is that the joy displayed during the celebration of that victory is groundless, since the kingdom of Israel is doomed.

In v. 13b, the anonymous addressees are quoted as boasting (in poetic style) that they have indeed managed to capture an Aramean city called Karnaim (mentioned in

Gen 14:5) on their own, "by our own strength (*běḥozkēnû*)."[79] Notably, these braggarts do not give any credit to the national deity, YHWH, for this military victory. According to a widespread notion in the ancient Near East, such arrogance was likely to incur divine punishment.[80] A further dimension is added when the semantic meaning of the name Karnaim—"two horns" (*qarnāyim*)—is considered. Evoking the image of a bull, this toponym is associated with power symbolism (with Paul 1991: 220). Thus, it becomes possible to interpret v. 13b as follows: "Did we not take the two horns (that is, the power) for ourselves (*lānû*) by our own strength?"[81] That really sounds like a piece of exaggerated self-praise.

It is likely that the place names Lodebar (or, Lo-Dabar) and Karnaim were chosen primarily because of their usefulness in an oracle based on wordplay (Jeremias 1998: 119; Lemaire 2009: 97–98). Hence, one may ask whether Israel actually captured these cities in the eighth century. In the absence of corroborating evidence from other textual sources, it is not possible to verify or to falsify the events alluded to in 6:13; however, the notion of such Israelite conquests is at least compatible with the general information concerning the reign of Jeroboam found in 2 Kings 14. Interestingly, as shown below, v. 14 seems to make an allusion to 2 Kgs 14:25.

6:14. In v. 14 readers are finally told what they may have already guessed, based on the recurring references to deportation and destroyed cities in the preceding passages. The impending disaster, sometimes described in very general terms (5:18–20; 6:3, 11), will take the form of military defeat and ensuing foreign occupation of the kingdom of Israel (here addressed as the "house of Israel") in its entirety.

Unambiguous references to an (Assyrian?) invasion are found only twice within the book of Amos, in 3:11 and here in 6:14. It is worth noting that the identity of the invading empire is not disclosed. According to v. 14a, this anonymous hostile "nation" (*gôy*) is not acting on its own. The formulation used, "I am raising up a nation," indicates that YHWH is the real agent, the one who brings about these events (cf. similarly Hab 1:6). In accordance with an ideological interpretation that appears to have been in vogue within prophetic circles in Judah during the late eighth century and later, Assyria is here (implicitly) portrayed as an instrument in the hands of YHWH (cf. Isa 10:5–15).[82] In addition, v. 14 can be read as a reversal of the exodus and conquest traditions (Jeremias 1998:119). Israel is about to lose the promised land.

While v. 14a offers a theological perspective on the end of Israel as an independent kingdom, claiming that it should be seen as the work of YHWH, v. 14b focuses mainly on the political and geographical aspects of this event. To begin with, the oppressive nature of the foreign (Assyrian) domination is underlined. The use of the verb *lḥṣ*, "press" or "oppress," might evoke associations with the traditions about the Israelites in Egypt (Exod 3:9). This time, however, they apparently are not going to be liberated by YHWH.

The concluding part of the oracle ascertains that the attacking enemy will gain control over the whole land of Israel (that is, the Northern Kingdom), from north to south, "from Lebo-Hamath to Wadi Arabah" (v. 14bβ). The southern border is indicated by Wadi Arabah (or, the brook of the Arabah), situated at the northern end of the Dead Sea, and the border to the north is marked by a place called Lebo-Hamath. Although Lebo-Hamath is mentioned in several other biblical texts as a point near the northern frontier (see, e.g., Num 13:21; 34:8; Josh 13:5; Judg 3:3; 1 Kgs 8:65; Ezek

47:20), its exact location is still a matter of dispute. For the interpretation of v. 14b, however, it does not matter much whether this toponym once referred to a city in the Lebanon valley (corresponding to the modern village of Lebneh) or to an area in the vicinity of Hamath ("the entrance to Hamath"), even farther to the north (see further Wei 1992).

The point made by the text is that the Assyrians will take every part of Israel; therefore, it refers to the maximal extension ever reached by this kingdom. In that connection, it is interesting to note that the closest parallel to the formulation in Amos 6:14 is found in 2 Kgs 14:25 (cf. Rudolph 1971: 228 and Paul 1991: 221). There it is said of Jeroboam II that he "restored the territory of Israel from Lebo-Hamath to the Sea of Arabah, in accordance with the word of YHWH, the God of Israel, spoken through his servant Jonah son of Amittai, the prophet from Gath Hepher" (2 Kgs 14:25). If, as seems likely, v. 14 was formulated with 2 Kgs 14:25 in mind, this utterance explains why the divinely sanctioned prosperity of Jeroboam's kingdom did not last longer than a few decades. According to Amos 6:14, the peaceful order presaged by Jonah was meant to be overturned, in accordance with a new (and allegedly more decisive) word of YHWH, spoken through Amos from Tekoa.

Visions (7–9)

"The plowman will catch up with the reaper" (Amos 9:13). This picture is
inspired by iconographic representations from the ancient Near East. For
the ox, see A. Mazar, *Archaeology of the Land of the Bible, 10,000–586 B.C.E.*
(New York: Doubleday, 1990), 351. For the plow, see M. Roaf, *Cultural Atlas
of Mesopotamia and the Ancient Near East* (New York: Facts on File, 1990), 189.
Drawing by Sverrir Ólafsson, published with permission of the artist.

The First Pair of Visions: Canceled Calamities (7:1–6)

7   ¹This is what the Lord YHWH showed me:
He was forming locusts when the late crops began to sprout—
the late crops, that is: after the king's mowing.
²And when they had finished devouring the vegetation of the land, I said:
"O Lord YHWH, please forgive! How can Jacob survive? He is so small."
³Then YHWH relented concerning this: "It will not happen," said YHWH.
      ⁴This is what the Lord YHWH showed me:
The Lord YHWH was summoning a judgment by fire.
It consumed the great deep and it devoured the land.
⁵And I said: "O Lord YHWH, please stop! How can Jacob survive?
He is so small."
⁶Then YHWH relented concerning this:
"This will not happen either," said YHWH.

INTRODUCTION TO 7:1–6 AND TO THE
SERIES OF FOUR VISION REPORTS

There is a major break between 6:14 and 7:1. Clearly, a new section begins in 7:1, comprising four vision reports (7:1–3 // 7:4–6 // 7:7–8 // 8:1–3) and one disputation narrative (7:10–17). New genres are introduced, as well as new questions and themes. Indeed, at this point the book of Amos changes character in a dramatic way. Until now, it has been possible to read it as an artistically composed collection of oracles attributed to a certain Amos (1:1). However, this person/prophet has remained in the background, as an invisible mouthpiece for the divine messages, throughout chapters 1–6 (with a possible exception for 5:1; see the Comments on that verse). Now, all of a sudden, a prophet/seer named Amos appears on center stage, as the protagonist in a drama in which the other main characters are YHWH, King Jeroboam, and the priest Amaziah. This drama is about the fate of the people of Israel (and Judah), personified as "Jacob" (7:2, 5) and "Isaac" (7:9, 16).

Much of the scholarly discussion on Amos 7–9 has centered on the so-called vision cycle, presumably consisting of *five* consecutive vision reports: 7:1–8 + 8:1–3 + 9:1–4. However, the fifth and last vision (recounted in 9:1) is so different from the others that I prefer to treat it separately (see "Introduction to 9:1–4, the So-Called Fifth Vision"). In the following, I therefore focus on the first four vision reports (7:1–3, 4–6, 7–8; 8:1–3), which exhibit extensive structural similarities.

For obvious reasons, scholars striving to reconstruct the life and career of the eighth-century prophet Amos have tended to treat the section 7:1–8:3 as a valuable biographical source. According to several exegetes, the series of visions, with its movement from divine mercy to irrevocable judgment, provides a key to the personal development of Amos, explaining how he eventually (and reluctantly) became a prophet of doom.[1] As noted by Georg Steins, the vision cycle in Amos 7–9 has been regarded as a kind of "birth protocol" for the entire phenomenon of biblical prophecy of doom (2010: 29–30). However, such a biographically oriented approach to the so-called vision cycle (usually thought to include five visions) suffers from serious weaknesses (see Wöhrle 2006: 102–4 and Steins 2010: 30–37). Quite obviously, it fails to do justice to the position and function of this section within the finally edited form of the book as a whole. If the vision reports supply information that is essential in order to understand chapters 1–6, why are they placed at the end of the book and not at the beginning?

To this one may add the important observation that an eighth-century dating of the vision reports cannot be supported by a systematic comparative examination of terminology and themes (Steins 2010: 57–67; see also Spieckermann 1997: 288–89). Moreover, if the narrative in 7:10–17 was written to convey actual information about Amos as a historical person, why does it not add anything substantial that the reader was not told already in the superscription? (see Steins 2010: 79–81). For a reader eager to find out the circumstances around Amos's call experience, the duration of his preaching activity in Israel, the king's reaction to Amaziah's report (vv. 10–11), or what happened to Amos after the short verbal exchange between him and Amaziah, this narrative (or, dialogue with narrative elements) must be quite disappointing (see further "Introduction to 7:10–17").

In order to be able to say something at all about the life and work of Amos, many scholars have simply filled in the gaps in the vision cycle and the interspersed narrative with the help of their own imaginations.[2] In my opinion, however, a responsible exegetical approach to Amos 7:1–8:3 should rather be based upon a careful analysis of the actual contents of the text: its terminology, its themes, and its theology. In addition, it is necessary to explore the intertextual ramifications of each motif or formulation and to search for links to specific genres and/or traditions. Refraining from biographical speculations (since that enterprise seems pointless, at least from a scholarly point of view), one should instead attempt to uncover the ideological (or, theological) dimensions of the text. From such a perspective, no part of Amos 7:1–8:3 can be said to be disappointing.

As regards the date of origin, I find it likely that both the series of four visions and the inserted narrative (7:10–17) were composed after the defeat and destruction of Jerusalem in 587 B.C.E. As demonstrated in the Comments below, this part of the book of Amos is preoccupied with some theological questions that are absent or extremely marginal in chapters 1–6, namely, the relation between divine anger and divine mercy, the effect of intercession, and the possibility of forgiveness (see also Steins 2010: 127–30). This can, I suggest, be explained in the following way: Whereas chapters 1–6 largely consist of texts relating to the downfall of Israel in 722 B.C.E. (texts foreshadowing this event, or explaining it, or interpreting it as a warning), the section that starts in 7:1 represents an attempt to come to terms with the situation after the downfall of Judah.

Before a detailed analysis, it is necessary to offer an overview of the structure of 7:1–8:3. As observed by other scholars, the four visions can be grouped into two pairs, here called A and B. While the first two visions (A1 and A2) are accompanied by (successful) prophetic intercession, the third and fourth visions (B1 and B2) are followed by divine interrogation and interpretation and a proclamation of judgment:[3]

A1 and A2 (7:1–3 // 4–6): Introductory formula—vision—intercession—
  YHWH relents
B1 and B2 (7:7–8 // 8:1–2): Introductory formula—vision—interpretation—
  no mercy

The first pair (A) would seem to contain immediately comprehensible visions of events (despite some interpretative difficulties; see below), but the more static B visions are apparently not intelligible without explication, which YHWH provides.[4] Both B1 and B2 feature some kind of pun (on the problems involved in reconstructing the wordplay in B1, see below). Each of these two visions is followed by an appended oracle, 7:9 and 8:3, respectively, which elaborates on the impending disaster. As regards the utterance in 7:9, it is of vital importance to recognize that it also serves as a bridge between the third vision and the narrative (7:10–17) that has been inserted before the fourth vision. This yields the following structure:

7:1–3 (A1): Vision report—intercession—YHWH relents
7:4–6 (A2): Vision report—intercession—YHWH relents
7:7–8 (B1): Vision report—interpretation—YHWH declares that no mercy
  will be shown
7:9: Elaboration, serving as bridge
7:10–17 (C): Narrative with dialogue, the encounter with Amaziah
8:1–2 (B2): Vision report—interpretation—YHWH declares that no mercy
  will be shown
8:3: Elaboration

At first glance, the insertion of the disputation narrative (C), which splits up the second pair of visions, would seem to disturb the otherwise perfect symmetry; however, as will be demonstrated below, 7:10–17 should not be regarded as loosely attached to its present context.

NOTES

7:2. *How can Jacob*. With most modern translators and commentators I presuppose that the interrogative participle *mî,* "who," here corresponds roughly to the English "how." A parallel case is found in Ruth 3:16. Alternatively, one might translate: "Who is Jacob, that he can stand/survive?" See Waltke and O'Connor (1990: 320, n. 10).

survive. The lexical sense of the verb *qûm* is "stand." Stuart (1987: 370) opts likewise for "survive" in this particular context.

7:4. *a judgment by fire*. The collocation לרב באֹש (*lārib bāʾēš*) has often been regarded as problematic. In my opinion, the best solution is to take רב as a defective spelling of *rîb*, "strife, lawsuit," and to translate "a judgment by fire" (with Paul 1991: 230–31 and Linville 2008: 136). This alternative has two obvious advantages: (1) It retains the text of the MT, and (2) it is supported by the LXX, which has ἐκάλεσεν τὴν δίκην ἐν πυρί. In addition, the notion of a judgment or lawsuit follows naturally after the participle *qōrēʾ*, "(was) summoning." Alternatively, one might consider making a different division of the consonantal text, לרבב אֹש, and translate either as "a rain of fire" (thus Wolff 1977: 292–93 and Jeremias 1998: 123) or as "an enormous fire," as suggested by Riede (2008: 65), who reads an otherwise unattested form, Piel infinitive, of the verb *rbb*, "to be great."

the land. With regard to the lexical sense of *ḥēleq*, "portion" (of territory), one might consider alternative formulations, such as "the portion of land." The translation "land" was chosen because it captures a certain ambiguity in the text. Although the scope of the vision appears to be cosmic, there might at the same time be a certain focus on the land of the Israelites.

COMMENTS

7:1. In 7:1–2, an anonymous voice (identified as "Amos" in v. 8), speaking in the first person, depicts a visionary experience. The introductory formula, *kōh hirʾanî ʾădōnāy yhwh*, "this is what the Lord YHWH showed me" (or, more literally, "thus has shown me the Lord YHWH"), which is repeated in the three ensuing vision reports (7:4, 7; 8:1), is not attested outside the book of Amos (but cf. the similar use of *hirʾanî*, "[YHWH] has shown me," in 2 Kgs 8:10, 13; Jer 24:1; 38:21; Ezek 11:25; cf. also Zech 2:3 [Eng. 1:20]; 3:1). This clause seems to have been modeled on the widely attested messenger formula, *kōh ʾāmar yhwh*, "thus says YHWH" (occurring eleven times in chapters 1–6 and once in chapters 7–9 [7:17]), which twice appears in a longer form, *kōh ʾāmar ʾădōnāy yhwh*, "thus says the Lord YHWH" (3:11; 5:3).[5] In this way, the reader is invited to make an analogy between the words recorded in chapters 1–6 and the visions described in 7:1–8:3.

The actual content of the vision is introduced by the deictic particle *hinnēh* ("behold!" or "see!").[6] The report that follows, in vv. 1aβ–2aα, can be divided into three parts. At first, the speaking "I" witnesses a peculiar act of divine creation. YHWH (no one else could be the implicit subject) is "forming" (*yôṣēr*) a swarm of locusts (v. 1aβ).[7] Within biblical disaster depictions the motif of an invasion of grasshoppers is quite common (cf. Exod 10:12–19; 1 Kgs 8:37; Joel 1:4; Amos 4:9).[8] However, the lexeme used to denote (a swarm of) locusts, *gōbay*, is unusual. It occurs only here and in Nah 3:17. The verb *yṣr*, which denotes the work of a potter who forms things out of clay, is sometimes used in order to describe, metaphorically, how YHWH creates living beings (Gen 2:7–8, 19; Ps 104:26). Here, though, the work of the creator clearly aims at destruction.

Thereafter, the reader is informed that this locust invasion happened at a specific time of the year, "when the late crops (*halleqeš*) began to sprout" (v. 1aγ). Because the lexeme *lqš* occurs in the Gezer calendar (from the tenth century B.C.E.), we know that it denoted a period roughly corresponding to February–March, when the late-sown crops (including vegetables) were growing (see Riede 2008: 39–41). It is conceivable that a locust attack during that time of the year would be particularly devastating (Paul 1991: 227 and Sweeney 2000: 252). However, the main function of this calendric reference appears to be related to the literary structure of 7:1–8:3. Taking its departure, in 7:1, at the time of the first harvest (*lqš*) and ending, in 8:1–2, with the gathering of summer fruit (*qyṣ*), the cycle of four visions thus encompasses almost the entire agricultural year, from line 3 to line 8 in the Gezer calendar (Riede 2008: 30).

What follows next, in v. 1b, looks like an inserted gloss, stating that the word *leqeš* ("the late crops") signifies what remains to reap "after the king's mowing" (*gizzê hammelek*). Ironically, whereas the word *leqeš* in itself presents no problem to modern interpreters (thanks to the Gezer inscription), it is quite difficult to understand the "explanation" offered in v. 1b.[9] It seems likely that the phrase "the king's mowing" refers to a royal prerogative that allowed the king (or, the state) to "cut" (*gzz*) the first of all crops as some kind of levy (cf. 1 Sam 8:15).[10] But this can be no more than a guess. Quite possibly, the interpolator wanted to connect the divinely decreed disaster to one of the central themes in the book, namely, oppression of the poor. One might thus paraphrase v. 1b as follows: What had not already been taken by the king would surely be eaten by the locusts (see Garrett 2008: 207).

7:2. In v. 2aα, a later stage of the vision is described. The locusts have finished their job; all green plants (*ʿēśeb*) in the land have been devoured. But since this is a vision, offering the prophet a preview of a catastrophe planned by YHWH, there is still time to cancel the locust invasion. Hence, it is not illogical that the prophet's intercession comes only after the depiction of the completed destruction (with Paul 1991: 228, n. 20).[11]

Nevertheless, the motif of intercession comes as a surprise. Nothing in the preceding parts of the book of Amos has prepared the reader for this. Until now, forgiveness has not been an option. All of a sudden, Amos (or, the "I" of the text) begins to act like Moses in the golden calf episode (Exod 32:11–14), as he prays for the people, trying to avert the disaster (v. 2aβ): "O Lord YHWH, please forgive (*sĕlaḥ-nāʾ*)!"[12] It is worth paying close attention to the vocabulary used. The verb *slḥ*, "to forgive," is almost exclusively attested in exilic and postexilic texts.[13] The formulation *sĕlaḥ-nāʾ* occurs only twice in the Hebrew Bible: here and in Num 14:19. An even closer parallel to Amos 7:1–2 is found in Exod 10:12–19, where it is recounted that a swarm of locusts, having devoured all green plants (*ʿēśeb*) in the land of Egypt, disappeared completely as a result of Moses's intercession. As regards the notion of prophetic intercession as such, Spieckermann has argued that it is a Deuteronomistic construction (1997: 287–90).[14]

Further indications that the first (and the second) vision report should be dated to the exilic or postexilic era are found in the continuation of the prayer (v. 2aγ + b), where "Jacob" designates the personified nation: "How can Jacob survive? He is so small (*qāṭōn*)." The affinity to Deutero-Isaiah, where "Jacob" stands for the afflicted exilic community (Isa 40:27; 41:14; 43:1), is intriguing (see Kratz 2003: 69, n. 40). Moreover, the allusion to the traditions in Genesis about Jacob as the younger (twin) brother should not be overlooked.[15] In his anxiety before the reunion with Esau, Jacob prays to YHWH, emphasizing his own unworthiness by means of the expression *qāṭōntî*, "I am (too) small" (Gen 32:11 [Eng. 32:10]). Against this background, the formulation in Amos 7:2, "he is so small," takes on additional nuances.

7:3. In v. 3 it is stated that "YHWH relented concerning this" (*nḥm* + *ʿl*) and that he answered, "It will not happen" (*lōʾ tihyeh*), in response to the prophet's intercession. It should be noted that the same phrase (*nḥm* + *ʿl*) is used about YHWH's repentance in Exod 32:14 (cf. also 32:12).

On the basis of the observations concerning vocabulary and intertextuality presented above, I find it likely that Amos 7:1–3 (as well as the remaining three visions in the cycle) was written as a piece of theological reflection after 587 B.C.E. (with Becker 2001: 148, 150–56, 163, and Steins 2010: 57–67). Against that background it becomes possible to make sense of the ambiguity that characterizes this passage. On one level, indicated by the literary context (especially 7:9–17), it refers to the downfall of the Northern Kingdom. On another level, it concerns the situation after the destruction of Jerusalem. Whereas the little and weak figure of Jacob is an unfit metaphor for the kingdom of Israel (especially during the reign of Jeroboam II), it is a congenial representation of the exiled Judean community in the sixth century.[16] It may seem strange that 7:3, with its bold declaration that the deity was persuaded to change his mind, is placed after all of the uncompromising prophecies of doom in chapters 1–6. However, if it is read as an expression of exilic (or postexilic) theology, 7:3, and the vision cycle as a whole, makes excellent sense in its present position.

7:4. The second vision report, in 7:4–6, repeats the pattern of the first (7:1–3). A terrifying sight provokes prophetic prayer, and YHWH relents once more. This time, the destruction is brought about by fire. Depending on how one chooses to solve the problem posed by the MT in v. 4aβ, *lārīb bāʾēš*, the vision depicts either (1) a "judgment by fire" (taking *rb* as a defective spelling of *rîb*, "strife, lawsuit"), the option preferred in this commentary (with Limburg 1973 and Paul 1991: 230–31), (2) a "rain of fire" (Wolff 1977: 292–93), or (3) "an enormous fire" (Riede 2008: 65).[17] In my opinion the first alternative, which is supported by the Septuagint, is the most attractive solution (see the Notes above). In favor of the rendering "judgment by fire" one may add the observation that divine punishment by means of fire is a common motif in the Hebrew Bible and especially in the book of Amos (see 1:4, 7, 10, 12, 14; 2:2; 4:11; 5:6).

Regardless of which translation one prefers, however, this vision undoubtedly depicts an enormous fire.[18] Its proportions are cosmic (Riede 2008: 69–73). Echoing mythological *Chaoskampf* motifs, v. 4b narrates that the fire "consumed the great deep (*ʾet-těhôm rabbâ*)"; that is, the subterranean waters were dried up.[19] Then the fire goes on to consume the land. Because the word *ḥēleq* is used, which denotes a territorial portion, one may perhaps trace an allusion to the conquest tradition (cf. Josh 18:5–10). In that case, it is implied that the people of Israel are about to lose the land that YHWH had allotted to them.

7:5–6. Once again, the prophet's reaction comes rather late, when the preview has reached the level of total destruction (cf. v. 2). With very few exceptions, the dialogue that follows, in vv. 5–6, is an exact copy of the verbal exchange between the prophet and YHWH in vv. 2–3. The result is the same: YHWH relents and withholds the destructive fire. Once again, land and people have been saved by the prophet's intercession. Still, the threat has apparently not been removed.

Repetition can be a way of reinforcing a message. Thus interpreted, vv. 5–6 would seem to reinforce a message of forgiveness conveyed by the passage 7:1–6 in its entirety (especially vv. 3 and 6). However, in this case the effect of the rhetorical device of repetition is far from reassuring, as observed by Francis Landy: "the divine retraction is provisional, itself rhetorical" (1987: 227; see also Linville 2008: 135–37).

Apparently, no permanent change has occurred as regards YHWH's attitude to the people. If YHWH had been wholeheartedly determined to show compassion after the first vision with subsequent dialogue, no further terrifying vision and no further intercession would have been necessary. It is probably significant that a different verb is used in the prophet's second plea to YHWH. Instead of *slḥ,* "to forgive" (v. 2), he now uses *ḥdl,* "to cease," as he supplicates: "O Lord YHWH, please stop!" (v. 5a). If forgiveness and restored relationship cannot be obtained, then all one can do is to ask for a temporary respite (thus also Wolff 1977: 299).

The Third Vision: A Riddle Made of Metal (7:7–8)

7   [7]This is what he showed me:
The Lord was standing on a tin wall, holding tin in his hand.
[8]YHWH asked me: "What do you see, Amos?" and I answered: "Tin."
Then the Lord said: "See, I am about to set tin in the midst of my people Israel. I will no longer spare them."

INTRODUCTION TO THE SECOND PAIR OF VISIONS (7:7–8 AND 8:1–2)

The third and the fourth vision reports (7:7–8; 8:1–2) have several features in common that distinguish them from the first pair (7:1–3, 4–6). What the speaker claims to have been shown by YHWH is no longer a graphic scene of massive destruction. Instead, it is a kind of picture puzzle, involving an element of wordplay. Interpretative help is needed.[20] The conversation is initiated by the deity, not by the seer. In the words of Landy (1987: 228), "God steals the initiative in the dialogue." In 7:8 and 8:2 YHWH asks: "What do you see (*mâ ʾattâ rōʾeh*)?" At this crucial stage, Amos (who is being called by name), does not make any attempt to intercede on behalf of the people. Instead of revoking the punishment, the deity renounces pity and pardon, as he abruptly ends the conversation.

There are several conspicuous similarities between the second pair of visions and two passages in the book of Jeremiah: Jer 1:11–14 and 24:1–5 (as noted by Steins 2010: 65–66). For Jeremiah, too, the vision he receives is hard to understand. Before assisting in the interpretation, YHWH asks Jeremiah, "What do you see?" (Jer 1:11, 13; 24:3), using exactly the same phrase (*mâ-ʾattâ rōʾeh*) as in Amos 7:8 and 8:2.[21] The prophet's answer follows promptly. To these formal resemblances one may add the element of wordplay in Jer 1:11–12 (cf. Amos 8:1–2). The affinity to passages in Jeremiah is an important indication as regards the theological horizon and the date of composition of the vision cycle in Amos 7–8 (see further Steins 2010: 65–67, 72–75).

NOTES

7:7. *standing on.* Because of the multiple functions of the preposition *ʿal,* it is uncertain whether YHWH is said to stand over, on, at, or by the wall.

7:7–8. *tin.* Within vv. 7–8, a somewhat enigmatic word spelled אֲנָךְ (*ʾnk*) occurs four times. Until recently, most commentators and Bible translators have adhered to the theory that the lexeme *ʾănāk,* through metonymic extension of its putative sense "lead," here signifies a plumb line (see, e.g., Cripps 1929: 224–25, Mays 1969: 132, Wolff 1977: 300, and Niditch 1983: 21–22, 28). The translation "plumb line" goes back to suggestions made by two Medieval Jewish scholars, Rashi and Kimchi (see Brunet 1966: 388–89). This is, admittedly, an attractive hypothesis, since a plumb line in the hand of a deity can be seen as a forceful metaphor for judgment. The people, one may infer, will be measured in accordance with divine standards. However, the act of placing a plumb line in the land (v. 8b) looks like an anticlimax. Moreover, this theory fails to account for the first occurrence of *ʾănāk* in this text (v. 7a). It is doubtful whether *ḥômat ʾănāk* really could mean "a wall built with the help of a plumb line," as claimed by several scholars (e.g., Mays 1969: 131, Soggin 1987: 115, and Williamson 1990: 112). Some commentators make an emendation in v. 7a (thus, e.g., Rudolph 1971: 234). Others delete the first occurrence of אֲנָךְ (thus, e.g., Harper 1905: 165; see Brunet 1966: 390, n. 3). The problem arises because these scholars believe that *ʾănāk* denotes an instrument (a plumb line). It is more reasonable to assume that *ʾănāk* refers to the material (probably some kind of metal) that the wall was made of. Such an interpretation is supported by the Septuagint. The Greek word ἀδάμας denotes a very hard metal or mineral, such as steel or diamond.

During the past decades, several scholars have argued that the correct translation of *ʾănāk* is "tin." As far as I can see, this is convincing. Despite a few dissenting voices (such as Noonan 2013), one might speak of a near consensus among recent commentators (see Stuart 1987: 372–73, Paul 1991: 233–34, Jeremias 1998: 130–32, and Linville 2008: 138–39; see also Ouellette 1973). The main arguments in support of this hypothesis can be summarized as follows: (1) The Hebrew lexeme *ʾănāk* is an Akkadian loan word, and (2) in Akkadian, *annaku/anāku* means "tin," not "lead" (see Landsberger 1965 and Holladay 1970; see also *CAD* vol. 2, 127–30, s.v. *annaku*). Remarkably, the tin theory, with its strong support among modern philologists and biblical scholars, has not been included in the major Hebrew dictionaries (see *HALOT,* Ges[18], and *DCH,* s.v.). This conservative attitude on the part of the lexicographers (as well as the Bible translators) has been criticized by Weigl (1995: 376–80). See also Jeremias (1998: 131, n. 19).

COMMENTS

7:7–8. Interpretation of the third vision (7:7–8) is, to some extent, obstructed by the fact that the lexical sense of the key word, *ʾănāk,* is disputed. This term, which does not occur in any other biblical text, is repeated four times within the range of two verses. In v. 7a, YHWH ("the Lord") is seen standing on or at a wall of *ʾănāk.* According to v. 7b, he holds *ʾănāk* in his hand. Having been asked, in v. 8a, what it is that he sees, Amos answers with one single word: *ʾănāk*. Finally, YHWH declares that he is going to place *ʾănāk* "in the midst of my people Israel" (v. 8b).

Because of the uncertainties involved, an abundance of suggestions have been advanced. As shown in detail in the Notes above, recent scholarship has abandoned the hypothesis that *ʾănāk* (allegedly denoting "lead") here signifies a plumb line. According to an emerging consensus, the lexical sense is "tin" (thus, e.g., Paul 1991: 233–34, Jeremias 1998: 130–32, and Linville 2008: 138–39). However, even if this new consensus may solve the issue of translation, several crucial questions concerning the interpretation of the vision report in 7:7–8 are still open to debate. Which associations linked to the metal tin should be seen as most relevant in this context? Granting that "tin" is the correct translation, is it possible to make sense of all parts of this vision? Does the conversation on *ʾănāk* between the deity and the prophet involve some kind of wordplay?

Since tin is rather soft compared with other metals, and therefore easily melted, some scholars have suggested that the tin wall symbolizes the people's vulnerability and defenselessness.[22] But if tin stands for weakness, it becomes very difficult to explain why the deity holds it in his hand (v. 7b) or why he threatens to place it among the people (v. 8b). Tin is, on the other hand, an essential ingredient in bronze, an alloy associated with strength and warfare. Hence, it is conceivable that YHWH is seen as a warrior wielding a bronze weapon (for instance, a sword) in v. 7 and that the tin mentioned in v. 8 refers to the arsenal of an invading enemy.[23]

But how should the image in v. 7aβ be understood? What could possibly be signified or symbolized by a vision of a deity standing on/at a wall made of tin/bronze? The wall might stand for protection. Thus, YHWH has been seen as a defender, standing on the city wall, who suddenly turns into an enemy attacking his own people (Beyerlin 1988: 40–48 and Riede 2008: 115–20). It may perhaps seem preferable to presuppose that YHWH is portrayed as an attacker throughout vv. 7–8. In support of such an interpretation, Christoph Uehlinger has called attention to the pictorial representation of an attacking goddess, positioned above a city wall, found on a terracotta plaquette from Larsa (1989: 96–99, 104.) However, I find it unlikely that the strangely unrealistic image of a tin wall should be taken as representing an ordinary city wall.

Perhaps it is not necessary, after all, to figure out exactly which qualities or uses of the metal tin the author had in mind. An intertextual investigation of the motif of a metallic wall opens up new possibilities. Interestingly, the closest parallels are (again!) found in the book of Jeremiah. Twice, in Jer 1:18 and 15:20, the prophet Jeremiah is told that YHWH will make him into a "wall of bronze (*nĕḥōšet*)." In both cases, the context makes it clear that this is a metaphor for the invincibility of the prophet and the prophetic word. In Jer 1:19 (and in 15:20, too), YHWH adds the following exposition: "They will fight against you, but they shall not prevail against you" (NRSV). I find it likely that Amos 7:7–8 contains a similar metaphor, as proposed by Martha Campos (2011: 17–21). According to Campos, the opening scene (v. 7) shows YHWH in the process of constructing the wall: standing in front of it, with an amount of building material, tin, in his hand. This metal (or, this wall?), which serves as a metaphor for the prophet and/or the prophetic message, will then be placed "in the midst (*bĕqereb*) of my people Israel" (v. 8).[24] Further support for this reading is found in the literary context.

In 7:10, Amaziah complains against the oppositional activity of Amos, taking place "in the midst of (*bĕqereb*) the house of Israel." This looks like an explanatory comment on v. 8 (see Campos 2011: 8 and Steins 2010: 97).

In terms of their metaphorical function, one may conclude, there seems to be no major difference between the tin wall in Amos 7 and the bronze (or copper) wall in Jeremiah 1 and 15. For the author of Amos 7:7–8, tin apparently symbolized strength (despite the objections made by several modern scholars). Presumably, this is due to the fact that tin is a component of bronze; nevertheless, it remains to be explained why the author chose to speak of tin instead of bronze. Further, why did the author use an unusual term of Akkadian origin, *'ănāk,* rather than *bĕdîl,* the Hebrew word for tin (used in Ezek 22:18, 20; 27:12)?

In light of the structural similarity with the fourth vision, an attractive solution suggests itself. In 8:1–2 the visual display is inextricably connected to a wordplay (see the Comments on that passage). It is likely, as commonly acknowledged by modern commentators, that the third vision likewise contains a double entendre. In that perspective, the word *'ănāk,* and the very sound of that word, becomes more important than the word's referent (a specific kind of metal). It has thus been suggested that the pronunciation of *'ănāk* evoked associations to a similar word denoting sighing (a form of either *'nḥ* or *'nq*) among the first readers/listeners.[25] They would hear two messages simultaneously, about YHWH bringing tin to the people, but also sighing and mourning.

Alternatively, picking up a proposal made by Praetorius (1915: 23) one hundred years ago, one may perceive a double entendre involving *'ănāk* and the first-person pronoun *'ānōkî* (see also Coote 1981: 92–93). This could be taken to mean that YHWH declares that he is about to place himself (the divine "I") "in the midst of my people" (v. 8b). A corresponding play on assonances is attested in an Akkadian hymn, where the goddess Ishtar praises herself with the help of metal metaphors, including the expression *a-na-ku anâ-ku,* meaning "I am tin" (see Riede 2008: 123–24).[26] In the Hebrew language, the similarity in sound is admittedly less striking (but see Novick 2008: 122–25); nevertheless, some features in the literary context suggest a wordplay between *'ănāk* and *'ānōkî.* In that case, however, the pronoun would seem to refer to Amos, not YHWH.

As noted above, v. 10 indicates that the tin placed in the nation's midst should be understood as a metaphor for Amos. Moreover, in 7:14, where Amos speaks about himself and his mission, *'ānōkî* occurs three times. Almost inevitably, the reader recalls the fourfold repetition of *'ănāk* in vv. 7–8 (Campos 2011: 6–7; see also Williamson 1990: 117). Thus, the wordplay *'ănāk—'ānōkî* can be integrated within the metaphorical interpretation outlined above.[27] In addition, the presence of such a pun might help to explain why Amos refrains from intercession. As the prophet answers YHWH's question in v. 8a, "What do you see, Amos?," he is trapped.[28] Amos says, "tin/myself," and then it dawns upon him that he himself is an instrument for the divine judgment—like tin in YHWH's hand.

According to a literal translation of the concluding clause of v. 8, YHWH says, "I will no longer pass him by (*lō' 'ôsîp 'ôd 'ăbôr lô*)." Arguably, this should be interpreted as a declaration that forgiveness (or, passing by without punishment, as if nothing had happened) has ceased to be an option.[29] Hence, one may translate, "I will no longer spare them" (see Wolff 1977: 301 and Paul 1991: 236, n. 82).

A Bridge between Two Passages (7:9)

7   ^{9}The high places of Isaac will become desolate,
and the sanctuaries of Israel will become ruins.
I will attack the house of Jeroboam with the sword.

COMMENTS

7:9. In v. 9, the divine punishment is described more concretely than in the preceding passage (vv. 7–8). This oracle was probably composed after the collapse of the Northern Kingdom. It is stated that all cultic places in Israel—the local open-air sanctuaries ("high places") and all temples—are going to be demolished (v. 9a). According to v. 9b, YHWH himself will attack the ruling dynasty "with the sword." The formulation "house of Jeroboam" seems to indicate that one and the same royal family had been ruling Israel through the centuries, from Jeroboam I to Jeroboam II. In fact, however, the latter king belonged to the "house" of Jehu, who finished off the dynasty of Omri.

Arguably, the point made by v. 9 is of an ideological nature. Thus, it implies continuity from Jeroboam (I) to Jeroboam (II), not in a strict dynastic sense, but in terms of apostasy, in the vein of the Deuteronomistic History: "King Jeroboam, son of Joash of Israel . . . did not depart from all the sins of Jeroboam, son of Nebat" (2 Kgs 14:23–24). The mention of "high places" (*bāmôt*), along with the main temples in the Northern Kingdom (most likely a reference to Dan and Bethel), supports the hypothesis that v. 9 expresses a Deuteronomistic standpoint (with Levin 1995: 309). According to this oracle, then, the divinely decreed destruction will befall Israel because of the "sins of Jeroboam" (1 Kgs 15:30; 16:31; 2 Kgs 3:3; cf. also 1 Kgs 12:30 and 13:34), an expression referring to diverse cultic practices that were perceived as persistent violations of the principle of cult centralization (as laid down in Deuteronomy 12).

With regard to its function within the literary context, the utterance in 7:9 can be called a bridge, since it connects the third vision report (vv. 7–8) with the disputation narrative in vv. 10–17.[30] On closer examination, though, the traffic runs mainly in one direction. Whereas vv. 7–8 and 9 do not share vocabulary, it is possible to make a rather impressive list of lexical links between v. 9 and the narrative in vv. 10–17 (especially vv. 11 and 16), as shown by Table 6.[31]

Table 6. Verbal Correspondences Linking 7:9 to 7:10–17

7:9	7:10–17	Comments
yiśḥāq	16 *yiśḥāq*	Unusual spelling of "Isaac"
ûmiqdĕšê (*yiśrāʾēl*)	13 *miqdaš* (*-melek*)	*miqdāš*, "sanctuary" (P; Ezek; 1–2 Chr)
yiśrāʾēl	10–11 (x3), 15–17 (x3)	"Israel"
ʿal-bêt	16 *ʿal-bêt*	v. 9, house of Jeroboam; v. 16, house of Isaac
yārobʿām	11 *yārobʿām*	"Jeroboam"
beḥereb	11, 17 *beḥereb*	"With the sword"

Note: "P" indicates Priestly source.

It is reasonable to assume that v. 9 had an important role in the editorial process whereby the disputation narrative (vv. 10–17) was inserted into the vision cycle. However, it is difficult to determine whether v. 9 was composed by the editor or was rather creatively reused as a bridge verse.[32]

A Narrative Interlude: Amos versus Amaziah (7:10–17)

7 [10]Then Amaziah, priest in Bethel, sent word to Jeroboam, king of Israel:
"Amos has conspired against you in the midst of the house of Israel.
The land cannot bear all his words.
[11]For this is what Amos has said:
'Jeroboam will die by the sword, and Israel will surely be exiled from its land.'"
[12]And Amaziah said to Amos:
"Go away, seer! Flee to the land of Judah! Eat your bread there, and prophesy there!
[13]But do not prophesy in Bethel again,
for it is a royal sanctuary, a state temple."
[14]Amos answered Amaziah:
"I (am/was) not a prophet, nor a prophet's son.
I (am/was) a herdsman and a tender of sycamore trees.
[15]But YHWH took me from behind the flock.
YHWH said to me: 'Go! Prophesy to my people Israel!'
[16]Now then, listen to the word of YHWH!
You say: 'Do not prophesy against Israel and do not preach against the house of Isaac!'
[17]Therefore, thus says YHWH:
'Your wife will prostitute herself in the city,
your sons and your daughters will fall by the sword,
and your land will be divided up by a measuring line.
You yourself will die in an unclean land,
and Israel will surely be exiled from its land.'"

INTRODUCTION TO 7:10–17

The prophetic legend recounted in 7:10–17 is commonly regarded as an insertion into the series of vision reports. I tend to agree; however, I find it likely that this addition was made shortly after the composition of the vision cycle, in the exilic or the early postexilic era. Quite obviously, the narrative in 7:10–17 separates the two visions that constitute the second pair in the cycle (7:7–8 + 9 and 8:1–2 + 3). Moreover, there are important differences in perspective between 7:10–17 and the surrounding visions. While the latter would appear to be consciously formulated in such a way that they could apply to either of the two national disasters, in 722 and 587 B.C.E., the depiction of the encounter between Amos and the priest Amaziah is characterized by a historicizing tendency, focusing on the reign of Jeroboam II (cf. 1:1). Further, whereas the vision reports can be read as theological reflections focusing on the role of YHWH as a divine judge, constantly choosing between judgment and mercy in any given situation, the narrative in vv. 10–17 focuses entirely on the role of the prophet.

Still, this narrative is well integrated into its present literary context.[33] I find it likely that it was inserted exactly here in order to solve a theological problem posed by the sequence of the vision reports. Since no other reason is given for YHWH's change of mind, from compassion (in the second vision) to pitilessness (in the third vision), this sinister development appears to be due to the cessation of prophetic intercession. But why did Amos stop praying for the people? Why was he not, in the end, able to prevent the catastrophe? The story about Amos and Amaziah would seem to provide an answer to those questions.[34]

The reader is told that Amos was prohibited to act as a prophet in Israel (vv. 12–13, 17). Ironically, one may infer, the political and religious leaders pronounced an irrevocable doom over themselves as they rejected Amos, the messenger of doom.[35] In his capacity as efficacious intercessor (vv. 2–3, 5–6), Amos turned out to be their last hope. I suggest that the main theological point made by 7:10–17 in conjunction with the vision reports could be formulated as follows: Rejection of YHWH's prophet, and of YHWH's word, makes forgiveness unthinkable (see similarly Steins 2010: 84–85).

In addition, the narrative in 7:10–17 serves to authorize the message of (or, the message associated with) Amos (so Paas 2002: 263–64 and Behrens 2002: 92). As regards the portrayal of Amos as an ideal prophet, there is a high degree of coherence between the vision reports and the narrative in 7:10–17. Throughout the entire section 7:1–8:3 Amos is consistently portrayed as a "prophet like Moses"—or, perhaps even more to the point, as a prophet like Jeremiah.[36] The resemblances between Amos and Jeremiah as literary characters are striking. Essential aspects of the image of Jeremiah have close counterparts in the portrait of Amos in chapters 7–8. Thus, these two prophets (or, literary characters) (1) deliver similar messages concerning an impending disaster and (2) receive visions of the same type, reported in the same style (Jer 1:11–14; 24:1–5; Amos 7:7–8; 8:1–2). In addition, both of them are described as (3) intercessors with the power to exert influence on YHWH (Jer 7:16; 11:14; 14:11; Amos 7:2–3, 5–6). Finally, both Amos and Jeremiah (4) are involved in a conflict with a priest who tries to silence the prophetic message (Jer 20:1–6, cf. also 29:24–32; Amos 7:10–17).

The parallels between the narratives in Jer 20:1–6 and Amos 7:10–17 are conspicuous. Generally speaking, the plot is the same. Primarily on political grounds, a priest (who acts as an overseer of the local prophets?) attempts to silence the prophetic message (Jer 20:2; Amos 7:12–13). In each case, the confrontation ends with an oracle, uttered by the prophet, which threatens the priest, along with his family or friends, with deportation (Jer 20:6; Amos 7:17). However, the author of 7:10–17 has not simply substituted Amos for Jeremiah and Amaziah for Pashhur. On the level of textual details, these two texts are too different to permit such a conclusion.

Apparently, the (postexilic?) author of Amos 7:10–17 reworked motifs from more than one source. Besides Jeremiah 20, the strange story in 1 Kings 13, about an encounter in Bethel between King Jeroboam I and an anonymous "man of God," stands out as the most important intertext that might throw light on Amos 7:10–17. The similarities between these narratives include (1) the location of the confrontation, Bethel; (2) the appearance of a prophet from Judah (1 Kgs 13:1, 12; Amos 7:12); (3) a message directed against the Bethel sanctuary, its priesthood, and the king (1 Kgs 13:2–3; Amos 7:9, 11, 13); and (4) an (abortive) attempt to stop further prophesying (1 Kgs 13:4–6; Amos 7:12–13). In addition, there is a common theme—that is, of "eating bread"—which is developed in strongly divergent ways. In 1 Kings 13, the man of God meets a violent death because he is tricked (by another prophet) into disobeying the command given by YHWH: "You must not eat bread or drink water, or return by the way that you came" (1 Kgs 13:9, 17). In Amos 7, it is the priest in Bethel, Amaziah, who tells Amos to go to Judah and "eat your bread there" (7:12). The reader gets the impression that Amos intends to disobey this command (7:16).

How should these intriguing correspondences and differences between the two texts be evaluated? Although several studies have been devoted to this topic, there is no scholarly consensus concerning the nature of the relationship between the narratives in 1 Kings 13 and Amos 7.[37] Is this a case of literary dependence? If so, in which direction does the dependence go?[38] Or are both texts drawing on a common source? Did the original story feature Amos or an anonymous man of God? Was it associated with Jeroboam I (1 Kings 13) or Jeroboam II (Amos 7)? These questions will have to remain unanswered. However, I am inclined to agree with Utzschneider that it makes excellent sense, in light of the textual evidence, to regard the narrative in Amos 7 as alluding to the legend in 1 Kings 13, or to some version of that legend (1988: 95–96).[39] In (deliberate?) contrast to the protagonist of that story, the wretched "man of God," Amos is here portrayed as successfully resisting any attempt to persuade him to disobey the words of YHWH.

In terms of genre (and genre expectations), Amos 7:10–17 has often been treated as a "piece of prophetic biography" (Mays 1969: 134).[40] However, such a genre label must be seen as a misnomer (see similarly Troxel 2012: 44–45). The reader is told very little about the life and career of Amos.[41] As a matter of fact, 7:10–17 adds almost nothing to the scanty information provided in the book's superscription (1:1). In the words of Tucker (1973: 429), "the biographical concerns of our story are not as high as those of the superscription to the book (1:1), which in the scope of a single verse contains more information about the life and times of Amos than do 7:10–17 and the remainder of the book combined."

Because the narrative in 7:10–17 is dominated by dialogue, it has been called "a little drama" (Tucker 1973: 425; see also Steins 2010: 78–80). I suggest the more specific label "dispute narrative."[42] At the center of this piece of prose is a heated debate between two characters, Amaziah and Amos. The geographical and historical setting of this discussion is described in an indirect and sketchy manner. No major events are recounted. This is a story about the power of words. It revolves around conflicting messages and rival claims. Whereas Amaziah represents the authority of the state, Amos allegedly acts and speaks with the authority of YHWH.[43]

Before the details of this dispute narrative are discussed, something should be said about its structure. The episodic structure is simple, consisting of two scenes: (1) Amaziah's letter to Jeroboam (vv. 10–12), and (2) the encounter between Amos and Amaziah (vv. 13–17).

In order for the dynamic complexity of this text to be grasped, it is more helpful to obtain an overview of the communicative structure.[44] It is possible to distinguish between three different levels of discourse: (a) the narrative frame; (b) the level of direct speech, that is, the words uttered by the characters (as reported by the narrator); and (c) the level of indirect or embedded speech. On the (c) level, the words (allegedly) spoken by one character are quoted within the speech of another character. In the following, the translated text is marked and indented in accordance with such a three-level analysis: level (a) in boldface, level (b) indented, and level (c) in italics:[45]

10 Then Amaziah, priest in Bethel, sent word to Jeroboam, king of Israel:
Amos has conspired against you in the midst of the house of Israel.
The land cannot bear all his words.
11 *For this is what Amos has said:*
Jeroboam will die by the sword, and Israel will surely be exiled from its land.
12 And Amaziah said to Amos:
Go away, seer! Flee to the land of Judah! Eat your bread there, and prophesy there!
13 But do not prophesy in Bethel again,
for it is a royal sanctuary, a state temple.
14 Amos answered Amaziah:
I (am/was) not a prophet, nor a prophet's son.
I (am/was) a herdsman and a tender of sycamore trees.
15 But YHWH took me from behind the flock.
YHWH said to me: Go! Prophesy to my people Israel!
16 Now then, listen to the word of YHWH!
You say:
Do not prophesy against Israel and do not preach against the house of Isaac!
17 Therefore, *thus says YHWH:*
Your wife will prostitute herself in the city,
your sons and your daughters will fall by the sword,
and your land will be divided up by a measuring line.
You yourself will die in an unclean land,
and Israel will surely be exiled from its land.

One may observe that the narrative frame is confined to a minimum, which means that the reader is informed only about the identity of the speakers. On that level, only one event is narrated, at the very outset, namely, that Amaziah sent a message to the king (v. 10a). If this had been a biographical or historical legend, the reader would certainly have been told about Jeroboam's reaction. Even more important, the reader would have learned what happened to Amos, and to Amaziah, subsequent to the dramatic verbal exchange. Apparently, however, the author of 7:10–17 found such details irrelevant. Clearly, this is a debate rather than a legend. Hence, it is of vital importance to study *how* things are said, and how the two combatants quote, or misquote, each other.[46]

Amos, the eponymous hero, is quite unsurprisingly pictured as the winner of the debate, the one who gets the last word (with Hardmeier 1985: 70–71). Hence, one may suspect that his opponent, Amaziah, is indirectly portrayed as a particularly unreliable character. As will be shown, however, Amos's quotation technique also seems to be governed more by his own rhetorical purposes than by an intention to be absolutely accurate. This is a verbal war, in which words are wielded as weapons, and in which the one with access to the words of YHWH is going to win.[47]

NOTES

7:11. *For this is what Amos has said.* One might also consider rendering *kî kōh ʾāmar ʿāmôs* by "For thus says Amos."

7:13. *a royal sanctuary, a state temple.* A more literal rendering of v. 13b would be, "for it is the king's sanctuary (*miqdaš-melek*), and the temple of the kingdom (*ûbêt mamlākâ*)."

7:14. *I (am/was).* The double Hebrew noun clause in v. 14a, *lōʾ nābîʾ ʾānōkî wĕ lōʾ ben-nābîʾ*, can be interpreted in two ways with regard to temporality. The same applies to the double noun clause in v. 14b. These utterances may be construed as referring to either the past or the present. Interestingly, the LXX opted for the former alternative: οὐκ ἤμην προφήτης ἐγὼ οὐδὲ υἱὸς προφήτου ἀλλ᾽ ἢ αἰπόλος ἤμην καὶ κνίζων συκάμινα ("I *was* not a prophet, nor the son of a prophet, but I *was* a herdsman and a gatherer of sycamores"). Arguably, though, the default interpretation of a noun clause without temporal markers is as a statement in the present tense. See further the Comments below.

7:16. *do not preach.* Or, more literally, "do not drip." See the Comments below.

COMMENTS

7:10. There is a small but significant catchword connection between v. 9 and v. 10: Jeroboam. To a certain extent, this name (although probably referring to two different kings) makes it possible to read vv. 10–17 as a logical continuation of 7:1–9. It enables the reader to construe the following chain of events: Amos had predicted misfortune for the royal house (v. 9). This could be interpreted as a subversive activity; hence, a loyal priest informed King Jeroboam. Such a scenario would have been seen as realistic by ancient readers.

In both Mari and Assyria it was the duty of royal officials to report any potentially disturbing prophetic messages that they came across (see Couey 2008). Concerning the attitude of Zimri-Lim (king of Mari) toward prophets, Couey has made this remark: "The fact that his officials felt compelled to report so many instances of prophetic activity, both at home and abroad, indicates that he was particularly concerned with what the prophets were saying" (2008: 301). In his succession treaty, the Assyrian ruler Assurbanipal instructed his subordinates to report any "evil, ill, and ugly word that is mendacious and harmful to Assurbanipal . . . may it come from the mouth of his enemy, from the mouth of his ally . . . from the mouth of a *raggimu* [prophet]."[48]

In Jerusalem, in the late monarchic era, one of the high-ranked priests was apparently endowed with the task of supervising the local prophets and diviners. We know from Jer 29:24–32—a passage that cites a letter from a certain Shemaiah to a priest called Zephaniah—that the priestly supervisor was expected to take action against potential troublemakers among the prophets (such as Jeremiah): "YHWH has appointed you priest in the place of the priest Jehoiada, so that there may be overseers in the house of YHWH to control any madman who prophesies; you should put him in the stocks and the collar" (Jer 29:26). Elsewhere in the book of Jeremiah, a priest named Pashhur acts as a supervisor of this kind (Jer 20:1–3). Arguably, the brief introduction provided by Amos 7:10a, "Then Amaziah, priest of Bethel, sent word to Jeroboam, king of Israel," implies that the literary character Amaziah was thought to perform a similar role in the administration of the Northern Kingdom.[49]

In the opening line of Amaziah's report (v. 10bα), it is stated that Amos has "conspired" (*qāšar*) against the king. This would have been regarded as a severe accusation, indeed. At the same time, from an inner-biblical perspective, the use of the verb *qāšar* ("to conspire") invites the reader to make a comparison with characters such as Elisha and Jehu (see 2 Kgs 9:1–15, especially v. 14; 10:9).[50] As noted above, the phrase "in the midst of the house of Israel" (*běqereb bêt yiśrāʾēl*) echoes the utterance in 7:8. This could be taken as an implicit interpretation of the third vision: the tin (wall) stands for Amos and his prophetic message. According to the next clause, Amos's words were considered unbearable: "the land cannot bear (or, 'contain'; Hiphil of *kûl*) all his words" (v. 10bβ). Possibly, the land of Israel is here metaphorically depicted as some kind of vessel, or cistern, that cannot contain more than a certain amount of fluid (thus Jeremias 1998: 138.) This expression thus would seem to imply that Amos's prophetic activity was characterized by verbosity, in addition to its subversive potential.

One may add a reflection on the history of interpretation. In 7:10 it is indicated, for the first time in the book, that Amos went to the Northern Kingdom and prophesied there. It is in fact perfectly possible to read chapters 1–6 as a collection of oracles concerning Israel, uttered by a prophet who was active in Judah (see Isa 28:1–4). If it had not been for 7:10–17, the entire book of Amos would have been susceptible to such an interpretation. Clearly, this narrative has had an enormous impact on the book's reception throughout the centuries.

7:11. The remainder of Amaziah's letter to Jeroboam contains a short summary of Amos's message. The king will be killed and the population driven into exile. Formally, this is a quotation, introduced by the so-called messenger formula, *kōh ʾāmar ʿāmôs* (v. 11aα; literally, "thus says Amos"). However, the fact that the formulation in v. 11aβ, "Jeroboam will die by the sword," differs slightly, yet significantly, from the (supposedly accurate) words of Amos in v. 9, hints at an element of distortion in Amaziah's quotation technique. Apparently, a somewhat diffuse saying concerned with the future of the ruling dynasty (v. 9b) has been transformed into a direct threat against the king (v. 11a). Clearly, Amaziah aims at presenting Amos as extremely dangerous, "to make him seem a worse threat than he actually is" (García-Treto 1993: 120).

One may observe that it is due to the change made by Amaziah that a certain (perceived) problem arises. If v. 11 is read as an actual oracle, one has to admit that this prophecy was only partially fulfilled. The people of Israel went into exile, as presaged in 7:9, but contrary to the prediction made by Amos in v. 11 (according to Amaziah), King Jeroboam II died peacefully (2 Kgs 14:29). However, it is unlikely that the author of 7:10–17, or the editor of 7:1–17, found this apparent inconsistency problematic.[51] For an observant reader, the discrepancy between what actually happened and the words of Amos, *as reported* by Amaziah, does not diminish the trustworthiness of Amos. On the contrary, it is Amaziah who comes out as unreliable. Whereas Amaziah cites what Amos has said (*kōh ʾāmar ʿāmôs*) in a dubious way, Amos is the only one in the debate who proclaims what YHWH has said (*kōh ʾāmar yhwh*, v. 17), as other scholars have also observed (Hardmeier 1985: 67–69 and Miller 1986: 85).

7:12. Filling in the gaps in the story, one may guess that King Jeroboam, in his reply to the priest's letter, urged Amaziah to silence or expel the rebellious prophet named Amos; but nothing is said about this in the text. As already noted, the narrator's conspicuous silence regarding the king's reaction (or regarding any further interaction with Jeroboam) indicates that this narrative focuses on words, not events.

In vv. 12–13, Amaziah speaks directly to Amos, addressing him as a "seer" (*ḥōzeh*). This designation can be seen as more or less synonymous with *nābîʾ*, "prophet."[52] It is often maintained that Amos was prohibited by Amaziah to prophesy any more. This is not correct. In v. 12, he is told to leave the country and to continue (!) to prophesy, but in another country. For the interpretation of the second part of this narrative (vv. 12–17, and especially vv. 14–15), I believe it is essential to acknowledge that the topic of the debate is not *whether* Amos should be allowed to act as a prophet, but *where* he should be allowed to act as a prophet (with Werlitz 2000: 240 and Steins 2010: 82).

Amaziah's order to Amos in v. 12 contains a sequence of four admonitions (two imperatives, followed by two *weqatal* forms serving the function of imperatives): "*Go* away, seer! *Flee* to the land of Judah! *Eat* your bread there, and *prophesy* there!" The clause "eat your bread there (*weʾĕkol šām leḥem*)" has been variously interpreted.[53] It has sometimes been taken to mean "earn your living there," with reference to the Akkadian idiom *akalam akālu,* which may carry that sense (thus, e.g., Paul 1991: 242). Alternatively, and perhaps more likely, it should be interpreted as a way of saying, "Stay there!"[54] The seemingly redundant repetition of *šām,* "there," is a rhetorically efficient device. It underscores the main point Amaziah makes: Amos must by no means stay "here," in Bethel.[55]

7:13. In order to avoid any misunderstanding, Amaziah adds that Amos must not ever "prophesy in Bethel again" (v. 13a). It is implied that he, in his capacity as priestly supervisor of all prophets in Bethel, had the authority to issue such a prohibition. According to v. 13b, the main reason was political. Subversive prophecy could not be tolerated at "a royal sanctuary, a state temple." Evidently, Amaziah claims to be a spokesman for the king. Notably, in his definition of Bethel (which means "the house/dwelling of El/God") as *miqdaš melek,* literally "the king's sanctuary," and as *bêt mamlākâ,* literally "the house/temple of the kingdom," Amaziah forgets to mention the deity who presumably resided in that temple. By such subtle means, the narrator pictures Amaziah and Amos as representing two allegedly conflicting authorities, King Jeroboam and YHWH (Dijkstra 2001: 118–19 and Miller 1986: 84–86).

7:14. The remainder of the debate, as reported by the narrator in vv. 14–17, contains Amos's answer to Amaziah. This response consists of three distinct yet connected parts:

1. A self-presentation with a brief call narrative (vv. 14–15)
2. A quotation ascribed to Amaziah, introduced by an admonition (v. 16)
3. An oracle of disaster, directed against Amaziah and his family (v. 17)

The first part of this complex and multistaged reply, the utterance in v. 14, has engendered an intense scholarly discussion. Much of the debate has focused on the translation and interpretation of Amos's opening words (v. 14aβ). What is he saying? Does Amos the prophet deny that he is a prophet? If so, for what reason would he deny that? Or could his words be taken to mean something else? In the following, I briefly describe and evaluate the main scholarly hypotheses. Then, I outline an interpretation based on the presupposition that 7:10–17 is a dispute narrative, not a piece of prophetic biography (see the genre discussion above). I argue that the utterance in v. 14 (and its continuation in v. 15) should primarily be understood as an answer to Amaziah's commands and prohibitions (in vv. 12–13).

Amos's self-presentation in v. 14 in the Hebrew consists of a series of four noun clauses. By default, if the immediate context does not suggest otherwise (for instance, a past or future orientation), such verbless predications are interpreted as temporally neutral. Hence, noun clauses are as a rule translated with the present tense (when translated into English, or some other tense-based language that does not allow this type of verbless utterance). Since these are Amos's opening words, and since Amaziah did not formulate any question concerning his past experience, it is therefore reasonable to understand v. 14aβ, *lōʾ nābîʾ ʾānōkî wĕ lōʾ ben-nābîʾ ʾānōkî,* as a twofold negative assertion relating to conditions prevailing at the time of speech: "I (am) not a prophet, nor a prophet's son."

Such an understanding of v. 14aβ has often been seen as problematic (see the Notes). Interpreted as a denial, this utterance would seem to contradict the saying in 3:7, which clearly implies that Amos should be counted among "his (YHWH's) servants the prophets (*hannĕbîʾîm*)." Within the narrower literary context, moreover, this appears to create the paradoxical notion of a nonprophet with a mission to prophesy (Niphal of *nbʾ,* vv. 12, 15). Among the suggested solutions to this (perceived) problem, some stand out as too speculative. Thus, Amos's answer has been construed as a syntactically unmarked question, "Am I not a prophet?" (so Driver 1955 and Ackroyd 1956; 1977: 83.) If such a reading of v. 14aβ is adopted, however, it becomes impossible to make sense of v. 14b (with Linville 2008: 144).[56] The hypothesis that v. 14aβ in fact expresses a positive affirmation, "I am a prophet," suffers from a similar lack of syntactic and contextual support.[57]

A more attractive option is to translate with the past tense. Although Amos *was* not a prophet (v. 14), he *became* a prophet when YHWH appointed him (v. 15). Going back to the Septuagint, this reading of v. 14aβ is popular also in modern exegesis.[58] However, even this seemingly ingenious solution creates problems. In terms of logic (or lack thereof), a past tense understanding of the last clause in v. 14aβ implies that Amos through his calling to act as a *nābîʾ* (recounted in v. 15) also obtained the status of *ben nābîʾ,* literally "son of a prophet," a technical term for a member of a prophetic guild (see 2 Kgs 2:3, 5, 15).[59] On the level of communication, moreover, this alternative entails that listeners or readers revise their first, intuitive interpretation (that the utterance referred to the speaker's present), retrospectively, in light of the preterital (*wayyiqtol*) forms in v. 15.

With several other scholars, I therefore prefer a present-tense translation and interpretation of the noun clauses in v. 14.[60] This reading is supported by the syntax and fits the immediate context.[61] In addition, it can be supported by an instance of inner-biblical exegesis. In Zech 13:15, where the statement *lōʾ nābîʾ ʾānōkî* is quoted verbatim from Amos 7:14a (and immediately followed by a phrase similar to Amos 7:14b), a present-tense reading ("I *am* no prophet") is ascertained. This gives an important hint as to how Amos's answer to Amaziah was understood by competent readers at a very early stage of its history of interpretation (thus also Linville 2008: 144–45).

In order for the rhetorical function of v. 14 to be understood, I believe it is essential to keep in mind that, so far, the topic of the debate has not been whether Amos is a prophet or whether he has the right to prophesy (see the Comments on v. 12). The issue discussed by Amaziah was rather *where* and *how* Amos should be allowed to prophesy. This raises the question of authority: Who has the right to decide about Amos's prophetic activity? It is against this background that we need to interpret the first part of Amos's answer in vv. 14–15.

The rhetorical strategy used by (the literary character) Amos in vv. 14–15 can, I suggest, be reconstructed as follows.[62] To begin with, Amos offers a self-presentation that is compatible with Amaziah's description of him as a "seer" (*ḥōzeh*) who is prophesying. For some reason, Amaziah did not use the term *nābî'*, "prophet." Making a point out of this seemingly unimportant omission, Amos seizes the opportunity to express his opposition to Amaziah's claims to authority in a clever way, in apparent agreement with his opponent: "I am not a prophet (*nābî'*)."[63] By means of the ensuing statement, that neither is he "a son of a prophet," he adds further precision, as well as further nuances.[64] As noted above, disciples of senior prophets (such as Elijah and Elisha) were called "sons of the prophets" (see, e.g., 1 Kgs 20:35). Hence, it is likely that the final clause of v. 14a makes the following point: Since Amos is not a member of a local prophetic guild, he is not the kind of prophet whom Amaziah has the authority to supervise. In terms of profession, Amos explains (perhaps to his opponent's surprise) that he is involved in various agricultural enterprises (v. 14b). In this way, he emphasizes even more efficiently that he does not stand under Amaziah's jurisdiction. Most important, though, Amos does not deny that he actually is what Amaziah called him (in v. 12): a *ḥōzeh* ("seer"), one who receives prophetic visions, a man with a mission to prophesy.

Although the two participles used to describe Amos's occupation(s) in v. 14b, *bôqēr* and *bôlēs*, are both *hapax legomena*, the translation "a herdsman and a tender of sycamore trees" has a high degree of plausibility. That *bôqēr* carries the sense "herdsman," or the like, is supported by the ancient versions. Most probably, the verb *bqr* is a denominative, constructed on the basis of *bāqār*, "cattle" (see *HALOT*, s.v.). As regards *bôlēs*, the literary context clearly indicates that the term denotes some aspect of the cultivation of sycamore figs. This supposition is confirmed by comparative philology: while Arabic *balasu* denotes a kind of fig, Ethiopic *balasa* may refer to both sycamore trees and figs.[65]

The question of how it was possible for one person to combine these two occupations need not detain us here, since 7:10–17 is not treated as a biographical account in this commentary.[66] In fact, it is possible to explain this strange juxtaposition of terms for agricultural occupations in purely literary terms. Whereas the image of Amos as a herdsman is linked to a literary motif in v. 15 (cf. also *nôqēd* in 1:1), the notion that he was dealing with figs could have been derived from the fourth vision, which is related to the harvest of summer fruit, such as figs (8:1–2).[67]

7:15. Having argued that he is not one of the local professional prophets, and that he therefore is not taking any orders from Amaziah, Amos now turns to the heart of the matter. He claims that he has the right to prophesy in Bethel concerning the fate of Israel because YHWH, representing the highest of all authorities, has commanded him to do that (v. 15b). Indeed, Amos cannot obey Amaziah's order to go away (*lēk*, v. 12) because that would amount to disobedience to YHWH, who had said to him: "Go (*lēk*)! Prophesy to my people Israel!" (v. 15b).

The episode recounted in v. 15 serves the function of a call narrative. With the aim of legitimizing the prophet, biblical call narratives usually stress that the initiative was solely YHWH's and that persuasion was needed (see, e.g., Exod 3:7–4:17 and Judg 6:11–18). The latter aspect is especially prominent in the case of Jeremiah (Jer 1:4–10; 20:7–9). Hence, the expression "YHWH took me" (v. 15a), which implies coercion, would seem to contribute to the process, discernible throughout 7:1–8:3, of portraying Amos as a prophet like Jeremiah.

At the same time, it is possible to detect an allusion to traditions about Moses and David in v. 15a: "YHWH took me from behind the flock (*mēʾaḥărê haṣṣōʾn*)." The (young) shepherd who receives a grand mission is a literary motif, attested in both biblical and extrabiblical texts (Schult 1971).[68] Moses was tending Jethro's flock (Exod 3:1) when he came across the burning bush. Likewise, David started his career as a shepherd (1 Sam 16:19; 17:15). A particularly close counterpart to the formulation in Amos 7:15 is found in Nathan's oracle in 2 Samuel 7, where YHWH says to David: "I took you from the pasture, from behind the flock (*mēʾaḥar haṣṣōʾn*)" (2 Sam 7:8).[69]

It is easy to see how a comparison with Moses suits Amos's (that is, the literary character's) rhetorical agenda, as he sets the authority of YHWH against that of Jeroboam (represented by Amaziah). But what could be the purpose of making an allusion to David? I suggest that it might be related to the author's deuteronomistically inspired, pro-Judean ideology. According to this text, Jeroboam's dynasty was doomed (vv. 9, 11). In contrast, as implied by v. 15a, the Davidic dynasty was seen as elected and protected by YHWH.

7:16. The roles have suddenly been reversed. Now Amos is the one giving orders to Amaziah. Within its context, the admonition in v. 16a, "listen to the word of YHWH," does not serve as an introduction to an oracle. Before actually uttering an oracle, in v. 17, which is properly introduced by the messenger formula, Amos cites the words of Amaziah (v. 16b). This juxtaposition of admonition and quotation has an ironic effect. Amaziah is reminded that he should have listened to the deity whose worship he was administering instead of rejecting his words. He has tried to throw out Amos, YHWH's mouthpiece. Now his own words are thrown back at him.

However, Amos has changed (or, distorted) his opponent's formulations. This is, I suggest, his *interpretation* of Amaziah's words. First, Amos claims that Amaziah has said, "Do not prophesy against Israel" (v. 16bα). To be precise, Amaziah had prohibited Amos to prophesy *in* Israel, but this is correctly (as the reader knows, because of the information provided by vv. 10–11) understood as an attempt to silence prophetic messages that are perceived as being *against* (ʿal) the kingdom of Israel. As stated in v. 15, Amos was acting in accordance with a divine command to prophesy *to* (ʾel) "my people Israel."

The second part of Amos's paraphrase looks like a poetic variation on the first part: "and do not preach (*taṭṭip*) against the house of Isaac" (v. 16bβ). Whereas Israel has been replaced by Isaac (a catchword link to v. 9), the verb *nbʾ*, "to prophesy," has been substituted by *ntp*, a verb with two interestingly interrelated senses: "to drip" and "to preach" (see, e.g., *DCH,* s.v.). Scholars have often taken *wĕlōʾ taṭṭip* ("do not drip/ preach") in v. 16bβ as a pejorative expression, alluding to the observation that ecstatic diviners sometimes slaver in an unsavory way (thus, e.g., Jeremias 1998: 141, n. 13).[70]

This interpretation is probably erroneous, however, as indicated by the use of *ntp* as a near synonym to *nb?* in Ezekiel 21 (vv. 2 and 7) in the context of a divine order to prophesy.

The relation between the two lexical senses of *ntp* ("to drip" and "to preach") is, I suggest, metaphorical. The underlying metaphorical concept can be defined as "speech is (like) fluid" (see *HALOT*, s.v.). Thus, words spoken by a person could be likened to drops of life-giving dew (Job 29:22, with *ntp* in Qal).[71] This would certainly apply to favorable prophecies, but in certain situations, prophetic speech would probably be experienced as an irritating dripping (see Mic 2:6, with a close parallel to the formulation in Amos 7:17). Hence, it makes sense that Amos puts the words "do not drip/preach" in Amaziah's mouth.

Additional nuances emerge if v. 17b is read in light of Amaziah's complaint to King Jeroboam concerning Amos's oracles: "The land cannot bear all his words" (v. 10). As noted above, the country is here metaphorically pictured as a vessel or container that is filled up and therefore cannot take more water (or some other fluid). Against this background, the conventional metaphor "words are drops" becomes vivid, and Amaziah's demand that Amos should stop dripping can be heard as an expression of desperation. By such subtle means, the author implies that Amos knew the contents of Amaziah's letter to the king.

7:17. Finally, the confrontation has reached its climax. In flagrant defiance of Amaziah's decree (v. 13), Amos delivers yet another oracle against Israel (v. 17). The main theme would seem to be possession of land. According to the concluding clause (v. 17bβ), the people will be exiled from "its land (*?admātô*)." However, the bulk of this prophecy concerns Amaziah, the priestly opponent, and his family. He himself (who wanted to see Amos deported) will lose his landed property (*?admātĕkā*), be deported to "an unclean land (*?ădāmâ ṭĕmē?â*)," and eventually die there (17aδ–ba). One may note the irony that a priest, presumably always busy avoiding ritual impurity, would end up in a land that could be considered impure.

Further, it is stated that Amaziah's wife will prostitute herself (v. 17aβ) and that their children will be killed "by the sword" (17aγ; cf. vv. 9 and 11).[72] Possibly, the idea is that the priest's wife "will be forced to support herself as a prostitute, since she will be deprived of children and husband" (Hayes 1988: 240). As indicated by the initial word of v. 17, *lākēn* ("therefore"), all these misfortunes are proclaimed as a punishment for Amaziah's disobedience to YHWH, when he attempted to prohibit the uttering of prophecies deriving from the supreme national deity.

This is the end of the story. Clearly, Amos must be seen as the winner of the debate from the narrator's point of view. Even more important, the invincible power of the prophetic word has been demonstrated, over against the words spoken by representatives of political power (King Jeroboam and Amaziah).

As noted above, the dispute narrative in 7:10–17 was probably inserted in order to provide answers to questions raised by the surrounding vision reports, such as: Why was YHWH unable to forgive the people of the Northern Kingdom? Why did the prophetic intercession cease all of a sudden? This happened, the reader of the narrative may infer, because the political and religious leaders rejected the words of YHWH. They even tried to banish and silence the one person who might have been able to persuade YHWH to cancel the catastrophe (vv. 2–3, 5), namely Amos.

Nothing is said about the fate of Amaziah. Were all parts of the prophecy fulfilled? The reader also is not told what happened to Amos. Was he arrested and executed?[73] Or did he return to Judah?[74] Apparently, the author of 7:10–17 had no interest in such matters. However, one remarkable feature of this story deserves a further comment. In v. 12, Amos is in fact ordered to prophesy in Judah. As pointed out by Steins (2010: 83, 86–87), this might be read as alluding to the process whereby words originally directed to (or against) the Northern Kingdom were later redirected and addressed to audiences in Judah.

The Fourth Vision: A Basketful of Bad News (8:1–3)

8 [1]This is what the Lord YHWH showed me: A basket of summer fruit. [2]He asked me: "What do you see, Amos?" and I answered:
"A basket of summer fruit."
Then YHWH said to me: "The end has come for my people Israel.
I will no longer spare them."
[3]The songstresses of the palace will wail on that day, says the Lord YHWH.
Many corpses, cast out everywhere. Hush!

NOTES

8:2. *spare them.* More literally, "spare him."

8:3. *songstresses.* The main interpretative problem in v. 3a concerns the grammatical subject of the wailing. The MT שִׁירוֹת וְהֵילִילוּ (*wĕhêlîlû šîrôt*) could be taken to mean "the songs will wail." Some scholars advocate such a translation (thus, e.g., Schart 2009: 266); however, such an expression would be an unparalleled case of metonymy. According to the LXX (τὰ φατνώματα) and the Vulgate (*cardines*), the whining sound will be produced by various parts of the building, which seems even less likely. An attractive alternative, which has informed the translation offered here, is to read a feminine plural participle, *šārôt*, "songstresses," in analogy with other texts (2 Sam 19:36; Qoh 2:8; 2 Chr 35:25). This solution has been advocated by, for instance, Wolff (1977: 317) and Jeremias (1998: 143). In order to avoid emendation, one might perhaps postulate the existence of an otherwise unattested lexeme, *šîrâ*, "female singer," as proposed by Paul (1991: 255). However, this can be seen as highly speculative. Alternatively, if the MT is retained, the subject (an unspecified "they") might be incorporated in the verbal form. This has been suggested by Garrett, who translates, "they shall wail temple songs" (2008: 230). The weakness of this reading is that it requires that an otherwise intransitive verb, *yll* (in Hiphil), takes on a transitive function.

of the palace. The lexeme *hêkāl* can denote either a palace or a temple. In most cases, this can be determined with the help of the context. Here the choice between those two alternatives is difficult. See further the Comments on v. 3.

cast out. This rendering presupposes a slight emendation, from הִשְׁלִיך (Hiphil of *šlk*) to הֻשְׁלַך (Hophal of the same verb), an operation that other commentators also advocate (see, e.g., Paul 1991: 255, n. 21). If the MT is retained, however, a similar sense can be obtained: "one has cast out," or the like (see Wolff 1977: 317–18).

COMMENTS

8:1–2. The fourth vision report (8:1–2) connects to the third (7:7–8) as if there had been no interlude (7:10–17). In terms of structure, the pattern from the third vision is repeated: introductory formula—vision—dialogue with interpretation—a final declaration made by YHWH (see further "Introduction to the Second Pair of Visions" above). The message conveyed by the fourth and last vision in the cycle is uncompromisingly harsh, yet far from unexpected, in light of the preceding passages. YHWH's verdict is definitive. A major catastrophe will befall the Northern Kingdom: "The end has come (*bāʾ haqqēṣ*) for my people Israel" (v. 2bα). This could, of course, also be read as a reference to the destruction of Jerusalem in 587 B.C.E., as indicated by the occurrence of exactly the same phrase, *bāʾ haqqēṣ*, "the end has come," in Ezekiel 7 (vv. 2, 6).[75]

If the concluding verbal message of the fourth vision report is straightforward, the same cannot be said about the relation between visual display (v. 1b) and interpretation (v. 2b) in this report. Amos is shown a basket, containing "summer fruit" (*qayiṣ*), most probably fresh figs.[76] He could hardly guess that this picture, a rather idyllic still life, was meant to symbolize violent destruction.[77] In his struggle to make sense of what he is seeing, Amos is assisted by the divine creator of this pictorial puzzle. Basically, the interpretation offered by YHWH consists of a pun, *qayiṣ*—*qēṣ*. When asked what he sees, the prophet answers, *kělûb qayiṣ*, "a basket of summer fruit" (v. 2aβ). Picking up on the last word, YHWH says, *bāʾ haqqēṣ*, "the end has come" (v. 2bα). Possibly, these two words, *qayiṣ* ("summer," or "summer fruit") and *qēṣ* ("end"), were pronounced in a similar way in the northern dialect.[78]

The vision described in 8:1–2 can, I suggest, be seen as a congenial representation of the catastrophe(s) that it refers to. In one respect, the reader of this text faces a situation similar to a national disaster: In both cases, it is only in retrospect that one may begin to try to make sense of the experience. With access to the interpretative key provided by YHWH in v. 2b, the reader may start searching for links between the pictorial motif of "summer fruit" and the message concerning "the end." In the Gezer calendar, *yrḥ qṣ*, the month when the figs were gathered, marks the very end of the agricultural year.[79] Thus, the vision cycle, which started with a reference to the beginning of the agricultural year (*lqš*) in 7:1, has come to a logical end. One may also construct the following chain of associative links: basket used for gathering—harvest of fruits—divine judgment. In some other prophetic passages, the image of fruit harvest stands, metaphorically, for judgment (Isa 17:5–6; 28:4).

8:3. The oracle in v. 3 elaborates on the preceding vision (vv. 1–2). In this respect it is analogous to 7:9, which is closely connected to the vision reported in 7:7–8. In both cases, the appended utterance focuses on the scope of the impending disaster. According to 8:3, a mass carnage will occur. Corpses will be on display in all public spaces (v. 3b). Wailing will be heard everywhere, even in the *hêkāl*, which may refer to either the palace or the temple (v. 3a).

Unfortunately, some details of the Hebrew text are obscure. In particular, it is difficult to determine the grammatical subject of the verb *wěhêlîlû*, "(they) will wail" in the opening clause (v. 3aα). With several other commentators, I find it likely that the text refers to female singers (see the Notes). According to other biblical texts, the royal personnel included songstresses (2 Sam 19:36 [Eng. v. 35]; Qoh 2:8). Their main task, one may infer, was to entertain the ruling elite; however, they would also be expected to participate in the lamentation over a deceased king (2 Chr 35:25). Against this background, I propose the following rendering of v. 3a: "The songstresses of the palace will wail on that day." This utterance continues a thematic thread, "singing," which has surfaced twice before. In 5:23, the songs of the addressees were denounced since they were part of a rejected cult. In 6:5, an association was made between the irresponsible attitude of the rich and the musical entertainment at their banquets. According to 8:3 (and 8:10, see below), all merry songs will be replaced by wailing and whining.

In v. 3b, interpretation is made difficult by a strange, staccato-like syntax. This can be seen as an apt way of depicting a situation characterized by traumatic stress. It is conceivable that v. 3b consists of a series of exclamations expressed by witnesses to the disaster: "Many corpses! Cast out everywhere! Hush!" The concluding "hush" (*hās*) is puzzling.[80] Who commands silence, and why? Arguably, this short interjection should be understood in the light of 6:10. It expresses the fear that words uttered may make things worse (see the Comments on 6:10). At the same time, *hās,* signifying speechlessness, serves as an efficient ending to the entire series of visions and words comprising 7:1–8:3. The end of it all, says 8:3bβ, will be unspeakable horror and deathly silence.[81]

Reinterpretations of the Words of Amos (8:4–14)

8   ⁴Hear this, you who trample on the poor
and do away with the afflicted of the land,
⁵saying: "When will the new moon be over, that we may sell grain,
and when will the Sabbath end, that we may market wheat?"
—making the ephah smaller and the shekel bigger,
dealing deceitfully with false scales,
⁶buying the poor for silver and the needy for a pair of sandals—
"and that we may sell the sweepings of the wheat."
    ⁷YHWH has sworn by the pride of Jacob:
"Never will I forget any of their deeds."
    ⁸Shall not the earth quake because of this, and all its inhabitants mourn?
Shall not all of it rise like the Nile, be stirred up and then sink like the Nile in Egypt?
    ⁹On that day, says the Lord YHWH, I will make the sun go down at noon
and thus darken the earth in broad daylight.
¹⁰I will turn your feasts into mourning and all your songs into dirges.
I will put sackcloth on everyone's loins and baldness on every head.
I will make it like the mourning for an only son,
the end of it will be like a day of bitterness.
    ¹¹Yes, the days are coming, says the Lord YHWH,
when I will send a famine over the land:
not hunger for bread, or thirst for water,
but for hearing the words of YHWH.
¹²They shall stagger from sea to sea, from north to east,
they shall roam around seeking the word of YHWH, but they shall not find it.

¹³In that day, the beautiful young women and the young men shall faint from thirst.

¹⁴Those who swear by the guilt of Samaria
or say, "As your god lives, O Dan," or, "As the way of Beer-Sheba lives,"
they will fall to rise no more.

INTRODUCTION TO 8:4–14

The section 8:4–14 consists of a string of somewhat loosely connected sayings: vv. 4–6 // v. 7 // v. 8 // vv. 9–10 // vv. 11–12 // vv. 13–14. According to Wolff, these oracles, which are quite disparate in terms of form and content, can all be read as comments on "the theme of the fourth vision, which is spelled out in 8:3: the end of Israel's life, and the mourning which that entails" (1977: 324). However, such a statement would seem to overstate the degree of coherence within chapter 8 as a whole. As a matter of fact, the theme of disaster, which unites 8:1–3 and 8:4–14, pervades the entire book.

On a closer examination, the utterances within 8:4–14 echo a number of motifs and formulations from chapters 1–6 (and, to some extent, from 7:1–8:3) in such a way that one may speak of deliberate quotations and allusions: (1) mistreatment of the poor, sending them into debt slavery "for a pair of sandals" (8:4–6, especially v. 6; cf. 2:6); (2) mention of "the pride/arrogance of Jacob" in the context of a divine oath (8:7; cf. 6:8); (3) a day of darkness (8:9; cf. 5:18–20 and 5:8); (4) national mourning instead of feasts, with songs of joy being replaced by dirges (8:10; cf. 5:1, 16–17, 21–23; 8:3); (5) people staggering because of (literal or metaphorical) thirst (8:11–12; cf. 4:6–8); and (6) young women (and men) who fall and cannot rise again (8:13–14; 5:2).[82]

Against this background I suggest that 8:4–14 is best characterized as a compilation of scribal prophecy, mainly consisting of comments on preceding passages in the book. In other words, the oracles within this unit should be read as reinterpretations of (an earlier collection of) the words of Amos, made in order to accommodate the message to new situations (with Jeremias 1998: 144–45 and Hadjiev 2009: 102–110).[83] This indicates a late (possibly exilic, but more likely postexilic) date of origin for the entire section, although it is possible to discern successive stages of growth, especially within vv. 9–14.[84]

The first unit within this section, 8:4–6, provides something that has been missing so far in the third part of the book (chapters 7–9), namely, accusations that could somehow justify the divine judgment proclaimed in 8:2. However, as mentioned already, this passage is hardly an independent prophecy. It is best described as an exegetical exposition, which reformulates the message of an existing prophecy, Amos 2:6–8 (especially 2:6b–7a), for a later readership (with Jeremias 1998: 146–48 and Levin 2003: 271–73).

As indicated above, the remaining parts of 8:4–14 can also be read as expositions or developments of topics treated in previous parts of the book. (More details will be provided in the Comments.) In this respect, however, an exception needs to be made for v. 8, which does not echo preceding passages. This complex rhetorical question is, above all, strikingly similar to an utterance in a subsequent section (9:5). Apparently, 8:8 serves as an editorial bridge between 8:4–7 and 8:9–14.

It furthermore can be argued that vv. 9–14 constitute a bridge between the preceding parts of the book and chapter 9. As far as I can see, these utterances introduce a stronger eschatological orientation into the discourse. In this connection it is worth noting that a study of other attestations in the prophetic literature of the phrase "on that day" (*bayyôm hahû*ʾ), which occurs in 8:9 and 8:13, shows that it often serves as an introduction to late additions with a more or less eschatological outlook. However, the individual oracles within 8:9–14 differ from each other in several respects. Whereas 8:11–12 provides a metaphorical and "spiritualizing" version of the scenery depicted in 4:6–8, transforming lack of food and water into hunger and thirst for divine words, the ensuing prophecy, in 8:13–14, seems to (re)interpret the metaphorical utterance in 5:2 rather literally.

NOTES

8:4. *afflicted*. I am reading עניי (plural of *ʿānî*) with the Qere; thus, apparently, also the LXX. Alternatively, if one chooses to follow the Ketiv, ענוי (plural of *ʿānāw*), "humble" might be a more apt translation. The Ketiv is attested also in MurXII. Arguably, though, the semantic difference between the lexemes *ʿānî* and *ʿānāw* is not great.

8:5. *saying*. Or "thinking," since the verb *ʾāmar* ("to say, speak") may carry that sense, as well.

8:8. *like the Nile*. Evidently, the MT is corrupt. Probably because of a scribal error, an original כיאר (*kayʾōr*, "like the Nile," cf. 9:5!) has become כאר (*kěʾōr*, "like the light"), which hardly makes any sense. This correction, adopted by most modern commentaries, is supported by the ancient versions.

and then sink. I am reading ונשקעה (Niphal of *šqʿ*, "to sink") instead of ונשקה (Niphal of *šqh*, possibly "to be watered"), in accordance with the Qere.

8:9. *I will make the sun go down*. According to the LXX (καὶ δύσεται ὁ ἥλιος μεσημβρίας), the sun will apparently set at this unusual hour without YHWH's direct involvement.

8:10. *like a day of bitterness*. Or "like a bitter day." The lexeme *mar* can be taken either as a noun ("bitterness") or as an adjective ("bitter").

8:14. *the guilt of Samaria*. This is the most plausible translation of the MT's *běʾašmat šōmrôn*. According to several scholars, it is preferable to interpret this phrase as referring to a goddess. The reading "by Ashima of Samaria" involves a minor emendation. However, the MT is supported by MurXII, as well as by the ancient versions. See especially the Targum (*běḥôbat šōmrôn*) and the Vulgate, *in delicto Samariae*. Possibly, the LXX rendering, κατὰ τοῦ ἱλασμοῦ Σαμαρείας ("by Samaria's expiation"), can be explained as an association evoked by a Hebrew *Vorlage* that did not differ from the MT. See further the Comments on v. 14.

the way. This interpretation of דרך (*drk*) is uncertain. The consonants of the MT are confirmed by MurXII. For alternative suggestions, see the Comments on v. 14.

COMMENTS

8:4. In v. 4, the addressees are described (and implicitly denounced) as oppressors of the poor. This echoes several previous prophecies in the book (2:6–8; 4:1; 5:11–12). By means of a quotation of the rare expression *haššō'ăpîm* ("you who trample") from 2:7a, an explicit link is made to the greedy evildoers mentioned in 2:6b–8. However, the vocabulary used, "the poor" (*'ebyôn*) and "the afflicted of the land," might denote marginalized groups of pious people, as well as groups of poor people in a strictly economic sense.[85] Perhaps the author of Amos 8:4 reinterpreted the mention of the "innocent" (*ṣaddîq*) in 2:6 as a reference to those who could be called "righteous" (*ṣaddîq*) in a religious sense?

8:5. Verses 4 and 5 appear to be linked by means of a wordplay based on different meanings of the stem *šbt*. Those who wish to "do away with" (Hiphil of *šbt*, v. 4b) the poor and the meek are now said to make evil plans on the Sabbath (*šabbāt*, v. 5a).[86] Direct address (v. 4) has been replaced by the rhetorical technique of constructing a (fictitious) quotation that purportedly reveals the inner thoughts of the speaker's (or, writer's) opponents (cf. 4:1; 6:13).[87] It is difficult to decide exactly where the direct citation ends.

On the basis of syntactical and structural observations, I regard vv. 5b–6a, containing a series of infinitives, as an artfully placed authorial comment, which belongs to the same level as the introductory infinitive *lē'mōr,* "saying/thinking." This insertion divides the quotation into two parts, v. 5a and v. 6b. One might speak of a chiastic structure or an *inclusio*. Hence, contrary to the opinion of many commentators, it is not necessary to delete or transpose some lines or to rearrange the text in any other way (with Paul 1991: 259). While the direct quotations (in vv. 5a and 6b) express the merchants' eagerness to make money, the interspersed comments (vv. 5b–6a) contain explicit accusations concerning their methods.

Read as "exegesis" of 2:6b–8, v. 5 can be characterized as both expansion and explanation. The identity of the evildoers who oppress the poor (2:6–7; 8:4) is revealed. The reader is told that they are grain traders.[88] In addition, the reader learns about their motives and methods. According to v. 5a, these merchants are so eager to do business (that is, to make more money) that they lack respect for the monthly and weekly holidays: the cultic celebration at each new moon, as well as divinely ordained rest on the seventh day of each week, the Sabbath.[89]

In v. 5b, the author adds the information that these greedy merchants are dishonest as well. They manipulate measures and weights so that they can sell less grain (less than a full ephah) and get more silver (more than an exact shekel).[90] Apparently, they tamper with the scales, as well. Far from being regarded as a trifle, the use of deceptive weights and balances is sharply condemned in several biblical texts (see, e.g., Lev 19:35–36; Deut 25:13–16; Prov 11:1; 20:23). It can be seen as a paradigmatic example of the kind of immoral behavior that was supposed to provoke the wrath of YHWH.

8:6. What follows, in v. 6a, is an almost verbatim quotation from 2:6b; however, there is a notable difference. Instead of *selling* the innocent (2:6), it is now about *buying* the poor (*dallîm*) for money (or, silver, *bakkesep*) "and the needy for a pair of sandals" (8:6aβ = 2:6bβ). In this way, an important nuance is added to the text that is being commented upon and updated (2:6b–8). It is emphasized that buying fellow Israelites or Judeans is as reprehensible as selling them.

But how does v. 6a connect to v. 5? What looks like a sudden move from the grain market to the slave market has often been seen as problematic.[91] However, it is possible to reconstruct a reasonable causal chain. Poor families (v. 4) who could not pay the high food prices (v. 5) would eventually end up in some kind of debt slavery (or, indebtedness that entailed dependency).[92]

Hence, what this text says, in a rhetorically skillful way, makes perfect sense: Those who sell grain using immoral methods (vv. 5 and 6b) are, at the same time, "buying" the poor (v. 6a), as they bring them into indebtedness or outright enslavement (cf. similarly Jeremias 1998: 148). It could begin with a small debt or pledge, just "a pair of sandals." It is likely that such processes of impoverishment were regarded as a severe societal problem during the postexilic period, and especially during times of famine or food scarcity. Interestingly, such a situation is described in Nehemiah 5. Various groups in the population complain that they have been forced to mortgage their homes, or even to sell their own children, in order to get food (Neh 5:1–5). Amos 8:4–6 condemns those who profit from such tragedies. The final clause, v. 6b, which continues the fictitious quotation from v. 5a, adds a further detail to the picture of the merchants' unscrupulousness as they exploit the poor: They sell the sweepings for the same price as high-quality wheat.

8:7. In prophetic texts in the Hebrew Bible, accusations such as 8:4–6 are as a rule followed by proclamations of judgment. The divine declaration in v. 7b, "Never will I forget any of their deeds," would seem to fulfill that function (see similarly 5:12). However, it is uncertain whether these words refer primarily to the devious merchants denounced in vv. 5–6 or whether they concern the entire people. Possibly, the immoral deeds of the grain traders are here seen as symptoms of a general state of depravity. At any rate, such an interpretation of v. 7 would seem to lie behind the insertion of v. 8 (see below).

The implicit threat of punishment (v. 7b) is introduced in a peculiar way. According to v. 7a, "YHWH has sworn (*nišbaᶜ yhwh*) by the pride of Jacob (*bigᵊʾôn yaᶜăqōb*)." Almost inevitably, this formulation recalls 6:8, but it is difficult to determine the nature of the allusion. Is it ironic, or even sarcastic, as suggested by Wolff (1977: 328)? Or should 8:7 be understood as some kind of correction, or counterproposition, in relation to the earlier text? In 6:8 YHWH swears (*nišbaᶜ ʾădōnāy yhwh*) "by himself," and then he declares: "I abhor Jacob's arrogance (*gᵊʾôn yaᶜăqōb*)." How can one and the same phrase, *gᵊʾôn yaᶜăqōb*, be used in so starkly contrasting ways? How can YHWH swear a solemn oath by something that he hates?

Arguably, the author of 8:7 wanted to rehabilitate the "pride of Jacob" phrase. After all, it was used in the cult (see Ps 47:5 [Eng. v. 4]). Hence, the highly polemical usage in 6:8, which exploits the semantic ambiguity (pride/arrogance) of the lexeme *gāʾôn*, should not be allowed to diminish the solemnity of this formula. In the light of Ps 47:5 (Eng. v. 4) and Nah 2:3 (Eng. v. 2), it is likely that the expression "the pride of Jacob" was associated with the land and more precisely with the notion that the land was a gift from YHWH (with Jeremias 1998: 148–49 and Fleischer 2001: 252).[93]

8:8. The utterance in v. 8 looks like an insertion, intended to elevate the discourse on divine retribution (v. 7) to a cosmic level, on par with v. 9. Thus, it serves as a bridge between vv. 4–7 and 9–14 (with Jeremias 1998: 149). Because of the juxtaposition of a divine oath (v. 7) and a rhetorical question (v. 8), one may understand the latter as spoken by either YHWH or the prophet/writer. The imminent punishment, apparently caused by all human transgressions mentioned earlier in the book (a plausible interpretation of "because of this," v. 8aα), will take the form of an earthquake (cf. 1:1; 2:13–16).[94]

A rather odd metaphorical comparison is made, as an exceptionally devastating quake is likened to the seasonal, gradual (and far from devastating) rising and sinking of the water level of the Nile. At any rate, this image conveys the notion of a cosmic upheaval. Interestingly, this strange image recurs, with almost exactly the same formulations, in 9:5, which is part of the third and final doxology (9:5–6). It is not easy to determine in which direction the literary dependence goes.[95]

8:9. The oracles in vv. 9 and 10 refer back to 8:1–3. More details and nuances are added to the depiction of a disaster that brings about death and mourning. At the same time, the eschatological element becomes more prominent in 8:9–10. Within the prophetic literature, the introductory phrase "on that day" (*bayyôm hahû²*, v. 9a) is a hallmark of additions displaying an eschatological tendency (cf. 2:16; 8:3, 13; 9:11).[96] Recalling 5:18–20, as well as the hymnic fragment in 5:8, v. 9a predicts that there will be complete darkness "on that day." This prophecy may be interpreted quite literally as a prediction of a solar eclipse occurring around noontime. Such an event would have been interpreted as ominous, as a sign of divine wrath (cf. Isa 13:9–11 and Joel 4:14–15 [Eng. 3:14–15]).[97] Alternatively, the prediction in v. 9 may be taken metaphorically (cf. Jer 15:9), as a depiction of a state of sudden and immense despair and hopelessness.

8:10. In this utterance, the thematic thread of mourning and lamentation resurfaces (see 5:1–2, 16–17; 8:3, 8). It is announced that, as a consequence of YHWH's punitive actions, there will be mourning ceremonies throughout the land. The affinity to 8:3 is especially striking. There it is said that the palace songstresses will be occupied with wailing instead of entertaining the ruling élite. Here, in v. 10a, the reader is told that the entire society, and especially the temple sphere, will go through a similar transformation (note the use of the verb *hpk;* cf. 4:11; 5:7), from joy to lamentation. Instead of participating in lavish feasts (5:21–22) accompanied by merry music (5:23), the people will have to sing dirges (v. 10aα) and perform the traditional mourning rituals: cut (or shave) their hair, tear their garments, and put on sackcloth (v. 10aβ; cf. Isa 3:24; 15:2–3; 22:12; Ezek 27:31).

A state of utter hopelessness is depicted. This is accentuated by the comparison with the grief occasioned by the death of an only child (v. 10bα).[98] Several biblical texts indicate that such a loss was seen as the most terrible tragedy that could befall a family (see, e.g., Gen 22:2, 12, 16, about Isaac; and Judg 11:34, about Jephthah's daughter). For the parents, the effect would be immense shock and sorrow. In addition, they would have to face the fact that their family had no future (unless a new child, preferably a male heir, was born). In Amos 8:10, the message is therefore in line with 8:1–2: The end is coming. And the "end of it (²aḥărîtāh)" can be compared to a dark day filled with sorrow and bitterness (v. 10bβ).

8:11–12. In comparison with many other passages in the book, and especially 4:6–8, which contains similar (but nonmetaphorical) motifs and formulations, the prophecy in vv. 11–12 stands out because of its focus on spiritual rather than physical needs. The disaster that it anticipates (by means of the introductory phrase "the days are coming") is not an ordinary famine but a metaphorical hunger and thirst for divine instructions, "for hearing the words of YHWH" (v. 11).[99] However, this need not be interpreted as referring to a religious revival movement, focusing on the inner life of the individual.

Throughout the book of Amos (at least, subsequent to its Deuteronomistic redaction), the possibility of obtaining messages from YHWH in a given situation is exclusively connected to prophetic mediation.

Thus, it is asserted that when YHWH makes plans of importance for the nation, he will always inform the prophets in advance, but only them (3:7). As a consequence, the prophets had the opportunity, and responsibility, to warn the people and their leaders (3:13). Apparently, a prophet/seer such as Amos was even thought to have the power to persuade YHWH to withhold punitive measures (7:1–6). In this perspective, attempts to silence (true) prophets (2:12; 7:10–17) could be seen as acts of disobedience, but also as examples of self-destructive behavior.

I suggest that 8:11–12 can be read as a theological exposition of 7:10–17, which underscores the dire consequences of expatriating Amos (7:12–13). Without access to the life-sustaining drops represented by his prophetic words (see the Comments on 7:16), both people and leaders would perish. Facing terrible disasters (cf. 8:1–3, 8–10), the population in the north would realize that they had lost the possibility to communicate with the deity who might avert further disasters.

Apparently, this postexilic prophecy retains the book's consistent focus on the region to the north of Judah (or, Yehud), the former kingdom of Israel that had become the province of Samaria. Such a supposition would explain the otherwise mysterious omission of one point of the compass in v. 12, where it is declared that a futile search for "the word of YHWH" will be conducted in various directions: "from sea to sea (*miyyām* *ʿad yām*), from north to east." It is worth noting that *yām* means both "sea" and "west." In other words, all geographical directions are mentioned, except for the south. Arguably, this is because the author was convinced that the word of YHWH could be found there, in Jerusalem (cf. 1:2; with Rudolph 1971: 267 and Paul 1991: 266).

As observed by Steins, Amaziah's order to Amos in 7:12—"Flee to the land of Judah! Eat your bread there, and prophesy there!"—can be read on more than one level. In addition to its immediate function within the narrative, this utterance seems to indicate that, according to the editors of the book, the prophetic word, having been rejected in the north, was henceforth at home only in Judah, where it was continually studied and (re)interpreted (see Steins 2010: 82–85, 94–95, 102–3).

8:13–14. In the last unit within 8:4–14, comprising vv. 13–14, further nuances are added to the vision(s) of the "end" of Israel (cf. vv. 1–3, 8–12). Likewise, further accusations are added, in order to justify the divine judgment (cf. 8:4–7).

Despite the fact that v. 14 is syntactically connected to v. 13, one may ask whether vv. 13 and 14 originally constituted a unit. There is a certain discrepancy between these utterances, since v. 14 does not focus especially on young people. Hence, v. 13 can hardly be understood as a description of the consequences of the various cultic acts alluded to in v. 14a. Moreover, v. 14b provides a renewed prediction of collective death, but now without any age limit. However, it is likely that this apparent discrepancy is due to the author's ambition to allude extensively to 5:2, an utterance that contains the motif of a young woman (*bĕtûlâ*, see v. 13b), as well as a close counterpart to the phrase "will fall to rise no more" in v. 14b. Moreover, if these two utterances are read together, it is possible to discern an *inclusio* structure, with v. 14a at the center (cf. Jeremias 1998: 151).

8:13. According to the oracle in v. 13, once again introduced by the formula *bayyôm* *hahûʾ*, "in that day" (see v. 9a), the young women (*habbĕtûlōt*) and the young men (*habbaḥûrîm*) will "faint from thirst" (v. 13b). I suggest that this can be seen as a literalizing comment on vv. 11–12, where the motif of thirst served as a metaphor. Although the formulations used focus, stereotypically, on female beauty and male strength, the main point made in v. 13 is probably that the young generation of the nation will die. The message intoned by 8:1–3 is thus repeated: there will be no future for this people (see also the Comments on v. 10b).

8:14. According to v. 14, a tragic end awaits all those who (regularly?) swear certain oaths at three major cultic sites: Samaria, Dan, and Beer-Sheba. In geographical terms these places represent the center of the (former) kingdom of Israel (Samaria, the capital), a temple at its northern border (Dan), and a pilgrimage site far to the south (Beer-Sheba). Notably, Jerusalem (situated between Samaria and Beer-Sheba) is not mentioned. Hence, one may reasonably assume that these three sites were selected because the Judean author regarded them as illegitimate (cf. Deuteronomy 12).

The act of swearing is probably not condemned as sinful in itself. I find it more likely that this prophecy denounces active participation in the cult at the sanctuaries mentioned. Possibly, v. 14a contains more specific accusations as well, concerning various cultic aberrations and transgressions. Unfortunately, however, the modern interpreter has to resort to guesswork when it comes to some details of this prophecy.

To begin with, the consonantal text of the MT in v. 14aα has been variously interpreted. If slightly revocalized, it can be read as a reference to the cult of a goddess named Ashima (see the Notes on "the guilt of Samaria"). In the light of 2 Kgs 17:29–30, where it is stated that people from Hamath introduced the cult of a certain Ashima (literally, "made Ashima") in the region of Samaria in the wake of the catastrophe in 722 B.C.E., this interpretation may seem attractive.[100] However, a goddess with this name is not attested in any other biblical or extrabiblical source.[101]

Weighty arguments can in fact be adduced in favor of retaining the reading of the MT, "the guilt (*ʾašmat*) of Samaria" (see Wolff 1977: 323, 332 and Paul 1991: 269–70). Most important, it is supported by the ancient versions (see the Notes). The expression "guilt (or, perhaps, sin) of Samaria" might be understood as a distortion of "YHWH of Samaria" (Olyan 1991: 149). I suggest that it alludes to allegedly heterodox aspects of the YHWH cult, perhaps a bovine statue (cf. Hos 8:5–6).[102] Alternatively, it could be taken as a pejorative reference to some other deity. It is worth noting, however, that in Hos 4:15, a close parallel to Amos 8:14a, the only deity mentioned is YHWH. Clearly, what is condemned in Hos 4:15 is primarily the YHWH cult performed at certain sites, not the worship of other gods. It is likely that this applies to Amos 8:14 as well (cf. 4:4–5; 5:4–5). Elsewhere in the Hebrew Bible, both Dan and Beer-Sheba are primarily associated with worship of YHWH (see, e.g., Gen 21:33 and 1 Kgs 12:28–30).[103]

It is impossible to ascertain to which deity the next expression, "as your god lives, O Dan" (v. 14aβ), originally referred. However, since no other name is mentioned, YHWH (or, El) must be regarded as the prime candidate. Arguably, the problem addressed is that large groups among the worshipers of YHWH went to Dan instead of Jerusalem (cf. 1 Kgs 12:28–30). It is likely that the words cited reflect actual, and long-standing, cultic practice. An inscription (in Aramaic and Greek) from the Hellenistic era found at the site of the temple in Dan contains the phrase "to the god who is in Dan."[104]

Finally, the reference, in v. 14aγ, to people swearing by "the way (*derek*) of (or, to) Beer-Sheba," would seem to make sense in a pilgrimage context. This expression is often compared to similar phrases used by Muslim pilgrims who swear by the road to Mecca (so, e.g., Paul 1991: 272). Nonetheless, the MT's formulation in v. 14aγ looks suspicious. What is the point in speaking about a road or route as though it were a living being? How could such an oath provide a parallel to the other oaths cited in v. 14? Several emendations therefore have been suggested.[105] In analogy with the oath associated with Dan (v. 14aβ), and in the light of the Septuagint's rendering of the Beer-Sheba oath (ὁ θεός σου Βηρσαβεε, "your god, O Beer-Sheba"), one might expect a reference to a deity (with, e.g., Olyan 1991: 122–27). In this vein, Linville has argued that the most likely reading is *dōrēk,* a verbal participle meaning "the one who treads/ strides," which is used as a divine epithet (of YHWH) in Amos 4:13 (2008: 156–57). One might, accordingly, translate "the strider of Beer-Sheba." In my opinion, however, swearing by the one who treads a cultic site sounds as strange as taking an oath by the pilgrimage route leading to that site.

According to Jeremias, it is preferable to read *drkt,* a noun attested in the Ugaritic language (with the sense "dominion"), and to translate "by the power of Beer-Sheba" (1998: 152; see also Stuart 1987: 382). Arguably, *drkt* ("power") would be a fitting divine epithet. But this solution, which requires a change of the consonantal text, lacks clear parallels in the Hebrew Bible. Thus, the question of whether the worshipers at Beer-Sheba were swearing by the road, or by the "strider" or the "power" of that site, has to be left open.

As regards the interpretation of v. 14b, however, there is little uncertainty. According to the concluding part of this prophecy, all worshipers at the sanctuaries mentioned in v. 14a (or, at least all those who have taken one of the oaths cited) will be put to death (presumably by YHWH himself). It is worth paying attention to the actual wording: "they will fall to rise no more" (*wĕnāpĕlû wĕlōʾ yāqûmû ʿôd*). The allusion to 5:2 is unmistakable; however, whereas 5:2 depicts the downfall and death of the personified nation of Israel (probably with reference to the disaster in 722 B.C.E.), the utterance in 8:14 focuses on the allegedly illicit cultic practice of certain individuals (most likely in the postexilic era).

A Vision of Inescapable Destruction (9:1–4)

9   ¹I saw the Lord standing by the altar, and he said:
Strike the capitals so that the thresholds shake!
Cut them off—on the heads of them all!
The remainder of them I will kill with the sword.
Not one of them shall be able to escape, not one fugitive shall survive.
²Though they dig down to Sheol, from there my hand will take them,
and though they climb up to heaven, from there I will bring them down.
³Though they hide on the top of Carmel, there I will search them out and seize them, and though they conceal themselves from my sight at the bottom of the sea, there I will command the serpent and it will bite them.
⁴Even if they go into captivity in front of their enemies,

there I will command the sword to slay them.
I will fix my eye upon them, for harm and not for good.

INTRODUCTION TO 9:1–4,
THE SO-CALLED FIFTH VISION

The passage 9:1–4 (or, primarily, 9:1a) is often counted as the fifth and last vision report, the grand finale, within a vision cycle comprising 7:1–9 + 8:1–3 + 9:1–4 (thus, e.g., Paul 1991: 273, Jeremias 1998: 154–55, and Schart 2003: 46–47).[106] However, several observations speak against this popular hypothesis. Whereas the four vision reports in 7:1–8:2 share an easily detectable structural pattern—in each case, the vision is introduced by a specific formula (kōh hir'anî 'ădōnāy yhwh, "this is what the Lord YHWH showed me") and accompanied by a dialog between YHWH and the prophet—it is difficult to find any formal similarities between this group of four and the so-called fifth vision of the cycle in 9:1–4 (with Willi-Plein 1971: 48; see also Behrens 2002: 77).

In 9:1, the introductory formula "this is what the Lord YHWH showed me" has been dropped (cf. 7:1, 4, 7; 8:1) and replaced by a simple "I saw" (rā'îtî, v. 9:1aα). Moreover, the depiction of the visual experience is not followed by a dialog between YHWH and the prophet/seer (cf. 7:2–3, 5–6, 8; 8:2). In fact, the prophet says nothing. Instead, a divine command is given (9:1aβ). In striking contrast to the two preceding visions, within the hypothetical cycle of five reports (cf. 7:7–8; 8:1–2), the vision depicted in 9:1 does not require any heavenly assistance in the process of interpretation.[107]

These structural differences indicate that 9:1 (or, 9:1–4) should not be regarded as a direct continuation of 8:1–3. Another argument against the standard theory is based on rhetorical analysis. Subsequent to 8:1–2, which clearly constitutes a climax, as it proclaims that "the end has come," no continuation of the series of visions is expected.[108]

One of the reasons why some scholars have insisted that the cycle originally consisted of *five* vision reports, despite the formal differences between 9:1–4 (or, 9:1a) and the preceding visions, is that this would make it structurally similar to the (hypothetically reconstructed!) original cycle of oracles against *five* nations placed at the beginning of the book (in chapters 1–2). According to Jeremias, both cycles were composed according to a 2 + 2 + 1 pattern.[109] As demonstrated by Steins, however, this theory is based on a number of questionable presuppositions (2010: 30–37). Most important, the alleged structural analogy, with two pairs, in each case followed by a surprising climax, founders when one observes that the sharp contrast between the first and the second pair in the vision cycle (7:1–6 mercy // 7:7–8; 8:1–2 no mercy) lacks any correspondence whatsoever in the oracles against various nations in chapters 1–2.

Nevertheless, it is a fact that within the final structural arrangement of the book of Amos, the passage 9:1–4 recalls the preceding vision reports. From the reader's perspective, it is the fifth vision. It is most naturally read as some kind of continuation of the series, despite all formal and stylistic differences. Although 8:1–2 appeared to be the definitive vision of destruction, 9:1–4 provides yet another climax. But how should the relation between the fifth vision, with its independent character, and the series of four be understood from a scholarly perspective? Does 9:1–4 represent a late addition?[110] Or is the fifth vision older than the others? As shown below, some formulations and motifs in 9:1 have close counterparts in Isaiah 6.

In my opinion, the most cogent hypothesis on this complex issue is the one presented by Steins (2010: 67–71). According to his reconstruction, 9:1 contains a fragment of a vision report from the monarchic era. This prophetic vision (which formed part of the book's first version?) served as a source of inspiration for the postmonarchic author who composed the cycle of four. In this way Steins manages to explain the intriguing similarities between the third vision (7:7–8) and 9:1. In both cases, YHWH is seen standing upon or by something (a wall or an altar), prepared to launch an attack (see also Bergler 2000: 459–66).

As I demonstrate below, some details in 9:1 seem to allude to traditions associated with the sanctuary at Bethel. At the same time, the vision report in 9:1–4 can be read as referring, in a somewhat veiled fashion, to the destruction of the temple in Jerusalem (with Becker 2001: 147). In its present shape, I suggest, the "fifth" vision serves as an important supplement to the preceding four, which also makes it easier to apply them to the situation after 587 B.C.E.

So far, very little has been said about 9:2–4. I find it likely that vv. 2–4a constitute a secondary expansion, which has been inserted between 9:1 and 9:4b (with Steins 2010: 68). Several observations indicate that 9:2–4a should be regarded as a distinct unit of postexilic origin (so also, e.g., Willi-Plein 1971: 52–54 and Weimar 1981: 66–67). Although there is a thematic connection to v. 1b, the differences in style and vocabulary are notable. In terms of topic, the unit 9:2–4a consists of a string of variations on the motif of "no escape" (cf. v. 1b).

From a formal point of view, the unit 9:2–4a consists of a series of five conditional sentences, all of them following the same pattern. In each case, the protasis is introduced by the particle *ʾim* ("if"), while the apodosis commences with the adverbial *miššām*, "from there." By means of poetic variations and rhetorical exaggerations, one and the same message is repeated throughout 9:2–4a: It is impossible to escape the divine punishment. Wherever the people may attempt to hide, YHWH will find them. Owing to the hyperbolic and hypothetical character of this passage, it is probably pointless to try to determine whether it depicts acts of punishment targeting a certain group or nation (Noble 1997) or whether it envisions divinely decreed destruction of global proportions (Linville 2008: 165–68).

In vv. 2–3 it is possible to detect a neat chiastic structure (Paul 1991: 277–79 and Irsigler 2004: 194–96). The first four refuge places have been arranged in two pairs representing the highest and lowest points along the vertical axis within a mythically constructed cosmos (v. 2) and within the geographical world (v. 3), respectively:

Lowest: Sheol (2a)—Highest: heaven (2b)
Highest: top of Carmel (3a)—Lowest: bottom of the sea (3b)

The series ends rather unexpectedly, however, with a reference to forced migration along the horizontal axis (v. 4a). Not even deportation to distant countries can provide protection.

The theme of "no escape" has surfaced in two previous passages, 2:14–16 and 5:18–20 (especially v. 19). In order for the theological profile of 9:2–4a to be grasped, it is instructive to make a comparison with 2:14–16. Whereas the latter passage can be read as a description of a more or less "ordinary" disaster, such as a military defeat or an earthquake, 9:2–4, a passage replete with mythological allusions, seems to depict an event of cosmic proportions. Clearly, this prophecy was composed in an apocalyptic (or proto-apocalyptic) milieu, with the purpose of applying the prophecies in this book to the eschatological era. In addition, the author may have had an editorial intention. By means of the reappearance in 9:3 of "the top of Carmel (*rōʾš hakkarmel*)" (see 1:2), an *inclusio* is created, which encapsulates the bulk of oracles in the book.

To sum up: While 9:1 and 9:4b may have formed part of the book's second version (during or shortly after the exile), 9:2–4a most likely represents a rather late postexilic addition.

NOTES

9:1. *Strike the capitals . . . Cut them off.* The two imperatives *hak* ("Strike!") and *ûbĕṣaʿam* ("[and] cut them off") lack a clearly identified addressee. In order to eliminate this mysterious anonymous agent, several scholars have suggested emendations. As a rule, these two imperatives are changed into verbal forms (finite forms or infinitives) that are consonant with the hypothesis that YHWH originally was seen as the sole agent of destruction. For various examples, see Rudolph (1971: 240–41), Soggin (1987: 119–20), and Jeremias (1998: 153). See also Koch et al. (1976a: 227), Wolff (1977: 334–35), and Hadjiev (2007). For a critical discussion of some of the most important textual emendations and transpositions that have been proposed, see Riede (2008: 169–71). It is worth noting that the LXX has imperative forms, like the MT (whereas the Vulgate has an initial imperative, followed by a passive form). Moreover, as regards the contested verbal forms, *hak* and *ûbĕṣaʿam,* the consonantal text of the MT is, interestingly enough, attested in MurXII.

on the heads. This translation is somewhat uncertain. See the Comments on v. 1.

COMMENTS

9:1. Because of a combination of various factors—mainly the use of an extremely terse style and the occurrence of some uncommon expressions—9:1 is commonly regarded as one of the most difficult verses in the book of Amos. It is possible that the text of the MT was damaged at an early stage of transmission. Many emendations have been suggested in order to make the depiction more coherent, but usually without any support from other textual witnesses (see the Notes).

In agreement with several recent studies, I prefer to retain and try to make sense of the MT.[111] After all, it seems to be possible to reconstruct the main aspects of the course of events described in 9:1: Positioned near an altar, the deity commands someone to strike the pillars of a building (probably a temple) and to cut off something (possibly their capitals). These acts will cause the thresholds (that is, the ground) to shake. Apparently, this is the beginning of an enormous disaster and massive carnage. Those who survive the quake and try to escape will be killed by YHWH's sword.

Even if such a reconstruction is accepted, several questions remain unanswered. Who is the anonymous addressee and agent? What is being cut off? Where (that is, in which temple) does the destruction take place? Is this vision report purely eschatological, or does it refer to some historical event(s)? Given the lack of conclusive contextual clues, an attempt to reach plausible answers to these questions has to be based, to a large extent, on a combination of lexical and intertextual considerations.

According to the opening line, the speaker (presumably the prophet) has seen YHWH (who is not mentioned by name but referred is to as ʾădōnāy, "the Lord"), "standing by/on the altar" (niṣṣāb ʿal hammizbēaḥ, v. 1aα). It is difficult to decide whether one should translate the preposition ʿal with "(up)on" or "by/beside" in this context. Both alternatives can be supported by relevant parallel texts (Garrett 2008: 256–57). The formulation in v. 1aα recalls 7:7, where YHWH was seen standing at/on (niṣṣāb ʿal) a wall. In this way, an allusion is made to the third vision (and, by extension, to the preceding vision cycle in its entirety).[112] In addition, the expression niṣṣāb ʿal echoes Gen 28:13, where YHWH is seen standing on the top of the stairway connecting heaven and earth. Hence, Amos 9:1 may allude to notions and traditions associated particularly with Bethel (Jeremias 1996: 256 and Schart 2003: 48–49).

The remainder of v. 1 has the form of divine speech, introduced by "and he said" (wayyōʾmer). While v. 1aβγδ can be characterized as an instruction, v. 1b constitutes a declaration made by the deity. At first, someone is given the order: hak hakkaptôr, "strike the capital(s)!" (v. 1aβ). The destructive intent appears to be underscored by the assonance (hak—hak). Although kaptôr stands in the singular, it should probably be taken in a collective sense (with Andersen and Freedman 1989: 835). For some reason, the lexeme kaptôr, "knob," is used, instead of the term that is otherwise used to denote capitals, kōteret (see 1 Kgs 7:16–20). At any rate, it is reasonable to assume that the blow will affect more than one single capital in the rows of pillars, since it is stated that this action will cause the foundations of the edifice to shake. Attention should be paid to the precise formulation used at the end of v. 1aβ: wĕyirʿăšû hassippîm, "so that the thresholds shake."

Interestingly, this depiction is reminiscent of Isa 6:4, where it is reported that the thresholds (hassippîm) of the temple start shaking at the sounds made by the praising seraphs. The lexical link between these two texts is admittedly weak, since Isa 6:4 uses another verb to describe the movement (nwʿ instead of rʿš). Nevertheless, the occurrence of this motif in two prophetic temple vision reports is conspicuous. One may add the observation that both visions are introduced in similar ways (in Isa 6:1a and Amos 9:1aα), by means of a form in the first-person singular of rʾh ("to see"), with "the Lord (ʾădōnāy)" as its direct object, which is followed by a participle describing the deity's position. It is highly unlikely that the author of Isaiah 6 was inspired by the dystopia envisioned by Amos 9:1–4 (contra Jeremias 1996: 251–52). However, a case of literary dependence in the other direction is conceivable.[113] If, as seems likely, 9:1a makes an allusion to Isa 6:4, this may have implications for the interpretation of the "fifth" vision in the book of Amos.

Thus far, the intertextual connections indicate that 9:1 can be read as referring to the sanctuary in Bethel (Genesis 28), as well as to the temple in Jerusalem and/or YHWH's heavenly palace (Isaiah 6).[114] This ambiguity may be intentional. In 7:10–17, the "royal" temple in Bethel was a focal point in the controversy between Amaziah and Amos (see especially 7:13). The destruction of the sanctuary in Bethel (which allegedly happened during the reign of King Josiah; see 2 Kgs 23:15–18) was presaged already in 3:14: "I will deal with the altars of Bethel. The horns of the altar will be cut off and fall to the ground." The event depicted in 9:1 can be read as a fulfillment of that prophecy. At the same time, 9:1–4 would seem to describe a disaster (an earthquake?) of cosmic proportions, involving a total collapse of divine-human communication and interaction (Hartenstein 1997: 114). In the words of Jeremias, "it means the end of all contact with God" (1998: 157).[115]

In previous passages, such as 4:4–5 and 5:4–5, it is made clear that Bethel had been abandoned by YHWH before its destruction. Thus, the notion that this holy place served as a point of contact between heaven and earth (Gen 28:11–16) is emphatically denied elsewhere in the book of Amos. Hence, I find it more likely that the passage 9:1–4 alludes to similar ideas, associated with the temple in Jerusalem, and that it describes the cosmic consequences of the destruction of that temple in 587 B.C.E.

As regards the identity of the anonymous agent of destruction in v. 1, no definite answer can be given. On one hand, the analogy with Isaiah 6 makes it plausible that YHWH is commanding one of his celestial servants (thus Andersen and Freedman 1989: 680, 835 and Hartenstein 1997: 111–112). On the other hand, the same analogy might support the idea that it is the prophet/seer who is being commissioned, as in Isa 6:8–9 (so Bergler 2000: 451 and Schart 2003: 49). Arguably, though, the focus lies on the actions decreed by the deity, not on the agent.

According to a plausible reading of v. 1aγ, *ûbĕṣaʿam bĕrōʾš kullām*, this clause provides a close parallel to the order to strike against the capital(s): "Cut them off—on the heads of them all!" However, within its immediate context, this formulation—and in particular *bĕrōʾš*—becomes deeply ambiguous. Since the lexeme *rōʾš* may denote both "top" and "head," v. 1aγ could describe the act of either severing the capitals from the columns or decapitating human beings.[116] The verb *rʿš* ("to shake, tremble") indicates that the disaster described is an earthquake (cf. 1:1!). Apparently, the collapse of the temple is accompanied by the death of numerous human beings; otherwise, YHWH's words in v. 1aδ would fail to make sense: "The remainder of them (*wĕʾaḥărîtām*) I will kill with the sword." In conjunction with 1aγ, this utterance involves an untranslatable wordplay, based on the multiple senses of the word pair *rōʾš* ("head," "top," "first")— *ʾaḥărît* ("end," "remnant," "last"). In this way, the totality of the destruction is underlined: from top to bottom, from the leaders to the remainder of the people.[117]

Amos 9:1a implies, rather than describes, a truly horrible event, staged by YHWH. Language becomes laconic, yet replete with allusions. Although the identity of the one who is supposed to strike against the pillars remains unclear, the final words of this utterance leave no doubt that the one who kills (his own people!?) indiscriminately with his sword is YHWH himself. This massacre scene is perhaps best described as proto-apocalyptic.

In v. 1b, YHWH declares that no one will be able to escape. This utterance picks up formulations from a previous passage, 2:14–16. While the form *yānûs*, "will (not) escape," appears in 2:16, too (cf. also *mānôs* in 2:14), a close counterpart to the phrase *lōʾ yimmālēṭ*, "will not survive" (but with the verb in Piel instead of Niphal), is attested three times within 2:14–15. In this way, I suggest, the catastrophe depicted in 9:1–4 is presented as the fulfillment of yet another earlier prophecy (in addition to 3:14).

9:2. According to the passage 9:2–4, all attempts to flee from the deity's punitive wrath will be futile. Using hyperbole, v. 2 explains that YHWH will find the refugees even if they somehow manage to travel to places that were considered inaccessible for (living) mortals. Those who dig their way down to the netherworld will be dragged up by the deity (v. 2a), and those who climb up to heaven will be pulled down again (v. 2b). As in Job 14:13, the realm of the dead is imagined as a hiding place. However, in contrast to a notion attested in several psalms (e.g., Pss 6:6 [Eng. v. 5]; 88:6, 11–13 [Eng. vv. 5, 10–12]; Isa 38:18), Sheol is here not thought to lie outside YHWH's sphere of activity. In my opinion, this observation supports the hypothesis that 9:2–4a is a late postexilic text.

Mythological motifs are used, but they do not seem to be connected to a consistent mythic worldview. Thus, somewhat surprisingly, the author constructs a scenario with people trying to hide from YHWH's wrath in heaven, the place where this deity was believed to reside. This can be seen as a (less fortunate) transformation of the motif of arrogant human beings (often associated with Babylon) attempting to climb up to heaven and to become godlike (see Gen 11:1–9; Isa 14:4–21; Jer 51:53). Nonetheless, the message conveyed by v. 2 is clear. YHWH supervises and controls the entire universe, and he has the power to reach the most remote parts of the world. As noted by Hubert Irsigler (2004: 199–216), the portrait of YHWH in this passage has solar traits.

The reader of v. 2 (and vv. 3–4a) is reminded of a number of other biblical passages that emphasize YHWH's virtual omnipresence or inescapability in a similar way (see, e.g., Ps 139:7–12; Jer 16:16–17; 23:24). The points of contact with Ps 139:7–12 are particularly striking (see Irsigler 2004: 184, 197 and Paul 277–78). Despite the lack of direct quotations, I find it likely that the author of Amos 9:2–4a borrowed a group of three extreme locations (Sheol, heaven, and the sea) from Psalm 139.[118] In addition, the author borrowed the motif of the divine hand that seizes the runaway(s) and gave it a more sinister touch. Whereas the psalmist is confident that YHWH's hand will lead and hold him or her, even in the most remote and dangerous places (Ps 139:10), the phrase in Amos 9:2a, "my hand will take (or, seize) them (*yādî tiqqāḥēm*)" means that there is no hope of rescue for the fugitives.

9:3. Presumably, the next pair of places of refuge (in v. 3) are meant to represent extreme depth and height, just like the two locations mentioned in v. 2, Sheol and heaven. One may admittedly wonder why Mount Carmel was chosen as a contrast to the sea bottom, as it is certainly not the highest mountain peak in the region of Palestine and Syria. One or several of the following factors may have influenced the author's decision in this case: (1) Carmel lay within the borders of the Northern Kingdom, (2) this mountain was an ideal hiding place because of the caves and the forest, and/or (3) Carmel is situated near the sea (cf. v. 3b).[119]

However, the text in v. 3a does not focus on any such aspect of Mount Carmel. It merely states that those who try to hide there (v. 3aα) will be detected and caught by the deity (v. 3aβ). As noted above, the phrase "the top of Carmel" (*rō³š hakkarmel*) looks like a quotation from 1:2. The author's intention to create an intertextual link to the book's opening motto might thus be the main reason why Carmel was selected, rather than, for instance, Mount Hermon.

If Carmel could be regarded as a realistic destination for Israelite escapees, the same cannot be said about the bottom or "floor" (*qarqaʿ*) of the ocean (v. 3b). Once again, the author would seem to use hyperbole (unless he or she actually imagined that human beings could breathe and live somewhere beneath the ocean). For the first time, interestingly, it is indicated that some places may be hidden even from YHWH's sight

(v. 3bα). However, it is affirmed that the deity will somehow spot the runaways, even if he cannot see them. In this case, he will be assisted by a creature, referred to as "the snake/serpent" (*hannāḥāš*), which is going to "bite them" (*ûnĕšākām*).

The vocabulary used in v. 3bβ is noteworthy in at least two respects. First, it is not at all suggestive of a sea dragon of the chaos monster type, such as Rahab (Ps 89:10–11 [Eng. vv. 9–10]) or Leviathan (Ps 74:13–14; Isa 27:1). On the contrary, this sea serpent appears to obey YHWH's order. Second, the formulations in v. 3bβ evoke a previous utterance in the book of Amos, namely 5:19. In both cases, the story of an unsuccessful escape ends with the bite (*nšk*) of a snake/serpent (*nḥš*). If, as seems likely, 9:3b alludes to 5:19, this could be interpreted as an attempt to establish a connection between the motif of the day of YHWH, in 5:18–20, and the vision of a major (cosmic?) catastrophe and its consequences, in 9:1–4.

9:4. In v. 4a, the series of conditional sentences ends in an unexpected way. The final example of attempted escape from YHWH's judgment is far from unrealistic or hypothetical. Still, the scenery described is rather grotesque. According to v. 4a, even those who "go into captivity in front of their enemies" will be tracked down and killed by "the sword." The latter expression might refer to a personification of YHWH's sword (see Isa 34:5–6; Jer 46:10).

This utterance stands in sharp contrast to other passages in the book (4:2; 5:27; 6:7; 7:17), where forced migration to distant territories ruled by foreigners is considered a severe punishment, almost on par with a death sentence. For the author of v. 4a, apparently, deportation was not enough. Somewhat surprisingly, it is implied that such a fate could be seen as a potential rescue (cf. Wolff 1977: 341). In my opinion, this is an indication that 9:2–4a was composed much later than passages such as 4:1–3 and 6:1–7. For this postexilic author it was a well-known fact that Jews could live and thrive in the Diaspora. Hence, he wished to emphasize that exile would not exempt anyone from the future judgment.

The portrayal of YHWH as an all-seeing judge, which was implicit throughout vv. 2–4a, is made explicit in v. 4bα, where the deity declares: "I will fix my eye upon them (*wĕśamtî ʿênî ʿălêhem*)." In another context, such an assertion might have a reassuring function, as evidenced by several texts in the Hebrew Bible (Gen 44:21; Jer 39: 12; 40:4; cf. also Ps 139:16). The closest parallel to Amos 9:4b is found in Jer 24:6, where exactly the same phrase, spoken by YHWH, is part of an unconditional promise of restoration. Here, "I will fix my eye upon them (*wĕśamtî ʿênî ʿălêhem*)" is followed by the qualifier "for good (*lĕṭôbâ*)." In the Amos passage a complete reversal has occurred: The divine promise has become an unambiguous threat. YHWH will be watching "them" (the entire people, or rather all evildoers?), "for harm (*lĕrāʿâ*) and not for good (*wĕlōʾ lĕṭôbâ*)" (v. 4bβ).[120] The theme of YHWH's "evil eye" will recur in 9:8, in a slightly more hopeful passage.

The Last Doxology (9:5–6)

9   ⁵The Lord YHWH of hosts,
the one who touches the earth so that it trembles, and all who live in it mourn,
and all of it rises like the Nile and sinks again like the Nile in Egypt,

⁶who builds his stairs in the heavens and founds his vault on the earth,
who calls for the waters of the sea and pours them out on the surface of the earth,
YHWH is his name!

INTRODUCTION TO 9:5–6

The unit 9:5–6 contains the third and last hymnic fragment in the book—the other two being 4:13 and 5:8(–9) (see further "Introduction to 4:13 and the Doxologies in the Book of Amos"). This passage can be seen as a fitting continuation of 9:1–4. It develops the theological theme of YHWH's sovereign power, with an emphasis on the deity's ability to bring about catastrophes (v. 5). At the same time, this passage contrasts with the preceding vision (vv. 1–4), which was characterized by utter hopelessness. Arguably, the very genre of doxology implies that at least some people may have reason to praise this powerful god, despite all disasters.[121] Moreover, it is affirmed that the one who acts as destroyer (v. 5; cf. vv. 1–4) is also (one may infer, first and foremost) the creator, the cosmic architect and builder (v. 6).

If one puts the three fragments (4:13 + 5:8 + 9:5–6) together, the dominant theme of the resulting hymn is, arguably, YHWH's role as creator of the universe (Pfeifer 1991). However, the doxologies extol the creator in a way that is consistent with the book's many prophecies of judgment, as they state that he has the power both to preserve and to destroy (Gillingham 1993: 120–21).

According to a relatively widespread hypothesis, an earlier version of the book ended at 9:6 (so, e.g., Rottzoll 1996: 288 and Jeremias 1998: 159–60.) Together with 1:2, these scholars aver, the doxology in 9:5–6 once constituted an outer framework. At a later stage, though, the oracles in 9:7–15 were appended. In my opinion, this hypothesis is not entirely convincing. To begin with, it is based on the questionable presupposition that 1:2 somehow belongs to the same category as the three hymnic fragments. Further, it seems to overstate the structuring function of the doxologies. It is true that 5:8 is placed near the center of the book; nonetheless, it "can be said to be clearly structurally intrusive" (McComiskey 1987: 141). Moreover, the first doxology, 4:13, which is far removed from the book's beginning, does not fit neatly into such an overall structure.[122] Hence, it would seem to owe its position to thematic considerations (see the Comments on 4:13). A similar case could be made for 9:5–6. In its present position, at least, 9:5–6 serves as a transition, not a conclusion.

NOTES

9:5. *the one who touches.* The Hebrew verbal participles in vv. 5–6 are not marked with regard to temporality or aspect. Hence, it would be possible to translate "the one who touched" (v. 5a), and likewise, in v. 6a, "who has built" and "who has founded" (v. 6a), as well as "the one who called" (v. 6b). Arguably, a present-tense rendering (with its broad and general scope) is more adequate in a hymnic piece such as this.

so that it trembles. Among the lexical senses listed for the verb *mûg* in the dictionaries one finds "to waver" and "to tremble," but also "to dissolve" and "to melt" (see, e.g., *DCH* and *HALOT*, s.v.). Thus, וַתָּמוֹג (*wattāmôg*) may alternatively be rendered "it melts" (cf. the Vulgate).

9:6. *his stairs.* Many commentators, deleting the first *mēm* in מעלותו as a case of dittography, read *ʿăliyyātô,* "his upper chamber" (thus, e.g., Harper 1905: 187, Hammershaimb 1970: 134, and Wolff 1977: 336). This reading can find support in the LXX and the Vulgate. However, as argued in the Comments on v. 6, the MT makes perfect sense. Interestingly, the dittography hypothesis finds no support in the earliest extant manuscripts from the Judean desert. While MurXII attests to the consonantal text of the MT, מעלותו, 4QXII^g indicates a plural form, מעלותיו.

his vault. This translation of *waʾăguddātô* is uncertain, yet generally accepted (see, e.g., Paul 1991: 280 and Jeremias 1998: 154). The attested lexical senses of *ʾăguddâ* are "bunch" and "bundle" (see the dictionaries). Possibly, the use is metaphorical. For another line of interpretation, based on the observation that bunches of plants feature in architectural ornamentations, see Paas (1993: 320–21).

COMMENTS

9:5. Unlike the two preceding doxologies in the book (4:13 and 5:8[–9]), the third one is framed by an *inclusio* arrangement: the divine name is mentioned both at the beginning (v. 5aα) and at the end (v. 6bγ). The first clause of the hymn proper, v. 5aβ, draws on traditional theophany depictions, which often include the motif of an earthquake (Jeremias 1998: 159). More precisely, it states that YHWH may cause the earth to teeter by touching it (see Pss 46:7; 104:32; Nah 1:5). In reaction to this demonstration of power, all its inhabitants will "mourn" (*wěʾābělû*). Thus, a connection is made to previous passages in the book where the theme of mourning is prominent (see 5:1–2, 16–17; 8:3, 8, 10). It is also possible that 9:5a alludes to 1:2 where the expression *wěʾābělû* occurs in a depiction of the consequences of YHWH's roar. In that context, however, the verb *ʾbl* should probably be translated "dry up" (see the Comments on 1:2).

In v. 5b, a rather far-fetched comparison is made. The movement associated with the earthquake (v. 5a) is likened to the rising and sinking of the waters of the Nile. Within the final shape of the book, this utterance constitutes an almost verbatim repetition of 8:8b. However, it is likely that the author of 8:8 borrowed this phrase from 9:5 (see the Comments on 8:8). Alternatively, 8:8 and 9:5–6 should be ascribed to the same editorial layer, as suggested by Schart (1998: 93).

9:6. Although some details are obscure, there is no doubt that v. 6a portrays YHWH as an architect constructing various edifices on a cosmic level. According to Stefan Paas (1993), this is a depiction of the dais in the heavenly palace. Within that perspective, the expression "his stairs" (*maʿălôtāw*) probably denotes the stairway leading to the divine throne (cf. 1 Kgs 10:18–20). The word *ʾăguddâ,* "bundle," may refer to some kind of vault (see the Notes on "his vault").[123]

If this interpretation is roughly correct, v. 6a can be read as a comment on the vision recorded in 9:1. YHWH may tear down (one of) his earthly temple(s), or order someone else to do it (v. 1a), but his celestial abode remains perfectly intact (v. 6a).[124] The earth may tremble (v. 5), yet the fundamental cosmic order and stability is not threatened. To some extent, then, v. 6a may inspire hope.[125] However, the *Gottesbild* (that is, the image of God) of this doxology is characterized by profound ambivalence. Its concluding part, v. 6b, which is identical to 5:8b, reminds the reader that the deity has the power to bring about a devastating flood.

The Turning Point (9:7–10)

9 ⁷Are you not like the Cushites to me, you Israelites? says YHWH.
True, I brought Israel up from the land of Egypt,
but also the Philistines from Caphtor, and Aram from Kir.
⁸Behold, the Lord YHWH's eyes are set upon the sinful kingdom.
I will destroy it from the face of the earth,
except that I will not completely destroy the house of Jacob, says YHWH.
⁹For I am about to give the order
and shake the house of Israel among all the nations,
as one shakes with the sieve and not a pebble falls to the ground.
¹⁰They shall die by the sword, all the sinners among my people,
those who say: "Disaster will never come near us or confront us."

INTRODUCTION TO 9:7–10

The section comprising 9:7–10 has a crucial function within the overall composition of chapters 7–9. Clearly, the final turnaround from total despair (9:1–4) to hope, the reversal of all reversals, comes in 9:11. However, the process of transition would seem to take its beginning in the prophecies that precede 9:11–15.[126] The utterance in 9:7 has a pivotal position. Placed at this juncture, it is intriguingly ambiguous. As I demonstrate below, 9:7 can be interpreted either as a negation of the exodus and election tradition or as an indication that YHWH might perform new acts of liberation.

The ensuing utterances, in vv. 8–10, are characterized by a sophisticated technique that involves the repetition of phrases and motifs from previous passages but with significant variation (Rüterswörden 2010: 212–15; cf. Nogalski 1993a: 102–4). Step by step, these prophecies introduce new perspectives into the discourse. The vision of massive destruction that no one can escape (9:1–4) is replaced by the notion of limited or differentiated judgment, which is illustrated by a (somewhat obscure) sieve metaphor (v. 9). Suddenly, distinctions are being made between nations and groups, as well as between individuals. According to v. 8, YHWH's ominous gaze (cf. 9:4b) is fixed on "the sinful kingdom" (probably the Northern Kingdom), which is said to be destined for destruction, whereas it is declared that "the house of Jacob" will be spared. According to v. 10, which modifies 9:1 (and v. 4a), only the sinners among the people are going to be slain by the sword.

According to my reconstruction of the successive growth of the book of Amos, the section 9:7–10, or an earlier version of this section, formed part of the second major version of the book (see Table 2). In other words, I suggest that the bulk of this section was composed during or shortly after the exile; however, this is far from certain. Alternatively, 9:7–10 should be ascribed to a somewhat later editorial strand.

NOTES

9:7. *True, I brought.* A more literal translation of v. 7b would be: "Have I not brought Israel up from the land of Egypt, the Philistines from Caphtor, and Aram from Kir?"

Caphtor. The geographical reference of *kaptôr* is somewhat uncertain; hence, the term is just transliterated, as Caphtor. The Old Greek translator of 9:7 identified Caphtor with Cappadocia (see further Wainwright 1956). However, Crete would seem to be a better guess, as regards the original point of reference. For arguments in support of Crete, see, for example, Wolff (1977: 347–48), Delcor (1978), and Paul (1991: 283, n. 13).

9:8. *set upon.* The verb "to set" lacks an equivalent in the Hebrew, which has a noun clause: "the Lord YHWH's eyes (are) upon the sinful kingdom."

9:9. *one shakes.* Or, more literally, "(it) is shaken" (Niphal of נוע).

a pebble. Since the mention of a "bundle" (*şĕrôr* I) does not fit the context, one should probably take this as an instance of *şĕrôr* II, "pebble" (see *HALOT* and *DCH,* s.v.; cf. 2 Sam 17:13, where *şĕrôr* is rendered by λίθος in the LXX). This translation is supported by the Targum (אבן) and the Vulgate (*lapillus*).

9:10. *those who say.* Or "those who think."

Disaster will never come near us or confront us. Alternatively, if the verbal forms are analyzed as second-person singular masculine instead of third-person singular feminine, this clause could be rendered: "You will not let the disaster come near us or confront us." However, such a direct address to YHWH is quite unlikely in a quotation designed to illustrate unawareness of the deity's warnings.

COMMENTS

9:7. Because of its position and its rhetorical structure, the prophecy in 9:7 can be read in more than one way. On one hand, it can be interpreted as an elaboration on the preceding oracles of judgment and disaster (8:4–14; 9:1–4), since it somehow relativizes the entire exodus and election tradition (v. 7b). On the other hand, this utterance appears to relativize the perspective of inescapable judgment and full-scale destruction, as well.

The saying in 9:7 consists of two rhetorical questions, construed with *hălô'* (an interrogative particle followed by a negation): "Is it not [the case that] . . . ?" On a closer examination, though, the structure is more complex. While v. 7a consists of one single question, v. 7b contains three. Because *hălô'* (or *hălō'*) often expresses added emphasis rather than genuine inquisitiveness, these questions can be treated as affirmations in dialogic disguise. This function of *hălô'* is reflected in the English translation of v. 7b above.

If all the rhetorical questions in 9:7 are "converted" into positive statements, we get the following series of assertions: (1) The Israelites are like the Cushites, from YHWH's perspective (v. 7a), and (vv. 2–4) YHWH has brought up (2) Israel from Egypt (v. 7bαβ), (3) the Philistines from Caphtor (v. 7bγ), and (4) Aram from Kir (v. 7bδ). It is reasonable to assume that these four assertions should be read together, as parts of a (more or less) consistent argumentation. But how are they related? And what point is being made?

To a large degree, the interpretation of v. 7 as a whole depends on the understanding of the first rhetorical question, in v. 7a, which has caused an intense scholarly discussion. One may ask: What is the purpose of making a comparison between the Israelites and the Cushites? Unlike the nations that appear in v. 7b, Cush, roughly corresponding to Nubia (or, Ethiopia), a region to the south of Egypt, was not mentioned in the section containing oracles against other nations (1:3–2:3).[127] So, why Cush?

The answer given by biblical scholars has often been that the Cushites were drawn into the discussion precisely because they did not belong to Israel's or Judah's neighbors. They lived in a distant country, and they were (culturally and ethnically) different. The following comment of Jörg Jeremias can be seen as representative of mainstream exegesis during the past century: "From the perspective of Palestine, the inhabitants of Cush, encompassing geographically modern Ethiopia and the southern Sudan, were the southernmost, most distant, and at the same time—because of their skin color—the strangest people with whom one came into contact (cf. Isa 18:1f.)" (1998: 164).

In earlier scholarship, the rhetorical force of this comparison was frequently seen as disparaging for the Israelites. Sadly enough, a study of this passage's history of interpretation, especially during the first half of the twentieth century, reveals that several commentators have been (anachronistically) influenced by the racist prejudices of their own time.[128] Despite the fact that the text of interest, Amos 9:7, says nothing about skin color or cultural inferiority, scholars have assumed that the Israelites are being compared to a "far-distant, uncivilized, and despised black race," that is, the Cushites, and that "their color and the fact that slaves were so often drawn from them added to the grounds for despising them" (quotations from Harper 1905: 192).[129]

As shown by several recent studies, however, the depictions of the Cushites in the Hebrew Bible are never characterized by contempt, but sometimes, on the contrary, by admiration (see, e.g., Isa 18:1–2).[130] Nothing in the immediate context of Amos 9:7 suggests that any specific cultural or ethnic traits are relevant to the discussion. Hence, there is no reason to assume that the author of v. 7 regarded Cushites as despicable (for instance, because of their skin color) or that the comparison was meant to be offensive (with, e.g., Vogels 1972: 232–33 and Paul 1991: 282). On the other hand, the literary context does not support the idea that v. 7a conveys an unambiguous message of hope and encouragement to the Israelites (as maintained by Holter 2000: 125).[131]

According to some commentators, the phrase *ʾattem lî*, "you (are) to me" (v. 7aα), expresses a relation of affiliation or belonging. They aver that this phrase should be translated "you belong to me," or the like.[132] This translation is certainly plausible from a semantic point of view (cf. Isa 43:1, with reversed word order), but it is not applicable in the two remaining attestations of the collocation *ʾattem lî* in the Hebrew Bible, Judg 14:13 and Joel 4:4 (Eng. 3:4). The most serious weakness of this reading is that it fails to account adequately for the prominent position of the Cushites in v. 7a. A literal translation that follows the Hebrew word order might look like this: "indeed, like sons of Cushites you (are) to me, sons of Israel." If the rhetorical aim of the utterance really had been to underscore that the Israelites belong to YHWH, no matter what (thus Steins 2010: 113–15), one would have expected another word order. Moreover, such an interpretation presupposes that the idea that the Cushites belonged to YHWH (or, had a close relationship to this deity) was common knowledge among the first readers and that this idea therefore could be used as an argument. I find this hypothesis highly unlikely.

An interesting alternative interpretation has been suggested by Brent Strawn, who argues that the formal structure of v. 7 ("staircase parallelism") implies that reference is made to a Cushite exodus in v. 7a, in analogy with the three cases mentioned in v. 7b (2013: 103–16). A weakness in Strawn's hypothesis is that it rests on the questionable assumption that the takeover in Egypt by a dynasty from Cush involved a large-scale movement of people, comparable to (the tradition about) the Israelite exodus from Egypt (Strawn 2013: 116–21). Still, one cannot exclude the possibility that Amos 9:7 alludes to the rise of the Twenty-fifth Dynasty in Egypt, an event that made Cush a political factor of importance to the Syro-Canaanite region, including Israel and Judah (thus also Koch 2007: 199).

On the basis of contextual and intertextual considerations, I find it likely that the rhetorical question in v. 7a is designed to make two points:[133] (1) that the Israelites are just like any other people to YHWH, and (2) that this equality before YHWH includes even geographically distant peoples, such as the Cushites (see Isa 18:1–2; Zeph 3:10).

In v. 7b, the exodus motif is introduced but only in order to be relativized immediately. The text does not deny that YHWH led the people of Israel out of Egypt; however, it maintains that similar things can be said about other nations, such as the Philistines and the Arameans, two archenemies of Judah and Israel. Notably, these two nations form the first pair in the oracles against neighboring nations in chapters 1–2 (see 1:3–8). The author of 9:7 appears to have relied on existing traditions concerning the original homelands of the Philistines, in "Caphtor," and of the Arameans, in "Kir" (see Amos 1:5). While Caphtor probably should be identified with Crete (see Jer 47:4 and the Notes), Kir seems to have been located in the east, possibly in the vicinity of Elam (see Isa 22:6; and see Thompson 1992). From a theological point of view, the assertions made in v. 7b, that YHWH brought "the Philistines from Caphtor, and Aram from Kir," are unparalleled in the Hebrew Bible. One may perhaps speak of a (limited) universalization of the exodus principle. In the words of Strawn, this text depicts YHWH as "an exodus kind of God—not just for Israel, but also for others" (2013: 122–23.)

In a Diaspora setting, the utterance in 9:7 could be given a rather positive interpretation. One might perhaps make this paraphrase: "You think you are far away from YHWH, but you're not—and a new exodus might be hoped for" (cf. similarly Coote 1981: 117–20.). Strawn's idea of YHWH as "an exodus kind of God" may indeed sound hopeful. Arguably, though, the "universal" perspective of this utterance is double-edged. YHWH appears to be pictured as a universal judge who punishes sins and crimes without regard to national or ethnic boundaries (cf. Carroll R. 1996: 66).[134] In line with 3:1–2, the prophecy in 9:7 therefore dismisses the idea that the people of Israel (or Judah) could claim special privileges because of the exodus from Egypt.[135]

Further, the intertextual link to Amos 1:5, where it is said that "Aram will be exiled to Kir" as a punishment for their crimes, allows for a more sinister reading of v. 7b. YHWH seems to be described as a God of reversals; that is, he might be prepared to reverse the Israelite exodus tradition. To sum up, 9:7 is a profoundly ambiguous prophecy. It is probably not by coincidence that it has been placed at this pivotal position in the book (with Rüterswörden 2010: 216).

9:8. At first glance, the utterance in v. 8 appears to continue the themes that dominated the section 9:1–6, namely, inevitable judgment and wholesale destruction. However, some important modifications have been made. The opening statement is a case in point: "YHWH's eyes are set upon the sinful kingdom (*mamlākâ haḥaṭṭāʾâ*)" (v. 8aα). Here, a motif from 9:4b, the all-seeing eye(s) of the divine judge, is reused. But the object is now defined differently. The unspecified "them" (v. 4b) has been replaced by "the sinful kingdom" (v. 8a). It has been suggested that this implies that YHWH is prepared to strike against any nation that could be described as "sinful" (thus Mays 1969: 159 and Paul 1991: 284–85). Alternatively, the scope is thought to be confined to the nations mentioned in v. 7 (Koch 2007: 202–3), but the formulation used would rather seem to refer to one particular nation.

In that case, the prime candidate is Israel, the Northern Kingdom (so, e.g., Hayes 1988: 220 and Rüterswörden 2010: 216–17). Since the ensuing statement, "I will destroy it from the face of the earth" (v. 8aβ), looks like a quotation from 1 Kgs 13:34 (cf. also Deut 6:15), it is possible that the expression "the sinful kingdom" in v. 8aα alludes to the "sins" of Jeroboam, a central topos in the Deuteronomistic History (1 Kgs 13:34; 15:30, 34; 16:31; 2 Kgs 3:3; cf. also the Comments on Amos 7:9). At any rate, v. 8aβ clearly describes a total, yet delimited destruction: "I will destroy it." As a consequence of this reinterpretation (in relation to v. 4), there is room for hope.

What follows next, in v. 8b, is in fact a complete reversal of the message conveyed by 9:1–4 (with Koch 2007: 207). In contrast especially to 9:2–4, where it is emphasized that no one will survive, it is now stated that YHWH is willing to make exceptions: "I will not completely destroy the house of Jacob (*bêt yaʿăqōb*)" (v. 8b). In the light of Amos 3:14, which contains an instruction to "warn the house of Jacob," and some other attestations in the Hebrew Bible (Isa 2:5; 14:1; 46:3; 48:1; Obad 1:17–18), it is likely that the expression "the house of Jacob" stands for a postmonarchic community of faithful YHWH worshipers.[136] Thus, a differentiation is made between "the sinful kingdom" (v. 8a), which is doomed to destruction, and "the house of Jacob" (v. 8b), where at least some will be spared. One may add the observation that a similar differentiation was made already in the vision cycle, in 7:1–8:2. Whereas the prophet's intercession concerns "Jacob" (7:2, 5), the proclamations of unrelenting judgment concern "Israel" (7:8; 8:1).

9:9. In the first clause of v. 9, the participle *měṣawweh* ("commanding" or "giving order") looks strangely redundant, since it lacks an object. Therefore, the primary function of this reiteration of the motif of divine commanding (cf. 9:3bβ, 4aβ) seems to be to provide a catchword link to the passage 9:2–4. In the remainder of v. 9, the process of limiting the scope of YHWH's destructive actions is continued (see the Comments on v. 8). Arguably, the statement that YHWH will "shake (*wahănîʿōtî*) the house of Israel among all the nations" (v. 9aβ) presupposes a relatively large number of survivors.

The dispersal of the Israelites is here depicted metaphorically—and perhaps literally as well. It is worth noting that the verb *nwʿ* in Hiphil can mean either "to shake" or "to cause to roam" (see the dictionaries). YHWH is apparently portrayed as a farmer who is shaking grain in a sieve. Unfortunately, the elaboration of this metaphor in v. 9b is opaque, at least to modern interpreters (cf. Koch 2007: 205). To begin with, the lexeme *kěbārâ* is a *hapax legomenon*. There is general agreement that this word denotes some kind of sieve.[137]

To make things even more complicated, it is difficult to make sense of the concluding clause, "and not a pebble falls to the ground" (v. 9bβ), within the framework of the sifting imagery. Do the small stones (or, kernels), which stay in the sieve, represent those who are spared by the divine judge (so Marti 1904: 225)? Or do they stand for the sinners? In the latter case, those grains that fall through must represent those Israelites who manage to escape (but only in order to become scattered among the nations?). According to an emerging consensus, some version of the latter alternative is preferable.[138] So far, however, a satisfactory solution to this interpretive problem is still wanting (see Lieth 2007).

9:10. In v. 10, the process of reinterpreting 9:1–4 is brought to an end. This utterance can be regarded as a milder version, or as a correction, of the terrifying visions of YHWH's sword in vv. 1b and 4a (Weimar 1981: 86). According to 9:10, the sword is not going to kill indiscriminately after all. Only "the sinners" will fall victim to YHWH's purging punishment. Thus, an ethical dimension seems to have been introduced into this discourse on divine violence.[139] However, it is instructive to study the description of these evildoers, which takes the form of a fictitious quotation: "Disaster will never come near (*lōʾ taggîš*) us or confront us" (v. 10b). This implicit accusation does not primarily concern unethical behavior against other human beings, such as oppression or corruption (as in 4:1 or 8:5–6). The main issue seems rather to be a matter of (in)correct attitude toward YHWH and the prophetic word (with Jeremias 1998: 166; cf. also 7:10–17).

One may further note an intertextual connection to the utterance in 6:3, which uses similar language to make a related point: "you who want to ward off the day of disaster, yet you bring near (*wattaggîšûn*) a reign of violence." I suggest that 9:10, "They shall die by the sword, all the sinners among my people, those who say: 'Disaster will never come near us or confront us,'" can be paraphrased in the following way: Those who believe that they can avoid the impending disaster (by themselves) are in fact the ones who will be hit by it. Conversely, one may infer, those who have taken the prophetic message seriously may hope to survive the impending catastrophe.

A Hopeful Epilogue (9:11–15)

9 [11]On that day I will restore David's fallen hut.
I will repair its breaches, restore its ruins,
and build it up as in the days of old,
[12]so that they may possess the remnant of Edom
and all the nations over whom my name has been called,
says YHWH who will do this.
[13]Yes, days are coming, says YHWH,
when the plowman will catch up with the reaper,
and the one who treads grapes will catch up with the planter,
when the mountains will drip grape juice, and all the hills will flow.
[14]I will restore the fortunes of my people Israel:
They shall rebuild deserted cities and inhabit them,
they shall plant vineyards and drink their wine,
they shall grow gardens and eat their fruit.
[15]I will plant them on their own land,
and they shall never again be uprooted from the land that I have given them,
says YHWH your God.

INTRODUCTION TO 9:11–15

Ever since the days of Julius Wellhausen, scholars have debated whether the book's epilogue, comprising 9:11–15, is a secondary addition. If one compares this passage with the bulk of chapters 3–6, for instance, the differences in style and content are certainly striking. Harsh and uncompromising oracles of doom have been replaced by idyllic depictions of peace and prosperity. On the basis of such observations, Wellhausen formulated his famous verdict that these verses were like "roses and lavender instead of blood and iron."[140]

According to the stance taken in this commentary, however, the entire third part of the book of Amos, comprising chapters 7–9, can be seen as "secondary" (that is, postmonarchic). Hence, the question needs to be reformulated: Is Amos 9:11–15 a fitting conclusion to 7:1–9:10 and, by extension, to the entire book? In my opinion, the answer must be in the affirmative (with Linville 2008: 173–74).

As demonstrated above, the section 9:7–10 serves as a transition from uncompromising judgment and total destruction (9:1–4 + 5–6) to an emerging hope for restoration. Moreover, the possibility of forgiveness was introduced already in 7:1–6 (see Steins 2010: 57–75). Hence, 9:11–15 cannot be regarded as an unexpected or unnecessary postscript to the book. The epilogue should rather be seen as an essential part of the book of Amos viewed as a literary composition. With its affirmation that there is a bright future for "David's fallen hut" (9:11; referring to the Davidic dynasty and/or the temple/city of Jerusalem), the epilogue spells out the pro-Judean and pro-Davidic bias that is inherent in several previous passages in the book that criticize the kingdom of Israel.[141] However, it does so from a perspective that is far removed from the political realities of the eighth century B.C.E. I suggest that the passage 9:11–15 can be seen as a logical outcome of a process of reorientation, whereby the main purpose of the collected words of Amos was changed. Arguably, in order to serve not only as an explanation of the downfall of the Northern Kingdom, but also as a reflection on the history of both Israel and Judah, the book needed some kind of happy ending.

I find it likely that an earlier version of the epilogue, consisting of v. 11 and possibly vv. 14–15, too, once constituted the hopeful ending of the book's second version; however, this cannot be established with certainty. At any rate, the passage 9:11–15 as we now have it should probably be seen as the product of postmonarchic scribal circles. These scribes seem to have had access to large parts of the evolving Hebrew Bible. The literary style of this passage has been aptly described as "Mosaikstil" (Rüterswörden 2010: 219). In the Comments I show that it is indeed a mosaic, made of pieces (allusions and quotations) drawn from a large number of biblical texts. The pictures created with the help of this mosaic technique can be characterized as reversals of the images of doom and destruction that dominate the rest of the book. Several formulations and motifs in 9:11–15 evoke the image of a paradise, or "a recreated cosmos" (Linville 2008: 173). Thus, a utopian vision is constructed, in stark contrast to the message conveyed by most of the preceding passages, yet at the same time in continuity with some of the book's central themes and metaphors.

NOTES

9:11. *fallen hut.* An alternative translation of *hannōpelet* (feminine participle of *npl*) would be "collapsing." Arguably, though, a perfective sense is more likely in this context. See Nägele (1995: 169).

I will repair. Or, more literally, "wall up."

its breaches . . . its ruins. The inconsistent use of suffixes in the MT is confusing: first comes *pirṣêhen* ("their breaches," third-person feminine plural), then *wahărîsōtāyw* ("his ruins," third-person masculine singular), and finally *ûběnîtîhā* ("I will build it/her up," third-person feminine singular). In order to obtain a more coherent text, it is preferable to follow the LXX, which apparently read a feminine singular suffix also in the two first instances (see BHSapp). As pointed out by Nogalski (1993c), the LXX may in fact have harmonized a *Vorlage* that contained both singular and plural suffixes (cf. the Peshitta and the Vulgate). For pragmatic reasons, however, I have decided to adopt the same strategy as the Old Greek translator.

9:12. *Edom.* Reading *'ādām,* "human(ity)," instead of Edom, and *drš* ("to seek") instead of *yrš* ("to inherit, possess"), the LXX translator managed to downplay the nationalist motif of territorial expansion. According to this reinterpretation, the prophecy in v. 12 is about the conversion of the gentiles: ὅπως ἐκζητήσωσιν οἱ κατάλοιποι τῶν ἀνθρώπων καὶ πάντα τὰ ἔθνη. See Glenny (2007: 545–47 and 2009: 224–28); also Gelston (2002: 498–99).

9:13. *flow.* Or, more literally, "melt, dissolve" (Hithpolel of מוג).

COMMENTS

9:11. In 8:13, the formula "on that day (*bayyôm hahûʾ*)" introduced a prediction of drought and death. Here in 9:11, by contrast, it heralds a vision of future restoration that promises life in abundance. The next phrase, "I will restore David's fallen (or, collapsing) hut (*'āqîm 'et sukkat dāwîd hannōpelet*)" (v. 11a), evokes a plentitude of intertextual associations. To begin with, it recalls the portrayal of "virgin Israel" in 5:2, as "fallen, to rise no more (*nāpělâ lōʾ tôsîp qûm*)" (cf. also 8:14). In the future envisioned by 9:11, YHWH will raise the fallen.

But how should the expression "David's fallen hut" in v. 11a be interpreted? It might be an allusion to "the house of David" (*bêt dāwîd*), the standard designation of the Davidic dynasty (see 2 Samuel 7; cf. also 2 Sam 3:1; 1 Kgs 12:20; 2 Kgs 17:21). After 587 B.C.E., the "fallen hut" metaphor would certainly be a fitting description of the dethroned and decimated royal dynasty (thus Kellermann 1969: 174 and Jeremias 1998: 166–67). This vision of restoration could thus be compared to the prophecy in Isa 11:1, with its image of a stump (rather than a tree).

However, the ensuing references to repair and rebuilding projects (in v. 11b) would rather seem to support an alternative interpretation of David's "hut" (*sukkâ*), as (primarily) a metaphor for the city of Jerusalem (with Wolff 1977: 353 and Troxel 2012: 49).[142] An interesting parallel is provided by another passage in Isaiah, where "daughter Zion" is said to be "like a shelter/hut (*kěsukkâ*) in a vineyard" (Isa 1:8). The image of a collapsing or already fallen *sukkâ* (hut, booth, or shelter), the very opposite of a magnificent house in perfect condition, suggests a situation of decline and despair. This illustration serves as a prelude for a vision of restoration. If, as seems likely, v. 11b refers to Jerusalem's ruined city wall, there might perhaps be a connection to the rebuilding achievements ascribed to Nehemiah (see Nehemiah 2–4). At the same time, the mention of "breaches (*pirṣêhen*)" in the walls echoes 4:3a: "Through the breaches (*pěrāṣîm*) you will depart." Hence, the utterance in 9:11 can be read as a reversal of the passage 4:1–3, with its predictions of defeat and deportation.

On another level, finally, one may note a significant shift in the agency of YHWH. Throughout the preceding parts of the book, the deity's destructive power has been emphasized. In 9:6, however, the image of a deity devising disasters was balanced by the portrayal of YHWH as a cosmic architect. Here, in 9:11, the deity is pictured as unambiguously constructive, also on earth. Downplaying notions of destructiveness, YHWH declares that he is going to build up Jerusalem (and/or the Davidic dynasty?), "as in the days of old" (v. 11bγ). As noted in the introduction, 9:11 was cited and interpreted as an eschatological promise in the texts from Qumran (the *Damascus Document* and 4QFlorilegium), as well as in the New Testament (Acts 15:16–17).[143]

9:12–13. For a number of reasons, vv. 12 and 13 appear to represent a later insertion into the epilogue.[144] Formally, these two utterances interrupt YHWH's speech in the first person. In terms of content, they are arguably more utopian than the surrounding oracles (vv. 11, 14–15). In addition, these verses seem to have a common editorial purpose related to the emerging book of the Twelve. As noted by Nogalski (1993a: 113), they "tie the ending of Amos to the book which follows (Obadiah) and the book which precedes (Joel)." Thus, while the topic of possessing Edom links 9:12 to Obadiah (see especially vv. 17–19), the similarities between Amos 9:13 and Joel 4:18 (Eng. 3:18) are striking.

9:12. In v. 12, the focus of attention shifts from Jerusalem and Judah to the international scene. This utterance spells out the geopolitical consequences of the restoration described in v. 11. It is stated that "they" (most probably, the people in the province of Yehud) will "possess (*yîrĕšû*) the remnant of Edom" (v. 12aα). This recalls the opening chapters of the book, where several oracles reflect animosity against Edom, a sentiment that appears to have been widespread in Judah/Yehud after 587 B.C.E. (see 1:6, 9, 11–12, and the Comments on those passages). Notably, the formulation "the remnant (*ʾet-šĕʾērît*)" implies either that Edom had suffered a military attack or that this nation had already lost parts of its territory to the Nabateans (cf. Mal 1:2–5).[145]

According to the fantasy depicted in 9:12, YHWH's people will also be able to take possession of "all the nations over whom my name has been called" (v. 12aβ). This vague definition, which explains that YHWH is the owner or overlord of these countries, does not help the reader to draw a map of the imagined empire. However, it is likely that the author had Amos 1:3–2:3 in mind, where a series of accusatory oracles, each time introduced by the formula "thus says YHWH," are directed against six nations bordering on Israel and/or Judah, including Edom. Alternatively, because David was mentioned in v. 11, the utterance in v. 12 could be understood as a vision of a revival of those "days of old" (v. 11bγ) when (according to the legends in 2 Samuel and 1 Kings) David and Solomon reigned over a united kingdom and several neighboring nations had been subjugated (Firth 1996 and Jeremias 1998: 167). In practice, though, these two scenarios are almost identical (see Carlson 1966).

In the concluding part of this oracle, v. 12b, the standard formula *nĕʾum yhwh* ("says YHWH") has been expanded by means of a unique phrase, *ʿōśeh zōʾt*, "(the one) who will do this." One may detect an intratextual link to the so-called doxologies here, since the participle *ʿōśeh*, "maker," is used as a divine epithet in 4:13 and 5:8.

9:13. According to v. 13, life in this new era will be characterized by agricultural abundance. Because of the excessively rich and frequent harvests, there will be no intervals between the seasons (see Paul 1991: 292–93): "the plowman will catch up with the reaper, and the one who treads grapes will catch up with the planter" (v. 13aβγ). The hyperbolic image of activities that overlap, or overtake each other, is probably inspired by the blessing in Lev 26:5. Apparently, there will be no period of drought at all. In other words, the epilogue of the book transforms the arid landscape envisioned in the prologue (1:2). Using formulations that echo Joel 4:18 (Eng. 3:18), v. 13b asserts that all mountains and hills shall overflow, not with water, but with "grape juice" (ʿāsîs)—that is, with wine!

From an intratextual perspective, one detail in v. 13b deserves further attention. It is declared that "the mountains will drip (wĕhaṭṭîpû)" (13bα). The verb nṭp, "to drip," occurs also in Amos 7:16, as a way of referring to prophetic speech. According to the narrative in 7:10–17, the leaders in Israel rejected the words of Amos. Apparently as a consequence of this, it is later on stated that the people will suffer from (metaphorical) hunger and thirst, as they search in vain for YHWH's words (8:11–12). I suggest that 9:13b can be read as a reversal of these previous passages (cf. also 4:7–8). In the future, this vision proclaims, there will be no thirst. Instead of prophets who "drip" words of judgment, the people will be surrounded by mountains that drip life-sustaining liquids (see similarly Linville 2008: 173).

9:14. In v. 14, the element of reversal is particularly prominent. As suggested by James Linville, the initial clause, wĕšabtî ʾet šĕbût ʿammî yiśrāʾēl (v. 14a, rendered here as "I will restore the fortunes of my people Israel"), could be translated as "I will reverse the reversal of my people Israel" (2008: 171). Judgment, accompanied by a repeated lōʾ ʾăšîbennû, "I will not hold it back" (1:3, 6, 9, 11, 13; 2:1, 4, 6), has now been replaced by salvation, expressed by means of a contrasting usage of the verb šûb. In the present context, the phrase šûb šĕbût (literally, "turn the turning") probably refers to the return from exile (see also Deut 30:3; Jer 30:3; 31:23).[146] Reversing the curse pronounced in 5:11, v. 14b promises that the repatriated Israelites (most probably this refers to repatriated Judeans) will be able to rebuild destroyed houses, to plant new gardens and vineyards, and to enjoy their fruits and wine.

9:15. The drama approaches its end. After all the outbursts and upheavals, the last scene presents a kind of still life, a static vision of permanent residence. Instead of simply "two years after the earthquake" (1:1), the setting seems to be a world where earthquakes are unknown. Apparently, all dangers have disappeared. No roaring lions are mentioned (cf. 1:2 and 3:8). Indeed, nothing happens. But much remains unspoken. The reader may well ask: What happened to the people's proclivity for oppression and corruption, or to the deity's inclination to punish human crimes with acts of large-scale violence?

In a final metaphorical move, YHWH declares that he shall "plant" the people in their land (v. 15a, nṭʿ; cf. Exod 15:17; 2 Sam 7:10; Jer 31:28). In other words, the blessed planters who were mentioned in v. 14 are themselves going to be planted. Furthermore, YHWH assures that "they shall never again be uprooted" (v. 15bα). Implicitly, the future ideal Israel is here depicted as a forest of trees, or perhaps as one single, gigantic tree (Paul 1991: 295). This evokes the image of the Amorites, the ones who were (allegedly) "tall as the cedars and strong as the oak trees" (2:9) and whose land YHWH once decided to give to Israel (2:10). According to the deuteronomistically inspired ideological perspective that informs large parts of the book of Amos, Israel later forfeited this gift through disobedience and sinfulness (7:17b; cf. 1 Kgs 9:6–7). The threat of deportation casts its shadow over several previous passages. As shown by 7:17, being cut off from one's *ʾădāmâ* ("land" or "soil") was seen as a severe punishment, comparable to death. Here in 9:15, the book's concluding oracle, the people's connection to "their land (*ʾadmātām*)" is once again restored. According to this vision, they will stay there forever, in "the land that I have given them" (v. 15b; cf. Jer 16:15).

This utopian promise is given further confirmation by the concluding phrase of v. 15b, "says YHWH (*ʾāmar yhwh*)." However, these are not the last words. For some reason, "your God (*ʾĕlōhêkā*)" has been added to the traditional formula. This sudden switch to the second-person singular is enigmatic, since it lacks an obvious referent within the epilogue. Possibly, the entire community of YHWH worshipers, the new Israel, is being personified (Jeremias 1998: 169). Thus interpreted, the end of 9:15 might recall an ominous admonition in a previous passage, "prepare to meet your God (*ʾĕlōhêkā*), O Israel" (4:12). Alternatively, the reader of the book of Amos is being addressed (Linville 2008: 173). At any rate, it is up to the reader to decide whether the concluding words of the epilogue are altogether reassuring or not.

Notes

Introduction

1. See Werlitz (2000: 237) and Barton (2012: 163–64).
2. S. R. Driver (1897: 94) continues: "the days spent by him [Amos] amid these wild surroundings left, we may be sure, their impress upon his character, sharpened his powers of observation, inured him to austerity of life, made him the keen and unflinching censor of the vices which flourish in the lap of luxury."
3. Thus, e.g., Soggin (1970), Wolff (1977: 124), and Paul (1991: 35–36).
4. Several Amos commentators refer to Yadin's excavation report from Hazor (Yadin et al. 1960) in support of their claim that the quake which followed upon Amos's prophetic activity can be dated with exactness. See Soggin (1970: 117), Wolff (1977: 124), and Paul (1991: 35). However, if these biblical scholars had studied the archaeological documentation more carefully, they would have noticed (1) that the destruction layer in question could result from either an earthquake or some other disaster, (2) that the archaeological data indicate that this layer should be dated roughly to the first half of the eighth century B.C.E., and (3) that a more exact date, around 760 B.C.E., was explicitly suggested with reference to a chronological interpretation of Amos 1:1! See Yadin et al. (1960: 36). As a matter of fact, earthquakes occurred rather frequently in ancient Palestine. It is by all means possible that Amos 1:1 refers to a major quake during the reign of Uzziah (cf. Zech 14:5), remembered by later tradition (see Josephus, *Jewish Antiquities* 9:225; cf. Soggin 1970: 118–20), but this remains hypothetical. See further the Comments on Amos 1:1.
5. Cf., similarly, Morgenstern (1936; 1937–38), who based his calculations on the following presuppositions: (1) that the utterance in Amos 8:9 refers to a solar eclipse that occurred in the year 753 B.C.E., and (2) that Amos delivered his prophetic messages on the very day of that eclipse. Morgenstern claimed, furthermore "that the prophet Amos delivered, not a series of addresses or prophetic utterances, but one, single, closely unified address, that he delivered this at the Northern national sanctuary at Bethel, that he delivered it upon the great, solemn New Year's Day, and this likewise two years to the very

day before the New Year's Day upon which the great earthquake in the days of Uzziah happened" (1937–38: 40).

6. See, e.g., Andersen and Freedman (1989: 5–9, 83–88), Watts (1997: 3–6), and Würthwein (1950: 19–40).

7. Thus S. R. Driver (1897: 95), Sellin (1929a: 189–90), G. A. Smith (1906: 120), and Weiser (1956: 128, 130).

8. For an English translation of *Vitae Prophetarum* (The Lives of the Prophets), with an introduction to this work, see Charlesworth (1985: 379–99; the translation was made by D. R. A. Hare). According to this legend, Amos was first tortured by Amaziah, the priest in Bethel (see Amos 7:10–17), and later killed (Charlesworth 1985: 391). For further discussion, see Martin-Achard (1984a: 187–88) and Werlitz (2000: 237).

9. Thus, e.g., Kapelrud (1956) and Reventlow (1962). For an overview of this line of research with a critical discussion, see Eidevall (2012c and 2016). See also Koch et al. (1976a: 285), Woude (1982: 34–36, 38), and Carroll R. (2002: 12–17).

10. This was maintained by, e.g., Haldar (1945: 79, 112). For a pointed critique, see Craigie (1982).

11. To the best of my knowledge, the theory that Amos belonged to the cult's personnel has not been defended in any major scholarly publication during the past forty years. Ward (1969: 92–140) can be seen as a late, but very cautious, representative of this line of research.

12. See Eidevall (2012a: 105–18 and 2013). As shown by Naiden (2006), the phenomenon of situation-bound rejection of sacrifices is attested in several ancient cultures. The extrabiblical examples discussed by Naiden are mainly drawn from Greek sources.

13. In addition, it is conceivable that some passages in the book of Amos denounce cultic practices performed at sanctuaries other than the temple in Jerusalem, in accordance with the principle laid down in Deut 12. See my Comments on the following passages: 4:4–5; 5:4–5; 7:9; 8:13–14.

14. See, e.g., Dines (2001), Linville (2008), and Radine (2010).

15. For an insightful discussion on criteria for identifying poetry in ancient Hebrew texts, see Berlin (1985: 1–9).

16. For analyses of the vast array of metaphors in the book of Hosea, see Eidevall (1996), Seifert (1996), and Oestreich (1998).

17. For a pointed critique of Limburg (1987) and O'Connell (1996), as well as some other scholars who tend to exaggerate the importance of certain numerical patterns, such as heptads and 7 + 1 constructions, see Möller (2003a: 83–88). For a discussion of additional stylistic features that may contribute to the sense of a carefully constructed literary composition, see Koch et al. (1976b: 105–20).

18. In this respect I disagree somewhat with T. Collins (2001: 94–95, 102–3).

19. Mention should be made of the anthology *Thematic Threads in the Book of the Twelve* (Redditt and Schart 2003), which does not, however, contain any analysis of "threads" running through the book of Amos. The purpose of the volume is to point to a certain degree of thematic coherence within the book of the Twelve, not to study the degree of coherence exhibited by individual books among the Twelve, such as Amos.

20. For a more extensive discussion of the applicability of the terms "comedy" and "tragedy" to the book of Amos, and in particular to the successive editorial stages of the book, see Rilett Wood (1998). On the question of whether the happy ending in 9:11–15 really turns the book of Amos into a comedy, see also Linville (2008: 8): "Like the restoration of Job's fortunes, one can ask if the ending of Amos is not deliberately superficial, leading the reader to probe ever deeper the themes of the book as a whole."

21. Thus, e.g., Mays (1969: 2–3) and Paul (1991: 1–2). See also Hayes (1988: 21–23). However, Hayes maintains that a number of factors may have made the situation somewhat more turbulent toward the end of the reign of Jeroboam II (1988: 23–27).

22. The description provided by Andersen and Freedman (1989: 18–23) is arguably more realistic. Focusing entirely on the absence of major wars and military threats during these decades, these two commentators abstain from speculations regarding increasing income gaps and widespread corruption.

23. Such a discrepancy between meager textual (and other) evidence and grand theoretical construction was, to some extent, admitted by B. Lang himself, who wrote the following as a kind of postscript to the essay on Amos and rent capitalism: "In saying all of this I am well aware that I am going slightly beyond the information given in the biblical sources. But read in the light of anthropology, the scattered bits of social and economic information fit into a definite and clear picture known as rent capitalism. Everything finds, so to speak, its natural place" (1983: 127). Perhaps it is needless to point out that these scattered bits of information could fit into some other model of Iron Age economy, as well. See further the discussion in Fleischer (1989: 359–67). See also Jaruzelska (1998: 14–23).

24. With Fritz (1989: 41), Levin (1995: 316–17), and Kratz (2003: 81, 85).

25. Thus, e.g., Fritz (1989), Möller (2003a: 104–52), and Radine (2010: 46–79, 130–69). See also Rilett Wood, who claims that Amos was a performing poet who "recited or sang his tragic poetry in the seventh century . . . during the reign of King Manasseh in Judah, a confident and peaceful age in which people could afford the luxury of listening to tragic poetry " (2002: 113).

26. See the sections "Introduction to the Second Pair of Visions (7:7–8 and 8:1–2)" and "Introduction to 7:10–17" in this commentary.

27. See further the pioneering study by W. H. Schmidt (1965).

28. See further the insightful discussion in Law (2012: 181–237). For a critical review of redaction-critical studies of the book of Amos, see Möller (2003b).

29. For an insightful discussion of criteria and principles for the identification of different redactional layers, see Hadjiev (2009: 25–40). See also Brettler (2006). Focusing his discussion on the passage 2:4–5, Brettler includes the examples of 3:7 and 8:11 as well, in order to demonstrate the necessity of a redaction-critical approach to the book of Amos.

30. See also Mays (1969: 61–62) and Wolff (1977: 181).

31. For more details, see the Comments on 3:3–8.

32. The following works have been important dialogue partners when it comes to reconstructing the book's redaction history: Coote (1981), Rottzoll (1996), Jeremias (1998), Schart (1998), Kratz (2003), and Hadjiev (2009). Mention should also be made of Loretz (1992) and Lescow (1998, 1999).

33. See Kratz (2003: 81) and Levin (1995: 310, 315–17). According to an interesting theory advanced by Philip Davies, the book of Amos (composed in the Persian period) was based on a preexisting collection of prophetic words, "probably preserved in Bethel," which contained "oracles that denounced Israel's depravity" (2006: 129). In my opinion, however, it is unlikely that a collection containing anti-Bethel propaganda (see 3:14; 4:4; 5:5) was stored in the Bethel sanctuary. Why not in Jerusalem? According to Davies (2006: 129), the prophetic message ascribed to Amos "had little relevance in Judah." In this commentary I aim to demonstrate the very opposite.

34. See further Becker (1997: 282), Jong (2007), and Eidevall (2009: 190–91).

35. For a more elaborate argumentation along these lines, see Scherer (2005: 7–14), Blum (2008: 88–96), and Radine (2014). See also Dijkstra (1995).

36. See, e.g., Mays (1969: 4–14), Coote (1981: 11–45), and Jeremias (1998: 2–5).

37. According to Rottzoll (1996: 288), the concentric structure was created at a late stage by the same editor who inserted the doxologies at 4:13, 5:8, and 9:5–6; however, I cannot see that he adduces any convincing arguments for this hypothesis.

38. A couple of recent studies, by Dines (2001) and Linville (2008), treat the entire book as a product of the Persian era. As far as I can see, however, both of them fail to find Persian era settings for a number of central topics and themes in the book.

39. Since the eschatological outlook in some of these additions is far removed from what we find in the book of Daniel and other apocalyptic texts (see J. J. Collins 1998), I find no reason to date the third and final version of Amos to the Hellenistic era.

40. See, above all, the works of Nogalski (1993a and 1993b), Schart (1998), and Wöhrle (2006 and 2008a).

41. See Nogalski (1993a: 278–80) and Wöhrle (2006: 51–53; 2008b). See also Jeremias (1998: 11), Schart (1998: 39–46), Sweeney (2000: xxxviii), Albertz (2003), and Kratz (2011: 276–77).

42. See further the predominantly negative evaluation of this line of research in Möller (2003b: 407–18). See also the contrasting views that have been juxtaposed in Ben Zvi and Nogalski (2009).

43. For an extensive and detailed overview, see Martin-Achard (1984a: 163–242). See also Markert (1978: 484–85) and, more recently, Barton (2012: 161–80).

44. See further the insightful comments on the Tobit passage in Barton (2012: 164).

45. For an insightful discussion of similarities and differences between the Amos-Numbers Midrash and 4QFlorilegium as regards the interpretation of Amos 9:11, see Kratz (2011: 370–79). According to Kratz, it is likely that the passage in 4QFlorilegium is dependent on the Amos-Numbers Midrash in the *Damascus Document*.

46. See further Richard (1982), Bauckham (1996), and Glenny (2012).

47. Cf. also the LXX and the Targum to Amos 9:11–12.

48. For more detailed overviews, see Martin-Achard (1984a: 186–99) and Neusner (2007). See also Park (2001: 207–14).

49. The contributions to Amos exegesis made by medieval Jewish scholars are not covered by this short survey. See, e.g., Ruiz González (1987). However, a number of philological and interpretative proposals advanced by such scholars as Kimchi and Rashi are discussed below, in the Notes and Comments on specific passages in the book of Amos.

50. A treatment of the Amos commentaries authored by Cyril of Alexandria, Theodore of Mopsuestia, and Theodet would exceed the limits of a short survey such as this. For a helpful discussion of some aspects of these works, see Kelly (1977).

51. Mein (2011) provides an insightful analysis, especially of the sermons on Amos 2:6–8, which relates Savonarola's exegesis to the political and religious context in Florence that he was addressing. See also Martin-Achard (1984a: 211–19), with lengthy quotations from one of the sermons, and Barton (2012: 172–74), with an English translation of the French translation used by Martin-Achard. The complete Italian text of Savonarola's sermons is available in a publication from 1971: G. Savonarola, *Prediche sopra Amos e Zaccaria* (Rome: Angelo Berdeletti). For an extensive treatment of Savonarola's life and work, see Weinstein (1970).

52. According to Barton, Luther's interpretation, with its focus on the sins of the people and the concomitant consequences for the relationship between God and Israel, nonetheless represents "something of a return to the original intentions of the prophet" (2012:

175). This assessment strikes me as both ill-founded and biased. For one thing, we know very little about the "original intentions" of the eponymous prophet, which may not have coincided with the intentions of the authors and editors who shaped the book of Amos. Furthermore, it should be obvious to modern readers that this prophetic writing presupposes a strong connection between righteousness and actual practice (in Luther's terminology, between "righteousness" and "works").

53. The notion of predestination has a particularly prominent role in Calvin's exposition of Amos 5:4–6. See Martin-Achard (1984a: 232–33, 241).

54. Perhaps needless to point out, all interpretations of this prophetic book from the past two centuries have not shared this emphasis on ethics and social justice. Some further aspects of modern Amos reception are covered by Martin-Achard (1984a: 243–60).

55. For a brief overview, see Martin-Achard (1984a: 266–70) or Barton (2012: 177–80). A helpful survey of literature reflecting liberationist perspectives, from different parts of the world, is provided by Carroll R. (2002: 53–72). For some examples of such interpretations, see Ceresko (1992: 180–84), Reimer (2000), and Wafawanaka (2003).

56. See, e.g., Fleischer (1989) and Reimer (1992). Mention should also be made of Dempsey (2000: 7–21), who examines the book of Amos critically from a liberationist point of view. In my opinion, her problematizing analysis represents a step in the right direction, when compared with earlier, less critical presentations of Amos's social message. See, e.g., Ceresko (1992: 180–84).

57. See Reimer (1992: 23–24, 54–58, 63–64, 81–85, 229).

58. For the following, see Reimer (1992: 118–22).

59. For two rather recent examples of the standard interpretation of this passage, see Paul (1991: 178–81) and Jeremias (1998: 96–97).

60. See the discussion in Carroll R. (1992: 38, 198, 238–40). See also Wolff (1971: 54–67) and Fendler (1973: 48–52).

61. The ongoing Oxford Hebrew Bible project will provide a critical edition. This is certainly to be welcomed as an important supplement to the diplomatic editions represented by *BHS, BHQ,* and the Hebrew University Bible project (which is based on the Aleppo codex). So far, the only modern editions of the Hebrew Bible containing the text of Amos are *BHS* and *BHQ.*

62. See the convenient presentation in Ego et al. (2005: 47–69).

63. I am aware that "the Septuagint," in a strict sense, is a designation of the Greek translation of the Pentateuch, which was begun in the third century B.C.E. When referring to the earliest Greek translation of a book belonging to some other part of the Hebrew Bible, experts within this field often use the term "Old Greek." However, the modern standard editions of these translations are usually called "Septuaginta." Therefore, I have chosen to speak about the Septuagint (or the LXX), rather than the Old Greek, of Amos. Cf. the discussion in Glenny (2009: 2–3).

Oracles against the Nations (1–2)

1. See further the section "Thematic Threads" in the introduction. See also T. Collins (2001).

2. For the following, see above all the well-argued analysis in Fuhs (1977). See also Schart (1998: 50–54) and the comments on 1:1 in Wolff (1977: 116–24).

3. The idea that there once existed such a collection, which might be called the "book of the Four" was, as far as I know, first advanced by Nogalski (1993a: 84–89, 176–78, 278–80).

This hypothesis has been accepted by several scholars. See, e.g., Schart (1998: 39–46; 156), Sweeney (2000: xxxviii), Albertz (2003), and Wöhrle (2006: 51–53).

4. For illustrative examples of this rather uncritical approach to the information provided by Amos 1:1 and 7:14, see Sellin (1929a: 179–89), Watts (1997: 64–68), and Andersen and Freedman (1989: 83–88).

5. With Auld (1986: 38–40) and Levin (1995: 307, 314). For a more elaborate argumentation concerning the speculative character of all attempts to reconstruct the life and career of Amos, see "From the Prophet Amos to the Book of Amos" in the introduction.

6. On these Phoenician theophoric names, as well as other parallels to the name Amos, see further Stamm (1980). See also Paul (1991: 33–34).

7. For a more elaborate argumentation against the position of Haldar and others, see Craigie (1982) and Paul (1991: 34).

8. According to Bič (1951), the designation nōqēd indicates that Amos was a "hepato-scoper" (inspector of livers). Convincing counterarguments were produced by Murtonen (1952). See also Segert (1967: 282–83).

9. See the intricate but in my opinion far too speculative argumentation in Rosenbaum (1990: 35–46, 99–102).

10. The prime representative of this approach is probably Linder (1922), who offers a detailed description of the view from Tekoa, in all directions. Clearly, the underlying idea is that all exegesis of the book of Amos should be informed by this perspective. See also the landscape-based speculations in S. R. Driver (1897: 94).

11. See, e.g., Wolff (1977: 89–90) and Jeremias (1998: 1–2). Thus also Stuart (1987: 283, 297), Hayes (1988: 26–27, 38), and Fleischer (2001: 121–29).

12. On the significance of the earthquake theme within the book of Amos, see Ogden (1992) and, more recently, Dell (2011).

13. The term "motto" has been used as a label of Amos 1:2 by, e.g., Harper (1905: 9), Hammershaimb (1970: 19), Wolff (1977: 119), and Paul (1991: 36).

14. See further Wolff (1977: 118–19, 121–22) and Jeremias (1998: 13–14).

15. On various aspects of lion metaphors in the Hebrew Bible, see Eidevall (1996: 86–88). For a more detailed discussion, supplemented with lavish documentation of iconographic representations of lions from the ancient Near East, see Strawn (2005). See also Nahkola (2011: 95–97, 99–101).

16. This term seems to have been coined by Robert Alter (1985: 144). It captures an important aspect of the rhetorical strategy in a number of passages in the prophetic literature. As to the applicability of the term "rhetoric of entrapment" to the series of oracles against neighboring nations in Amos 1–2, see Chisholm (1990: 188–90) and Linville (2000a: 407).

17. With Wolff (1977: 135–41), Barton (1980: 22–24), Fritz (1987: 27–28), and Fleischer (2001: 142–51).

18. The affinity with Deuteronomistic language and ideology was pointed out in an influential study by W. H. Schmidt (1965: 177). Additional arguments in support of this view have been adduced by Gosse (1988: 29–31, 39–40).

19. For an extensive survey and discussion of the anti-Edomite passages in the prophetical literature in the Hebrew Bible, see Cresson (1972). See also Eidevall (2009: 154, 157).

20. Thus also Jeremias (1998: 22), Paul (1991: 46), and Möller (2003a: 178–80).

21. Apparently, then, the oracle in Isa 41:15 endorses the type of brutality that Amos 1:3 condemns. See Dines (2001: 582). Cf. also the similar use of threshing imagery in Mic 4:13.

22. For a more detailed discussion of the location of Kir, see Thompson (1992).
23. See further Eidevall (2009: 133–36, 141–45).
24. On the Edom oracle's use of the term "brother" in light of treaty terminology in the ancient Near East, see Fishbane (1970) and Barré (1985). See also Coote (1971).
25. See Isa 34:5–15; Jer 49:7–22; Ezek 25:12–14; Joel 4:19 [Eng. 3:19]; Mal 1:2–5. See further Cresson (1972).
26. Akkadian attestations are cited by Cogan (1983). See also Wolff (1977: 161).
27. The textual variant attested in 4QXII[g], "the day of *the* battle" (with the article before *milḥāmâ*), could perhaps be taken to refer to a specific military attack (see the Notes).
28. For an illustrative example of this type of Phoenician burial chamber inscription, see *KAI* 14, lines 20–22. For transliteration, translation, and discussion of the inscription from the cave in Jerusalem, see Aḥituv (2008: 44–47).
29. On this Assyrian practice, see Olyan (2015: 138, n. 16), with further references.
30. Thus also, e.g., Rilett Wood (2002: 204). For a detailed investigation in support of the view that the oracle against Judah betrays Deuteronomistic influence, see Gosse (1988: 29–31, 39–40).
31. Thus, e.g., Harper (1905: 49), Mays (1969: 45), B. Lang (1981: 482–83), and Sweeney (2000: 214–15).
32. For a critical examination of this unlikely hypothesis, see the discussion in Viberg (1992: 148–51, 157–58).
33. Cf. similarly the LXX version of 1 Sam 12:3.
34. With, e.g., Rudolph (1971: 141), Fendler (1973: 38), Hayes (1988: 110), Fleischer (1989: 55–56), and Jeremias (1998: 35–36).
35. An alternative interpretation has been proposed by Avi Shveka (2012). Referring to a Hittite law which prescribes that a person who returns an escaped slave shall receive either silver or a pair of shoes as reward, Shveka claims that Amos 2:6b condemns those who were chasing runaway slaves in order to get the reward (2012: 99–103). However, in view of the context, as well as the close parallel in 8:6, this reading of 2:6 is unconvincing. In my opinion, the Hittite text cited by Shveka (2012: 99–100) actually supports the mainstream interpretation, since it proves that the payment of a small sum of money, in some instances, was replaced by the act of handing over a pair of sandals.
36. So also, e.g., Wolff (1977: 166) and Jeremias (1998: 36). The topic of corruption surfaces later in the book of Amos. See the Comments on 5:7 and 5:10–12.
37. See further the discussion in Paul (1991: 82), with references to Akkadian parallels. See also Bronznick (1985).
38. A complaint concerning a creditor's failure to return a worker's garment is recorded on an ostracon from Meṣad Ḥashavyahu. See Aḥituv (2008: 156–60).
39. A rather speculative interpretation has been suggested by Delbert Hillers (1995). Referring to a cognate word in Palmyrene Aramaic, he argues that *ʿănûšîm* (commonly translated as "the fined") here denotes the temple treasury (1995: 59–60).
40. According to Rilett Wood (2002: 206), who argues that 2:11 must be understood in the light of the Deuteronomistic History, this utterance may allude to both Samson and Samuel.
41. Such a translation has been suggested by Gese (1962: 417–23), with reference to the Arabic verbal stem *ʿqq*.
42. For the same reason, the solution suggested by Stuart (1987: 307), "bog down," fails to persuade me.

43. Several commentators advocate this interpretation of the motif of nakedness. Thus, e.g., Marti (1904: 171), Paul (1991: 98), and Jeremias (1998: 44).

The Words of Amos (3–6)

1. According to Jeremias (1998: 47–49, 57), this phrase has a structuring function only in 3:1 and 5:1. He suggests that whereas 3:1 introduces a section containing words spoken by YHWH, 5:1 marks the beginning of a collection of words spoken by Amos. However, this hypothesis cannot be sustained by a closer examination of the text. Throughout chapters 3–6, all oracles (also 5:2–3) are presented as words spoken by YHWH and transmitted through the prophet. For a more detailed critique, see Steins (2004: 36–37). From a different perspective, Wöhrle (2006: 80) has argued that the imperative in 3:1 belongs to another structural level than those in 4:1 and 5:1. According to Wöhrle, 3:1a is part of the oldest layer of the book (the *Grundschicht*), whereas 4:1 and 5:1 represent later additions.
2. According to Paul (1991: 109), the verb *yᶜd* (in Niphal) here denotes an accidental meeting, when people "bump into each other by chance without prearranging either the time or the place." However, this statement concerning the lexical sense of *yᶜd* is not supported by the dictionaries. Besides, this interpretation turns 3:3 into a tautology.
3. So, e.g., Mays (1969: 61–62) and Wolff (1977: 181). See also Mittmann (1971: 136), Pfeifer (1983: 342, 345–46), and Jeremias (1998: 54–55).
4. See further Moeller (1964: 32) and Möller (2003a: 239–42). Cf. also Jeremias (1998: 59).
5. Less likely, the addressees are non-Israelites, perhaps the same as in v. 9, and their task is to testify against Israel, as averred by Wolff (1977: 200).
6. As noted by Paul (1991: 124), there is "no compelling reason to deny the existence of multiple altars in Bethel." After all, this was a national sanctuary (Amos 7:13). One of these altars, however, would have been the central one. See further Davis (2013: 164–65).
7. In Hos 10:11, similar bovine imagery is used about the entire nation of Israel (called Ephraim) and in a basically positive sense: "Ephraim was a trained heifer, willing to thresh; I passed by the beauty of her neck; I will harness Ephraim." See further the analysis in Eidevall (1996: 159–61).
8. For a critical discussion of further examples of scholarly comments on this text with a misogynist tendency, see Linville (2008: 82–83). See also the discussion of this passage in Sanderson (1998: 218–19, 221–22).
9. Paul (1991: 134) has adduced a passage from the Mari letters, where similar imagery is used in a depiction of a transport of captives, conducted by the god Dagon (for the text, see Dossin 1948: 130). In that case, however, it is evident that the metaphorical comparison centers on the writhing movements of the fish. See further Kleven (1996: 221–22).
10. For a more elaborate discussion, see Eidevall (2012a: 105–18 and 2013: 34–41, 45).
11. Thus, e.g., (Paul 1991: 141–42). See also Harper (1905: 96), Carroll R. (1992: 210), and Möller (2003a: 270).
12. For an overview of such hypotheses, see Ulrichsen (1992–93: 285–88).
13. According to Andersen and Freedman (1989: 450–52) the *yiqtol* forms in v. 12 should be understood as expressing the past tense; however, their argumentation fails to persuade me.
14. See further Koch (1974), Foresti (1981), and McComiskey (1987). Cf. also Jeremias (1998: 76–79) and Schart (1998: 234–37).

15. So already Horst (1929: 50–54), who even claimed that it was possible to outline a very specific ritual setting, within the sphere of sacral jurisdiction. For a more nuanced position, see Koch (1974: 536), who observes that this "Gebrauch geprägter poetischer Stücke legt liturgische Verwendung nahe." Jeremias (1998: 78) speaks of an "exilic/postexilic penitential ritual."

16. It has been suggested by Crenshaw (1972: 39–44) that the terminology used in the phrase "(the one who) treads on the heights of the earth" alludes to a motif in Canaanite mythology: Having defeated his enemies, the weather god treads on their backs. In Ugaritic, as pointed out by Crenshaw (1972: 39), *drkt* denotes dominion, *bmt* can refer to someone's back, and *arṣ* may stand for the netherworld.

17. According to the hypothesis propounded by Rottzoll (1996: 243–50, 288), the concentric structure in 5:1–17 underwent no such expansion, since it was created by the editor who inserted the doxologies. In that case, however, one might have expected smoother transitions within vv. 7–10, as well as more elaborate lexical and thematic links between v. 8 and the surrounding parts of the composition.

18. In the parallel texts cited, from the book of Isaiah, the female (*bětûlâ*) metaphor is used about cities, rather than nations (Isa 23:12, Sidon; 37:22, Jerusalem; 47:1, Babylon). Hence, as Schmitt (1991) argues, it is conceivable that the metaphor in Amos 5:2 refers primarily to the city of Samaria. However, the context (v. 3) makes clear that a disaster of national scope is described.

19. For a detailed discussion of the interpretation suggested by Weiser (1929: 190–94), see Hesse (1956).

20. See further the discussion in Eidevall (2012a: 109–10).

21. Arguably, Bethel, which is mentioned first and last in 5:5, has a more prominent position than the other two sites. Quite possibly, 5:5 attests to the continuing significance of Bethel after 722 B.C.E. It seems to have been a prominent cultic site during the sixth century. See further Blenkinsopp (2003).

22. It has been noted by Fleischer (2001: 194) that there is an element of paronomasia in v. 5aγ, as well, since the verb ʿbr plays on consonants from the first syllable in Beer-Sheba.

23. So, e.g., Jeremias (1998: 89). It is possible, as suggested by Lust (1981: 137), that the redactor responsible for 5:6 wanted "to warn the 'house of Judah' through a reference to the downfall of the 'house of Joseph.'"

24. Thus, e.g., Wolff (1977: 233, 247). According to Levin (2003: 283–84), 5:11–12a is a very late addition to the book of Amos.

25. The challenge of making this saying fit within the concentric structure is not addressed by Goff (2008), who suggests that 5:13 can be seen as thematically connected to the surrounding utterances.

26. So, e.g., Wolff (1977: 249–50) and Jeremias (1998: 93–94). As observed by Ina Willi-Plein (1971: 36), the use of *maśkîl* as a self-designation for members of a marginalized pious group recalls the book of Daniel. Thus, it might point in the direction of apocalyptic circles. Alternatively, the commentator who penned 5:13 may have belonged to postexilic wisdom circles, as suggested by Martin-Achard (1984b: 43).

27. Tromp (1984: 78) lists three different interpretations. In addition to one that is similar to the one proposed here, he mentions the possibility that the sage resorted to silence either as an expression of grief or because the situation was "unspeakably bad."

28. A less likely hypothesis has been propounded by Gary Smith (1988). According to him, Amos 5:13 criticizes the "prosperous" (*maśkîl*) in society for not speaking up on behalf

of the poor. Similarly also Jackson (1986). But why would someone use the word *maśkîl*, with its positive connotations, as a designation for rich oppressors?

29. According to Neubauer (1966: 297–308), Amos 5:14 alludes primarily to the so-called salvation oracle in the cult. However, in that context the worshipers are told, even assured, that YHWH is with them; they do not claim that themselves.

30. On the basis of observations regarding the vocabulary used, Lust (1981: 133–37) has argued that the passage 5:14–15 is postexilic, whereas 5:4–5 is preexilic or exilic. Focusing on occurrences of *ʾûlay* in the Hebrew Bible, Schorch (2012: 462) draws a different conclusion, namely, that 5:15 cannot be dated later than the sixth century.

31. According to the LXX, however, divine mercy is indeed the most likely consequence of the people's repentance. This looks like a theological reinterpretation. See Schorch (2012: 460).

32. For transliteration, translation, and discussion of the relevant lines in the Deir ʿAlla plaster texts (Combination I, either lines 6–7 or 8–9, depending on the numbering system), see Hoftijzer and van der Kooij (1976: 173, 179, 196; lines 8–9) and Seow (in Nissinen 2003: 209, 211; lines 6–7).

33. See the overview in Norin (2009). A helpful summary of the discussion up to the beginning of the 1970s is offered by Leeuwen (1974).

34. See Leeuwen (1974: 115–16) and McLaughlin (2001: 92–94). See also Schart (2009: 260–62), with a detailed analysis of the function of the particle *hôy* in Amos 5:18 and 6:1.

35. For critical reviews of these two theories, see Leeuwen (1974: 120–25) and Norin (2009: 33–36).

36. With, e.g., Barton (2004) and Oswald (2009: 21); see also R. Müller (2010: 587). With reference to these observations, the hypothesis put forward by Meir Weiss (1966) can be discarded. Weiss suggested that the phrase *yôm yhwh* was coined by Amos and that it had negative connotations from the start. But why describe someone as desiring something he or she has never heard of? And why bother to reverse the understanding of a brand new concept? Thus interpreted, the utterance loses all of its rhetorical force. According to another hypothesis, propounded by Yair Hoffmann (1981), the expression "day of YHWH," with its origin in the theophany tradition, was intrinsically ambiguous. This theory is compatible with the analysis presented here, but it tends to reduce the rhetorical force of 5:18. Arguably, this utterance represents an attempt to reverse positive expectations. See also the evaluation of Weiss's and Hoffmann's theories made by Norin (2009: 35–37, 41).

37. It is possible that the author of Isa 1:11–15 reused (and rearranged) motifs and formulations from Amos 5:21–24. Thus, e.g., Fey (1963: 70–74) and Weiss (1995: 200–201). Alternatively, both passages draw on some kind of common source or tradition. See Ernst (1994: 161–78) and Niditch (1980: 518–20).

38. Translation of Smith and Pitard (2009: 463).

39. The Ugaritic passage takes the form of a numerical proverb, and more precisely of an "abomination saying." For a brief discussion, see Smith and Pitard (2009: 475).

40. According to Wolff (1977: 263), *minḥâ* should be taken in a generic sense, as a reference to various types of offerings. However, I find this unlikely, since the other terms in v. 22 are not generic.

41. Thus Sellin (1929a: 235) and Berquist (1993: 57). Cf. similarly Weiss (1995: 211–12).

42. See further Kratz (1998: 105–6, 111–12).

43. See W. H. Schmidt (1965: 188–91). According to Wolff (1977: 260, 265), vv. 25–26 belong together, comprising a coherent unit (ascribed to a Deuteronomistic editor). Soggin

(1987: 97) suggests that "the whole section vv. 25–27" is "secondary" in relation to the preceding section.

44. See the sections "Amos at Qumran" and "Amos in the New Testament" in the introduction above.

45. On the *zebaḥ* as a sacrifice of communion, see Marx (2005: 112–17). For various aspects of the vegetable offering, see Marx (1994). There is no reason, in my opinion, to assume that *minḥâ* carries the more general sense of "gift" in 5:25. Notably, the verb *ngš* in the Hiphil is used about the presentation of cultic offerings also in other texts (Exod 32:6; Lev 2:8; 8:14).

46. See further Eidevall (2012a: 149–71, 219).

47. For yet another possible exception, see the Comments on Amos 8:14.

48. In a similar vein Hertzberg (1950: 222) has suggested that the purpose of adding vv. 25–26 was to soften the harsh critique against the sacrificial cult in vv. 21–24, by means of a reinterpretation: It did not concern the cult of YHWH, only "Fremdkult," that is, sacrifices offered to *other* deities.

49. It is uncertain whether Amos 5:8 was part of the text when 5:26 was added. At any rate, the relation between these two verses is intriguing.

50. See Jeremias (1998: 105). It should be noted, though, that this hypothesis requires a revocalization of the MT in 2 Kgs 17:30, from *sukkôt* to *sakkût*.

51. According to some Greek manuscripts, the final destination is Babylon.

52. See McLaughlin (2001: 1–79). See also Greenfield (1974) and Maier and Dörrfuss (1999: 48–54). The term *marzēaḥ* is even attested on the Madaba map, a mosaic from the sixth century C.E., as noted by McLaughlin (2001: 64).

53. Interestingly, McLaughlin (2001: 70–79, 104) was not able to establish a firm connection between the *mrzḥ* and funerary rituals, or a cult of the dead. Such a connection has been postulated in previous scholarship, by, e.g., Pope (1981: 176) and Loretz (1982 and 1993: 140–42). For a critical review of such hypotheses, see B. B. Schmidt (1996: 144–147). See also Maier and Dörrfuss (1999: 57).

54. McLaughlin (2001: 103) concedes that "two elements commonly seen in connection with the extra-biblical *marzēaḥ* are not mentioned in this text: the *marzēaḥ* leader and the *marzēaḥ* house."

55. See also Maier and Dörrfuss (1999: 57) and McLaughlin (2001: 106). Some scholars have pointed out that the *marzēaḥ* institution, with YHWH as its patron deity, may have been accepted by Yahwist circles. Thus, e.g., Fleischer (1989: 238–39) and Polley (1989: 89). See also Fabry (1998: 14). According to Ackerman (1989: 279–81), the *marzēaḥ* in Amos 6:4–7 was "not condemned . . . as religious apostasy, but as social abomination" (quotation on p. 279).

56. Mention should also be made of the unsuccessful attempts by Weiser (1956: 175–76) and Fohrer (1964: 294) to retain the text but still claim that the inhabitants of Jerusalem are not addressed in parallel to the population of Samaria in 6:1. Whereas Weiser claimed that v. 1aα refers to an Israelite victory over Judah and Zion, Fohrer suggested that "Zion" here stands for the capital of Israel, that is, Samaria. For critique, see Wolff (1977: 269) and Blum (1994: 29, n. 17). As far as I can see, the additional arguments that McLaughlin (2001: 102–3) has adduced in favor of Fohrer's harmonizing solution are not convincing.

57. I thus agree to a certain extent with the thought-provoking analysis of 6:1–7 that has been presented by Blum (1994). However, I find it unnecessary to postulate, as he does, that an oracle which originally concerned only Samaria was later updated and adapted

to a Jerusalem audience, at some point between 711 and 705 B.C.E. (see Blum 1994: 41–44).

58. See also Maier and Dörrfuss (1999: 47).

59. See Carroll R. (1992: 256, n. 3).

60. See the discussion in Eidevall (2009: 47–48).

61. For a helpful survey and discussion of hemerology in the ancient Near East, with particular emphasis on the distinction between "good" and "evil" days, see Spieckermann (1989: 201–3). I do not agree with him (1989: 197–200) that the phrase "the day of YHWH" in Amos 5:18–20 should be understood against this background (see the discussion in R. Müller 2010: 583–84). On the other hand, the extrabiblical material adduced by Spieckermann throws light on the formulation in Amos 6:3.

62. See further Snyman (1995 and 1996).

63. A similar view is taken by Fleischer (1989: 239–40).

64. See King (1988: 142–46). According to King, "Samaria yielded over 500 ivory fragments, dating to either the ninth or the eighth century B.C.E." (1988: 143). See also Jaruzelska (1998: 79–82, 164–65).

65. For a detailed discussion on the role of meat in the diet of the population in Palestine during the biblical period, see MacDonald (2008: 47–64). See also Altmann (2011: 102–6).

66. For the lexeme *marbēq DCH* lists the senses "stall" and "fattening." According to *HALOT,* "fattening" is the primary lexical sense. Apparently, the expression in 6:4b refers to the practice of keeping cattle tied in enclosures in order to fatten them. See further King (1988: 149–51).

67. According to Helga Weippert (1985: 7–9), who refers to an Egyptian picture of a calf being tied to its mother cow, the expression *mittôk marbēq* indicates that the calves in question were still nursing. Drawing on Weippert's hypothesis, and developing it further, Stefan Schorch (2010: 128–29) has suggested that the practice described amounts to a violation of the prohibition in Exod 23:19 and Deut 14:21. For a pointed critique of Schorch's theory, see Guillaume (2011).

68. In addition, it is possible that *kĕdāwîd* ("like David") functions as a "pivot word," and as such is "serving both colons" (that is, both 6:5a and 5b), as suggested by Goswell (2011: 249).

69. The second alternative requires that the preposition *ʿal* in v. 5a is understood as doing double duty. See Andersen and Freedman (1989: 563). Cf. also Freedman (1985).

70. As regards Ps 151:2, one should note the different formulations in 11QPsᵃ and the LXX.

71. The word *mizrāq* occurs seventeen times within descriptions of the tabernacle: Exod 27:3; 38:3; Num 4:14, and no fewer than fourteen times in Num 7. In the remaining fourteen instances outside the book of Amos, there is always a close connection to rituals taking place at an altar, or to a sanctuary, primarily the temple in Jerusalem (1 Kgs 7:40, 45, 50; 2 Kgs 12:14 [Eng. 12:13]; 25:15; 1 Chr 28:17; 2 Chr 4:8, 11, 22; Neh 7:69 [Eng. 7:70]; Jer 52:18, 19; Zech 9:15; 14:20).

72. Cf. Greer (2007: 261): "Thus, this Yahwistic purist's root cause of 'woe' was the offense of syncretism, rather than simply the symptomatic neglect of the poor." In my opinion, the idea that "idolatry" or alleged heterodoxy is the main reason for the prophetic critique delivered by this text lacks solid foundation in the wording of the text itself. Notably, the drinking vessels are called "bowls of wine" (*mizrĕqê yayin*). Hence, they are not explicitly defined as cultic vessels. Contrary to what Greer (2007: 261) claims, his study therefore has not "established that the Samarian loungers were emulating their neighbors in the act

of drinking from their own sacred vessels." It is indeed doubtful to what extent the iconographic material from Mesopotamia and Phoenicia adduced by Greer (2007: 251–59), showing that bowls of the type used for libations were used as drinking vessels in banquets, is relevant to the interpretation of Amos 6:6. If this was the source of the biblical author's indignation, why didn't he mention that the "wine bowls" of the loungers were also used for libations?

73. This statement is based on statistics. As observed by Seybold, "The majority of texts refer to the anointing of kings, so that in the OT the verb has become a technical term with this specialized sense" (1998: 45).

74. As observed by Wolff (1977: 280), the introductory *wĕhāyâ* might also indicate that vv. 9–10 is a later addition. One may further note that there is no *atnaḥ* sign in v. 9. This is merely registered by Rudolph (1971: 222), without any further discussion.

75. Schart (2009: 265) conjectures that this survivor is in fact dying. In this way he avoids the problem that v. 9 states that all ten would die.

76. For a detailed study of all rhetorical questions in Amos, with special emphasis on recurring structural patterns, see Allen (2008).

77. Since 6:13 begins with a participle, it is possible that it once was preceded by a woe exclamation. Thus Wolff (1977: 286). See the Comments on 5:7.

78. Wordplay involving place names does admittedly occur in Amos 5:5, too. But in the case of 5:5 the author primarily employs alliteration and assonance.

79. On the site of Karnaim, see Wolff (1977: 288) and Paul (1991: 219, n. 17).

80. On this frequently attested topos in Assyrian texts, see Cohen (1979: 39–42).

81. With regard to the Hebrew word order, which gives prominence to *bĕḥozkēnû*, I suggest that one might also translate 6:13b as follows: "Was it not by our own strength that we captured Karnaim (the two horns) for ourselves?"

82. For an elaborate analysis of the metaphorical portrayal in Isa 10:5–15 of Assyria as an instrument in the hands of YHWH, see Eidevall (2009: 45–47 and 2014: 115–16).

Visions (7–9)

1. For different versions of such a biographical approach to the cycle of visions, see, e.g., Würthwein (1950), Wolff (1977: 295–96), and Jeremias (1998: 2–3, 124–26).

2. See, e.g., Würthwein (1950), Watts (1997: 1–7, 64–68), and Andersen and Freedman (1989: 83–88).

3. Similar analyses of the structure have been provided by Behrens (2002: 78–83) and Riede (2008: 29–30).

4. Waschke (2012: 421) makes a distinction between "Ereignisvisionen" (in the first pair) and "Zeichnisvisionen" (in the second pair).

5. The longer form is, above all, typical for the book of Ezekiel, with 123 attestations. The remaining occurrences are found in Isaiah (nine times), Jeremiah (once), and Obadiah (once).

6. See further the discussion on the function of *hinnēh* in the context of vision reports in Behrens (2002: 48–54). According to Behrens, this Hebrew particle may signal an element of surprise; however, as far as I can see, such a supposition lacks firm textual support.

7. In this case the explicit grammatical subject of the verbal participle precedes the interjection *hinnēh*. A similar syntactic construction is found in Gen 41:1.

8. For helpful factual background concerning the damage caused by locust swarms in Palestine, see Riede (2008: 36–38).

9. Obviously, the LXX translator did not have a clue, since she/he came up with a reference to "Gog, the king" (Γωγ ὁ βασιλεύς).

10. Thus Wolff (1977: 297) and Sweeney (2000: 252). In addition to 1 Sam 8:10–18, see 1 Kgs 4:1–5:18.

11. The lengthy discussion of this issue in Riede (2008: 54–56) is thus unwarranted.

12. Steins (2010: 59–60) has suggested that Exod 32 serves as a subtext for Amos 7:1–6. Cf. similarly Becker (2001: 164). As pointed out by Becker, it is highly unlikely that Exod 32 has borrowed the motif of intercession from Amos 7. Thus Aurelius (1988: 82, 203–4).

13. See Spieckermann (1997: 288–89) and Steins (2010: 58). Although Riede (2008: 87) makes exactly the same observation as these scholars concerning the distribution of the verb *slḥ* in the Hebrew Bible, he is unwilling to conclude that the two first visions are of exilic or postexilic origin.

14. Cf. also Becker (2001), who argues that, although the motif of prophetic intercession may be preexilic, the use of it in Amos 7 is clearly postexilic.

15. See further Brueggemann (1969: 386–90). See also McConville (2006: 139–43) and Riede (2008: 91–94).

16. For a discussion of the theological usage of the name Jacob in the book of Amos, see Jeremias (1996: 257–71).

17. As regards the second alternative, the metaphor "rain is (like) fire" is in fact attested in some biblical texts, albeit with the use of different terminology (Gen 19:24; Ezek 28:32). However, such a metaphor is not suggested by the immediate context.

18. One may note that, just like the locust swarm in the first vision, fire is a literary topos in biblical disaster depictions. See Spieckermann (1997: 288).

19. In ancient Hittite and Greek myths, fire in the form of lightning was often used as a weapon by deities combatting chaos monsters associated with the sea. See Hillers (1964: 223–24).

20. In this respect, these vision reports resemble accounts of dream interpretation. See Niditch (1983: 28–32).

21. The two remaining occurrences of this phrase in the Hebrew Bible, Zech 4:2 and 5:2, are found in similar contexts. In some respects, there are points of contact between these prophetic vision reports.

22. Thus, e.g., Landsberger (1965: 287). See also Uehlinger (1989: 101–2) and Paul (1991: 235).

23. An interpretation along these lines was first proposed by Brunet (1966: 390–95), whose ideas were developed further by Beyerlin (1988). See also, more recently, Jeremias (1998: 131–32), Bergler (2000: 457–58), and Waschke (2012: 426).

24. According to an alternative theory, propounded by Ina Willi-Plein (1999: 46–47), the motif of YHWH placing an amount of tin in the midst of something alludes to a critical moment in the process of bronze production. In this way, Willi-Plein avers, the third vision illustrates a critical moment for the nation. A weak point in her interpretation is that it makes the initial motif, the tin wall, quite irrelevant.

25. For various versions of such a theory, see Gese (1981: 81–82), Stuart (1987: 373), and Novick (2008: 125–26).

26. For transliteration and translation of the relevant parts of this Ishtar hymn, K 41, with a discussion of its possible significance for the interpretation of Amos 7:7–8, see Riede (2008: 123–24). See also Jeremias (1998: 133, n. 27). The complete line quoted reads: *šu a-na-ku ana-ku a-na-ak si-par-ri* ("I am tin, I am bronze," line 23/24). It is worth noting that tin appears to be associated with strength and power in this text.

27. I am indebted to Martha Campos (2011), who was the first scholar to present a consistent interpretation of Amos 7:7–8 as a vision focusing on the role of the prophet.
28. In some respects, I agree completely with the rhetorical analysis offered by Novick, who argues that "the third and fourth visions are constructed not to silence Amos but to co-opt him; to entrap the prophet, and make *him* pass judgment on Israel by (unknowingly) mouthing the fateful word" (2008: 118, emphasis in the original). In one important respect, however, I disagree. According to Novick (2008: 125–26), the wordplay involves *ʾănāk* and the verbal stem *ʾnq,* denoting the act of sighing.
29. Such a use of *ʿbr* + *l* is unparalleled in the Hebrew Bible; however, this expression denotes forgiveness of transgressions in Mic 7:18 and Prov 19:11.
30. With Andersen and Freedman (1989: 754–55). Cf. similarly Steins (2010: 96), who refers to v. 9 as a "Brückenvers."
31. Similar observations have been made by Steins (2010: 96–97). See also Utzschneider (1988: 81–83).
32. Hugh Williamson has argued that v. 9 is an integral part of a passage comprising vv. 9–17, which "owes its present position to an editor who shared many of the views normally characterised as Deuteronomic" (1990: 113). According to Steins, it is necessary to reckon with successive stages of redaction: "7,10–17 ist unter Aufnahme sprachlichen Materials und konzeptioneller Ideen unter anderem auch aus 7,9 heraus entwickelt worden" (2010: 99). See also Werlitz (2000: 238–39) and Levin (1995: 309–10).
33. As shown by Bulkeley (2009), Amos 7:1–8:3 can indeed be read as a coherent composition. However, in his article Bulkeley also demonstrates that such a reading requires that one downplay the theological tensions between 7:10–17 and the visions.
34. See Jeremias (1998: 137): "Amos 7:10–17 . . . stands between the third and fourth visions in order to show later readers why Amos' intercession, which in the first and second visions was yet successful, is silent beginning with the third vision, and why it is no longer able to dissuade God from carrying out his acts of disaster." See also, in a similar vein, Behrens (2002: 88) and Paas (2002: 263).
35. In the words of Coote (1981: 60): "The prophet warns. Catastrophe results from the rejection of the warning and the spurning of the warner as much as from the transgression itself. To heed the warning is to avert catastrophe. To spurn the warning is to invite catastrophe." See also Landy (1987: 234): "Israel damns itself, through the mouth of its most sacred functionary."
36. For a more elaborate discussion of possible points of contact between the image of Amos in 7:9–17 and the Deuteronomic notion of "a prophet like Moses," see Dijkstra (2001: 121–22, 127–28). Steins (2010: 65–67, 73–74) has called attention to the far-reaching parallels between the portraits of Amos and Jeremiah.
37. For detailed discussions, divergent conclusions, and references to further literature, see Ackroyd (1977), Utzschneider (1988), and Levin (1995). See also Rilett Wood (2002: 194–99).
38. It has often been assumed that the story in 1 Kgs 13 represents a reworking and recontextualization of the Amos tradition preserved in 7:10–17. Thus recently Werlitz (2001). See also Levin (1995: 311–13), with references to Wellhausen, Eichrodt, and others. However, against this hypothesis, Ackroyd (1977: 80) has argued that "it is easier to see an anonymous narrative coming to be attached to a known prophet (cf. 1 Samuel 9), than to suppose that an Amos narrative lost its identity."
39. The ingenious interpretation offered by Utzschneider can be illustrated by the following quotation: "Mit der Anspielung auf die Erzählung von 1 Kön 13 (genauer wohl: auf

eine ihrer Vorstufen) läßt die Erzählung Am 7, 10ff den Priester sagen: Nun geh' du aber wirklich, und iß dein Brot in Juda, wie es jener vorhatte!" (1988: 96).

40. For other examples of the biographical approach to this narrative, see Sellin (1929a: 253–56), Weiser (1956: 190–92), and Andersen and Freedman (1989: 763–94).

41. This has been recognized by a number of scholars in recent decades. See, e.g., Ackroyd (1977: 84–85), Werlitz (2000: 234–38), Wöhrle (2006: 111), and Steins (2010: 79–81).

42. This comes close to the designations "judgment narrative" and "conflict narrative" employed by Ackroyd (1977). However, Ackroyd's labels do not accentuate the element of verbal debate. Tucker (1973: 428, 430) speaks of a reported "dispute," but he settles for the genre classification "story of prophetic conflict."

43. With Miller (1986: 84–85) and Werlitz (2000: 241). This aspect of the drama has been accurately analyzed by Hardmeier (1985: 68): "Im szenischen Vordergrund stehen sich zwar Amos und Amazja, auf dem legitimatorischen Hintergrund aber Jahwe und die durch den König repräsentierte Staatsmacht konträr gegenüber." See also García-Treto (1993: 119–20, 123–24).

44. For the following, see Hardmeier (1985: 64–68), who introduced this kind of three-leveled analysis of Amos 7:10–17.

45. Except for the translation of the Hebrew text, the text presented here is virtually identical to a number of displays of the communicative structure of this text that have been published by other scholars. See Hardmeier (1985: 64–65), Bulkeley (2009: 523–24), and Steins (2010: 79). Apparently, this is the most adequate way of doing and presenting such an analysis.

46. Cf. Landy (1987: 235), who points out that characters who are "misquoting each other" can be seen as a subtle device employed in "the wonderfully nuanced world of biblical prose."

47. Cf. the analysis in Eidevall (2009: 68–72) of another text in the prophetic literature that represents a war of words, viz. Isa 36–37. See also Eidevall (2014: 116–19).

48. Quoted from Nissinen (2003: 150–51); lines 108–11 and 116 of SAA 2.6.

49. For the interpretation of the narrative, it is a moot question whether Amaziah should be seen as an entirely fictitious character or not. According to Levin (1995: 310), the somewhat strange title "priest of Bethel" (there were, of course, many priests at a major sanctuary) suggests that Amaziah was invented by the author.

50. See further Ackroyd (1977: 77–78). Cf. also Schmid (1967).

51. It is therefore misguided to use the actual wording of 7:11 as an argument in favor of a very early dating, before the death of Jeroboam II. Such a theory has recently been propounded by L. Schmidt (2007). Obviously, Schmidt has failed to distinguish between different levels of communication in 7:10–17.

52. These two lexemes appear to be used synonymously in Isa 29:10 and 2 Kgs 17:13. See further Zevit (1975: 785–89), Jepsen (1980: 284–88), and Wolff (1977: 310–11). See also Sweeney (2000: 258), who maintains that *ḥōzeh* was "a standard professional designation for a prophet or oracle giver in both ancient Israel/Judah and in the pagan world."

53. For the possibility that Amos 7:12 contains an allusion to the story in 1 Kgs 13, where the theme of "eating bread" is more prominent, see Utzschneider (1988: 96) and the discussion of intertexts in "Introduction to 7:10–17."

54. According to Steins (2010: 82), a survey of all biblical attestations of this expression shows that it stands for "Partizipation/Zugehörigkeit zu einer sozialen Einheit."

55. Cf. similarly Miller (1986: 86, emphasis in original): "For Amaziah's command to Amos is essentially: If you want to prophesy and criticize, then go back home and do it *there* (the Hebrew is emphatic at this point); but don't do it here in our territory."

56. In addition, one may consider these two alternatives, both rather nonsensical: "Am I not a prophet? Am I not a prophet's son? I am a herdsman", or: "Am I not a prophet? Am I not a prophet's son? Am I a herdsman?" The paraphrase proposed by G. R. Driver (1955: 92), "do you suppose that I am not a true prophet because I'm a seasonal labourer," presupposes that a "because," which lacks correspondence in the Hebrew, may be inserted.

57. This theory comes in two different versions. According to Richardson (1966), the word לֹא, which occurs twice in v. 14, is not a negation (*lōʾ*) but an emphatic particle, attested in Ugaritic. According to Zevit (1975: 789–90; 1979), the first *lōʾ* should be taken as a free-standing negation, "No!," whereas the second instance of *lōʾ* should be interpreted more conventionally. This adventurous operation yields the following translation/interpretation: "No [I am not a *ḥōzeh*]! I am a *nābīʾ*" (1979: 508). A translation of the next clause is provided in an earlier article by Zevit: "I am not even a *ben nābīʾ*" (1975: 789). For a more detailed critique, see Viberg (1996: 103–4). See also Y. Hoffmann 1977).

58. See, e.g., Mays (1969: 134, 137–39) and Jeremias (1998: 135, 139–40). Cf. also, more cautiously, Paul (1991: 238, 243–47).

59. One should note, however, that all other biblical instances of this expression are in the plural, "sons of the prophets" (*bĕnê hannĕbîʾîm*).

60. Thus, e.g., Wolff (1977: 306, 312–13) and Linville (2008: 144). For further arguments in favor of such a present tense interpretation, see Utzschneider (1988: 89), Rottzoll (1988), and Campos (2011: 14–15).

61. Rottzoll (1988) has convincingly argued that the syntactically closest parallel to Amos 7:14–15 is found in 2 Sam 14:5. It is evident that the initial noun clause in 2 Sam 14:5, which is followed by a reference to an event in the past, must be interpreted as referring to the speaker's (that is, the widowed woman's) *present* status. Accordingly, the concluding part of 2 Sam 14:5 can be translated as follows: "I am a widow, my husband died." Arguably, the theoretically possible alternative "I was a widow, and then my husband died" makes no sense.

62. A rhetorical approach to Amos 7:14–15 has been adopted also by other scholars. See, e.g., García-Treto (1993: 121–23). In some respects, my own analysis comes close to the reading outlined by Viberg (1996: 107–13), although I do not agree with Viberg that 7:14 is best understood as "an example of irony" (1996: 107). Alternatively, as suggested by Radine (2010: 193–97), this text downplays the role of prophets, in the same vein as Zech 13:14–15. According to Seleznev (2004: 256–58, quotation on p. 257), who likewise points to affinities with Zech 13:14–15, Amos employs the "rhetorical device of disguising" himself. However, I find it unlikely that the narrator presents Amos as hiding his true identity, as if he were able to win the debate only by means of deception. A similar critique can be delivered against the interpretation proposed by Schmid (1967: 72–74).

63. Cf. García-Treto (1993: 122): "The rhetorical, performative strategy of seeming to agree with the one who 'puts you down' in order to 'put him on' is what appears to be at work here."

64. Probably, as suggested by Jeremias (1998: 135), the conjunction at the beginning of the second clause in v. 14a should be regarded as an explicative *waw*.

65. See further *HALOT*, s.v., and the extensive treatment in Steiner (2003: 35–47). According to a common theory, in part based on the LXX rendering (κνίζων), the verb *bls* refers to the act of gashing the figs, presumably in order to promote ripening. See the learned

discussion in Wright (1976). See also Keimer (1927), with illustrations showing ancient Egyptian pictorial evidence for the practice of incising figs. As far I can see, however, it is not necessary for the textual interpretation of Amos 7:14 to determine the precise denotation of *bôlēs*.

66. Readers who take a special interest in such issues are referred to the work of Steiner (2003). On the basis of a thorough investigation, and guided by his ambition to harmonize the information concerning Amos's occupations in 1:1 and 7:14, Steiner arrives at the following hypothesis: "the herdsmen from Tekoa rented fields containing sycomore trees at the end of the summer, when the trees were full of figs. While keeping an eye on their animals, they harvested the figs, selling the edible ones and storing the others. When winter came, they fed their animals the stored figs" (2003: 115). Similarly also King (1988: 117).

67. I owe the idea that there might be such a connection to the fourth vision to Karin Tillberg, one of my doctoral students.

68. See also Utzschneider (1988: 90–91), who criticizes Schult's thesis that the shepherd motif is primarily associated with the legitimation of outsiders without institutional affiliation.

69. According to Dijkstra (2001: 126), it is evident that the author of Amos 7:15 "had this ancient prophecy of Nathan in mind."

70. See also Cripps (1929: 237) and Rudolph (1971: 251).

71. Cf. also Deut 32:2, with different terminology.

72. There is no reason to assume that Amaziah's wife is depicted as an immoral woman. It is possible, on the contrary, that this utterance alludes to the hardships women suffered during war. Thus Sweeney (2000: 260–61). See also Sanderson (1998: 220).

73. According to Andersen and Freedman (1989: 86–87), Amos was certainly put in jail. "The only question is whether he was martyred or just kept under restraint" (1989: 87). The tradition that Amos became a martyr can be traced back to *Vitae Prophetarum,* a work dating to the Hellenistic era. See Charlesworth (1985: 379–99). See also the discussion in Werlitz (2000: 237). According to this legend, Amos was tortured by Amaziah, the priest in Bethel, and eventually put to death: "at last his son also killed him with a club by striking him on the temple." Apparently, however, he did not die immediately: "And while he was still breathing he went to his own district, and after some days he died and was buried there" (cited from Hare's translation in Charlesworth 1985: 391).

74. This supposition was often made in earlier exegesis, sometimes in combination with the idea that he wrote down his prophecies, or transmitted them orally to his disciples, upon his return to his hometown, Tekoa. See, e.g., G. A. Smith (1906: 120): "Amos silenced wrote a book--first of prophets to do so--and this is the book we have now to study." See also Sellin (1929a: 189–90), Weiser (1956: 128, 130), and Watts (1997: 5, 65–67).

75. See further Steins (2010: 63–64). A similar phrase occurs in the flood story, in Gen 6:13. However, it is unlikely that the Genesis text alludes to Amos 8:2, as suggested by Smend (1986b).

76. The fruits gathered at the end of the summer were figs, pomegranates, and grapes; see Num 13:23. See Riede (2008: 135). On the importance of such "summer fruits" as ingredients in the daily diet, see, e.g., 2 Sam 16:1–2 and Jer 40:10, 12. See further MacDonald (2008: 29).

77. Yvonne Sherwood stresses that "no discourse of naturalness can ease the friction of the union between summer fruit and mass carnage" (2001: 7). She even makes a comparison between the fourth vision and modern surrealistic art (2001: 10–12).

78. The Samaria ostraca indicate that "diphthongs were monophthongized" in the northern region, as pointed out by Paul (1991: 254). See also Wolters (1988) and Novick (2008: 119–20), with references to further literature.

79. For a more extensive discussion in relation to this text, see Riede (2008: 39–40, 140–41). See also Rahtjen (1964).

80. According to Landy (1987: 230–31), who translates "He has cast hush," YHWH is the implied subject of v. 3bβ. See similarly Linville (2008: 152). I find this possibility intriguing, but unlikely.

81. See the following insightful comment made by Schart (2009: 267): "Das *has* schließt, oder besser gesagt: bricht, die Szenerie ab. Danach kommt nichts mehr. *has* steht für die Totenstille, in der von YHWH nichts mehr erwartet wird" (emphasis in the original).

82. Hadjiev (2009: 102) provides a similar list.

83. To some extent, this special character of Amos 8:4–14 was also recognized by Wolff, who referred to a process of interpreting the message of Amos "in a new situation" (1977: 325). However, he nevertheless insisted upon a date of origin in the eighth century B.C.E. for this series of reinterpretations, allowing a very short time for that process.

84. See Jeremias (1998: 145). Similarly also Kratz (2003: 67–68) and Troxel (2012: 46–47). Hadjiev (2009: 104–110, 201–7) suggests an exilic provenance for the entire section 8:4–14.

85. See the elaborate discussion in Levin (2003: 268–75). The lexemes *ʾebyôn* and *ʿanāw/ ʿānî* occur frequently in the Psalms (אביון twenty-three times, ענו eleven times, and עני forty times), and in several cases it is clear that these words are used as (self-)designations of the pious and righteous. See esp. Ps 37:14, where the collocation *ʿānî wĕʾebyôn* stands in synonymous parallelism to *yišrê dārek*, "those who walk uprightly" (NRSV). Cf. also, for the use of this collocation, Pss 40:18 (Eng. 40:17); 70:6 (Eng. 70:5); 74:21; 86:1; 109:16, 22.

86. According to Linville (2008: 153), this formulation "evokes the 'Sabbath of violence' of 6:3." However, his interpretation presupposes a different reading of Amos 6:3 than the one adopted in the present commentary.

87. This technique is common in the Psalms. See, e.g., Pss 2:3; 10:6, 11, 13; 22:9 (Eng. 22:8).

88. According to Kessler (1989), it is more likely that the perpetrators denounced by this passage were rich landowners. Rich merchants appear only in later texts, e.g., in Zeph 1:10–11. However, the problem that Kessler attempts to solve evaporates if one assumes a postexilic date of origin for Amos 8:4–6.

89. The collocation "new moon and Sabbath" occurs in a few biblical texts (2 Kgs 4:23; Isa 1:13; Hos 2:13). Evidently, they were seen as the two main regular holidays. Some scholars have suggested that the Sabbath originated as a monthly counterpart to the new moon festival, as a feast celebrating the full moon, but this can be no more than speculation. Advocating a preexilic dating for 8:4–6, Fleischer (1989: 190–92) has argued that "Sabbath" in 8:5 refers to a cultic full moon festival. However, I cannot see how this might help the interpretation.

90. An ephah was roughly forty liters, and the weight of a shekel was about twelve grams. See, e.g., Paul (1991: 258, n. 22).

91. For a survey of various exegetical solutions to this perceived problem, see Kessler (1989: 13–18). Some scholars have found it particularly awkward that slavery is mentioned almost in passing, in comparison with the detailed description of the allegedly minor crime of manipulating weights and scales. However, this smacks of anachronism. It is worth noting that the institution of debt slavery is seen as legitimate in Exod 21 (see

also Deut 15), whereas the use of false balances is condemned as a crime by a number of biblical passages (see, e.g., Deut 25:14). See further the Comments on 8:5.

92. An elaborate argument for the plausibility of such a reconstruction has been provided by B. Lang (1981: 483–84). Cf. similarly Fendler (1973: 39–42). See also Fleischer (1989: 195–198), who adds further details.

93. It has also been suggested that the phrase "the pride of Jacob" was used as a divine designation, the underlying idea being that YHWH was (or ought to be) the real "pride" of the nation. Thus Marti (1904: 217) and Mays (1969: 145). Cf. the use of somewhat analogous phrases as divine epithets in 1 Sam 15:29 and Mic 5:3 (Eng. 5:4). In that case, 8:7a would say almost the same thing as 6:8a: "YHWH has sworn by himself." For critique of this line of interpretation, see Wolff (1977: 328) and Paul (1991: 259–60).

94. I find it unlikely that the author saw this cosmic upheaval primarily as a punishment for the crimes committed by the merchants who tampered with weights and measures (vv. 5–6), as suggested by Gese (1989).

95. For the position that 8:8 draws on 9:5, see, e.g., Willi-Plein (1971: 50). According to Jeremias (1998: 149), the literary dependence goes both ways, in two successive stages. See also Gese (1989: 64–65), who argues that 9:5 quotes 8:8. In my opinion, 8:8 is likely to be the younger of these two postexilic passages. It appears to be the product of a scribe who provided a lengthy quotation from 9:5 (8:8aβ + b = 9:5aβ + b) with a new introduction (v. 8aα) in order to connect the utterance to the preceding verses. However, it is also conceivable that Amos 8:8 and 9:5–6 belong to the same editorial layer, as suggested by Schart (1998: 93).

96. This phenomenon is frequently attested in the book of Isaiah. See Isa 2:20; 3:18; 4:2; 7:18, 20, 21, 23, etc.

97. For examples from Mesopotamian literature, see Paul (1991: 262–63).

98. See similarly Jer 6:26, where the same phrase, *ʾēbel yāḥîd*, is used. Although the masculine form in *yāḥîd*, "only," may be interpreted inclusively as referring to both boys and girls, it is likely that the author of Amos 8:10 primarily had the death of an only son in mind. After all, this text was written in a patriarchal society.

99. The introductory formula *yāmîm bāʾîm*, "days are coming," which occurs also in 4:2 and 9:13, is above all linked to the Jeremiah tradition. Out of a total of twenty attestations in the Hebrew Bible, fourteen are found in the book of Jeremiah.

100. Such a reading is adopted by, e.g., Soggin (1987: 140), and Jeremias (1998: 144, 152).

101. Barstad (1984: 167–78) has argued that Ashim-Bethel, who is mentioned in the Aramaic letters from Elephantine (ArPap 22, 124), should be seen as a male counterpart of this goddess. I find this hypothesis too speculative.

102. The observation that the lexeme *ʾašmâ* is attested only in rather late biblical texts poses no problem, once it is accepted that Amos 8:13–14 most probably is postexilic, like the rest of 8:4–14.

103. For a detailed discussion, see Olyan (1991: 136–41).

104. See Biran (1981) and Jeremias (1998: 153). The Greek text reads θεόι τοι εν Δανοις.

105. For an overview of various scholarly proposals, see, e.g., Wolff (1977: 323–24). See also the detailed discussion provided by Olyan (1991: 122–35), who advocates the reading *dôdĕkā* (assuming that this is one of many cases of d/r confusion in the history of textual transmission). Thus also Lehmann and Reichel (1995: 30–31), who aver that "Dod" was a divine epithet used in Beer-Sheba.

106. For two elaborate (yet very different) arguments in support of this hypothesis, see Jeremias (1996: 157–71) and Riede (2008: 305–30).

107. Because of these troubling observations, some scholars have resorted to substantial rewriting of 9:1–4, without any support from extant textual witnesses, in order to make this vision conform to the general pattern of the first four (so, e.g., Rottzoll 1996: 99–100).

108. See Waschke (2012: 419–20) and Steins (2010: 34–35). While Waschke observes that "die vierte Vision schon durch ihr Bild und seine Deutung als Schlussvision verstanden werden will" (2012: 419–20), Steins describes the fourth vision as a concluding "Paukenschlag" (2010: 35). Similarly Willi-Plein (1999: 42–43) and Becker (2001: 147 and 2011: 216). See also Bergler (2000: 450). According to Bergler (2000: 461–71), however, both the third and the fifth visions are secondary additions to a cycle that originally contained only three vision reports.

109. Jeremias (1996: 158–61 and 1998: 6). Thus also Wolff (1977: 338) and Gese (1981).

110. The hypothesis that 9:1–4 represents a secondary addition to the vision cycle, a "Nachinterpretation," has been propounded by Waschke (1994).

111. Thus, e.g., Andersen and Freedman (1989: 832, 835–36) and Linville (2008: 159–63). For further interpretations based on the MT, without resort to emendations, see Waschke (1994: 440–41), Schart (2003: 48–51), Garrett (2008: 236, 256–60), and Riede (2008: 169–73). See also Paul (1991: 273–76), who, however, leaves parts of v. 1aγ untranslated.

112. This link between the third and the "fifth" vision has sometimes been interpreted as an indication that they belong to the same stage of composition or redaction. According to Bergler (2000: 454–71), these two visions were added by the same editor in order to serve as a framework around 8:1–3. They should be read as two separate stages of one and the same vision/event, the idea being that YHWH wielded the *ʾănāk* that he was holding in his hand (7:7–8) as a weapon as he struck the pillars in the temple (9:1). Reversing Bergler's order of redactional stages, Steins (2010: 67–71) has suggested that the third and "fifth" visions contain fragments of two preexilic vision reports that existed before the creation of a cycle comprising four visions. Thus, the present separation of 7:7–9 and 9:1–4, which originally belonged together, would be due to later editorial activity. Given the striking structural dissimilarities between these two visions, however, it is more likely that the author of 9:1 reused a phrase that he found in 7:7.

113. With Waschke (1994: 442) and Bergler (2000: 452). See further the elaborate argumentation in Bartczek (1977: 96–100) for the hypothesis that Amos 9:1 is secondary in relation to Isa 6.

114. According to the Targum, which here deviates considerably from the MT, 9:1 predicts (in retrospect, clearly) the violent death of King Josiah, as well as the destruction of the Jerusalem temple and the transportation of its vessels to Babylon.

115. Cf., in a similar vein, Gese (1981: 83). In an attempt to spell out the theological implications of the oldest layer of Amos 9:1–4, Aaron Schart has made the following comment: "Since the temple is the center that gives refuge, stability, and prosperity . . . to the land, its elimination sets off disorder and death" (2003: 51).

116. In addition, there is a homonym, *rōʾš* II, with the lexical sense "poison," that occurs elsewhere in the book, in 6:12. Hence, there are even further interpretive possibilities. See Cathcart (1994) and Linville (2008: 161–63).

117. Similarly Paul, who comments: "Just as the temple is about to be destroyed entirely, from top to bottom, so, too, the people, from their ראֹשׁ ['heads,' that is, their leaders] to their

אַחֲרִית [all the 'residue,' that is the 'rest' of the population]" (1991: 276). See also Hadjiev (2007: 388–89).

118. According to Irsigler (2004: 197), Amos 9:1–4 may rather have influenced Ps 139. Blum (2008: 106, n. 30) has called attention to a hymn (to Pharaoh) in the Amarna letters that might provide parallels to Amos 9:2. This passage (EA 264, lines 15–16) reads, in my translation (which is based on Knudtzon's): "Whether we rise to heaven or descend to the netherworld, our head is in your hands."

119. On the location and the vegetation of Mount Carmel, see further Mulder (1995).

120. See further Paul (1991: 279), with references to the notion of the "evil eye" in Akkadian texts.

121. Cf. Schart (1998: 236), who speaks of "der Hoffnungsakzent des Hymnus."

122. According to Rottzoll (1996: 4–5), the book has two parallel structures. Whereas 5:8–9 constitutes the center of the concentric composition, 4:13 marks the division between two major sections, 1:3–4:12 and 5:1–9:6. But why would the editor responsible for the insertion of the doxologies want to create two competing macrostructures?

123. Alternatively, ʾăguddâ might refer to a special type of ornamented column, known from Egyptian iconography, as argued by Paas (1993: 320–21).

124. For further correspondences and points of contact between 9:5–6 and 9:1–4, see Paas (2002: 260).

125. Cf. these comments made by Linville: "The third hymn may be viewed as a ritual of rebirth. By soliciting the involvement of the reader, a sacred space and time is created in which the eternal powers of creation can be accessed. Order can be restored" (2008: 168).

126. So Coote (1981: 117–21) and Steins (2010: 117–25). For the idea that a turn toward a more hopeful perspective starts already at 9:7, see also Neher (1950: 150–52) and Linville (2008: 169–70).

127. I agree with Holter that "the best solution for the translator is to let Cush remain 'Cush'; that is, to avoid the problems of finding a modern equivalent such as 'Ethiopia,' 'Nubia,' 'Sudan,' or even 'Africa,' and just transliterate it" (2000: 114; see further 107–13).

128. See Rice (1978), R. Smith (1994), and Holter (2000: 115–16).

129. More examples could be cited. See, e.g., Marti (1904: 223, "ein verachtetes schwarzfarbiges Sklavenvolk"), Sellin (1929a: 268, "wegen seiner schwarzen Hautfarbe besonders verachtetes"), and Hammershaimb (1970: 134, "Its dark-skinned inhabitants were held in contempt by the Israelites").

130. See further Rice (1978: 38–40), Holter (2000: 121–23), and Strawn (2013: 101–3, 122).

131. Omitting the mention of Cush, the Targum transformed 9:7a into an unambiguously reassuring utterance: "Are you not regarded as beloved children before me, you Israelites?" See Cathcart and Gordon (1989: 3–4).

132. So Neher (1950: 140–42), Vogels (1972), and Steins (2010: 111–15).

133. With varying emphasis, several modern commentators interpret 9:7a along these lines. Thus already Robinson (1954: 106). See further Wolff (1977: 347), Paul (1991: 282), Sweeney (2000: 271–72), and Fleischer (2001: 264).

134. In his discussion of Amos 9:7, Carroll R. discards simplistic notions, such as "divine involvement" in all migrations or YHWH as a universal liberator from oppression and settles for "the notion of sovereign intervention in the course of history" (1996: 66).

135. Most likely, 3:1–2 and 9:7 should be ascribed to different redactional layers. However, the tension between them, in terms of affirming or relativizing the exodus, should not be exaggerated. See Schullerus (1996: 58–60).

136. This has been argued by Jeremias (1998: 165) and Rütersworden (2010: 217). See similarly Rilett Wood (2002: 210–11). See also Davies, who maintains that, from the sixth century B.C.E. onwards, "Jacob" tends to be "used in prophetic texts to refer to Judah" (2006: 127). However, since Judah ceased to exist as a state after 587 B.C.E., it seems more likely that some of these passages refer to a community of Judeans in exile or in the land.

137. See Paul (1991: 286, n. 39). See also Lieth (2007: 53–54).

138. Thus, e.g., Wolff (1977: 349), Paul (1991: 286), and Jeremias (1998: 166).

139. For a more profound and provocative discussion of the theme of divine violence in the book of Amos, see Mills (2010). See also M. Lang (2004), with a more traditional treatment of this topic.

140. The German original reads "Rosen und Lavendel statt Blut und Eisen." See Wellhausen (1893: 94). For a recent, and basically positive, evaluation of Wellhausen's position concerning Amos 9:11–15, see Rütersworden (2010).

141. The view that the book of Amos as a whole expresses a pro-Judah and pro-Jerusalem perspective has gradually become more accepted. See, e.g., Carlson (1966: 74–78), Polley (1989: 66–74), Firth (1996), and Sweeney (2000: 194–95). See also Davies (2006), who suggests that "the end of the book may not be, after all, an afterthought or a correction, contradicting the 'social' message of the remainder; rather, it may be precisely the culmination of the book's main theme: the supersession of Israelite sanctuaries by Jerusalem within the context of a broader supersession of 'Israel' by Judah" (2006: 127).

142. Alternatively, this prophecy refers particularly to the destruction and rebuilding of the Jerusalem temple. Thus Davies (2006: 126–29). According to some other scholars, Amos 9:11 is about future rebuilding of Sukkoth, a small (but strategically important?) town on the east side of the Jordan valley. Thus Richardson (1973), Stuart (1987: 398), and Polley (1989: 72–74). However, this interpretation seems quite unlikely. See Homan (1999).

143. See "Amos at Qumran" and "Amos in the New Testament" in the introduction.

144. See Weimar (1981: 75–76), Jeremias (1998: 167–68), and Fleischer (2001: 270–72).

145. See further Bartlett (1992: 292–93).

146. As pointed out by Paul (1991: 294, n. 63), it is probably a misconception that the phrase *šûb šěbût* in itself denotes the act of returning (or being brought back) from captivity (*šěbît*). However, it does not follow that this phrase cannot be used to refer to such events.

Index of Subjects

accusation, 8, 11, 13, 14, 100, 101, 102, 104, 106, 107, 109, 110, 111, 114, 116, 123, 140, 144, 153, 155, 157, 159, 172, 178, 179, 187, 207, 216, 219, 221, 222

agricultural occupations, 5, 31, 210, 241, 266n.26

agricultural year, 146, 191, 195, 214, 241

altar, 115, 134, 142, 226, 227, 252n.6

Amaziah, 4, 6, 14, 118, 192, 200, 202–13, 221, 227, 246n.8, 260n.49, 262n.73

Ammon and Ammonites, 101, 102, 104, 108–9, 187

Amorites, 117, 242

Amos (person/prophet), 3–7, 9–10, 18, 22, 93–95, 154, 155, 189, 191–92, 204, 210, 221, 245n.2, 245n.5, 246n.8, 246n.11, 247n.25, 252n.1, 262n.66, 262n.73, 262n.74

Amos, as a literary character, 7, 13–15, 16, 23, 155, 191–92, 195, 197, 198, 200, 202–12, 214, 221, 259n.36

ancestor cult, 174, 255n.53

anointing, 181, 185, 257n.73

apocalypticism, 226, 228, 248n.39, 253n.26

Aram and Arameans, 17, 100, 101, 102, 104–6, 108, 187, 236

Ashdod, 106, 130, 131, 132

Ashima (goddess), 217, 222

Ashkelon, 106

Assurbanipal, 206

Assyria, 16, 17, 18, 19, 95, 104, 105, 106, 109, 110, 130, 131, 132, 139, 140, 163, 169, 172, 173, 176, 177, 178, 181, 182, 184, 187, 188, 189, 206, 251n.29, 257n.80, 257n.82

astral deities, 170, 171, 172

Aven, valley of, 105

Baal, 94, 165, 166, 167

Balaam, 23, 24, 103

banquet (*marzēaḥ*), 115, 138, 142, 167, 173–74, 178–81, 215, 257n.72

Bashan, 138, 140

Beer-sheba, 156, 157, 222, 223, 253n.22, 264n.105

Ben-Hadad, 104, 105

Beth-Eden (*bīt adini*), 105

Bethel, 6, 7, 14, 18, 19, 110, 116, 130, 132, 134, 135, 140, 141, 142, 143, 155, 156, 157, 165, 168, 201, 203, 204, 208, 210, 225, 227, 228, 245n.5, 246n.8, 247n.33, 252n.6, 253n.21, 260n.49, 262n.73

Bozrah, 108

bread, 141, 203, 204, 208, 221, 260n.53

breeder, of livestock (*nōqēd*), 3, 5, 6, 92, 93, 94–95

calamities, series of, 146, 147

call experience, prophetic, 93, 128, 192, 209

call narrative, prophetic, 22, 128, 208, 211

Calneh (Kullani), 173, 177, 178

269

fortress, 13, 104, 106, 112, 113, 129, 130, 131, 132, 184, 186
fruit (motif), 117, 195, 210, 214
funerary rites, 110, 155, 162, 174, 255n.53

Gath, 106, 177, 178
Gaza, 106, 107
Gezer calendar, 195, 214
Gilead, 100, 104, 105, 108
Gilgal, 140, 141–42, 156, 157
Gog, 34, 258n.9
grain offering, 141, 168, 170
grain trade, 218–19

Hamath, 173, 177, 178, 189, 222
harvest (motif), 210, 214
Hathor (goddess), 138
Hazael, 104, 105
hemerology, 178, 256n.61
Hermon, 13, 137, 140, 172, 229

injustice, 9, 10, 11, 28, 30, 31, 117, 152, 153, 158, 160, 167
intercession, 14, 16, 19, 23, 25, 193, 195, 196, 197, 200, 203, 212, 237, 258n.12, 258n.14, 259n.34
Isaac, 192, 201, 211, 220
Ishtar, 200, 258n.26
Israel and Israelites, 5, 7, 11, 13, 14, 16, 17, 18, 23, 24, 25, 26, 92, 93, 95, 96, 97, 99, 100, 101, 102, 104, 105, 106, 108, 110, 112–20, 122, 123, 125, 128, 129, 132, 134, 135, 141, 142, 143, 147, 148, 150, 153, 155, 156, 157, 158, 162, 163, 167, 168, 169, 171, 172, 175, 177, 178, 181, 182, 184, 187, 188, 189, 192, 193, 194, 196, 201, 203, 207, 210, 211, 212, 216, 218, 221, 222, 223, 229, 234, 235, 236, 237, 239, 242, 243, 252n.5, 252n.7, 255n.56, 267n.141
ivory, 20, 121, 135, 179, 256n.64

Jacob, 14, 108, 133, 134, 135, 184, 192, 193, 195–96, 219, 237, 258n.16, 264n.93, 267n.136
Jehu, dynasty of, 201, 207
Jeremiah (prophet), 9, 19, 21, 23, 25, 26, 139, 197, 199, 203, 206, 211, 257n.5, 259n.36, 264n.99
Jeroboam I, 201, 203, 204, 237

Jeroboam II, 5, 6, 16, 17–18, 95, 96, 188, 189, 192, 196, 201, 202, 204, 205, 206, 207–8, 211, 212, 247n.21, 260n.51
Jerusalem, 7, 16, 19, 25, 92, 97, 101, 105, 107, 108, 110, 112, 126, 127, 134, 135, 136, 147, 152, 156, 157, 161, 171, 173, 175–76, 177, 178, 181, 193, 196, 206, 214, 221, 222, 225, 227, 228, 239, 240–41, 246n.13, 247n.33, 251n.28, 253n.18, 255n.56, 255n.57, 256n.71, 265n.114, 267n.141, 267n.142
Joseph, 133, 157, 161, 181, 253n.23
Judah, 5, 7, 13, 14, 18, 19, 23, 24, 25, 26, 93, 95, 96, 97, 99, 100, 101, 102, 104, 105, 106, 107, 108, 111–12, 116, 130, 144, 155, 161, 171, 172, 175, 176, 177, 178, 188, 192, 193, 203, 204, 207, 213, 221, 236, 239, 241, 247n.25, 247n.33, 251n.30, 255n.56, 267n.136
Judah-oriented, perspective, 23, 97, 176, 267n.141
judgment, divine, 11, 12, 14, 16, 25, 100, 103, 105, 120, 136, 148, 150, 155, 158, 167, 192, 193, 194, 198, 200, 202, 214, 216, 221, 230, 231, 233, 234, 236, 237, 239, 242
justice, 3, 14, 25, 30, 116, 131, 132, 157, 158, 159, 161, 168, 169, 182, 185, 187, 249n.54

Karnaim (place), 187, 188, 257n.79, 257n.81
Kir (place), 105, 236, 251n.22

lament (genre), 8, 13, 18, 144, 153, 155, 156
lamentation, 10, 27, 97, 153, 158, 160, 161, 162, 164, 186, 215, 220
Lebo-Hamath, 188, 189
lion (motif), 9, 12, 13, 92, 97, 98, 126, 128, 133, 134, 165, 242, 250n.15
locusts, 144, 146, 194–195, 257n.8, 258n.18
Lodebar (Lo-Dabar), 187, 188

meat, 179, 256n.65
merchants, 218–19, 263n.88, 264n.94
mercy, divine, 16, 23, 161, 192, 193, 202, 224, 254n.31
Messiah 29, 34, 139
messianic interpretation, 28, 29, 149, 170
metaphor, 9, 12, 22, 92, 97, 104, 107, 108, 109, 115, 117, 119, 120, 128, 133, 138, 139, 146, 155, 156, 157, 158, 164, 165,

metaphor (*continued*)
181, 194, 196, 198, 199, 200, 207, 212,
214, 217, 220, 222, 233, 237, 239, 240,
242, 246n.16, 250n.15, 252n.9, 253n.18,
257n.82, 258n.17
Moab and Moabites, 100, 101, 102, 108,
109–10, 162
monotheism, 3, 30
Moses, 23, 128, 170, 195, 203, 211, 259n.36
motto, 91, 92, 96–98, 126, 149, 229,
250n.13
mourners, professional, 31, 161
mourning, 13, 29, 31, 97, 162, 164, 174,
200, 216, 220, 232
music, 12, 92, 167, 168, 178, 179, 220
musical instruments, 168, 175, 179, 180, 215,
220

narrative, 4, 5, 8, 12, 13, 22, 23, 27, 92, 98,
108, 118, 143, 147, 165, 185, 186, 191, 192,
193, 202–5, 207, 208, 211, 212, 221, 242,
259n.38, 260n.40, 260n.42, 260n.49
nations, oracles against (OAN), 8, 99–101,
103, 108, 110, 112, 131
Nazirite, 116, 118
Nile, 217, 220, 232
Northern Kingdom (= Israel), 5, 7, 11, 13,
14, 16, 17, 19, 20, 23, 25, 31, 95, 101, 104,
111, 112, 116, 130, 134, 142, 153, 155, 157,
160, 161, 163, 169, 172, 176, 181, 182, 184,
187, 188, 196, 201, 207, 212, 213, 214,
229, 233, 237, 239

oath, 8, 139, 184, 219, 222, 223
officials, 103, 109, 206
oil, 170, 178, 180, 181
Omri, dynasty of, 201
oppression, of the poor, 11, 13, 17, 19, 25,
29, 30, 31, 101, 113, 114, 115, 116, 131, 132,
136, 138, 139, 142, 159, 160, 162, 178,
179, 182, 184, 188, 195, 217, 218, 238,
242, 266n.134

palace, 13, 113, 129, 130, 135, 186, 213, 214,
215, 220, 232
Persian period, 20, 26, 28, 116, 160,
247n.33, 248n.38
Peshitta, 34, 130, 145, 154, 240
pestilence, 147, 185

Philistia and Philistines, 99, 100, 101, 102,
106, 107, 114, 130, 131, 132, 177, 234, 236
Phoenicia and Phoenicians, 94, 106, 107,
110, 114, 179, 250n.6, 251n.28
pledge, 116, 219
plumb line, 198, 199
power, divine, 14, 97, 149, 151, 152, 158, 159,
186, 229, 231, 232, 241
priest, 14, 19, 23, 31, 94, 167, 168, 180, 192,
203, 204, 206, 208, 212, 260n.49
Priestly source (P), 170, 201
prophetic guild, 15, 16, 128, 209, 210
prophets (category/group), 15, 19, 21, 25,
30, 116, 118, 127, 128, 134, 150, 180, 206,
208, 209, 210, 221, 242, 261n.62
prophets, anti-cultic, 7, 141, 168
prophets, cultic, 6, 9, 241n.11
prostitution, 212, 262n.72
protection, divine, 14, 94, 167, 169, 176,
177, 184, 211

question, rhetorical, 8, 11, 12, 13, 21, 124–28,
165, 170, 171, 177, 178, 183, 187, 219,
234, 236, 257n.76
Qumran, 27–28, 29, 32, 33, 104, 241

redaction criticism, 4, 20–23, 247n.28,
247n.29
rejection: of prophetic words, 203, 211, 212,
221, 242; of sacrifices, 7, 11, 142, 164,
166–69, 172, 215, 246n.12
restoration, promise of, 170, 230, 240
royal ideology, 25

Sabbath, 175, 218, 263n.86, 263n.89
sacrifice, 7, 9, 134, 140, 141, 142, 166–69,
170–71, 174, 246n.12, 255n.45, 255n.48
salvation, oracle of, 8, 254n.29
Samaria, 9, 11, 12, 13, 14, 17, 18, 19, 20,
95, 113, 127, 129–33, 135, 136, 138–40,
142, 155, 159, 163, 167, 173, 176–81, 184,
187, 217, 221, 222, 253n.18, 255n.56,
255n.57, 263n.78
sandals, 114, 216, 218, 251n.35
Sargon II, 106, 177
Septuagint (LXX), 28, 33–34, 92, 103, 104,
113, 114, 125, 130, 131, 137, 140, 145,
149, 150, 153, 154, 170, 175, 180, 183,
184, 194, 196, 198, 206, 209, 213, 217,

223, 226, 234, 240, 248n.47, 249n.63, 254n.31, 256n.70, 258n.9
sheep, 5, 6, 9, 12, 94, 133, 179
Sheol, 225, 229
shepherd (motif), 13, 92, 95, 98, 133, 211, 262n.68
sieve (metaphor), 233, 237
simile, 8, 9, 130, 133
site, cultic, 97, 134, 140, 142, 143, 144, 156, 201, 222–23, 253n.21
slavery, 17, 114, 115, 159, 216, 218–19, 235, 251n.35, 263n.91
slave trade, 106, 107, 111, 219
snake (motif), 12, 163, 165, 230
soldiers, 119, 145, 147, 156, 185
songstresses, 213, 214, 215, 220
superscription, 5, 6, 7, 8, 18, 23, 26, 91–96, 98, 118, 147, 192, 204
sycamore (figs/trees), 3, 5, 210, 266n.26
syncretism, 115

Targum (Jonathan), 34, 92, 110, 113, 120, 130, 137, 145, 153, 217, 234, 248n.47, 265n.114, 266n.131
taxes, 154
Tekoa, 3, 5, 6, 10, 19, 93, 95, 250n.10, 262n.66, 262n.74
temple, in Bethel, 19, 110, 116, 134, 140, 142, 143, 157, 165, 201, 203, 206, 208, 225, 227, 228, 245n.5, 247n.33, 252n.6, 253n.21
temple, in Jerusalem, 7, 16, 19, 25, 29, 112, 134, 152, 171, 225, 227, 228, 239, 246n.13, 256n.71, 265n.114, 267n.142
temple cult, 7, 9, 134, 164, 168, 184, 215
themes (thematic threads), in the book of Amos, 11–13, 15, 31, 92, 95, 96, 97, 98, 105, 114, 115, 117, 118, 120, 133, 144, 158, 159, 160, 161, 162, 164, 176, 182, 184, 186, 195, 215, 216, 220, 225, 230, 232, 246n.19, 250n.12, 267n.139
thirst (motif), 13, 22, 27, 97, 146, 216, 217, 220, 222, 242
Tiglath-Pileser III, 18, 105, 106, 109, 110, 163, 177

tin, 198–200, 258n.24, 258n.26
Torah, 25, 28, 29, 101, 111, 140, 170
trap (motif), 126
trumpet, sound of, 95, 109, 128
Tyre, 101, 102, 106–7, 130

Uzziah, 5, 94, 95, 96, 245n.4, 245n.5

vessel, cultic, 256n.72
violence, 18, 31, 103, 104, 117, 132, 158, 159, 175, 178, 238, 242, 267n.139
virgin, 155, 240
vision report, 8, 19, 22, 23, 135, 191–200, 201, 202, 203, 214, 224–28, 257n.6, 258n.20, 258n.21, 265n.105, 265n.112
vocabulary, Deuteronomistic, 19, 101, 111, 117, 122, 123, 250n.18

wagon (metaphor), 113, 119
warfare, 13, 17, 100, 101, 103, 104, 108, 199
warning, 9, 14, 15, 16, 19, 21, 25, 127, 134, 147, 150, 156, 157, 161, 169, 193, 234, 259n.35
weights, 218, 263n.90, 263n.91, 264n.94
wine, 115, 116, 118, 139, 162, 174, 178, 180, 242
wisdom tradition, 6, 9, 10, 93, 95, 102, 160, 184, 253n.26
women: powerful, 136, 138–40; as victims of violence, 103, 104, 108, 115, 262n.72
worship: of other deities, 25, 28, 111, 116, 136, 141, 160, 169, 172, 173, 180, 222, 255n.48, 256n.72; of YHWH, 100, 115, 116, 134, 141–42, 156–57, 166, 168–69, 172, 211, 222–23, 237, 243, 254n.29
wrath, divine, 16, 101, 157, 218, 220, 228, 229

Yehud, 116, 241
youth, 115, 118, 145, 155, 216, 221, 222

Zimri-Lim, 206
Zion, 12, 13, 92, 97, 126, 160–61, 173, 175–76, 180, 181, 240, 255n.56

Index of Authors

246n.20, 248n.38, 250n.16, 252n.8, 261n.60, 263n.80, 263n.86, 265n.111, 265n.116, 266n.125, 266n.126
Loretz, O., 94, 183, 247n.32, 255n.53
Lust, J., 10, 156, 253n.23, 254n.30
Luther, M., 30, 248n.52

Maag, V., 137, 157
Maier, C., 255n.52, 255n.53, 255n.55, 256n.58
Malamat, A., 105
Markert, L., 30, 248n.43
Marti, K., 237, 252n.43
Martin-Achard, R., 28, 29, 30, 141, 246n.8, 248n.43, 248n.48, 248n.51, 249n.53, 249n.54, 249n.55, 253n.26
Marx, A., 255n.45
Mays, J. L., 17, 106, 107, 119, 129, 132, 133, 139, 140, 141, 143, 150, 160, 162, 176, 198, 204, 237, 247n.21, 247n.30, 248n.36, 251n.31, 252n.3, 261n.58, 264n.93
McComiskey, T. E., 148, 231, 252n.14
McConville, J. G., 258n.15
McLaughlin, J., 10, 136, 174, 178, 179, 254n.34, 255n.52, 255n.53, 255n.54, 255n.55, 255n.56
Mein, A., 29, 30, 248n.51
Metzger, M., 187
Miller, P. D., 138, 207, 208, 260n.43, 261n.55
Mills, M., 31, 117, 267n.139
Milstein, S., 126, 128
Mittmann, S., 128, 131, 134, 252n.3
Moeller, H., 252n.4
Möller, K., 10, 13, 14, 19, 24, 92, 96, 98, 102, 119, 122, 126, 128, 132, 133, 139, 140, 141, 148, 150, 155, 246n.17, 247n.25, 247n.28, 248n.42, 250n.19, 252n.4, 252n.11
Montgomery, J. A., 12
Morgenstern, J., 245n.5
Moughtin-Mumby, S., 115
Mulder, M. J., 125, 266n.119
Müller, H.-P., 119
Müller, R., 163, 164, 165, 254n.36, 256n.61
Murtonen, A., 6, 250n.8

Nägele, S., 239
Nahkola, A., 165, 250n.15
Naiden, F. S., 166, 246n.12

Neher, A., 266n.126, 266n.132
Neubauer, K. W., 254n.29
Neusner, J., 248n.48
Niditch, S., 198, 254n.37, 258n.20
Nissinen, M., 254n.32, 260n.48
Noble, P. R., 103, 183, 185, 225
Nogalski, J. D., 26, 95, 96, 122, 233, 240, 241, 248n.40, 248n.41, 248n.42, 249n.3
Noonan, B., 198
Norin, S., 254n.33, 254n.35, 254n.36
Novick, T., 200, 258n.25, 259n.28, 263n.78
Nowack, W., 150

O'Connor, M., 194
Ogden, K., 250n.12
Olyan, S. M., 110, 222, 223, 251n.29, 264n.103, 264n.105
Osten-Sacken, P. von der, 28, 170
Oswald, W., 163, 254n.36
Ouellette, J., 198

Paas, S., 203, 232, 259n.34, 266n.123, 266n.124
Pakkala, J., 19
Park, A. W., 27, 248n.48
Paul, S. M., 17, 91, 95, 96, 97, 99, 103, 104, 105, 106, 107, 110, 113, 115, 116, 119, 123, 125, 126, 130, 131, 134, 137, 139, 140, 141, 143, 145, 146, 148, 149, 150, 151, 153, 154, 155, 156, 157, 159, 161, 165, 167, 170, 171, 172, 175, 176, 177, 180, 181, 183, 184, 185, 186, 187, 189, 194, 195, 196, 198, 199, 200, 208, 213, 218, 221, 222, 223, 224, 225, 229, 232, 234, 235, 237, 241, 242, 245n.3, 245n.4, 247n.21, 249n.59, 250n.6, 250n.7, 250n.13, 250n.20, 251n.37, 252n.43, 252n.2, 252n.6, 252n.9, 252n.11, 257n.79, 258n.22, 261n.58, 263n.78, 263n.90, 264n.93, 264n.97, 265n.111, 265n.117, 266n.120, 266n.133, 267n.137, 267n.138, 267n.146
Pfeifer, G., 125, 133, 148, 231, 252n.3
Pietsch, M., 19
Pitard, W. T., 104, 167, 254n.38, 254n.39
Polley, M. E., 174, 255n.55, 267n.141, 267n.142
Pope, M. H., 255n.53
Praetorius, F., 200
Priest, J., 107
Puech, E., 104

Rabinowitz, I., 131, 133
Radine, J., 24, 143, 246n.14, 247n.25, 247n.35, 261n.62
Rahtjen, B. D., 263n.79
Rashi, 198, 248n.49
Redditt, P., 246n.19
Reimer, H., 30, 31, 249n.55, 249n.56, 249n.57, 249n.58
Reventlow, H. G., 6, 9, 144, 246n.9
Rice, G., 266n.128, 266n.130
Richard, E., 248n.46
Richardson, H. N., 261n.57, 267n.142
Riede, P., 194, 195, 196, 199, 200, 226, 257n.3, 257n.8, 258n.11, 258n.13, 258n.15, 258n.26, 262n.76, 263n.79, 265n.106, 265n.111
Rilett Wood, J., 102, 103, 144, 155, 246n.20, 247n.25, 251n.30, 251n.40, 259n.37, 267n.136
Roberts, J. J. M., 181
Robinson, T. H., 266n.133
Rosenbaum, S. N., 95, 250n.9
Rottzoll, D., 11, 15, 24, 93, 231, 247n.32, 248n.37, 253n.17, 261n.60, 261n.61, 266n.122
Ruiz González, G., 248n.49
Rüterswörden, U., 267n.136, 267n.140

Sanderson, J., 139, 252n.8, 262n.72
Schart, A., 96, 97, 185, 186, 213, 224, 227, 228, 232, 246n.19, 247n.32, 248n.40, 248n.41, 249n.2, 249n.3, 252n.14, 254n.34, 257n.75, 263n.81, 264n.95, 265n.111, 265n.115, 266n.121
Schenker, A., 125
Scherer, A., 247n.35
Schmid, H., 260n.50, 261n.62
Schmidt, B. B., 255n.53
Schmidt, L., 260n.51
Schmidt, W. H., 21, 94, 111, 117, 123, 128, 142, 167, 247n.27, 250n.18, 254n.43
Schmitt, J. J., 253n.18
Schorch, S., 179, 254n.30, 254n.31, 256n.67
Schullerus, K., 266n.135
Schult, H., 211, 262n.68
Schüngel-Straumann, H., 171

Schütte, W., 101, 105, 106,
Schwantes, S. J., 137
Segert, S., 250n.8
Seifert, B., 246n.16
Seleznev, M., 261n.62
Sellin, E., 246n.7, 250n.4, 254n.41, 260n.40, 262n.74, 266n.129
Seybold, K., 257n.73
Sherwood, Y., 262n.77
Shveka, A., 251n.35
Smend, R., 262n.75
Smith, G. A., 246n.7, 262n.74
Smith, G. V., 253n.28
Smith, M. S., 167, 254n.38, 254n.39
Smith, R., 266n.128
Smith-Christopher, D. L., 109
Snijders, L. A., 167
Snyman, S. D., 129, 132, 256n.62
Soden, W. von, 176
Soggin, J. A., 96, 142, 157, 168, 198, 226, 245n.3, 254n.43, 264n.100
Spieckermann, H., 192, 195, 256n.61, 258n.13, 258n.18
Stamm, J. J., 94, 250n.6
Steiner, R. C., 5, 261n.65, 262n.66
Steinmann, A. E., 99
Steins, G., 23, 101, 106, 107, 158, 192, 193, 196, 197, 200, 203, 204, 208, 213, 221, 224, 225, 235, 239, 252n.1, 258n.12, 258n.13, 259n.30, 259n.31, 259n.32, 259n.36, 260n.41, 260n.45, 260n.54, 262n.75, 265n.108, 265n.112, 266n.126, 266n.132
Strawn, B. A., 14, 235, 236, 250n.15, 266n.130
Stuart, D. K., 115, 130, 141, 142, 149, 154, 183, 194, 198, 223, 250n.11, 251n.42, 258n.25, 267n.142
Sweeney, M. A., 19, 129, 135, 195, 248n.41, 249n.3, 251n.31, 258n.10, 260n.52, 262n.72, 266n.133, 267n.141

Tadmor, H., 106
Tawil, H., 153
Terrien, S., 10
Theodet, 248n.50
Theodore, of Mopsuestia, 248n.50
Thompson, H. O., 236, 251n.22
Torczyner, H., 154

Index of Ancient Sources

40:18 [Eng. v. 17]	263n.85	11:1	218
46:6	161	16:18	184
46:7	232	17:23	115
47:5 [Eng. v. 4]	184, 219	19:11	259n.29
50:2–4	97	20:23	218
50:3	145	22:5	137
65:13 [Eng. v. 12]	98	28:23	159
68:15 [Eng. v. 14]	145	30:1	93
68:20 [Eng. v. 19]	94	30:18	102
70:6 [Eng. v. 5]	263n.85	30:18–19	102
74:13–14	230	30:18–23	113
74:21	263n.85	30:21–23	102
77:10 [Eng. v. 9]	103	30:29–31	102
86:1	263n.85	31:1	93
88:6 [Eng. v. 5]	229		
88:11–13 [Eng. vv. 10–12]	229	**RUTH**	
		3:16	194
89:10–11	230	4:8	114
89:47	104		
91:3	126	**QOHELET**	
Psalm 104	149	1:1	93
104:15	162	2:8	213, 214
104:26	194		
104:32	232	**NEHEMIAH**	
109:16	263n.85	Chapters 2–4	240
109:22	263n.85	3:5	95
118:24	165	3:27	95
119:110	126	Chapter 5	219
124:7	126	5:1–5	114, 219
137:7	108	7:69	256n.71
Psalm 139	229, 266n.118	12:36	180
139:7–12	229		
139:10	229	**1 CHRONICLES**	
139:16	230	23:5	180
140:6 [Eng. v. 5]	126	28:17	256n.71
141:9	126		
		2 CHRONICLES	
JOB		4:8	256n.71
9:5–10	149	4:11	256n.71
9:8	151	4:22	256n.71
9:27	154	11:6	95
10:20	154	29:26–27	180
9:33	159	35:25	213, 215
14:13	229		
24:22	138	**Apocrypha and Pseudepigrapha**	
29:22	212	**PSALM 151**	
38:31	153	v. 2	200, 256n.70
PROVERBS		**TOBIT**	
8:13	184	2:6	27
10:19	160